Head
Letterbox

Peggy Bell

First Published in 2022 by Heather Shields Publishing
Copyright © 2022 Peggy Bell

Peggy Bell has asserted her right to be identified as the Author of this Work in accordance with the Copyright, Designs and Patent Act 1988 and Intellectual Property (Copyright and Related Rights) (EU Exit) (Amendment etc) Regulations 2019.

This memoir is a work of creative nonfiction. The events are portrayed to the best of Peggy Bell's memory. Everything here is true, but it may not be entirely factual. In some cases, the author has compressed events; in others made two people into one, some names and identifying details have been changed to protect the privacy of the people involved. All rights reserved. No part of this book may be reproduced, or stored in a retrieval system, in any form or by any means, without the prior permission in writing of the author.

Paperback ISBN: 978-1-8383820-4-9

Heather Shields Publishing
HeatherShieldsPublishing.com

Prologue

The Departures Lounge

In the space between lives, we sat on boulders around a campfire and talked. Low flames crackled, sending sparks into the twilight sky. Our gentle Guides watched from a respectful distance as we considered each image of potential lives illustrated in the dancing flames, places and faces flickering and fading. We have incarnated together many times before, as parents, siblings, offspring, friends. We have loved, lost, affected, rejected, grown old and moulded each other.

These are my soul mates. On Earth, the term soul mate has been desecrated by Hollywood. True soul mates challenge you to grow, whether through challenges or encouragement, but the celestial Doorway Effect, the Asphodel Fields, the River Lethe make us forgetful.

We settled on a two-parent family, four children, Ireland and revised the events that would provide the greatest opportunities for growth and change. These we saturated with white light so that we would remember - the inception of the magic of deja-vu.

The boldest of us had struggled with control in previous lives - self-control and the urge to control others. This soul chose a familiar form - a robust male, a father. Our guides whispered fail-safes.

The meekest of us chose to work on withstanding vulnerability. This soul was to experience loss and be forced to stand alone. She was to be the mother.

One of the souls was here to grow strong, to foster fortitude by weathering disapproval.

Two more souls would come, not to learn but to teach. Hopes and dreams would be built on these children, then ripped away, a vacuum for grief's alchemy.

Then there is me.

We swore our oaths, to each other and our guides, in the presence of others peripheral to our circle, then embraced our farewells and travelled one by one from the place of understanding to the low vibrations of Earth. We carried with us only who we are, the identity built over many lifetimes, our essence. We embroidered our contracts on our souls and descended into another school room: Belfast, to learn.

Four descended before me.

To Martin

The contract, your heart - changed everything.

Contents

Prologue	3
One	11
Two	25
Three	51
Four	71
Five	81
Six	93
Seven	105
Eight	113
Nine	123
Ten	131
Eleven	149
Twelve	165
Thirteen	183
Fourteen	195
Fifteen	219
Sixteen	251
Seventeen	279
Eighteen	305
Nineteen	327
Twenty	347
Twenty-One	365
Twenty-Two	379

Twenty-Three 395

Twenty-Four 411

Twenty-Five 435

Twenty-Six 455

Twenty-Seven 461

Twenty-Eight 481

Twenty-Nine 495

Thirty 505

Thirty-One 527

Thirty-Two 541

Thirty-Three 549

Epilogue 563

About the Author 571

Family Photographs 573

Acknowledgements 579

Index 581

Head Letterbox

Peggy Bell

One

Ben's proclivity for control was reinforced in the formative period of his childhood, when he was least provided for, least protected and seemingly least loved; taking the reins was the best way to ensure his own safety. He was born in 1943 as the Second World War raged on, two years after the Luftwaffe dropped a parachute bomb on their neighbourhood of Sandy Row during the Belfast Blitz, ripping the facades from the terraced houses and killing ten, including children. He was his mother's firstborn. Her maiden name had been Annabella Coates; Bell for short. After she married Jimmy Bell, she lengthened her name to Bella, deciding it was marginally less ridiculous than Bell Bell. Bella took on his two children (Peggy and Alfie – his first wife, May deceased) before bearing four of her own (Ben, Tucker, Hughie and Janet). In the lottery of genetics, Bella's children favoured her; the high cheekbones, strong chin and bulbous tipped nose – DNA that would trickle down generations.

Sandy Row was a small, working class, Protestant enclave in South Belfast. In the 1940s, the wide, arterial road of Sandy Row was flanked by tall brick terraces, the ground levels of which comprised over a hundred shops. The reputation for quality and variety drew shoppers from all over Belfast and beyond; awnings sheltered merchandise displayed outside and window displays were carefully curated. Neat, tightly packed rows of poverty lay behind the main road; two-up, two-down kitchen houses, gardenless, unless you counted the barren yard at the back, which was not much more than a few yards of stone, over which the women hung the boiled nappy cloths out to dry. Here too, in the yard was a cold outside toilet, where old newspaper was ripped into strips and pierced on a nail - rudimentary toilet paper. Winter evening toilet visits posed a conundrum: go without a candle and hope there were no rats waiting in the stall or watch in horror as a rat entered stage left, scurrying through the steam rising off a hastily dropped deposit. The yards backed onto narrow alleys, while the front doors opened directly onto the streets, the doorsteps polished daily in half-moon arcs by fastidious housewives, determined to dodge the shame of being outdone by her neighbour.

    The Bell family were poorer than many in Sandy Row, which is saying something given that the area was known for its poor socio-economic conditions. Bella's kids were tarred with the shame of wearing hand-me-down clothes and shoes with holes. Flapping shoes that looked like they were talking as you walked, trousers exposing ankles, seemingly half-mast (Here – did your dog die?!), jumpers made from wool that had been unwound from outgrown garments and re-knitted to fit. Ben was one of the kids that seldom had a penny for the open fire by the teacher's desk, when a contribution to the coal would earn you a seat at the front. Those whose parents had drank, gambled or simply didn't have a penny left over would shiver further back, with hours to reflect and lament their lot. Ben, whose wool socks had got soaked through ineffective shoes ruminated darkly. The school churned out leavers as poorly educated as their fathers before them, in the bald expectation that the boys would take on the menial professions of their fathers and the girls keep houses. Having little opportunity, few left to live elsewhere, ergo everyone was known or known-of; generations of families living in claustrophobic proximity in this village where reputations were known, and nothing was forgotten. Social immobility had everyone fucked, but those without a penny for the fire suffered the further insult of being fucking foundered.

Ben was a charismatic wee thing, with dark eyes that twinkled with mischief and a ready smile. An aged black and white school photograph shows him standing off to the far right of the lines of boys three rows deep, a head taller than most of the others, a whisper of the Bell bone structure on his boy face, already handsome in its symmetry. He was bright, but there was no money for books; a luxury item when food had to be put on the table and clothes on backs. His education was not fostered: a head full of facts was no use when you're labouring to bring in a wage. School was somewhere that kept the kids out of the house, and homework was his own business. A few streets over, the teachers at Linfield Secondary School delivered the curriculum unenthusiastically, with more emphasis on maintaining discipline than achieving potential. Any talent he had, if ever noticed, was not encouraged. One day, a very green or hopelessly optimistic door-to-door salesman knocked on the front door of their Utility Street mid-terrace and left an encyclopaedia sample for a week's loan in the hope that, once perused, the buyer would commit to taking the remaining bulky collection on tick. Ben pored over it, but the tome was hurriedly returned to the salesman before he even had a chance to begin his spiel. Ben cried. I imagine the salesman might have too; imagine a more frustrating task than that of trying to sell encyclopaedias in Sandy Row, where people were barely making ends meet.

It was the era of Mickey Marley, a man whose horse-drawn roundabout drew the children from the surrounding streets. In the words of "Mickey Marley's Roundabout" (a jaunty song which extolled the childhood glee of a visit from the eponymous ride) *If you haven't got a penny and your ma's gone out / You can still climb on his roundabout.* Well, that was a load of ballicks: Mickey insisted on a penny and if you didn't have one, you'd get told to fuck off, and a cuff round the ear if you were caught trying to slippy-tit on.

Ben's father, Jimmy was well regarded in the area, despite hushed speculations about his paternity (Here, he spent a lot of time with those Clintons from the Markets… and he has the look of them!) He worked in the bakery in Sandy Row and distributed leftover bread and kind words to neighbours on his way home. This generosity of spirit was not extended to his family; in local parlance; he hung his fiddle outside the door. He watched his second wife carefully for signs of giving preferential treatment to her natural born children and allowed evidence to the contrary to pass without remark. One cold, winter morning, treacherous patches of black ice peppered the route along Blythe Street as Bella was bringing her stepchildren to school. All three lost their footing, and Bella landed heavily on the hard, cold ground as she attempted to save Peggy and Alfie. Though the children were unscathed, Jimmy overlooked his wife's injuries and reprimanded her for a lack of due care.

He was quick to blame and quicker to anger. When he could not find his change in his work trousers, he leapt to conclusions and accosted Ben, his tall frame looming over his skinny son, long, thin face darkened with accusation.

"Did you lift money out of my pocket?"

Ben's shoulders stiffened, already braced to defend himself from blows.

"No, Daddy!"

"You're a lying wee bastard. Where is it?"

"I don't have it!"

"Don't fucking lie!"

Crack. Ben's ear was still ringing as the belt was slipped from the trouser loops. Bella ran upstairs to examine her husband's discarded work trousers and found the money deep in the very pocket Jimmy had believed it was stolen from. He had given only a cursory search before he leapt to conclusions and lost his temper.

"*Jimmy! Jimmy – the money is here! It was here in your pocket!*"

Ben, still cowering, looked up at his father, who lowered the belt and laughed.

"*Ha! I didn't even see it!*"

Ben raised himself to standing, cheeks red, his arms and back stinging. He knew there would be no apology and silently condemned his father as a sadist. The lack of remorse stung more than the belt and he understood that justice was not something he could take for granted.

His older half-brother Alfie, having shouldered the pain and upheaval of losing his mother, also understood the world to be an unfair place, but set out to take full advantage of the situation. He chose the path of the sneak. He wheeled and dealed, cheated and refused to honour debts. When Ben was nine, his older half-brother's nefarious antics brought a deputation of angry men to Jimmy's door.

"*Does Alfie Bell live here?*"

Jimmy saw the obvious danger and went on the defensive.

"*Who's asking?*"

"*Never you fucking mind who's asking. GET THE FUCK OUTTA HERE YOU STEALING BASTARD!*"

"*Fuck away off from my door!*"

Alfie didn't fancy his da's chances of holding them off for long, so he left him to it and scarpered out the back, hot footing it through the yard and down the alley, leaving his own father outnumbered, struggling to detain men younger and stronger than him at the door. Ben wasn't one to run. He jumped on one of the men's backs in an attempt to haul him off his father and threw whatever punches he could land during what was essentially a token beating: enough to say they wouldn't be dismissed by some aul' lad or messed about by his son. When they relented, the one who had been peppered with digs from a child threw a parting remark:

"Your wee lad has more guts than your big son."

    Ben didn't have time to wait until he was big enough to defend himself, so he learned to box. A distant relative, Alfie Pedlar had been a boxer back in the 1920s, so Ben decided to follow in his footsteps. In the stagnant geography of Sandy Row, everybody was looking for somebody to knock the rump out of, whether through personal vendetta or establishing pecking order, so it wasn't the worst idea. Once he knew how to handle himself, he never looked for a fight, but never avoided one, even if he saw it coming from a mile off. He was primed.

    He was ten when he and his friends were walking past a sweet shop and noticed that the sweet display, at arms-length from the open window, was unattended. They each thrust their hands through the gap to grab a handful of sweets. Only he was caught – his friends scarpered - and the police were called, resulting in a charge of petty theft and a date at the Magistrate's. On court day, stony-faced adults scrutinised him, as he stood afraid and ashamed on a dock; tall for his age, skinny in his threadbare clothes, wishing for an ally. The judge looked to his parents.

"What do you have to say in defence of your son?"

Ben hoped they would plead on his behalf, maybe even barter a beating in lieu of legal consequences. To Jimmy and Bella, the question reeked of accusation, and they were on the back foot; poor, from Sandy Row, feeling somehow complicit, having spawned an apparent criminal. His mother spoke.

"We don't know what to do with him, Your Honour, he's a bad boy."

His heart sank. They were publicly washing their hands off him, this child of ten. The words tore at him, as he felt the weight of being undefended and truly alone; a bad boy that not even a mother would step in to defend. Those sweets earned him a spell at borstal, where, younger than most, his bad boy reputation became his armour. Nobody would mess with a bad boy. This epithet could keep him safe.

By 1962, at 19, he had completed a very brief stint in the army. He was posted in Germany, and won the Boxing Cup for his Regiment, but this was to be the solo highlight of his career. His Leo pride, charm and natural leadership would have made for an excellent general, but having never taken so much as advice, never mind orders from another human being, the life of a soldier wasn't the best fit. He bristled at commands that he found unnecessary. If a commanding officer gave instructions that were chiefly meant to humiliate, or establish dominance, as is often the culture (Get down and give me ten! etc.); *"fuck off"* would be his merry retort. Behaviour which, predictably, culminated in him seeing out the end of his term in military prison and dishonourable discharge. He delighted in not bending the knee, his defiance a clear message that he would not be pushed around. During his time in solitary, he was isolated in a cell, featureless except for a fireplace. One day, he climbed up the flue and hid, while military police were called by panicked officers to address an apparent escape.

"One of you must have opened his cell door."

"I swear, we didn't. We've been here all along, he didn't come past us!"

"Well, where is he then? There's not even a window to climb out of…"

Silence, then footsteps towards the fireplace and a face-full of soot.

"Ah, for fuck sake. FOUND HIM."

Any attempts to repress or oppress him resulted in a variety of verbal and non-verbal fuck-yous. He was competent, but unruly, tough but defensive, smart but above taking arbitrary instruction. In short, he was a truly terrible soldier. However, one commanding officer saw potential:

"The SAS would be a good fit for you, son."

"Why's that, Sir?"

"You've to be made of strong stuff to survive the training alone. Mental fortitude. Physical fortitude. And down the line, an ability to

make hard decisions and see them through. I don't see you folding under pressure, son."

Ben thought about it. It sounded to him like a lot of bending the knee would need to happen for him to get to a place where he would thrive. "Not for me."

After discharge, he returned to Sandy Row, where he supplemented his meagre boxing income by working the doors of pubs. His reputation alone usually kept trouble from the door, and if it didn't, woe betide the idiot who fancied his chances. He tattooed HATE on the knuckles of his right hand. The threat of his fury made him invulnerable, so he called it hate, inked it onto his fist and sewed it into the fibres of his being. The warrior-spirit came to reacquaint himself with the old familiar ways. As one punter reflected at kick-out time: *"You're a bastard, Ben Bell...but you're a good bastard."* He wore this epithet as a badge of honour. He would protect everyone, even if he had to hurt them.

He appointed himself moral as well as physical guardian to the patrons. He watched men closing in on inebriated and dressed to impress women, attracted by their vulnerability and impaired judgement. Some were daughters of his friends or neighbours; these he threw into taxis and sent home to their da's. He listened to men boasting about their conquests; having given it up, these women were no longer objects of desire, they were used up, devalued. *The town bike. Had more pricks than a dartboard. It was like throwing a sausage down Royal Avenue.* Reputations lost and never regained. He saw a woman who got so drunk that she defecated in her knickers and swung them across the road. He decided that some people were beyond saving.

∞∞∞∞∞

Gloria was born a year later than Ben in a little two-up-two-down kitchen house in Sandy Row, the third of three children. Her mother, a talented dressmaker, made her sweet little dresses and kept the house fastidiously clean and tidy as she waited anxiously for her husband to come home from the war. Money was tight with the man of the house away, so Martha supplemented what little was coming in by taking in work. Her sewing machine sat pride of place on a table in front of the little window looking onto the street, where she could get the best light for her delicate stitching. She tailored and made alterations for people as poor as herself and only ever charged what was reasonable until a begrudging neighbour put a stop to it by tipping off the social.

By the time Gloria was born, her older sister Lily was a teenager. They looked nothing alike: the elder had blonde, tight curls and bright blue eyes and had been a chubby child and curvy teen, while Gloria was dark, small and slight. As a baby, Gloria was being held and rocked by her older sister when she slipped over Lily's shoulder and landed with a sickening thump, head-first on the floor. She was hospitalised and regained consciousness a couple of days later, with no obvious signs of damage.

Gloria's theme of loss began early. Her father returned from France alive, but not intact, having lost an arm to cannon-fire. Within a year, the wound on his stump turned gangrenous and he died of septicaemia when she was two years old. Martha eventually remarried: a kind, quiet man, Bob, who was traumatised by the war. He kept himself to himself, taking what comfort he could from the mundanity and predictability of a daily routine. Each summer holiday was a train ride from Belfast to Bangor for a picnic on the beach. Bob would sit and gaze at the water, lost in the peaceful rhythm of the lapping, pointing out the galloping white horses to his little stepdaughter as the surges unfurled towards them.

Back in Sandy Row, Gloria made herself useful by running errands for her mother or the neighbours, skipping off to buy 2d of snuff for old Minsy Maxwell, who was confined to a wheelchair, and occasionally getting a sweet for her service. She was a quiet wee thing who gave no one any trouble. Her dark hair was swept to the side with a clip, revealing large, brown eyes that searched faces for signs of approval. Her brow was often furrowed, her serious expression belying the nervousness she felt as she tried to please everyone by being good. She was lightly made-up, small and thin, conditioning her to the very thing she was tasked to overcome vulnerability. She was meticulously turned out in patterned dresses and white socks and she always jumped when her mummy shouted through the window, "Get up off that dirty cribby!" when she had forgotten herself and plonked down for a game of marleys.

Gloria found school unbearable. In the forties and fifties, dyslexia was not yet understood, and so she sweated and blushed through lessons, praying not to be called upon to read. Her teacher, Mrs Smith took umbrage to her; Gloria's difficulties were an affront to her teaching and so she set about trying to shame the child into becoming literate. *"Are you stupid?"* she would rage in front of the class, as Gloria bit her lip to suppress tears. She so badly wanted to be smart like the others, so that she could be seen as good, and to return to comfortable obscurity.

She was approaching double figures when her mother was diagnosed with throat cancer. Martha's condition deteriorated until she lay, bedridden in the bedroom at the top of the echoing, narrow wooden stairs. Gloria sneaked up to sit close by the sick bed, quietly so as not to be noticed, so she wouldn't be told to *go out and play, love*, by her mother torn with sorrow for the child missing her childhood, a child she'd soon leave. When Gloria was dismissed, she allowed her steps down the stairs to echo, then tiptoed back up to sit outside her mother's room, eavesdropping on conversations with the visiting aunts, loving her mummy secretly from behind the door, missing her already, and dreading a future without her.

She occasionally visited her aunts' houses on the way home from school. Gloria was having a cup of tea and a piece and jam at Minnie's house when a bird flew down the chimney and made an unholy mess of the parlour. Minnie looked at Vicky.

"*Our Martha.*"

A terse nod. A bird in the house meant death. Gloria was fourteen when her mother died, leaving her in the care of her unobtrusive, shell-shocked stepfather. They muddled along in a routine of sorts: she'd keep the house tidy and have his tea ready after work, they would go their separate ways to socialise in the evenings, return and bid each other goodnight. Each gave each the other no trouble, but Gloria was anchorless and yearned to belong.

Gloria noticed Ben. In fairness, everybody noticed Ben Bell: the bad boy, the boxer, the bouncer, the defender of underdogs, a self-appointed arbiter of justice. She decided she would quite like to position her seven stone frame of anchorless vulnerability firmly under his wing. Small and meek, she had made her home in the sidelines, where she remained unobserved and out of trouble, and though these qualities had thus far served her well, now this invisibility was a hindrance. Eyes are drawn by the ostentatious, the gregarious, even the quietly confident pull focus; Gloria was none of these things. To gauge Ben's attention she had to figure out a way to launch an assault from her position of obscurity. Everybody knew Ben Bell, but Gloria decided it was high time that Ben Bell knew Gloria Martin.

Two

"Away you and call for Tucker, then see if Ben wants to come out too."

Gloria's best friend Noleen wasn't sure about this plan of action. She knew Tucker; he was a geg, but Ben Bell was another matter altogether.

"I will not indeed."

Gloria sighed. Not one to be deterred once her mind was made up. She came up with another plan.

"Right, what about this…"

She was resourceful. It was a snowy day, so they gathered a mound of snowballs. Noleen went and rapped the door, asked for Ben and then – crucial to this dastardly plot – hid. Ben was effectively lured outside to search for his mystery caller, Gloria's cue to strike.

The plan went off without a hitch. Four foot eleven and a half inches in height, Gloria's determination made her feel six foot and bulletproof: attacking a boxer with a reputation was a bold move indeed. Ben, subjected to a barrage of snowballs, reluctant to suffer any kind of affront to his dignity, toppled his tiny assailant and rolled her thoroughly in the snow. Lying in close quarters to her crush was a better result than she had dared anticipate.

Having meted out the appropriate justice, Ben was ready with questions.

"*What did you do that for?*"

Gloria was giddy at her own boldness and buoyed up by its success.

"*Ack, sure, I only wanted to talk to you.*"

"*Did you, aye?*"

She looked familiar to him, then he placed her; the quiet girl who lived two streets over. She wasn't hard to look at; slim, long dark hair parted in the middle, big dark eyes.

"*Do you smoke?*"

She did not.

"*Oh, yes.*"

"*JANET!*"

Gloria jumped as he guldered back towards his house. His youngest sibling came out looking a bit annoyed.

"*What?*"

"*Here's 3d, away to the shop and get us ten Park Drive.*"

"*Do I get any?*"

He lowered his brows, but she held his gaze and didn't relent.

"*Get us a quarter of raspberry ruffles, too, and you can have some of them.*"

That was the beginning of their courtship. They were an odd couple: Ben was tall, handsome, muscular with an air of danger. Gloria was small, slight and shy. No matchmaker would put them together, and yet, there was no denying their affinity. Her attraction was predictable – what first attracted you to this tall, dark, handsome, strong man?! - and yet, a deeper magic was at work. She accepted him as he was, and somehow knew there was more than met the eye. For the first time, he felt understood. They would meet at the wall and freeze their bums off, puffing on Park Drives and gorging on Raspberry Ruffles. When he told her that he would have to travel for bouts in England, she told him she would wait, or step aside before coming between him and his passion. He knew that she meant it, that presented with the choice between doing what was best for her, or what was best for him, she would choose his welfare in a heartbeat.

After that, he gave her his Army Boxing Trophy as a token of his love and told her she was his girl. Say no more, thought Gloria, and nailed that shit down fast: not long after, she announced that she had rented them a house in Bentham Street and was ready to get married.

"Fuck me!" he exclaimed. *"That was the most expensive snowball I have ever been hit with."*

Their wedding was impromptu. They donned their Sunday best and headed for City Hall. Gloria had been warned by many not to get involved with Ben Bell – that bad boy, but it was a fait accompli the minute he face-planted her in the snow. Being together felt like home. Her brother Billy was concerned that a life with Ben Bell would be a life of trouble for his younger sister, but he was already in Fermanagh courting his wife-to-be, Geraldine, so lack of proximity made his contribution moot. Lily was similarly concerned, but no more successful.

Gloria wore a suit, because a dress on her diminutive frame would make her look childlike, and if there was one thing she hated, it was being mistaken for a child. She arranged her long, dark hair into a beehive, as was the style at the time, but allowed the front to sweep down to cover her ears before being gathered up into a twist above the nape.

Happily, there was a bun in the oven shortly after the wedding. When she announced the pregnancy to Ben, he put her on immediate bedrest with a steak and a mug of Complan: in the hope that she would grow a strong boy, another warrior. Jeanette thwarted expectations with her gender. Jeanette was bonny, she had the Bell charm: a ready smile and good looks. Billy was born a couple of years later, the longed-for son, his wee mate, his champ. Billy favoured his mother, a gentle demeanour, a shy, trusting gaze looking out from under long dark eyelashes.

Two children were plenty; there were now four hungry mouths to feed, not including Punchie, a flatulent Alsatian-cross mutt. Ben worked as a stager in the shipyards. The sporadic staging work was punctuated by the occasional boxing engagement, and they lived hand to mouth. Early each morning he took his greatcoat off the sleeping children to go to the gates of Harland and Wolff shipyards in the hope of being chosen for a day's work, handpicked by an impassive foreman, or dismissed on his whim. When he couldn't afford the bus fare, he walked the distance through the grey streets of Belfast. One day, he watched a childhood friend lose his balance and drop like a stone, thudding off the sides of the dry dock. They lifted his lifeless, broken body from the floor and worked on, traumatised but unable to lose a day's pay.

Gloria enjoyed nothing more than walking the length of Sandy Row with Billy in the pram and Jeanette in tow. One sunny afternoon, a lady stopped her to admire Billy.

"Would you look at him! My God, he has the face of an angel."

Gloria beamed with pride. He really was a lovely wee thing, so pleasant and serene. The lady fixed her with a steady gaze and added,

"He's not long for this world."

The words turned her blood to ice. She had never told a soul that for as long as she could remember she had intrusive visions of a small white coffin, just large enough for a child. She grabbed Jeanette's hand and hurried on.

It was the sixties and rumblings of political unrest were coming from Derry. The Civil Rights movement was gathering force and one dreadful Sunday the British troops, deployed to keep the peace in the Bogside, opened fire on a civilian march, killing many, including children. Across the province, working classes were beginning to polarise to Orange and Green. Gatherings and shows of strength in the Green Nationalist areas prompted the same in the Orange Loyalist areas. The Ulster Defence Association (UDA) gained strength in numbers in response to a burgeoning Irish Republican Army (IRA). There was no elaborate induction into the paramilitaries; pretty much every man in Sandy Row considered himself to be in the UDA - prepared to take up defensive arms should the need arise. Partisan lines were drawn; Nationalist was synonymous with Catholic, and Loyalist with Protestant. Ben's older half siblings had married Catholics and moved to Nationalist Twinbrook. Gone now were the easy days when family could babysit for their nieces and nephews in nationalist areas, or when Peggy and Alfie could visit their parents' or siblings' homes in Loyalist Sandy Row. Everyone was afraid.

Still, nobody messed with Ben. He laboured at the shipyard by day, trained by night and fought bouts. It was time to develop different muscles. One day at work, he was doing some heavy lifting and felt a sudden pain in his lower back. The pain was excruciating: he couldn't sit, stand or walk for any length of time. The GP diagnosed a herniated disc. A manager called to offer him a job as foreman, no lifting, shifting or exertion, just overseeing. He still needed to put food on the table, so was grateful for the opportunity and presented to work, only to leave the day unfinished; he was in too much pain to do anything but lie down. Showing up for half a day's work was later cited as evidence that he was still fit for work after the accident and therefore ineligible for an injury settlement. He had been duped.

Ben underwent a spinal operation on the damaged discs. The prognosis was not good: there was a chance that he may not be able to walk again. He refused to accept this and forced himself to regain mobility little by little, through gritted teeth and intolerable pain. As Billy took his first steps, Ben began to walk again.

The spinal injury left him in various states of incapacity: some days he could walk further than others with the pain remaining a low-level constant, on other days a sneeze could put his back out and have him bedridden, grey and drawn, unable to move, pissing into a bottle. Doctors assessed him to determine if he was fit for work. If he didn't present for his appointment, he couldn't be declared unfit for work or eligible for benefits, so no money. If he did present for his appointment, the rigour of the physical exam - the bending, the walking, the turning this way and that - was sufficient to convince the medic that he was fit for work, but enough to exacerbate the injury and put him in bed for a week: no money. So began the merry-go-round. He would be declared fit for work and forced out to earn, which would aggravate his spine. He'd be forced to leave the day half done and fired. More doctor appointments to determine his eligibility for sickness benefit. And on it went.

Might was entwined in both his essence and reputation, but now he couldn't perform physical labour or fight without incurring serious physical pain. Alternating between standing and sitting was the only way to alleviate the pressure on his spine.

Boxing had been integral to his sense of self: it was the birthplace of his self-esteem and the means by which he garnered respect. He reasoned that if he could work the doors, he could still fight bouts. Bobbing and weaving was no longer a possibility so he stood rooted in the ring like an oak, taking punishment until his opponent tired, before he landed the blows that would finish the match. He turned professional for a time and fought bouts in England, but soon became disillusioned; money changed hands to secure outcomes, making a pantomime of his beloved sport. He started his own boxing club to teach kids the basics of the sport and to give them the self-esteem it had bequeathed him. In a world where the weak were chewed up and spat out, he wanted to make everyone strong.

The Troubles were raging in seventies Belfast. People who considered themselves underdogs in family disputes, neighbour disputes or paramilitary disputes came to Ben to solicit advice or have situations handled. Problems that could not be solved with words were solved with fists. His take on justice incurred assault charges, which he was comfortable with, trusting that he never hit anyone that didn't deserve it. Word was that paramilitary leaders had decided that Ben could be of use to them. He ignored the rumour mill and carried on with his routine; work, pints and home. He mostly drank in the Lily Bar, a men's pub in Sandy Row, remarkable for the red telephone box inexplicably situated in the middle of the saloon. He knew the owner, James McNair well, and his old friend

Hearn was the manager. A notorious face took the stool beside him at the bar, and both knew there was no need for introductions. Smoke hung thick in the air, and nearby conversations hushed to best facilitate a decent eavesdrop.

"We need something handled and you're the man to do it."

Ben took a sip of his pint and licked his lips.

"Nah."

"I'm not asking. I'm telling you."

Ben continued looking forward towards the bar, stonewalling.

"You'll fucking do it or you're dead. You hear me?"

Slowly, Ben turned to look at the man whose paramilitary protection enabled him to talk to him this way. He allowed his cold stare to linger a while. Then he spoke.

"Fuck off," he said, quietly, confidentially, wishing to make his point without drawing further attention.

"You'll regret that."

Ben looked back at the bottles lining the wall behind the bar, a gesture of dismissal, but the man just stood there, trying to work out how to circumvent this apparent checkmate. Ben sat, motionless and defiant.

"I thought I told you to fuck off," he muttered.

The man scraped his stool as he disembarked, enraged.

"You're dead, you cunt."

Ben nodded and sipped his pint.

Within the week, men wearing balaclavas busted in the front door and dragged him to a waiting van. Gloria screamed and pulled at them but there was nothing she could do, except wait for word – that he was in hospital or found dead. He was dumped on the doorstep the following day, barely conscious, his face beaten to a purple pulp, teeth missing, and fingers broken by a breezeblock. Gloria rushed to him.

"*Oh, Ben!*"

She tried to help him up and into the house, but he was mumbling something through his bust lip.

"*What is it, Ben?*"

"*I.. didn't…*"

"*What is it? What are you telling me?*"

Blood flecked his lips and chin as he tried to enunciate through his broken mouth.

"*I didn't…bend…the knee.*"

He was left alone after the beating; it was clear that his UDA involvement was very much at an end. It was one thing to go and march with the boys in Sandy Row, or erect defensive street barricades, but he drew the line at being used to administer beatings at the whim of men using the cover of the cause to wield power.

Paramilitary attacks were getting closer to home and becoming more frequent. Nationalist paramilitaries killed two in a no-warning bomb at the Crescent bar and the historical Klondyke was blasted by a car bomb, killing one and maiming numerous others. Catholics were murdered at the interface of Sandy Row and the Falls; later an eighteen-year-old Catholic girl drinking with her Protestant friends was taken out the back by paramilitaries and her throat slit. The UDA had morphed into something else that Ben and many others wouldn't be a part of.

Ben continued to mete out justice according to his own moral code: he would not tolerate apparent unfairness or unnecessary shows of strength. He hit a UDA man who had gotten too big for his boots, but when word was ferried back to command, they refused to intervene. Perhaps, after the punishment beating, they realised what he was made of and backed off, perhaps it was simply easier to ignore him. There was even a possibility that he was inadvertently helping by taking upstarts down a peg or two. Whatever the reason, it had become apparent that senior UDA leaders wouldn't touch Ben Bell, and this piqued the interest of intelligence gathering police.

The 1970s saw the beginning of internment in Northern Ireland, when many people were detained or imprisoned without trial in the hope that isolating paramilitary leaders would prevent further violence in the conflict. The raid was swift: police choreographed raids to occur simultaneously at his house, his brothers' houses and at his mother's home. Doors were broken down and floorboards ripped up in the hope of finding guns. Neighbours ran into the streets and clanged metal bin lids off the kerbs to warn others of the police presence.

Two RUC men kicked in the front door and found Ben with Gloria, six-year-old Jeanette and four-year-old Billy, who were frozen with alarm in the front room.
"Ben Bell, you're under arrest!"

Ben stood and fixed them with a defiant glare. The speaker was an older officer, lines of stress etched deeply into his face. The younger one looked like he'd been on the job for one hot minute.

"*Oh aye? What for?*"

"*Suspected paramilitary involvement.*"

"*I'm no paramilitary. I'm going nowhere. I've done nothing wrong.*"

"*Aye, I know. Get out of this house and into the van.*"

"*No.*"

"*What?*"

"*No. Fuck off.*"

"*Fu…? Look. Do you understand me? You are under arrest. Get out!*"

"*No. I haven't done anything wrong.*"

Jeanette and Billy had been ushered out to the scullery and were craning their necks round their mummy, who had taken up a defensive position in the doorway. The officer was growing agitated with this cheeky fucker who was making his job harder than it needed to be. He didn't put his life on the line day in day out to have his authority undermined by some uppity cunt from Sandy Row. He turned and fixed his gaze on his colleague and lowered his voice.

"*Shoot him.*"

The words hung in the air for a moment. Gloria felt a sudden sting of white-hot alarm. The younger one stared wide-eyed at his colleague, hoping this was a ploy to get the unwilling ward to capitulate. He glanced at Ben who smiled back, daring him to act.

"He's resisting arrest," he repeated. *"Shoot him."*

Seconds stretched. All eyes were on the younger one, as he struggled to figure out what to do. Eventually, the would-be assassin found his voice.

"But…"

He pointed in the direction of an ashen-faced Gloria, and the staring children in the room beyond.

"Witnesses…"

His superior let out a bark of frustration and lunged at his unwilling captive, to drag him out. Hughie and Tucker were in the street outside, having run straight to Ben's as their houses were being turned over. They watched as he was hauled into a van.

"Ben! What the fuck…!"

Ben realised he was about to have the rump knocked out of him, and any resistance on their part could land them in the shit too, never mind making things significantly worse for him in the van.

"Don't antagonise them!"

"But –"

"Don't fuckin' antagonise them!"

He took the beating, after which he found himself in Long Kesh prison.

It wasn't all bad. There was a fair few familiar faces on the inside - it seemed like half of Sandy Row had been interned - and on visiting day, relatives did their damnedest to smuggle in alcohol or cigarettes. The families of UDA inmates received support in the form of food parcels; an act of charity which stirred animosity in one blow-in who, having become pregnant following an affair with a UDA commander, begrudged the parcel going to his wife and children. Eight weeks after her son was born, she was forced to account for her defamatory remarks by the wife, who ordered her to be kidnapped, brought to a UDA club in a former disused bakery and rompered, that is to say, tortured before being brutally murdered, all within earshot of the woman's terrified six-year-old daughter.

Gloria took the bus with the rest of the wives and tried to smuggle in miniature bottles of drink too, but her seven stone frame didn't afford her much of a bosom and the clanking gave her away. Her guilty conscience also determined that she probably wasn't the best accomplice. Ben resigned himself to a dry spell and requested books instead. By this stage, his interests were many: Philosophy - Ancient and Modern, Mathematics, Journalism, Poetry, Modern European History. Anyone else would have had the piss ripped out of them.

He figured that the best way to get by in jail was to walk up to the biggest, scariest inmate and punch him in the face. That way, you looked hard as nails or completely mental; either way, you'd likely be given a wide berth, and peace to read your books. Self-education had long been his means of escape; he would open a book and be transported. As for providing a means for a literal escape from the poverty, that ship had sailed. He took workshop and branded a broad leather belt with the names of his family; Ben, Gloria, Jeanette, Billy. He taught a fellow inmate how to read. Fascinated by human nature, he watched: wardens, fair and sadistic, inmates; defeated, contrite, the ones that kept their heads down and the ones that stabbed blocks of cheese because it had a similar give to that of human flesh. Gloria brought the kids to see their daddy, but after that first time, Ben told her not to bother again. As they sat at a table under the watchful gaze of prison officers, an excited Billy (his understanding of jail being gleaned from cowboy pictures) asked loudly,

"Daddy! When are you going to escape?"

The interest of the officers monitoring the visitation room was piqued. Ben tried to think of something to say that would placate his wee son while reassuring the guards that no such plan existed, but he drew a blank.

"Eh...don't be silly, son."

Gloria noticed the change in Ben's affect and realised that Billy was drawing unwanted attention. She panicked and shushed her son, which served only to make them seem more suspicious. Undeterred, Billy's eyes were lit up with enthusiasm for the imminent break-out.

"You are going to escape, Daddy! When will you escape?"

"Ah, fuck."

Gloria was no help. She just sat there, now mute with horror, making it look very much like a plan existed and they had been rumbled. By the time visitation was up, Ben's cell had been thoroughly turned over.

Billy wasn't entirely wrong, however. Escape plans emerged sporadically, a natural consequence of boredom and discontent. Word was ferried along from inmate to inmate, cell to cell, that there was a plan to break the prods out. A fellow inmate sought out Ben, speaking in a confidential tone.

"Ben…Ben!"

"What?"

"You looking out?"

"Wha'?"

"You looking out of this place? There's a few lads have a plan."

"What plan?"

"We are meeting at the rec area at 4. If ya want in, meet us there."

A conspiratorial wink and off he sauntered, a poor imitation of inconspicuousness. Ben instinctively knew it was bound to be a heap of shite, but curiosity and a healthy disdain for imprisonment was motivation enough to show up later that day. A sizeable group had collected; the anticipation was palpable. He stood back slightly and observed as a face he couldn't quite place began to talk.

"Right, lads, we are getting out."

"YEEEOOOO!"

"Shh! What the…keep it down, Dickhead!"

"Ah shite, sorry."

"I have a plan I have been working on but I'm going to need your co-operation."

"I'm in! Count me in. Whatever you need. I need to flit this shit hole."

Murmurs of agreement rippled through the gathering as a piece of paper was produced.
"What's that?"
"This, lads, is our way outta here."
"What is it, a map?"
"It's a blueprint."
"A blue…? What the fuck are you on about?"
"Look…here it is."
The piece of paper was carefully unfolded and discreetly passed along. Ben pushed in to get a better look and spoke for the first time.
"Ah, for fuck sake."
It was indeed a blueprint - for a hot air balloon.
"It's stuff like this that gives Prods a reputation for being thick. Hot air balloon. You're a fucking balloon!"

Gloria suffered the indignity of invasive searches every week and counted off the days until her husband came home. She brought the kids into her bed each night. They were no stranger to the big bed; before their daddy went to prison, they would bound in each morning and he would stretch his arms out in invitation.
"Take a wing!"
"I'm taking this wing!"
They would lay their heads down and breathe in the musty morning smell of their big daddy. Billy always had questions.
"Daddy, what are we doing today?"
"Well, you're going to school."

"Oh, Daddy?"
"What son?"
"What's that?"
He pointed to the rug of hair on Ben's chest.
"That? That's my chest, son."
Billy looked at it thoughtfully then snuggled in.

When it was just the three of them, Jeanette and Billy joined their mummy in the big bed, taking turns being warm in the middle, or wedged against the cold wall. Gloria saved up what little money they had to pay a photographer for a portrait of the three of them, for Ben to keep while he was away.

Release day came and Ben departed prison with the photograph and the belt he had made in the workshop. Things were back to normal, or whatever constituted normalcy during the Troubles. Her daddy was home, but little Jeanette seemed more anxious than her usual self. The other world clung to her like trailing cobwebs. She began coming downstairs after bedtime, to tell her mummy there was someone in her room. One night it was a young boy, looking out of the window, wearing a yellow top with a brown collar, and everything felt sad. Another night, she was drifting off to sleep when she felt her Granny Bell's hair tickle her face. She woke abruptly and ran downstairs.
"Mummy! I smelled Granny Bell's hair! It went past my face!"
"It's okay, love, just another wee dream. 'Mon back to bed."
Gloria brought her up the cold wooden stairs and tucked her back into bed with a kiss. Tucker and Hughie called to

the door within the hour with news that their mother had passed.

∞∞∞

Bombs were frequent occurrences. The deep, sonorous boom of an explosion, felt as much as heard, first prompted guesses as to the location and a race to the nearest television in the hope of catching the news to confirm your loved ones were safe. It was during such a bulletin that Gloria saw footage of a dazed man, leaning against a lamppost with a bleeding head wound. Her stepfather. Horror replaced dread as she sped to the hospital to see him. The wounds were superficial, but not everyone was so lucky. Nowhere was safe.

Gloria was walking up the Donegal Road with Billy when he asked her for a penny sweet, a request which she refused. He persisted. She stood firm, a little surprised as it wasn't like him to continue asking. She wasn't usually one to relent to whining, but something told her to do so and together they went into the shop.

"Just a wee penny sweet, Mummy."
"Alright, son, alright, 'mon and pick one."
Little Billy strained to see the counter.
"That one!"
"Alright, here you are."
Billy popped the penny sweet in his mouth and looked around the shop. A little old lady had come in, and his eye level was just above her sagging stockings.

"*Mummy?*"

Gloria was arranging her purse back in her bag.

"*Yes, son?*"

"*That lady has chest on her legs.*"

There was no time for embarrassment, because just then, a bomb detonated down the road – precisely where they would have been had they not stopped.

It is a rare parent who approaches the task unencumbered by their own early experiences; we are reactionary creatures. Ben projected the chinks in his armour onto his children. Their clothes and shoes were the best he could afford, they were not to know the vulnerability of being the poorest and least provided for. Janet had moved to the States and regularly sent back boxes of clothes which were passed around her brothers' families to see what fitted the various children. Ben wanted to be the sole provider for his family, but Gloria was happy to rifle through the parcel with her sisters-in-law, and found a few nice tops, purple for Jeanette, yellow with a brown collar for Billy.

Ben did his best to provide what he could but was determined that his children would get the education he was denied, and not be trapped, or without options. In the meantime, he put food on the table, made sure the homeworks were completed, and took both of his children to his club to teach them to defend themselves. Jeanette cut her hair short and fought with the best of them. He wanted her to be strong and independent, beholden to nobody.

The kids played around the streets of Sandy Row, making their own fun. Jeanette and Billy were inseparable. Jeanette was scrappy, like her daddy, while Billy was soft-hearted like Gloria. Sometimes they went to the park and swung high, kicking the stony ground beneath the swing to get high enough to point their toes at the ridge of Napoleon's Nose on the silhouette of Belfast's Black Mountain. Besides the games of chase or hide and seek, they were opportunists; a favourite game was jumping on the bar at the back of delivery vans that wended through the narrow streets. Jeanette, Billy and their friend caught up to a van and jubilantly mounted the bar for a wee ride. The vehicle slowed, then began to reverse towards a wall. The children panicked – Jeanette jumped off one side, their friend, the other, but little Billy was too slow. The van continued to reverse until it pinned Billy against a wall. Jeanette ran, horrified, to the driver's door and banged with her palm.

"Mister! Stop! Mister! My brother is at the back!"

The driver had only meant to frighten the children. He hurriedly drove forward and shouted out his window.

"Is he okay?"

She didn't want to get into trouble. She nodded as Billy clutched his stomach.

"Jeanette, I want Mummy."

Jeanette sprang into action and helped her brother up.

The driver left. Billy put his arm round his sister for support and walked as far as he could manage, until it became too much.

"I want Mummy."

Jeanette was breathless with panic and exertion.

"We are nearly there. It's okay, Billy."

But it wasn't. She wasn't so much supporting him as dragging him. She lifted him and somehow managed to get him over the wall they had climbed together earlier that day, but he was growing weaker, and she could carry him no further. She lay him down.

"Wait here, okay? I'm getting Mummy."

She ran as fast as she could and by the time Gloria got to Billy, his lips were turning blue. She saw that he had soiled himself and assumed he was in shock.

"Jeanette! Go and get Uncle Hughie and tell him we need a lift to the hospital!"

Jeanette ran, breathless and afraid. Gloria carried her son home and somehow stood him in front of the fire to wash him off over a bucket before Hughie arrived.

Word was sent to Ben to get to the hospital. There, in the sanitary white ward amid the bleeps and smell of disinfectant, the doctors quickly determined that the effluence had been forced from his bowel by the unrelenting pressure of the van, which had ruptured his little organs. His condition deteriorated. Jeanette fretted by her brother, his skinny seven-year-old frame lying tiny in the bed. Billy was sore but was distracted for a moment by something in the corner of the room. He pointed and his brown eyes grew wide as he smiled faintly.

"Look! There's Mary and Joseph."

He slipped into unconsciousness.

    Ben and Gloria watched, horrified and unbelieving, as the life ebbed from their son's little body. In the meantime, Jeanette was passed between her uncles' houses. At Uncle Tucker's house, she was watching TV with the cousins when suddenly she was seized with apprehension.
"*Aunt Anne, what time is it?*"
Aunt Anne checked her watch.
"*It's ten til', love.*"
"*Ten 'til what, Aunt Anne?*"
"*'Til four, love. Why?*"
Jeanette just nodded and let her gaze glaze over. She knew Billy was gone because everything felt different.

    Now her mother's only child, Jeanette was sure her mummy would gather her up in her arms when she was returned home from her uncles' houses. Instead, lost in the depths of her own pain, Gloria looked through her, remote and untouchable. Billy had been buried in the cold, packed earth with Granny Bell, and his parents didn't know how to live out their days until they could be with their dear, sweet boy again. Jeanette turned ten without Billy. Ten, when she was dressed in a too-hot formal overcoat and brought to court without warning, subjected to a barrage of blunt questions forcing her to re-live the most horrifying and painful day of her life under scrutinizing eyes, that seemed to watch with unblinking accusation. Ben refused to prepare his daughter for court lest it be seen as tampering with a witness and so she found herself on the stand, confused and scared. She identified the driver incorrectly. Outside the courtroom, she watched her daddy's friend give him a consolatory pat on the arm and learned that she could not be trusted with questions.

The pressure to provide for his family and honour his son while in the clutches of a vicious, unrelenting grief was overwhelming. He organised a Boxing Show and donated the proceeds to the hospital wing that cared for Billy in those last days. He worked the doors of bars to bring money in; he drank, staggered home and passed out in his clothes.

Gloria struggled on, racing back and forth to whatever work was available, running on tea and cigarettes. She cleaned schools and did auxiliary nursing to supplement Ben's income, made unpredictable by flare ups of the spinal injury. She cut off her signature long dark curtains of hair, now a pointless frivolity. Her grief stuck in her throat as she desperately tried to conceive another baby. After three years and five miscarriages, at last, a pregnancy looked like it might go to full term. She did not celebrate because she had learned that life ripped your joy away if you dared take anything for granted.

On Earth, skewed perspective casts long, dark shadows. They loaded a new arrival with meaning: a baby after five losses meant God cared again. They had prayed for a child, but to pray is to enter into a contract with the divine and an answered prayer can be what you need, which isn't always the same as what you want.

They wanted a boy but expressing this ingratitude could invite the wrath of the God who ripped Billy from the world. A baby girl meant that when God remembered their address, he also remembered their limitations and understood that a mere three years after Billy was taken, another boy would have expectations heaped upon him.

These were the circumstances of my arrival.

Three

I took on the temporary identity bestowed by genetics and environment, which shaped my core beliefs and dictated the themes I would be attuned to and explore throughout my life. That's how it is. There are no accidents.

This new assignment had me hitting the ground running; the stage was set, and frankly, it was a shit-show. I found my soul mates fraught and weary. They had taken many punches and had their guard up, anticipating further blows.

Jeanette was thirteen when I was born. When I squalled for milk, she pacified me by sticking her big toe in my mouth while Mummy rushed off to the kitchen to prepare a bottle. I'm not a foot fan to this day. She pushed me along in the pram when she went to meet her friends. By the time I was able to talk, she had a Catholic boyfriend, and I was issued strict instructions not to rat her out. Dating across the barricades was a good way to get yourself killed and our daddy would have knocked seven bells out of her for being so foolhardy. Despite having zero understanding of the stakes, I said zip. I worshipped Jeanette. Daddy was out all day and well into most evenings, Mummy was forever finishing a fag and running across Belfast to work, and I was fired across the street to our neighbour Moira's house, with a hasty *be good!* until Jeanette could collect me.

I shared one of the two bedrooms with Jeanette; Mummy and Daddy slept in the room across the square of the hall. Jeanette's bed was against the wall immediately beside the door and mine was at the opposite side, the foot of my bed reaching a disused fireplace from which a cold damp emanated. Mummy was the praying kind; when she prayed with me it was like we were paying our dues. We knelt by the side of the bed and did prayer hands – although she couldn't tell me why the hands were necessary - to recite the Lord's Prayer followed by God Bless Daddy, Mummy, Jeanette, Billy and Peggy, and All the Poor Children of the World. Billy's bequest to me was to initiate a lifetime of preoccupation with the other side. We never met in Earth's school room, but his absence was formative.

"Mummy, where is Billy?"
"Billy is in Heaven, love."
"Why?"
A sigh. Then quietly -
"Because God wanted him to be with Him."
I imagined playing with my brother, forever frozen at age seven. His photograph sat in the living room, the colourisation of the black and white photograph gave his gentle smile an otherworldly look. His dark eyes looked wistful and kind. I had heard the story of Billy, arm in a

sling, climbing a tree to help a sad little boy retrieve a ball and I knew he would be kind to me too.

"I wish he would come back. I want to play with him."

It was barely perceptible, but I felt Mummy withdraw.

"He can't come back. He is in Heaven. Now, Time to sleep, wee love."

"What if I have a bad dream?"

"Think nice thoughts and you will have nice dreams."

"Ni'-night, Mummy."

"Ni'-night, love."

Mummy stayed until I was asleep. I felt her warm beside me, breathing soft and steady, hypnotising me, relaxing me with her constancy. Her warm woollen cardigans smelled of talcum powder and stale cigarette smoke. On nights when I woke and found her gone, I lay in the dark, reassured by the chink of light across Jeanette's bed from the bulb on the landing, and thought about my brother. His presence in another realm sparked questions.

Who was this God?

Why did he take people away?

Would he take me away?

Where was Heaven?

What was it like?

We missed Billy - did he miss us?

This other place was behind an opaque curtain, governed by a capricious master, a terrifying and unfathomable Father.

I felt perpetually haunted, a fact which made night-time toilet trips infinitely worse. I left my bed, the warmth immediately dissipating from my thin body, and padded down creaking stairs that echoed hollow. I always felt eyes on my back as I trekked through the desolate living room and felt the shock of cold tile underfoot in the kitchen. It seemed impossible that anything could be colder than those tiles, and yet, somehow the tiles in the hall managed it, a biting cold that made the bones of my feet ache. My breath came in misty puffs as I shivered on the toilet. The return journey was never quick enough; those same eyes watched me climb the stairs, get into bed and try to thaw.

I was a strange wee fish, with ideas well above my station. When my aunts came to visit, they bowled in through the front door into our cramped, shadowy living room and exclaimed in their broad Belfast accents:
"Ack, would ya look at wee Paggy, you're your ma's double!"
My joy at having visitors would diminish and I would reply, witheringly, in a clipped accent,
"My name...is Peggy."
I couldn't abide the mispronunciation of my name, Paggy sounded uncouth. I had the idea that I was fancy and didn't enjoy suggestions to the contrary.
"Oh, pardon me...Pehhh-ggy."

I detected sarcasm, but was content that they had conceded, and snuggled in to enjoy hugs that smelled of different laundry powders and floral perfumes. I trotted off through the draughty kitchen, where the tap dripped metronomically, measuring my journey in hollow plinks to the square back hall, only large enough to allow a door straight ahead to the bathroom, another to the right which led to the garden and a space to the left with shelves, our pantry. I went into the yard, past the concrete coal bunker and onto the grass to collect wild roses from the hedges; a gift for our gracious guests and forgiveness for the Paggy affront.

As the aunts pointed out, I was a ringer for Mummy, every feature in miniature. She delighted in this and frequently dressed us in matching clothes to drive the point home. I remember itching as she wheeled me about Stewart's supermarket in our matching handmade Aran cardigans with the duffle coat buttons or begging for a wee ride in her tartan pull along trolley on the way home with the shopping, protected from the rain in our identical mint green anoraks.

"My legs hurt, Mummy."
"Uh hmm."
"Can I have a wee ride in the trolley?"
"No, you'll squash the food."
"I won't, I promise."
"No. Now give my head peace."
"Ack."

The return journey from the shops seemed never ending. Tates Avenue was a long, busy road lined with terraced houses on both sides. The upper end joined the busy shopping district of the arterial Lisburn Road. The houses at this end of our street were fairly well-proportioned townhouses. The bottom end consisted of two-up, two-downs; it was here we lived. Walking away from the Lisburn Road end was a downhill trek over the bridge, the apex of which was approximately two storeys high, the latticed wall allowing a view of the streets below. The height triggered Mummy's vertigo; here, she stiffened, held my hand more tightly and refused to look over the edge. There were steps flanking the bridge and I pulled away, eager to experience the cause of her discomfort, and gaze down, dizzied and exhilarated. Sometimes the journey made me sore and tired, and I cried. Her warm hand would give mine a squeeze.

"*That's enough of the gurning, we're near home nai.*"

Hot tears spilled down my cheeks, not from sore legs, but from the unfairness of having to walk so very far for so long. Surely it was too far for a little person? Anyway, I was only crying for some sympathy to feast on, which would give me enough energy to make the final furlong. Mummy was worn out herself, and this gurning was only sucking the life out of her faster.

"*That's enough of the crocodile tears. Come on, nai.*"

My Achilles heel was the unfounded accusation that I was putting it on. I'd pull my hand away to show that she had single-handedly destroyed our friendship, and we trotted on, the cliché of grim parent and wailing child. To add further insult, passers-by coming the other way gave Mummy the sympathetic eye-roll, that silent salute of comradeship, *Kids, eh?* wilfully oblivious to the tumult in my chest. It wasn't their business and they had picked a side that wasn't mine. Rude.

Memories of another life lingered. I had hazy recollections of a life as a boy with ringlets, a cropped coat and knickerbockers. Jeanette was training to be a hairdresser and offered to cut my hair into the page-boy style. I remember giddily thinking that she could make me look like myself again. I sat on a dining chair in the middle of our living room, newspaper spread out on the floor to catch the hair. There wasn't much room for Jeanette to navigate her client, between the coarse brown corduroy sofa behind and the chipped beige tiles of the 30s deco fireplace opposite. The TV was to my left, in the corner and beside the window looking onto the busy street beyond. I was thrilled with anticipation as one by one my sandy waves fell on the newspaper sheets covering the swirly orange and brown carpet. At one point I remember thinking, hold on, there's rather a lot of hair coming off here, but my concerns were dismissed with a curt *Hold still!* I was finally allowed to stand on the sofa to get a look at myself in the frameless mirror above the fireplace. Mummy had stuck rose transfers on each corner to try and make it fancy, and there was me in the middle. Profoundly disappointed barely covers how I felt upon viewing the final result. Jeanette had snipped my barnet into a bowl cut: a fringed bob with no distinction between what was fringe, and what was bob. I was only four, but even I knew I looked like a dick. I started to cry.

"Ah, here we go, wee gurny guh!"

I'd been cheated out of my ringlets by a hairdresser, but I could rely on Mummy the tailor not to muff short trousers. She made what she referred to as 'pedal-pushers' in, at my insistence, cornflower blue. I wore them constantly, even after the day a smelly bus backfired and covered them in soot spots that wouldn't wash out. In time, the memories and feelings faded, and I was just me, Peggy - old lady name and bad hair. Worse was to come when it was discovered that I needed glasses.

My sight was poor, and my left eye turned in when I tried to focus, a lazy eye. The optician recommended glasses with a patch over the good eye, to force the lazy eye to buck up its ideas. We were poor so frame options were limited to those provided free of charge by the National Health Service (NHS). In those days, that meant one recognisable style; plain, two thick plastic rectangles, straight edged along the top and slightly curved around the lower edges. In an attempt to ensure I wore the glasses, Mummy encouraged me to pick my own frame.

"What ones do you want, love?"

I looked around the Optometrist's shelves in the bright shop, flooded by light from the large window, underwhelmed by the options. I very much wanted a black or brown frame, like Daddy, or one of the Two Ronnies, so I began to make my way over to the Men's section.

"Those ones!"

"No love, they are boys' glasses. 'Mon over here 'til you see the girl's ones."

"But I want those ones!"

"No, love."

Mummy was growing flustered; she had a voucher for a pair of NHS children's glasses and didn't have the money for anything that was more expensive than free.

"You get to pick from these ones."

She drew my attention to a pearlescent range. I studied the three, translucent light pink, beige or light blue.

"I'll have those blue ones."

"What about the pink, or the beige?"

This second apparent veto dispensed with the illusion of choice. I felt my eyes sting and the glasses I was trying on began to steam up.

"No gurning, nai! That's enough."

I tried to swallow them back, but if there was one thing guaranteed to bring tears out faster, it was a lack of sympathy. I went from frustrated to frustrated and lonely. I wiped away the wet with the heel of my hand and sniffed back rivulets that weren't abating. In the coming months, I alternated between the pink and beige. How many pairs did I have, if alternating was possible? You may well ask.

I hated wearing glasses. I was already hearing impaired, presumably because both parents smoked, and second-hand fumes meant ear, nose and throat issues resulting in dull hearing from runny ears and constant catarrh. I had come to rely on lip reading, but now a brown orthoptic patch obscured my one working eye. It was no wonder, then, that by the time I attended nursery, I had a tendency to 'lose' my eyewear.

Mummy held my hand as we walked up Donegall Avenue, lined with tall, narrow terraced houses, stealing peeks in through the parlour windows that faced directly onto the street. Most had net curtains for privacy, some were boarded up and many long since bricked up, with tell-tale scorch marks of arson. Once we reached the Donegall Road, busy with traffic, the air thick with exhaust fumes, her hand tightened around mine as we approached the pedestrian crossing by the newsagents'.

"Mummy, can I have a wee sweet?"

"Get away o' that, what do you think I am, made o' money?"

On days when Jeanette was walking down to her apprenticeship at Hairlines, I held both their hands and pressed my luck for a wee swing, flinging my legs in the air.

"That's enough o' that, you've near me arm pulled outta the socket."

I loved Mummy, but by God, she could be a spoilsport.

The Arellian Nursery was a cacophony of bright colours and activity. The teachers wore blue checked pinnies, aprons that presumably saved their clothes from whatever filth us tinkers subjected them to.

"Morning, Miss!"

"Good morning, Paggy, and how are you today?"

"My name - "

Mummy would jerk me off to one side, before I could be marked as a cheeky child. A quick kiss and off I'd go to hang my coat up on the peg beneath a picture of a house, a useful symbol for a non-reader. I had a full-time place and after a morning of play we were all ferried off to the nap room and would then awaken groggily to the smell of a cooked lunch. We sat at long tables and went through the same charade each day.

"Who would like the skin of the custard?"

And all hands would go in the air, desperate for the accolade of being chosen to choke down the rubbery dairy flap. If the honour was not bestowed upon me, I felt it as a vicious affront.

The nursery teachers were committed to ensure that my glasses were fixed to my face at all times. At three, I attempted to negotiate this, but to no avail.

"I only have to wear them sometimes," I would venture.

"Now, Paggy, your mummy said you have to wear them all day."

The fools. Mummy had buggered off to work and what she didn't know wouldn't hurt her. It was profoundly unfair; the other children (I assumed, from their gleeful sounds) were having larks galore; I couldn't see to play and if they left suddenly, I had more chance of getting a sweet of a morning than of finding them. Instead, I developed solitary games. I found a small hill and stood on top with my arms outstretched, pretending to be Worzel, a scarecrow, staked to the ground. Just like in the opening credits to the programme, my imaginary stake would become loose, and I would fall off the hill, arms outstretched. *"Arghhh!"* I would exclaim. Well, there are only so many times you can amuse yourself with the same dramatic re-enactment. All things considered, I really wanted to be Aunt Sally anyway, pretty and popular, having a cup o' tea and a slice o' cake.

Eventually I'd engage myself in a more rewarding pursuit; losing the patch festooned joy stealers. I soon discovered that just leaving them around and walking off had limited success; I would be spotted enjoying myself and the situation quickly remedied. The solution was obvious; lose them irredeemably. There was a railway track running behind the wall of the nursery: the Botanic to City Hospital line. One day, I simply flung them on to the rails. Problem solved. The teacher was cross, a fact I can confirm because for once I could see her clearly and she looked livid. Sadly, for me, subsequent pairs kept appearing; my prescription was on file and Mummy grudgingly but diligently acquired replacements. She was a worthy adversary. I became aware of being watched more closely by the staff when I approached the railway-adjacent boundaries.

"Where are you off to, Paggy?"

I'd freeze like a rabbit in headlights and be brought inside to play. Every day was a new day. I bided my time, looking all innocent, like Emu waiting for the right moment to attack Grotbags. Sometimes I ran for the wall, but that drew attention. Often, I meandered, feigning aimlessness. On happy days, I'd make it to the wall and chuck them. The adrenaline rush would subside as I awaited the inevitable scolding, while the other children, having been able to form friendships without the impediment of near-blindness or burdensome task of having to dispose of glasses, would play on.

It had been Mummy's idea to move to Tates Avenue in the unspoken hope that a bit of distance from Sandy Row might be good for them, i.e., limit Daddy's opportunities for frequenting the pub. She took ownership of the keys from the Housing Executive and had to clean and redecorate extensively as the house had formerly been a knocking shop, the walls a lurid pink, the interior fetid with the stench of moral decay. Ever the home maker, she bleached it to clinical standards, and decorated in the orange and brown patterned fabrics of the era, teak furniture and a gargantuan cube of a television.

It wasn't enough. Daddy was locked off in his grief and anger. He amassed a group of cronies as disenchanted with life as himself. They drank heavily, for something to do, for a few hours of escape. They shouted, laughed, vomited and passed out. They used family homes like dives, they barged through lives and homes with respect equivalent to the amount they had for themselves. To a man, they were each a directionless shambles.

Mummy stuffed down her feelings, kept house, ferried me about and worked. Ben would not be told. She'd tried and earned herself a broken cheekbone. One morning, she left Daddy sleeping off a hangover in bed, dropped me off to nursery with the usual instructions to keep the specs on, and made her way towards the hospital. Halfway there, in Hunter Street, a familiar face stopped her.

"*Gloria?*"

Mummy motioned towards her uniform.

"*Hiya! I can't stop – I'm heading for work.*"

"*Gloria – wait a minute. I need to talk to you.*"

A sinking feeling hit her stomach.

"*What is it?*"

"*It's Ben. He is seeing a fancy woman and she's away round to your house now. I had to tell you. I'd want to know.*"

Mummy's head began to swim.

"*Right.*"

She spun on her heel and took off in the direction of home. Thoughts buzzed – *What if there is somebody there? What do I do? How can I stay? Where do I go?* As she raced down Donegall Avenue, everything seemed brighter, sharper; she felt sick.

The gate she had closed carefully earlier, so as not to wake him, was lying open. She mounted the narrow stairs slowly, quietly, as if she was the one in the wrong. There he was, lying with some sleekit bitch.

"*You bastard! You dirty, fucking bastard!*"

She ran out, thoughts spiralling. I was collected before I had a chance to think about Operation Spectacles and before I knew it, we were on a bus, going on holiday to her cousin, Pat, on the other side of Belfast. The textured plastic seats were slippy and sheets of cigarette smoke hung static in mid-air. Mummy didn't want to chat and by the time we disembarked, I was green and nauseous. Our holiday didn't improve once we arrived;

Mummy had a face on her like a slapped arse and I was sent to sit in Pat's front garden to blow broad blades of grass and find one I could make a whistle noise with, which was great craic, for two minutes. I eariwigged beneath the window as they had tea.

"Pat, I tried everything. I got that house to get him away from all that, but it just follows him about. And now this…"

"I know, love."

"It's too much. I had his children. I made him a home. Why can't he be happy with that?"

In the silence, I imagined them sipping their too-hot tea and taking drags of cigarettes.

"I know. You warned me. Yous all did. But he's not all bad…it's just…since Billy died…"

Her voice cracked. Thinking of Billy always made her sad.

It seemed like Mummy also realised our holiday was shit because we went back home after one night. His drinking continued, if a little less frequently. If he continued womanising, he must have been more discreet. I watched comings and goings from the sofa, where I also viewed my beloved Worzel and Sesame Street and the japes at the Pink Windmill. I sat with Jeanette as she watched Fame and I tried to enact the dance sequences of the opening titles. It confounded me that a dancer was able to maintain splits in mid-air courtesy of a freeze-frame, whereas when I catapulted myself off the sofa for a mid-air splits, I ended up in a heap on the carpet.

Mummy protected me from the worst of him. I'd be sent to bed once he came home from the pub or sent away with Jeanette. I saw Daddy so infrequently that he took on the mystique of a movie star. He was fun when he was sober. He threw me up onto his shoulders, where I would scream with excitement to be on the shoulders of the tallest man in the world. Sometimes he got a mischievous look in his eye, and silently beckoned me with a crooked finger for tickles. I'd laugh and say no, and he would lean forward more, and beckon again, because tickles were en-route and there was nothing either of us could do to circumvent them. The summoning finger would turn to tickle fingers, and he would end up giggling himself at my joyful peals of laughter as I tried unsuccessfully to defend my armpits, knees and sides. He had a talent for silliness and recited:

"*Late at night, when the stars are bright / The hens and the chickens come out to…*"

He looked expectantly at me to complete the rhyme. I would giggle and shake my head until he whispered -

"*Shite!*"

"*Ben!*"

"AH! No – *fight*! They come out to *fight*! Oh, my goodness, that's terrible language, don't be saying that now, sure you won't?"

He went quiet for a moment, then suddenly shouted.

"*Arr Jim-lad! Where be me hearties?*"

Right on cue, I completed the couplet.

"*They are up in the toilet, doing their farties!*"

Mummy tutted and we delighted in her disgust.

Daddy was fun and he awed me with his massive presence, but Mummy was my safe place. She was gentle and consistent. She sang lullabies and rocked me, and called me My Wee Woman (sometimes Wums, for short). When we were out doing the messages, people I didn't know would smile and boom at me:

"*You're just your mummy's wee stickin' plaster, aren't ye?*"

I cowered behind her legs, and she stroked whatever part of me she could reach.

"*She's my Wee Woman, aren't ye, Wums?*"

She's shy, she'd whisper, by way of unnecessary explanation, mouthing like Les Dawson's housewife character.

"*Shy, is it? Ack, you're not shy with me, sure you're not?*"

I pressed myself harder into her thighs, as if to ferret out an umbilical cord to shimmy back up to the safety of the womb. Anyone not in my immediate family could get in the bin.

Mummy was quiet and gentle. She jiggled me on her knee and sang,

"*Ack on the knee when I was wee, I used to sit on my mummy's knee her apron tore and I fell on the floor (here she would dip me dramatically to the floor and back) Ack on the knee when I was wee.*"

When her legs grew tired, she hugged me close, stroked my hair and kissed the top of my head. I felt cherished. She told me stories of a countryside neither of us had ever known, of fields and cows and cottages with roses growing around the door and I too felt this yearning for a quieter life, away from the stresses of ruminating, pustulating Belfast. She wrote maudlin poems and recited them to me in wistful tones as we snuggled.

We lived on a main road so playing outside was not an option. Our neighbours either side were old women; it felt to me like the entire street was populated by them, edging out potential playmates with their tweedy, whiskery presence. Our old lady neighbour to the left had a granddaughter visit her for a few hours on alternate Sundays; on these days I had a friend. I wasn't much used to playing, what with being a Cyclops, but I remember the first-rate entertainment of sitting on the freezing toilet and weeing together. I don't recall taking things to the next fundamental level, but that's not to say it couldn't have happened. Apart from having a companion to relieve myself with fortnightly, I was pretty much on my tod.

I would have been alone if it hadn't been for Reggie. Mummy referred to him as my imaginary friend, although, to me, he didn't exist in my imagination, he corporeally appeared and disappeared at whim. I knew the difference as I also had several imaginary cats, all white and long-haired. My arm often got tired stroking them, so I'd delegate that duty to Mummy, especially if we were on a packed bus going into town. I also enjoyed the company of All the Poor Children of the World, of night prayer fame. They sounded great – for one thing, they were children and for another, there was an absolute ton of them. They obviously wouldn't all fit on a bus (the bus would likely move off before they all got mounted, for a start, and separating the group was ludicrous) so they came along on foot journeys. The only issue was that it can be tricky marshalling a group of that size and hunger meant their stamina wasn't great. We were forced to stop periodically to allow them to catch up. *"Wait!"* I would implore, casting a backward glance at my band of chums. They only had little legs, like me, and sometimes we were all required to walk rather faster than we liked.

The cats and Poor Children are easily understood in the context of the life of a lonely kid; what child doesn't crave pets or playmates? Reggie was not so easily explained. He was a young, Native American boy; dark-haired, brown-skinned, wearing an animal hide skirt and one feather in his head-dress. I could see him and hear him speak, except when an adult was there. This wasn't ideal; if Reggie suggested a forbidden activity such as jumping on the bed, or using the coalbunker as a house, our discovery heralded his disappearance and I'd have to shoulder full culpability.

During another spinal operation, Daddy had his own experience with the un-manifest. He was on morphine and recalled doctors rushing to aid the man in the adjacent bed, saying in panicked tones: *"We are losing him!"* He strained to see what was happening to the poor sod, before noticing that the man in the bed was him. Suddenly he was floating above the scene, surprised, yes, but feeling curious more than anything, before he felt his attention pulled to a corner of the ceiling. There he saw a tunnel of peaceful, white light, at the end of which stood Billy with Granny Bell. Filled with joy at seeing his son, he willed himself to move closer to be with him. Billy didn't speak, but he smiled, and his eyes told Daddy that he had to stay to look after the girls. It wasn't his time. Torn between love for his lost son and the responsibility to us, he reluctantly moved away from the light and towards his body - one of the very few times he did as he was told.

∞∞∞

And so, my view of myself and my place in the world began to take shape. Billy's palpable absence was a reminder of the existence of a place beyond Earth, a home that we departed and will return to. My isolation - the dearth of playmates at home and nursery, difficulties with seeing and hearing caused an essential lack of distraction which made space for me to perceive. I grew adept at absorbing, reflecting, processing; acquired skills that served me so well later in life. I had Reggie, but I would have to wait years for him to explain why.

Four

It was so obvious, as to not need stating, that I was unlikely to be either particularly attractive or sporty like my older siblings. My sole pleasant feature was my dark eyes. Unfortunately, these big brown eyes and long, dark eyelashes were somewhat obfuscated by thick NHS specs, with lenses which gave me one ridiculously magnified eye and fuzzed the other out with translucent glass - apparently more cost effective than endless sticky patches. By this point it was evident that my lazy eye hadn't bothered to shift itself one iota. I imagined the Numskulls in charge of my left eye slumped on a sofa, watching TV.

These glasses dominated my round face under the aforementioned rage-inducing page-boy, which, let's face it, was a grandiose name for a bowl-cut, executed by an apprentice hairdresser using me for practice. As for sporty, I couldn't see to throw a ball or a punch. There was nothing else for it; I would just have to be clever. Daddy called me Professor Peg and availed of all opportunities to make me deserving of that label. He was big on positive reinforcement and soon I became a praise junkie, seeking approval like a Skinner's rat energetically pumping the button for a pellet. When I didn't get a big enough hit of parental awe I'd raise the stakes: any mug could complete a jigsaw, so I'd flip the pieces over and complete it with no picture to guide me and present a rectangle of featureless cardboard, eyebrows wiggling pointlessly behind my massive fringe.

Whether I had an innate love of books or if my love of books was shrewdly planted, the outcome was the same. Mummy took me to Donegall Road library regularly, to peruse and borrow. It felt like a long journey, the same arduous trek along Donegall Avenue that took us to the Arellian over in Sandy Row. We passed housewives doing their 'messages', or men going to or from a job or bar; some with the lowered eyes of someone needing to get somewhere without distraction, others with the furtive glances of someone hoping for a hello, or on the lookout for someone who owed them money. I watched everyone, hoping to be noticed, preferably admired. Only the very unusual would extract me from my self-obsessed musings, and one day it was an old lady in a wheelchair. Her hair was grey and pinned to her nape, she looked withdrawn and sad, and a red tartan blanket kept the cold from her motionless legs. My curiosity was piqued.

"*Mummy, what is wrong with that lady's legs?*"
"*Shh! Peggy. That's not nice.*"
"*But —*"
"*No. We don't comment on our differences, we say quietly to ourselves, There, but for the Grace of God, go I.*"
"*What does that mean?*"

"It means that we have to imagine what it feels like to be that lady. God gave you strong legs that work but decided that this lady wouldn't have strong legs that work, and she might feel sad about it."
"Why would He do that?"
"Ours is not to reason why."
"What does that mean?"
"It means give over and stop tormentin' me wi' questions."
"But – "
"Gi' my head peace."

All God seemed to do was make people sad. I wished he would just take a day off and be nice. Mummy would not be drawn into such discussions, seemingly afraid to give offense to her eavesdropping God, up there in the sky, slipper in hand, ready to punish miscreants. She attuned her heart to recognising and acknowledging the pain of others, as if this could inoculate her against further disaster, and offered up prayers to God in a sanctified Stockholm Syndrome.

Well, if there was a Heaven, to me, it would look like Donegall Road Library. The building was a huge and imposing presence with solid architectural features hewn in stone. Steps elevated it from the street, and the doors were over-large and made of thick wood, a portal from the dusty street with the blaring horns and exhausts and the hum of pedestrian hubbub. The library was a respite away from the creeping, sticky, fearful energy emanating from the City Hospital opposite to a place where other worlds beckoned silently amid the hush and peace and dusty paper smell.

When Mummy had chosen her books for the week, she would look and eventually find me huddled under a table or stuffed into a corner, lost in a story.

Reading afforded similar comfort at home, snuggled under a wing, or on a warm lap. Mummy read slowly and deliberately, her caution tended to impede flow, but Daddy gave dramatic performances and challenged me to read words, pointing at them with his distractingly gnarled, nicotine-stained fingers, with green letters by his knuckles.

"Daddy, what does that say on your fingers?"
"It says Kate. That was the name of my favourite teacher."
"No it doesn't!"
"It does! Good teachers are the best people in the world."

I used contextual cues and memory; he would pause mid-sentence with his finger on the next word and I would guess what it was. When I was correct, I was showered with enthusiastic praise. I'd pause mid-bask to memorise the shape of the word in case it came up again. I had built up quite a bank of words in this way and looked forward to starting school, so that I could add teachers to the list of adults (so far, two) who recognised my genius. My parents projected the narrative that I was bookish, and I strived to meet their expectations.

Mummy was frugal and used every last scrap of food. Leftovers from Sunday's roast dinner would be used in a stew, or a pie. Sometimes she let me seal the pie by crimping the edges of the uncooked pastry with a fork.

The bones of the roast were boiled up in a vegetable soup that was served with a giant boiled potato plonked in the middle.

Sometimes we had mince, which was later used in a pie. I didn't mind the mince, except when I chewed on the firm spring of cartilage, but I could not abide the onions she fried it up with. They were too strongly flavoured, squeaked against my teeth, chunky, slippery things that made me gag. Those onions gave me a horror of mince night.

"Eat your mince."

"I don't like onions."

"Sure, I didn't put any onions in it."

I poked around suspiciously.

"You did. Look!"

I pointed to a small, clear square, glistening in plain sight.

"That's not an onion, sure look at all the size of it. It's totey!"

I looked at Mummy with scepticism.

"What is it, then?"

She hesitated only briefly before announcing,

"It's…uhh…it's a squik. I made it with squiks because I know you don't like onions."

I narrowed my eyes.

"I don't like squiks."

"Sure, you haven't even tasted it. Taste a squik, 'til you see."

I took a moment to extricate one of these squiks onto my fork, ensuring that no mince came with it so that I could focus solely on this new ingredient, without the flavour of mince improving it. I raised it to my lips and nibbled at it a bit. There was no squeak. It didn't flop around my mouth.

"*I love squiks!*"

"*See?*"

"*Mummy, just do squiks with mince from now on.*"

"*Okay, love.*"

And that's how I was gaslit into eating onions.

If there was enough money, we would head across the zebra crossing to get a chippy from Beattie's on a Friday. Mummy and Daddy had fish suppers and I would have a sausage, with fat salt granules sticking to the crisp brown skin, and a few chips from Mummy's plate.

Beattie's chippy sat next to the Butcher's and Arnott's, a corner shop with thrilling rows of colourfully wrapped confectionery. I was a shy child who cowered mutely when addressed, perhaps because I hadn't been exposed to many social situations, or perhaps because in the social situations I had been exposed to it had been drummed into me that *Children Should Be Seen and Not Heard*. Shyness may not be in my nature; for all I know, I could be an extrovert who had all exhibitionism quashed, the latest in a long line of natural extroverts who had been similarly repressed in the name of tradition or social propriety. Attention-drawing behaviours - asking questions, making observations or joining in adult conversations were rude, and rude children were controlled with shame. Sharp words find their target in the soft underbellies of the young. Having pushed me into my shell with *Children Should Be Seen and Not Heard*, Mummy attempted to coax me out of it again by having me practise speaking to the shopkeeper at Arnott's. Like many parents, mine hoped I would become a confident and forthright adult, but focused on engendering obedience, hoping that on some destined day (perhaps the day I finally left home) the switch would magically flip from one state to the other.

Speaking to the shopkeeper was a foreboding task. Profoundly aware that one wrong word could bring down adult wrath, it was safer to stay mute behind Mummy's legs, occasionally peeping out to check if my coy behaviour had shut the situation down. Usually it did; few adults were inclined to indulge the obstinate silence of a wilful child; my failure to capitulate was felt as an affront. There was a chink in my armour, however, Milky Bar shaped. The prospect of a thin tablet of creamy white chocolate was all this four-year-old needed to go from sullen to charm personified. The flaw in this behavioural training was that instead of strengthening my social skills, I learned that the only adult worth chatting to was that nice one at the shop, who cheerily dispensed Milky Bars for nothing more than a please and thank you.

This misunderstanding had unfortunate consequences. One boring, nothing-to-do, no-one-to-play-with day in 189 Tates Avenue (even too boring for Reggie, apparently), I thought about a Milky Bar. I asked Mummy for a Milky Bar, but the answer was no. The Milky Bar thought got bigger. I wanted, no - needed a Milky Bar. I applied liberal sprinkles of explanation, repetition and pleading, but they landed on barren soil, leaving me with no other option but to take matters into my own hands. I shimmied a stool over to access the front door lock and soon I was outside. I opened the gate with dizzying trepidation, but that Milky Bar wasn't going to eat itself, so I proceeded to the zebra crossing. I wasn't altogether sure about how to cross it without an adult hand, but luckily there was an old lady. Before I could slip my hand into hers, I was whisked up by a frantic Mummy and carried back indoors. My Milky Bar! I had been so close. I struggled and hot tears sprung - for the lost Milky Bar and for the trouble I found myself in.

"I'm sorry, Mummy."

"You needn't start your waterworks nai! You're only sorry you were caught."

Mummy was locked-off from me, cross and upset, refusing to listen or talk to me. She wasn't my friend anymore and sent me upstairs with the ominous *Wait until your daddy gets home.*

It wasn't long until I heard the tell-tale open and slam of the front door. I strained to listen to the muffled sound of Mummy ratting me out.

"*She did WHAT?*" he guldered.

The door from the living room crashed open and heavy footsteps thundered up the stairs. I sat on the bed hugging my legs and pressed my back against the cold woodchip, making myself as small as possible in the furthest point from the doorway. He burst in, all fury.

"Did you disobey your mother?"
I nodded.

I flinchingly anticipated a smack round the ear, or a thorough barging, but instead he unlaced his belt from the trouser loops. I had never been hit by a belt before but had been threatened with it enough times to know that it was a big deal. I whimpered in panic.

Seven years earlier they had been all but destroyed by horror and grief when their gentle son had been killed. My wilfulness threatened their shaky sense of safety, their illusion of control. It seemed as though Daddy was looking through me, seeing only the possibility of revisiting the pain of Billy's loss, a possibility that he had to crush.

The belt was the one he had made in prison and branded with the names of another nuclear family that I was never a part of. This strap unleashed sharp, burning, breath-taking pain, and I didn't know when it would end. My tears couldn't stop it. My screams couldn't stop it. By the time it did, I was emblazoned with thick, red, raised marks, the reversed letters of their names. I was marked by this family that no longer was and left to cry alone.

The message was clear: I had to be obedient to be loved. The bad are beaten, the unforgiven left alone. Negative core beliefs *(I am bad, not good enough, unlovable)* branded my sense of self just as the belt had my skin. In the coming years, confirmation bias attuned me to further evidence of this being the case and my negative self-image solidified.

Choosing other perspectives is possible with a mature mind, but in the innocence of childhood as I sought to make sense of the world and my place in it, I couldn't know that other perspectives were available. It would be many years before I could jettison these unfair and unhelpful ideas about myself and adopt a kinder, less debilitating perspective, but in the meantime my best chance of survival was to buy love with obedience, and purchase acceptance at the cost of losing myself. Additionally, the threat of punishment made me a worried, risk-averse child, resulting in a hardwiring for stress that would prove just as difficult to get rid of.

Five

Daddy was still binge drinking when I was five. The term alcoholic didn't sit well with him because it implied that the drink had the better of him, rather than the other way round. He wanted to believe that drinking was a choice he made, a deliberate and justifiable escape from the cycle of grief and rage. It gave him a brief window of relief where he could say fuck it to the hand he had been dealt, maybe even briefly forget. I don't recall the frequency of his drunkenness, but I have a vivid recollection of palpable fear when he came home from the pub. He bowled in, unsteady and huge, smelling of stale smoke and leather, breath sour from whiskey. Sometimes late-night Daddy was also Fun Daddy.

"Daddy, let me pull your boots off!"

He swung his feet up and I wrestled with the Chelsea boots wedged on by the curve of ankle to foot, straining and pulling like a one-person re-enactment of the Enormous Turnip. Daddy got cross if I didn't pull them off fast enough, so the trick was to dispatch them quickly, to keep the fun going.

"Daddy – play with me!"

"Leave Daddy alone, now, he's tired."

He didn't like being told what to do at the best of times, and the implication that he was incapacitated registered somewhere in the fug behind his bleary, red eyes.

"Leave her alone, Gloria. Come 'ere, you!"

He tickled and rough-housed while Mummy watched, tight-lipped and coiled to intervene as inevitably irritation eclipsed his cheerfulness like a summer sun overshadowed by storm clouds, and I'd be whisked away to bed for my own safety. From this safe remove, I heard him ask for his dinner, which was dried out from sitting too long in the oven awaiting his return and hear the thud as the desiccated remains hit the wall and slid down onto the carpet.

"What the fuck is this shite?"

"Ben, no!"

"What the fuck did you just say to me?"

"I'm sorry. I said I'm sorry!"

Sometimes he had an incoherent rant before passing out. Sometimes he made it to bed to sleep in his suit. Often, the sofa did just as well.

Mummy was now more vulnerable under the wing than outside of it. His unpredictability or the increasing predictability of drunken rage forced her to become her own protector. Sick of watching the door for him to come home, of managing his drunken moods, of flinching from the rumbles of violence and of cleaning food from the walls and floor, Mummy knew something had to change.

When Daddy didn't make it home for dinnertime, Jeanette wore her shoes in bed, in case she had to do a bunk to Uncle Tucker's house. She had a plan of action if he blocked the stairs: out the window, drop to the corrugated roof of the toilet, jump down to the coal bunker and away down the alley like two men and a wee lad.

One night, Mummy had us pack our bags and we sneaked off to a Women's Refuge. Our new dwelling was a large building that reeked of impermanence. The room furnishings looked worn and cobbled together. I was excited by the promise of new pyjamas, but the ones I received were threadbare and smelled strange.

I brought my View Master, a red plastic binocular toy through which I viewed story reels of Sooty, Superman and Doctor Who. I had a fascination with Superman. The previous Christmas I had chosen to write him a letter instead of Santa, figuring that if you could communicate with a celebrity once a year, it might as well be the one you liked most. I left the letter under my pillow and kept running upstairs, hoping to stage an impromptu meeting for when Superman came to collect it. That first night in a strange room, I watched the window and imagined Daddy flying up to it dressed in a Superman costume to rescue us. I missed him and didn't understand why we weren't living with him anymore. I gazed at the window, anticipation dwindling with the fading light until sleep took me.

Things started to look up the next day when I discovered that there were other children living there. I made a new friend called Diane, impossibly sophisticated at a mature seven years old, sporting a space where two baby teeth once were. I wanted to play on the grass with her, but despite having moved us away from the dangerous Tates Avenue, Mummy was still a massive worry wart and didn't like me being out of her sight.

Diane's mummy didn't mind her playing on the grass. She fascinated me, with tattoos and sporting a black eye that I was warned not to ask about. I don't remember much else from that time, except that Jeanette brought home an enormous Easter basket, all for me, complete with numerous chocolate eggs, sugar shelled almonds and tiny, fluffy toy chicks.

We were living on the other side of Belfast and Mummy had to produce a copy of my birth certificate in order for me to change schools. Mine lay inconveniently in a drawer in Tates Avenue. She phoned her friend Eleanor.

"Eleanor, hiya love, it's me, Gloria. I need a favour."
"Ah, love, good to hear from you, love. Are yous okay?"
"Yes, we are, thanks. Look, could I ask you to go round to Ben's and get Peggy's birth certificate for me. I need it for her new school."
"Gloria, I don't think Ben'll let me in."
"Please, Eleanor. I can't go round there."
"I can't promise, love, but I will do my best."
"Thanks, love."

The next day we were on a bus to Eleanor's house to collect the certificate. Things were awkward on her doorstep. I stood quietly beside Mummy, unsure as to why we weren't coming in for a cup of tea and a wee bun. I'd been counting on a bun the whole way down on the bus. Eleanor could always be counted on for a perfume-y hug, treats and a cup of too-hot tea, in fact I usually left her house with a wee present or a 10p to get myself sweets.

"*Gloria, he is in a complete state round there.*"

Mummy looked alarmed.

"*The front door was wide open to the street and the house is a dive. I could hear him snoring upstairs.*"

Mummy stiffened.

"*Did you get the certificate, okay?*"

"*Gloria, I did, but I was quaking! I had Jack in the pram with me. I was afraid Ben was gonna wake up plastered and go beserk. I can't be doing that again.*"

"*No, I won't ask again, Eleanor, I'm sorry.*"

"*Gloria, he must have left the tap on and the whole house is flooded. He is gonna end up dead if he's left there on his own for much longer!*"

"*And what am I supposed to do, Eleanor? I can't help him!*"

"*You won't help him!*"

"*What would you have me do?*"

"*I don't know, Gloria. I really don't know.*"

"*I can't do this, Eleanor. I've Peggy with me.*"

I sidled out slightly, to demonstrate her point and hope that my presence could get us back into a tea and buns kind of situation, but it wasn't on the cards. Mummy held my hand tightly as we went back up to the Lisburn Road to wait for the next bus.

Carr's Glen Primary admitted me the next day. I had been disappointed to discover myself to be an unexceptional student as a P1 at Fane Street Primary. I hadn't entirely made my peace with obscurity and still harboured hopes of being acknowledged a mastermind. Unfortunately, I was already at a disadvantage having missed the end of P1 and beginning of P2 and was still chronically shy. I felt out of my depth during lessons and conspicuous as the new girl. Break-time provided a refuge from the stress, but the solace was short-lived. Break-time here was briefer than at Fane Street and I didn't have enough time to finish my crisps before we were being told to take our litter to the bin and resume lessons. The teacher eventually asked Mummy to send a smaller snack. A sensitive child, I perceived myself to be a nuisance, albeit a hungry nuisance, because a chocolate biscuit wouldn't fill a gap in your tooth. Instead of having a tasty bag of Gammon crisps to look forward to, I had to determine which was the least depressing option between Penguin, Blue Riband, Taxi and Club. (The answer is none, because not a single one competed with sucking salty pig flavour off of each individual crisp in those too brief moments of peace).

During this time Mummy happened to run into her old friend Sylvia, who had moved to Lisburn many years before. Sylvia advised her to apply for a house near her; they were recently built, and the area was quiet and pleasant, a welcome contrast to frenetic Belfast. We were being steered by an unknown power, a white light moment; something about moving to Lisburn resonated with Mummy. She still felt the strong magnetic pull of Daddy, the sense of belonging with him (in cynical moments, that better-the-devil-you-know certainty) but she found the strength to forge on. I once believed that she had chosen Lisburn because he was in Belfast and she'd had her fill of him, but perhaps taking his children and moving was a last-ditch attempt to entice him away from Belfast, and drinking. The failure of Tates Avenue to set Daddy on the straight and narrow was not his fault if the issue was proximity to pubs.

Mummy and I disembarked the bus at the bottom of this strange street and walked towards our new home at the top of the wide road, lined at both sides with terraces of four, grey plaster with white pebbledash. Trees bordered the boundaries of the estate and children played on two large greens amid birdsong. The houses had gardens - actual grassy stretches boundaried by low walls, not just the three feet of space between the door and the dusty footpath, as had been the case in Belfast. It was a council estate, but compared with Tates Avenue, it was an idyll. It reminded me of Mummy's poems.

"Are we in the country?"

"No, love."

"But there's fields! And trees!"

She knew it was just a council estate but could not refute the evidence before our eyes.

"We are a wee bit in the country, maybe."

"I told ya."

Ballymacash consisted of a large estate on one side of the Prince William Road, and Ballymacash Park, a tiny estate tucked away on the other. Ballymacash Park always had a considerable waiting list compared with Ballymacash Estate, being comparatively quiet and small enough that most people knew their neighbours. The main estate was livelier and had a higher turnover rate.

When Mummy applied to be re-housed, the Housing Executive proposed three different houses, with clear instructions that if none of those were to your satisfaction, hard luck, because you'll not be offered a fourth. It still amazes me that we were offered a house in Ballymacash Park. Living in the temporary accommodation of the Women's Refuge and being a single mother of two dependants catapulted Mummy up the housing list but being offered a house in peaceful Ballymacash Park with proximity to a great school, rather than the larger estate was statistically unlikely.

Acquiring this new home became a rather bold chess move. Jeanette was taking her bright orange quiff to work in Belfast everyday via the 103 bus that dropped off and picked up at the bottom of our street, and in the course of checking on Daddy from time to time, found herself ferrying information back and forth between her estranged parents.

"Tell your Daddy about our lovely wee house up here."
"Ack, Mummy."
"Tell your ma that there's a woman that wants to be with me and start a family."

"I don't want to tell her that, Daddy."
"Tell her! And tell her I'm here considering my options."

Daddy could play Mummy like a fiddle. The thought of losing him permanently was anathema, and reading between the lines, they were getting back together providing she was the one to do the asking. In this weird chess game, she acknowledged mate and fell pregnant. They were back together, both feeling a victory of sorts and neither having to lose face. For the second time, Mummy had acquired a house and constructed a new life, with Daddy at the centre.

The former inhabitant had painted most of the walls a pale apple green, a colour which Mummy despised almost as much as prostitute pink. She used her housing grant to slap all of the wood-chipped walls with brilliant white emulsion. Harry Corry's half-price bedding sale dictated the colour schemes in the bedrooms. We acquired matching rosebud patterned duvet sets; Mummy's in beige, Jeanette's in blue and mine in soft pink. Coordinating carpet was installed. My pink palace was the box room at the front of the house, above the front door and next to Mummy's bedroom, but I would have much preferred Jeanette's larger, blue-themed room. It was the blue glasses all over again. Mummy planted sweet-pea in two urn-style plastic planters flanking the concrete step at our back door. We had a tall tree that discarded orange berries in the back yard and lilac bushes at the side, each with an abundance of fascinating insects. Mummy saw me stamping on a beetle in the back garden and left her post at the sink to speak to me.

"*Peggy, don't be hurting those creepy crawlies, now.*"

"*It was just an aul' clock, Mummy.*"

"*Ack, don't be killing them, but.*"

"*Why not?*"

"*'Cause we're all God's creatures. Even the wee creatures. Especially the wee creatures, for they are only wee, so it's our job to do them no harm.*"

I dragged the sole of my shoe along the grey ripples of dusty concrete in an attempt to cleanse myself of beetle guts and guilt.

"*Sorry, Mummy.*"

"*It's alright, love. Just don't do it no more, okay? There's a good girl.*"

I'd like to be able to say it was the last time I injured one of God's creatures, but it wasn't. Having heard that a worm cut in half made two worms, I set about proliferating the worm population by taking the edge of the spade to an unsuspecting annelid lured onto our back step by the rain. It didn't make two worms. It made one very agitated worm into two bits, one of which writhed more energetically than the other, in a horrifying display of agony. I was seized with hot alarm, sickened by the torture I had inflicted and ran to Mummy to hand myself in.

"*Mummy! I cut a worm in two with the spade and it's wriggling in pain!*"

"*Ack, Peggy! You just have to put it out of its misery now.*"

"*NO!*"

"Yes. And do it quick if the poor wee thing is in pain."
I ran to the step and stamped like a crazed Michael Flatley, completely obliterating the parts into strings and mush, and vowed never to kill again. That was me done with the aul' murdering.

This new life was agreeing with me. I had friends to call for me and who I could call for, grass to play on and trees to climb. There was a play park in the neighbouring Army Estate. I still don't know if it was for the exclusive use of the army children as their parents periodically insisted as they chased us out, but we enjoyed many a day there, nonetheless. We played chase and found haunted houses, fell out and made up. I wasn't alone anymore, although I had been used to that state for so long that loneliness was my default, having seeped in and taken root at nursery. I no longer wore a patch and could see my friends to play or lip-read if needed. I still had my hearing issues and on days when I had them syringed, the world seemed too loud, and I held my hands over my ears while I played. The sense of being a person apart remained.

Reggie seemed to understand that I'd outgrown the need for him. I missed him though, and in quiet moments wondered if I'd ever see him again. As time wore on, I questioned whether I'd ever really seen him at all, while wishing fervently to do so again, if only to confirm his existence. By this time, societal filters had descended, and I understood that my imaginary friend was either childish or sinister, I woke up in the wee hours of one dark night, and as I turned to get comfortable on my other side, pulling my pink rosebud duvet cover around my shoulders, there, at arm's reach away on the sickly pink carpet was Reggie, side-on, creeping as if tracking an animal, holding his finger up to his lips in an entreaty to stay quiet. I ran into my parents' bedroom, crying in terror. Mummy returned me to bed, insisting it had been a dream, but it didn't feel like one. It would be decades before I would encounter him again.

It is difficult to imagine what direction my life would have taken had we stayed in Belfast, or whether my parents would have remained locked in their destructive cycle. The small seed sown during a chance meeting with Sylvia became the catalyst for change, but that wasn't the main reason everything altered. When I look back and try to identify the turning point at which things got better, when my parents chose to focus on family life over destructive grief and resentment, it wasn't the move to Ballymacash. It was the surprise pregnancy, Mummy's unlikely fertilisation at 42 that yielded Martin. Having a son was the balm they needed, he was their something to live for. Martin's coming to Earth at that time saved them, which saved me.

Six

I was six when Martin was born. After Billy died, God had given them a girl first because they hadn't been ready for another boy. If I was their lesson in patience, Martin was their reward. Jeanette was nineteen and jaded. She was disgusted that Mummy had taken Daddy back and didn't want to stick around to see the inevitable unravelling, so she took her colourful quiff and thick eyeliner to the States shortly after Martin's christening - on the very day of my seventh birthday, in fact. On the last day we lived together, the last day I had the loving attention and care of my big sister and the privilege of being a cossetted younger child, I wailed.

"This is the worst birthday ever!"

Coincidentally, I shared my birthday with Aunt Janet, who was waiting in Dallas Fort Worth airport for Jeanette's arrival, and assuaged any guilt my sister might have felt at ruining my special day by greeting her beloved niece with a delighted -

"This is the best birthday ever!"

And so began Jeanette's new life.

It heralded a new beginning for me, too. I went from being the younger child to being the middle child for what felt like five minutes, before becoming the older child in the house. It was the beginning of my understanding of perspective - how your position in a family changes expectations, behaviour and self-regard.

Martin was a lovely wee thing who wouldn't have looked out of place as an illustration of a bonny child in a vintage book of nursery rhymes. His white blond hair was shaped into the bowl cut once inflicted upon me (which proved that it wasn't personal). He had the round, dark eyes and thick black eyelashes we all inherited from Mummy, but without the throwback turn I'd been jipped with. Everybody doted on him. Family from Belfast and further afield began to visit more frequently, keen to share in the joy of my parents for their much-needed baby boy.

I was jealous of how easily he drew admiration, of how he was a cause for celebration, and I indulged in a highly personalised interpretation of this situation - I wasn't as important or as cherished because I wasn't enough. I was too young to see that babies are simply more demanding of time and energy, too young to understand that this boy child was a balm to two humans who missed their first son, too young to appreciate that this continued focus on Martin may have been a burden to him.

I didn't resent him, but I envied the lack of responsibility he enjoyed, having ousted me as the youngest child. Mummy was forever issuing instructions.

"Peggy, away to the shop for a few wee messages."

I was sent to the shop to buy a pack of twenty Berkley Red when my folks had run out of cigarettes and instructed to bring Martin in his pram - ironically for fresh air.

Mummy slipped him into his warm coat and shoes and buckled him securely in the pram. Martin invariably resisted. He didn't want to be stuck in a pram any more than I wanted to push one. His wee cheeks flushed red with the effort of straining against the buckles as he grunted through a downturned mouth. She slid the transparent pram cover over the top of the pram and secured it under his feet with two loud snaps of the metal buttons, as Martin wailed in defeat.

"*I don't think he wants to come, Mummy.*"
"*He'll relax once you're out walking him. G'wan quick now.*"
I bounced the pram down the back step and out the back gate, waiting until I was out of earshot to mutter,
"*Shut up your gurning, will ye?*"

Cars were fewer back then, so a seven-year-old pushing a pram across the road wasn't the hazard it has since become. As we rounded the corner that took us out of sight from the windows of home that felt like eyes in my back, I would pull the protective clear plastic cover back on to the top of the pram and break into a sprint, relishing the sound of Martin's reflexive, short little gasps as the rush of air hit him square in the beak.

I wanted to be the one to elicit his first unaided steps, so I snuck him out to the back garden and helped him steady himself by wrapping his chubby fists round my fingers. After practising this for a few minutes, I took my fingers away and watched him stumble across our grey paving for a few steps before gravity and ineptitude combined to topple him. A starfish in his padded romper suit, he was unable to put out arms to save himself and landed head-first on a jutting edge of an uneven flagstone, emitting an ear-splitting squeal. White hot panic seared through me as I scooped him up facing away from me and hurried towards the back door to get help. Mummy had already rushed to the door. I watched the colour drain from her face as she snatched him away and only then noticed the trail of blood, betraying our path like Hansel's crumbs. The flesh over his right eyebrow had split to expose bone. As we piled into a taxi for the hospital, I made plans to construct a hut in the bushes where I could live out my days as a fugitive. He received six stitches, his screams a treacherous lack of stoicism at a time when my sentence was pending. I was boggled when no punishment was forthcoming for my part in his injury but thought it wise not to pull at that thread.

When Martin started to walk Mummy always lumbered me with him, and I invariably attempted to run off with my friends and lose him, if only for a few minutes. He waddled after us, arms outstretched, cheeks wet with forlorn tears. Guilt and pity invariably drew me back.

Our row of houses backed onto the grounds of my primary school and the bell signifying break or lunch would bring him toddling to the perimeter fence of chicken wire, where he would shout for me until I had been fetched. Word would be ferried across the green -

Tell *Peggy her wee brother is at the fence!* I would trudge over with a band of friends and Martin fans to listen to him lisp and dribble his greetings. He always insisted on sticky kisses of farewell, which I secretly loved.

It wasn't long before we were back in casualty, having found him squatting guiltily in the middle of the kitchen floor with the pin-box from Mummy's Singer sewing machine. I had just come in from school to find Mummy frantically phoning a taxi and Martin crying. When he saw me, he said;
"It burnt me and went down."
"Peggy, get your coat ready for the taxi. Martin swallowed a pin."
"Is he gonna die?"
"That's enough o' that. Get your coat on."
I thought he was a goner for sure and cried in the waiting room until a fairly unimpressed nurse showed us the x-ray of a button, expected to pass in a day or two.

Martin and I sat on the rug in front of the fire, wrapped in towels, pink and damp from our bath. As we dried ourselves Daddy asked Martin to count his fingers. Tiny wee digits uncurled as he lisped;
"One…two…three…four…"
"Yes, son, well done, keep going…"
"Five, six, seven…"
"Ah, you're great, son. What else?"
"Nine…ten…eleven…"
Daddy's jubilation abated and his eyebrows lowered in confusion. He turned from his chair by the window.

"Eleven?"

Martin opened his towel and pointed proudly to his male digit. The stunned silence was broken by Daddy wheezing an insuppressible laugh which set us all off, even Martin, who loved a laugh as much as the next person. Mummy giggled nervously and insisted that he had only ten fingers and closed the matter without explanation. Daddy giggled intermittently for the rest of the night.

We shared the back bedroom that Jeanette had vacated when she left for America, our single beds separated by a bedside table. Martin's bed was closest to the window, mine to the door. I read a few pages of my book while Mummy told Martin a bedtime story, then the light was switched off. I lay in the dark with only my thoughts for company, and Mummy lay in the adjacent bed until Martin was safely over. One night, I lay on my back, folded my hands over my chest and imagined being in a coffin. I pictured the lid, mere inches from my face and envisaged my body lying undisturbed, unthought-of for years and years as my body – *this body!* – rotted. I knew that I wouldn't really be there – the real me, my soul, my awareness - would be elsewhere, but all the same, I had great sentimental attachment to my body and felt mounting horror that I would be separated from it as it mouldered. I started to sweat as my heartbeat faster – *how much longer will this heartbeat before it ceases forever?* I suddenly needed Mummy more than anything, so I whispered so as not to disturb Martin;

"Mummy!"

"Shhh!"

I panicked that she did not appreciate the urgency of my need for her, and before I could help it, I had called out in a half sob.

"I don't want to die!"

"Frig sake, Peggy, he was nearly over there."

Martin fidgeted and said, *"Peggy?"* and huffed out a sigh as he drifted off again. A couple of minutes later – that felt like an eternity – the bed creaked as Mummy rolled out to tiptoe away. She opened the door and light from the hall spilled in, illuminating her briefly as she exited.

"Mummy, I'm scared!"

I could tell that she was done for the day and was more than ready for a cup of tea.

"Peggy, you are not going to die. Now go to sleep, okay?"

Her tone indicated that this was the final word. She left the door slightly ajar to allow some of the landing light to pour in, a minimalist gesture of sympathy for an eight-year-old petrified with existential dread.

By the time he started school, Martin's white blond mop calmed to a light brown, dark blond, dull as dishwater colour, shaved close for expedience. After years of resenting his idolisation of me, of begrudging him my companionship, I began to really love him fiercely.

On the day that my friend called him a mean name, I punched her square in the face. When I glanced through a window and saw him getting grief from a bigger boy on a bike, I sprinted to the scene to rip that boy a new one. On slow days we lay on either end of the sofa, put the soles of our feet together and pedalled lazily. We squeezed into the same armchair by the window to watch TV, a custom which continued long after our hips had grown too wide for us both to fit comfortably, whereupon we took turns sitting tilted. When we fought, I generally had the advantage, being six years older, until one day he put his head down, came at me with fists flying and nearly put me through a wall. It was a strange feeling, having my pan knocked in, suffused with pride. I was his first friend, and he was my truest.

I continued to find school difficult. Inconsistencies in my schooling meant that by the time I got to P2 in Pond Park, my phonics skills were poor, and I was still relying heavily on knowing words from memory. I was in the bottom groups for Reading and Maths and had reluctantly accepted that I wasn't smart. When everyone keeps telling you that you're dead, eventually you'll lie down. Except, in my case I had one person who refused to call it, who stood in the wings with a set of inexhaustible defibrillators. Daddy.

I don't know whether he saw potential in me, was projecting his own talents where there were none or simply decided that because I didn't have much else going for me, I bloody well needed to be smart. Whatever his motivation, he didn't take his foot off the pedal for a moment. A bookcase was installed in my bedroom, replete with all the classics of children's literature: Treasure Island, Little Women, Lorna Doone, The Three Musketeers, What Katy Did. The bedtime story continued to be a dramatic performance, with exclamations, laments and accents. He hammed it up like he was headlining the Royal Opera House, rather than a parent charged with relaxing the children for bed, and predictably, by the end of a chapter I was left more awake than when he'd begun. His talents extended to writing - his vocabulary was extensive and his style lofty. In later years when I was issued a writing homework, he edited or rewrote each of my sentences until eventually I learned to save time by aping his style. As I submitted each written homework for his approval, he turned off the TV, put his reading glasses on and cleared his throat, ready to pass judgement.

"Instead of saying then, you should write subsequently."
"Okay."
"As a result of sounds better than because."
"Yes, Daddy."
"I think you need a Thesaurus."

I didn't know any other ten-year-olds whose daddy was banging on about a Thesaurus. I suspected nobody else's daddy gave as much of a toss about homework as mine did, and I was pretty sure they weren't hell bent on making the homework sentences sound like they'd been written by Shakespeare during a pretentious spell. Teachers began to credit me with being a proficient writer, when in fact I was a proficient mimic, motivated by the desire to make the homework ordeal as brief as possible.

The trauma of under-parenting meant that he equated love with intervention and committed to over-involvement in my education. To his mind, it was my job to produce a perfect piece of work and his job to ensure this occurred; the standard of the work I submitted to the teacher the following morning was not so much a reflection of my abilities as it was a reflection of his parenting. He commanded that I write out my homework twice - once on rough paper, to be inspected by him, then copied into my homework book upon his approval. If I was careless and made a mistake in the transcribing, he would draw a thick, crude line diagonally across the page, the deep divet of the ballpoint proportional to the depth of his displeasure. He wrote 'unsatisfactory' at the bottom of that page, beside a flamboyant signature, and instructed me not to spoil the next page. On such occasions, the teacher would call me up and insist that I didn't have to start again in order to correct a mistake, as if I had any say in the matter. It was hard enough trying to serve two masters without having to explain the ways of one to the other or vice versa. I felt hot with shame and suppressed anger whether I had drawn the attention of my father or my teacher.

Daddy had aligned himself with a new normal of a quiet life with his gentleman's family. Mummy lived with a quiet gratitude that her prayers had been answered. They seemed to relax into each other, Daddy content in a quiet home, Mummy orbiting him with cups of tea, food and the papers.

Sometimes, as Daddy sat minding his own business in the chair by the window, reading a book, puffing on a cigarette, she gave us a discreet wink.

"Ben."

"Hmm?"

She waited for him to look up from his book.

"Ben."

"What?"

He turned to see her serious face.

"Ben."

"What?!"

A pause. Then confidentially;

"Give us a wee laugh."

He would look away, irritated.

"Ack. Stap it, nai."

Mummy raised her eyebrows at us, and we all sat, rapt in anticipation, our eyes boring into the side of his face as he tried to get buried in his book again. The silence stretched, until eventually, a small, quiet giggle forced its way out.

"Was that a wee laugh?"

"No. Fuck off."

As seconds passed, his sense of humour staged a coup, and the more he tried to resist laughing, the funnier he found it, his chuckles gave way to great peals of laughter, until eventually he would be a wheezing, hysterical mess, tears brimming, all because Mummy had very solemnly asked for a wee laugh. It worked every time. Daddy wore the trousers, but every now and again,

Mummy liked to remind herself that she alone could play him like a fiddle.

Seven

My friend Carol, who also had straggly mousy brown hair and a pronounced squint, lived at the entrance of our street. When we chatted with our glasses off, it looked like we could hardly bear to look at each other. She was a character who gave not one fiddler's fart about rules and did precisely what she felt like at any given time. When accusations of wrongdoing were levelled at her, she steadfastly and merrily lied her way out of culpability. In the common parlance, you could see *the devilment hanging out of her*. She flashed a cheeky smirk when she got away with a lie, as well as when she was caught out. You could generally tell when Carol was lying, because her lips were moving. It was a source of consternation to me that Carol's spoofs had a 50% success rate, yet mine had zero. Somehow Mummy always seemed to know when I was stretching the truth.
"Ack, Mummy, how do you know?"
"I can see it in your eyes."
"What do you mean - you can see it in my eyes?"
"There's a wee spot in your eye when you lie."
I dashed off to the living room and stood on the squashy sofa to get a good look at myself in the mirror above it,

lifting my glasses up above my eyes and back down trying to get the fix on this alleged spot.

"There's no spot, Mummy."

"It's there when you lie."

It was a sophisticated Catch-22: I would give myself away if I dashed off to the mirror for a juke at my eyeballs, but if I didn't, I'd never see this elusive spot for myself.

Carol had a tendency to fix you with a stare as she lied, examining your face to see how convincing she was. Sometimes the intensity of her gaze triggered her squint, and her bad eye drifted in. I soon came to believe that what my mother could see in my eyes during a falsehood marathon was what I saw when I looked at serial spoofer Carol - a tell-tale squint, because when Carol lied, one eye looked at you and the other was too ashamed to. I tried avoiding eye contact with Mummy after a lie, but that tipped her off, too.

I didn't need any special technique to tell me that Carol was lying the day she said;

"My ma gave me a pound for the shop! Do you want to buy sweets with me?"

This was too good to be true. Ten pence was the very most you could expect for sweets, enough for a 10p mix up, or a chewy Wham bar, or a 5p packet of rainbow puffs and five penny sweets.

"Carol, did you pinch the pound out of your ma's purse?"

"No!"

She was all indignation as her one good eye searched my face for approval.

"Why is she giving you a pound then?"

"Alright, alright, she didn't. I found it in the drawer."

"She'll know you took it!"

"Sure, it's been there ages! I don't even think she knows it's there."

If her mum didn't know it existed, was it really stealing? If I could find a way to suspend my reticence, I too could be eating fifty pence worth of god knows what. Maybe even one of those exciting lollies pictured on the side of the freezer chest that started at 35p.

I had conducted a swift risk/benefit analysis where the risk of being discovered was minimal, while the benefit was a whole fifty pence worth of sweets, a prospect I had previously only dreamed of. Not to shift the blame entirely onto my parents, but because mistakes were punished rather than discussed or explored, I had begun to evaluate decisions on the basis of whether I'd be caught rather than any moral implications. I decided that what they didn't know wouldn't hurt them (or me).

Me and Carol skipped to that shop, giggling and giddy, taking a right out of Ballymacash Park along the grassy verge in front of the pensioners' bungalows lining the main road. The shop was at the far end of the road, an extension to the last private house in the row. We ran down the steep driveway alongside the children whose parents ran the shop, who were riding trolleys from the top of the incline, laughing and juddering along at quite a clip. The prospect of sweets made me marginally less jealous of them than I usually was. It felt strange to swerve the transparent plastic-covered penny sweet tray that sat beside the till, but 50p had us feeling like Daddy Warbucks, too rich to slum it at the mix-up counter.

Unfortunately, we had failed to analyse the crime past the acquisition of the sweets and were rumbled by our subsequent lack of discretion. The jig was up when Carol was spotted looking happy and a bit sick by her older sister, Lynn.

I was over Lynn. Just weeks before, Carol and I had been innocently sitting on the carpet listening to True Blue playing on their Hi-Fi for the umpteenth time, when Lynn thrust a birthday card at us, the front emblazoned with a giant willy. She immediately threatened to tell my mum that I was looking at pictures of men's willies, which was patently unfair given that this particular willy had been foisted on me without preamble and certainly not at my behest. I burst into tears – of both fear and indignation, and begged to just go home, my insides twisted with shame and fear. Lynn was now not only a foister of willies but a tout.

Nothing stayed secret for long in Ballymacash Park - news of my misadventure got back to my parents with astonishing speed. Daddy's angry bark carried to the other end of the street. I knew that tone, so I sprinted home, unwilling to earn further displeasure by dilly-dallying, past the greens and football, past skipping rope games and a kid playing tennis against the gable wall of her end-terrace. I let myself in the back door and feigned innocent curiosity.

"Daddy, did you call me?"
"You're fucking right I did."

His lips drew back to bare his teeth, his cheeks bloomed pink; he was furious. Not only had I disrespected him by transgressing a very obvious rule, but he stung from the ignominy of the crime itself; theft was sneaky and low. Perhaps he was triggered - no leniency was shown when the suspicion of theft had earned him a sound beating from his father, or when a handful of sweets landed him in borstal.
"Get up to your room and take off your trousers."
"Please, no, Daddy – "
"GO!"

Adrenaline coursed through me as I ran upstairs towards the inevitable. I removed my trousers, climbed onto the bed and adopted the now familiar position of hugging my legs with my back pressed against the flock wallpaper. He withheld nothing and punctuated each strike with a stream of consciousness tirade.
"Stealing bastard!"
Crack.
"Dirty thief!"
Snap.
"Fuck up squealing."
Whack.

Administering the beating put him in bed with back pain for a week. In his case, the adage, *this will hurt me more than it hurts you,* was literally true; he sabotaged his welfare in an attempt to ensure that I turned out right, seeing it as the noble sacrifice of a committed parent. His disability impeded his commitment to violence not one iota.

This beating was the first where I remember feeling conspicuous. I overheard children playing outside as I waited in my bedroom and tried desperately to muffle my cries of pain from potential eavesdroppers, unsure of whether I was more ashamed to have done something to deserve a beating, or to have a parent for whom discipline needed to be so extreme.

I stifled myself as best I could under the circumstances, but it was moot - as soon as he was finished lashing the leather, he instructed Mummy to escort me to Carol's house to apologise to her mum and show the bruising which had already bloomed on my poor legs and bottom. This public shaming was the greater punishment by far; I felt my opportunities for redemption lessen from the judgement of others, branded a thief. I was consumed with hot, sickening shame hiccoughing my way down the street, past games that seemed to slow, and kids bold enough to ask my mummy why I was crying. Once in Carol's house I was made to take my trousers down to show that justice had been served. Carol recoiled in the big puffy armchair and began to cry frightened tears. When I dared look up at Carol's mum - the victim of my crime -

she looked upset. This performance was for her benefit and her role was to acknowledge the retribution.

"Oh Gloria; there was no need for that."

I didn't know if she meant the beating, or the visit.

"There was. Ben says to tell you that we won't have thieves in our house."

"I know she's not a thief, it was just a wee mistake, wasn't it?"

I almost began to cry at this gesture of understanding, but I wasn't sure whether I was crying because I felt I didn't deserve it, or because I wished for that kind of compassion from my own parents. I was sore inside and out.

"Really, there was no need."

Well, that was a matter of perspective. If the objective had been to prevent me from choosing to steal in the future, then a thorough discussion of theft may have achieved this just as well, if not better, but Daddy's overarching objective had been to obliterate the taint of shame I had brought to his door. He wanted to send the message that he did not raise thieves, that he had rectified the situation and was once again above reproach. Maybe he understood what his father had felt, all those years ago when he relinquished his son for borstal, unwittingly choosing to perpetuate the cycle of violence that marred the generations.

I learned my lesson - that love was conditional, and mistakes were not learning opportunities but punishable offences, each one depreciating me incrementally as a human being.

Eight

An enamel plaque with the Serenity Prayer hung from a nail on the wall beside the little alcove that bore Billy's photographs and trophies; a petition to God to help my parents accept this thing that they couldn't change.

I was surrounded by the concept of God, this divine Where's Waldo that everyone could find but me. I looked for Him at church on a Sunday, during school assemblies and bedtime prayers. I hadn't seen hide nor hair, yet everyone spoke of Him casually, old pals on intimate terms. There was no sense of audience when I prayed and so I grew more certain that He didn't exist with each passing day. Surely adults wouldn't lie?

The strong moral component to belief - that having faith made you good - was troubling; I was an undercover Doubting Thomas, implicitly 'bad'. I didn't want to be bad. I wanted to be acceptable and accepted. I already had a dad spring loaded to punish behaviour he didn't like. The notion that a Heavenly Father was similarly attuned to my transgressions was unbearable, particularly when this treacherous doubt was something I couldn't shake.

Mummy was a typical Christian woman, her well-thumbed Bible sat on her bedside table along with the Al

Anon handbook. She loved the reassurance and poetry of the Psalms, and the wisdom of the Proverbs. We were registered with the Church of Ireland, but the services always seemed a bit too formal. The Minister's droning reverberated around the cold, stone architecture and the minutes stretched. She felt closest to God when she was at services that had the warmth of the wee Mission Halls of her childhood. The Salvation Army was a much better fit. There was a simple carpeted hall, stacking chairs, relatable sermons, happy-clappy songs with a joyful tambourine accompaniment and spontaneous testimonies from people who witnessed and sometimes cried with devotion. The warmth felt human.

Daddy never attended - a hard seat would likely trigger his bad back. All the same, I worried about his soul.

The church minibus took the rest of us to services each Sunday, alongside other families and old ladies from the Residential Homes who similarly did not have transport. The sliding door scraped open and whoever sat closest to the opening would offer a hand to help us up into the stuffy, claustrophobic tin. Each service began with prayer and singing, then Martin and I would be ferried off to crèche and Sunday school respectively, so the adults could focus on the sermon.

One Sunday afternoon, Mummy sent us on without her, claiming to have something she needed to do instead. Unbeknownst to us, Daddy had acquired a copy of the Exorcist on VHS and packing us off to church provided the perfect opportunity for a matinee. It had only been on for a few minutes when a picture slipped its hook and smashed onto the floor - the photo of Billy boxing. They turned it off immediately and Mummy took it as a sign that they were aligning themselves with the wrong energy. She prayed all afternoon, and that evening would've beat Linford Christie to the minibus.

At the end of each evening service the congregation were invited to visit the Mercy Seat, a long bench situated in front of the pulpit. Here we kneeled and prayed to be saved. We sang slowly, mournfully, *All your worries, all your cares, Come to the Mercy Seat, leave them there*, as people shuffled up to pray and cry. I visited that Mercy Seat several times in the hope that God would meet me there for once and remove all doubt from my heart. He was a blind date that kept standing me up. Others knelt to pray and came away looking relieved, lighter, but when I walked away, I felt hollow and fraudulent. I vacillated between feeling hurt at the abandonment, and foolish for railing at an evident nothing, while burning with an impotent rage - at God, if He existed, if not, at the Salvationists who colluded in this apparent myth. Sometimes I went home and screamed *fuck you!* into a pillow until my throat was raw.

Christianity made life a high stakes testing ground. Toeing the line yielded eternal salvation, coming up short, eternal damnation. I called myself a Christian and set about ensuring that my parents were Christian too, because it would be hard for me and Billy to enjoy Heaven if our parents were dodging pitchforks day in and day out. I wondered how anyone could really enjoy Heaven once they'd taken stock of the absentees. I saved my pocket money and bought Mummy a white leather-bound Bible for her birthday (as if God took inventory of Bibles as an indicator of piety) and begged both my parents to stop smoking. Mummy was having none of it.

"Look, this is our one vice. We are not out drinking or gambling like some do."

Mummy was stubborn but I figured there might be some leeway with Daddy, who was fond of a good argument. I turned to him and hit him with my best shot.

"Daddy, it says in the Bible, Your body is a temple of the Holy Spirit, you are not your own."

"Is that right?"

He hadn't countered, so I pressed my advantage.

"Yes, so that means stop smoking. You should probably stop swearing, too."

He reached for his cigarette packet and for a moment I wondered if he was going to throw them out then and there. He paused, formulating a response and then tapped a cigarette out of the box.

"Fuck off and give my head peace to smoke my feg."

This binary world of Christianity, with its right and wrong, good and bad, black and white absolutism was a dangerous concept to this child not yet able to think in shades of grey. Mummy may have been a straight-down-the-line, cover-your-bases, Bible thumping Christian, but Daddy's beliefs were not so cut and dried. He loved to pull at threads and explore tangents. He took a draw of his cigarette and set it in the ashtray as he stifled a cough.

"*Look. I don't need to be perfect. It says in the Bible, I am the Way, the Truth and the Life / No man cometh unto the Father but by me. If I accept Jesus as my Lord and Saviour, that is all that matters. That is the central tenet of Christianity.*"

I thought about that for a moment.

"*But Daddy…*"

He looked intently at me as I struggled to formulate a counterargument, willing ideas to present themselves and clarify.

"*That can't be the main thing. What about anyone that was born before Jesus arrived to die for their sins? Are they in Hell because they didn't know about Jesus?*"

I was attuned to fairness, and it stood out as patently unfair. All those ancient souls getting chased from blaze to blaze by demons would probably take issue with this new Get Out of Jail Free card.

"*That's a good point, kid. And what about people who have been bad all their lives, then just accept Jesus seconds before they die? Would that be okay?*"

I laughed at how ludicrous this was.

"*No! Sure, God would know they were trying to trick Him.*"

Daddy turned to the magazine table between his chair and the window, angling a lighter to line up with the remote control and box of cigarettes, placed neatly beside his book. Mummy called this area Daddy's Mucky Corner, but it was anything but. It was a collection of accoutrements sorted into regular formations, creating pleasing parallel placements as he marshalled his thoughts. Daddy foutered as his ideas brewed.

"We have to take the New Testament at its word. Jesus declaring himself as intermediary between Man and God is what matters to us."

"Yes, Daddy. But God won't be tricked by last minute Christians, right?" I asked, wishing for confirmation that fairness existed.

"No, He wouldn't be tricked."

I felt relief.

"Catholics try to trick Him, though."

"Ack, Daddy." I was disappointed that our high-minded philosophical musings were about to be tainted by the politics of them'uns versus us'uns.

"Wait 'til you hear, now. Remember earlier, I said, No Man Cometh Unto the Father but by Me?"

I nodded.

"Well, they get priests to speak to God for them in their confessionals."

"But they still believe in Jesus."

"Yes, but they are ignoring the Bible! They allow priests to act as intermediaries! It's unnecessary. Jesus said it himself."

He angled his chair towards me: a sign that he was just getting warmed up.

"Do you know what them bastards do?"

"Ben!" Mummy scolded from the kitchen.

There was a line between anti-Catholicism and bigotry, and Daddy wasn't much of a tightrope walker.

"Daddy, you don't hate the sinner, you hate the sin."

Daddy had a look on his face that suggested he had enough hate to stretch to both.

"Do you know what them b ..." he gathered himself – *"the priests did when IRA men came to confess their sins? Their sins of murder, bombing and shooting? Weemen and children?"*

I shook my head.

"Told them to say a few prayers for Absolution then kept the information from the police, hiding behind the sanctity of the confessional."

I floundered for an opposing argument.

"Maybe it's more important to surrender to God than to Man."

"Getting away with murder? Easing their consciences with a visit to the priest, and getting away with murder, then sleeping easy in their beds?"

"But they don't really get away with murder, because they'll be judged by God, right?"

Daddy grew shrill.

"They are walking about, free men, having killed and maimed and destroyed lives! Murdering bastards!"

The excitement started his cough off; great gutteral rasps that rattled through his chest and wracked his body. It sounded like a bad one, and sure enough it went on for a minute or so and culminated in dry heaving and gasping, red-faced and rheumy-eyed. It seemed like a demon was using his vitriol as a conduit to make its way out from his core, clawing and railing, bursting out from the confines.

Mummy left her doings in the kitchen to stand in the doorway and suggest, pointlessly, that he shouldn't get himself worked up. The notion lingered in the aftermath, as Daddy's breathing slowed, wheezing into regularity.

I eagerly anticipated Junior Soldiers summer camp, when kids from all over Northern Ireland would come together for a week of lessons, activities, worship and the overlooked midnight feast on the last night. We memorised Bible verses and prizes were awarded for being able to parrot them at the end of the week. During the final service of the week came the usual invitation to the Mercy Seat. One by one, each Junior Soldier made their way to the front to pray and to sign a Junior Soldier's Covenant. I sat in my pew waiting to feel moved to approach the Mercy Seat, as my friends visited the bench and left one by one, clutching their signed A4 certificate. As the last children were leaving, I dissolved into frustrated, fearful tears. Going through the motions of belief was not an option; I saw the inherent flaw in Pascal's Wager - an omniscient power would not be hoodwinked. If He existed, He knew of the doubts I had, and refused to allay them. If He didn't exist, I was crying into a void. I wasn't sure which was worse.

Jim, a kindly Senior Soldier, came to sit with me. He leaned forward so his eyes were level with my wet face as I hunched forward, hurt and embarrassed. He looked sad.

"Are you okay?"

I wasn't sure how to answer without outing myself as a heathen, so I simply nodded and sniffed. He sat beside me for a while, then asked quietly;

"Is there anything wrong at home?"

The question pulled me up short. I'd assumed he understood that the cause of my tears was a crisis of faith, but now I wasn't sure what to say because I wasn't sure what he was asking. He knew my mummy from Sunday services; I couldn't explain that sometimes I was deeply unhappy at home because there was a very real chance word would get back and I'd be accountable for anything defamatory. Besides, as Daddy occasionally reminded me, the Bible said *spare the rod and spoil the child,* understanding it to mean that physical discipline was divinely ordained. Jim's misplaced concern cemented the understanding that my burdens were very much my own; neither God, nor Jim, could help me.

It was bad enough that I couldn't feel God, but I was also burdened with worrying about Gatekeeper Jesus, condemning innocents to Hell on a technicality - those born before him, tribes too remote to ever learn about Jesus and the mentally disabled who mightn't understand what was required of them. I was upset that some people were born into situations of hardship, while others were granted what seemed to be a care-free, pleasant existence. I imagined it'd be easier for the second group to accept God while the others might rightly take umbrage with the stacked deck. Exposure to religious doctrine made me anxious at a time when my greatest concern should have been establishing which was the best Thundercat or seeing how many bogies I could deposit under my school desk by June.

Nine

School became a depressing cul-de-sac where I made little progress socially or educationally. I felt of little value to teacher or classmate and the hurt that saturated my days distilled to bitterness. One girl represented everything that I wanted but did not have. It seemed like everywhere I looked, there she was, mocking me with her comparatively easy existence.

Her name was Julie. A casual observer might have seen two quiet, pleasant, obedient girls. However, under the veneer, she battled shyness while I battled disaffection.

I hated Julie. Her mother was a supervisor who oversaw lunch and performed playground duty. My mother would never have courted such visibility. Schools - and any other authoritarian institution - made her nervous; she had a horror of responsibility rooted in a deep fear of messing up. Julie's mum was quiet and pretty. She wore lipstick and mascara and set her shiny, dark hair in waves. To me, using make-up and taking time to put in rollers were indicators of acceptability, of the good self-regard that my mummy lacked. It seemed like showing off when Julie ran across the tarmac to greet her lovely mother every lunchtime, as if she hadn't just seen her three hours before at breakfast. Adding insult to injury was Julie's splendid crimson hooded coat which she had no doubt been allowed to choose herself. My coats were always chosen for me, utilitarian and dull coloured to hide the dirt. She had lovely blonde hair and blue eyes, while my brown eyes still resided behind stupid overlarge glasses, beneath a mass of mousy brown straggles which Mummy called rats' tails as she pulled a brush through the tangles each morning in an attempt at making me presentable. I watched Julie from afar and brooded, consumed with jealousy for these advantages I would have gambled my good eye for.

Somehow, years of being unexceptional and lonely had not extinguished my annual September optimism. Once again, I was hopeful that this would be the year I would be smart, despite the mountain of evidence to the contrary. After a solid seven or eight years of circumstantial proof that I was thick and unappealing, somewhere in the deepest recesses of that bespectacled kid lived the conviction that I was an undiscovered treasure, and the right set of circumstances would unleash my magnificence onto the world.

In short, new pencil case, new room, new me.

The Primary Five room was similar to the Primary Four room in architecture and furniture, but a world apart. The brown and cream geometric patterned carpet was the same, and the lacquered beech tables gouged by the pencils of the bored, and the seats - beige moulded plastic affixed to a cold metal frame. In P5, however, the desks were a little bigger and the chairs a little taller. We had to raise ourselves up or grow into these new spaces. Miss Martin, whose first name was Margaret, reminded me of Princess Margaret; a regal bearing, pearls and expensive perfume.

We filed in with trepidation, searching the labelled desks for our allotted seat. Much to my surprise, Miss Martin had placed me in the back row next to lovely Julie, the unwitting target of my bile. I wasn't quite sure what to make of it. I was usually seated at the front of a classroom on account of my sub-par vision and hearing, while the educator's penchant for ability grouping usually dictated that I sat with the thickos. Didn't she know who I was? I was the kid without friend or talent, while Julie was sweet and smart. With whiplash speed, my feelings for Julie made an astonishing volte-face, and I resolved upon becoming as much like her as possible - neat, diligent, polite - in the hope that Miss Martin wouldn't realise her mistake.

Predictably, that first day yielded the annual embarrassment of the class register as the teacher asked for Margaret - the name on my birth certificate - rather than the diminutive Peggy, thereby providing the first giggles of the academic year. My classmates laughed rather harder than was necessary, while my cheeks flushed with the ignominy of uninvited attention from being the owner of not just one, but two antiquated names. I liked the idea of being in the back row in theory - the reputed refuge of the naughty, the trusted furthermost row from the teacher - but that day I discovered one huge drawback. If you were taking a beamer at the front, people could only see the backs of your ears reddening, if anything, but sitting at the back meant vulnerability to an audience capable of swivelling their heads faster than the kid from the Exorcist, to feed hungrily on your humiliation.

Miss Martin settled the class and rather than amending the register and moving on, as previous teachers had, she looked me in the eye and asked me which name I preferred. I felt dizzy. This was my chance to jettison the ridiculous Peggy, with its old lady connotations, Peggy-Sue, Peggy-Leggy, Eggy-Peggy and Peggy in the Middle. Peggy had proven to be dull academically and socially, a drudge who drew no admiration, but Margaret could be my ticket out of Pegsville. It was only the first day of P5, I was sitting next to Julie and now I had the opportunity for a new identity. Margaret, I announced. A few Philistine classmates wailed that my name was Peggy. To this day I do not know whether they had misunderstood Miss Martin's meaning when she asked my preferred name, or if I had. Either way, it was of no consequence because from that day on, and for a whole academic year, I was Margaret.

Being sat next to Julie was the first bit of extraordinary good luck since the serendipitous move to Ballymacash Park and Martin's arrival. I wanted so much to be like her, to enjoy the warmth of approval given for being good, to be celebrated instead of tolerated. I dusted off my mimicry skills. I set out my pencil case and books upon the table in the same methodical fashion she did. She had a large rectangular Staedtler rubber emblazoned with a butterfly, with sharp edges and barely a blemish on it. I took my no-brand rubber and removed the black marks by rubbing it on clean paper until they disappeared. I studied her handwriting, which looked like knitting, consistent loops and curls in cursive uniformity. I studied and simulated each letter and word, laboriously at first, until her pleasing penmanship became mine too. She had a charming technique for colouring her illustrations, using a series of pointillist dots to build up colour instead of merely shading. I aped that, too. Another kid might have grown irritated, declared me a copycat and curled their arm protectively around their work, but Julie simply accepted me, and allowed me to become more like her, which made me like both of us more. Miss Martin's pairing of us may not have been the oversight I'd originally believed it to be. Perhaps she felt I could learn from Julie. Perhaps she may have even seen a pair of pleasant girls who would fit well together. At the time though, I felt I was tricking her into honouring her mistake and spent every day working undercover as a likeable kid, dreading being exposed as the less admirable person that previous evidence had pointed towards.

Much to my amazement, Julie seemed to enjoy spending time with me as much as I enjoyed spending time with her. We became best friends. Each day after school I fired my schoolbag home and trotted on round to Julie's house, across the strip of green and through the hole-in-the-hedge – an inappropriately named intersection which had neither a hole nor a hedge, but which linked the bottom of her street to the estate. We played on her swing set and monkey bars, ate gingerbread biscuits, watched

Children's TV and played in her bedroom until time forced me home for my dinner.

I loved being at Julie's house. It had a light, easy atmosphere, whereas my own was permeated with gloom and loaded silence, the place where frivolity came to die. The weight of the unsaid hung in the air with the smoke of so many cigarettes as my parents sat in the dull room, lost in their own thoughts. When visitors called, my parents put on jolly facades, but this effort beyond their default inertia exhausted them. With all the hiding - of grief, of shame - they were unable to find socialising fun. I was attuned to the unsaid and instinctively knew when they had had enough. Other people's parents didn't seem to tire of pleasantness because it wasn't an act. My friends didn't tiptoe around their homes. When the joy was sucked from them so many years before, it created a vortex where happiness collapsed and suffocated under the weight of the vacuum.

We were clearing our desks ready for the lunch bell when Miss Martin exited her store with a large poster of a very sweet cartoon bunny.

"Would anyone like this?" she asked.

Eight hands shot in the air, all girls. She hadn't anticipated this enthusiastic response and paused for a moment, lamenting this inadvertent conundrum.

"Anyone who would like the poster, put your name on a piece of paper in this tub and I will pick the winner after lunch."

We wrote our names on post-Its and folded them neatly into little rectangles. I figured that I wanted it more than any of the other girls and decided that the best way to secure the favour of any eavesdropping deity was to demonstrate fealty. I committed to cross my fingers from that moment until the winner was announced. This posed no issues for lining up for dinners but made handling cutlery challenging. Uncrossing my fingers would convey a lack of commitment, so I soldiered on, cutting up food with my contorted digits, much to the amusement of my table mates. By the time we were enjoying the playground, my fingers had cramped, and I fervently wished for the bell. Once inside the classroom, my insides were squirming with anticipation. This was no longer just about a poster. If I won, justice existed and life was worth living; if not, life was brutal and pointless. Either there was honourability to the pain, or I was just an idiot with sore fingers. Miss Martin rifled about in the tub amid a hushed silence.

"The winner of the poster is..."

My fingers had crossed the threshold from painful into numb and were threatening to spring open without my volition. I heard a few mutters around me.

"Margaret has had her fingers crossed all lunchtime!"

Miss Martin carefully unfolded a square of paper and smiled.

"...Margaret!"

Vindication. Not only was life worth living, but I also had a poster for my bedroom wall. I walked to the front to collect the rectangle of card that confirmed my ability to tap into something bigger than me. Perhaps it was my crossed fingers and indiscreet classmates that prompted Miss Martin to call my name regardless of which piece of paper she unfolded, but isn't that a kind of magic, too?

Primary 5 saw me acquire the first A grades I ever achieved on a report card (two of them), one rabbit poster and my first real best friend. Julie's friendship allowed me to blossom, where before I had stagnated. Her friendship was alchemical.

Ten

The Eleven Plus was a high stakes transfer test administered in the first term of Primary 7, the finish line after a year of serious preparatory academic graft in Primary 6. In theory, it made it possible for a poor kid like me to access a Grammar school education, because admission was dependent upon academic performance rather than which postcode your parents could afford. Despite getting my first A grades in Primary 5, passing the Eleven Plus felt beyond my reach. Our class was to be entrusted to one of two teachers: humorous Miss Wright or strict Mr Vance. I already had one strict disciplinarian with a tendency for angry outbursts and prayed fervently to be in Miss Wright's class.

With the end of Primary 5 came the dreaded news that our class would be taught by Mr Vance. Our summer break from school was bittersweet, each warm summer day taking us closer to September and the commencement of two long years of being accountable to a stern taskmaster, both at home and at school.

Mr Vance was tall and solid, old, but not as old as my decrepit parents in their fifties. His voice was strong and carried well, not that it needed to, because (in stark contrast to previous years) our days were mostly spent in attentive silence. As it transpired, he had a dry sense of humour which flashed brilliantly on occasion, a joyful beacon on otherwise dull days of test-oriented grind. He had ginger hair around his balding head and a thick, bristly moustache. My daddy had always been clean-shaven; I wasn't sure what to deduce from that facial hair.

I was amazed to find that Mr Vance noticed and seemed to like me from the very beginning - shy, straggly, bespectacled me. Each morning during registration, we deciphered our morning anagrams, and he called each pupil's name in a formal monotone, until it was my turn, at which point he would joyfully exclaim, "PEGGYYY!" as if he had been looking for me all morning and was delighted to have discovered me hidden just out of sight. Everyone laughed, and not the sneering laughs I'd never become accustomed to when attention was drawn to my name. It seemed inexplicable to me, but somehow Mr Vance was under orders from heaven to be my friend.

He built me up with every interaction. We pupils lined up at his desk, set back slightly in a little storage alcove lined with files and books, to have completed work perused and marked. Time pressed teachers typically flew through marking and scrawled an abbreviated comment at the bottom; VG for 'very good' being most common. He riffed on this practice for me; having marked my work, he would pause and thoughtfully pen a summation. One day it was simply 'M'.

"What do you think that stands for?" he asked, eyes earnest and twinkling.

"*Marvellous?*" I dared to guess.

He smiled warmly and nodded, and I floated back to my seat.

When I wrote an epic and mawkish poem about First World greed and Third World starvation, he asked me to read it to the class, who had the dubious honour of listening to me pontificate for rather longer than necessary while rhyming peas with cheese. I became a prolific poet, thereafter, ever keen to bask in the warmth of his approval.

As Christmas approached, Mr. Vance asked us each to bring in an orange so that we could make Christingles by ramming a candle into the middle of the fruit, symbolically representing Christ as the light of the world. I'm sure there was more to this craft activity than I can recall, but these Christingles became memorable for another reason entirely. In typical kid form, I had forgotten to tell Mummy that I needed a big orange for school the next day and by the time I panic-announced it, daylight had started to fade. She undertook a hasty solo trip to the garage at the bottom of the main road rather than be saddled with mine and Martin's dilly-dallying.

Martin and I were happy enough with this plan, having wedged ourselves into the chair in front of the telly for the dregs of Children's BBC, tolerating Newsround and Blue Peter before the inevitable switch to the news. Mummy returned rather sooner than expected, enormous orange in hand. She muttered something to Daddy, then walked over to the window beside us and flicked the blinds closed. As she reached to pull the first red velveteen curtain across the window, a rumbling, deafening boom reverberated, shaking the house, vibrating through my body and shattering the window. The glass exploded inwards, hitting off the just-closed blinds before cascading onto the side table and carpet. I was momentarily deafened and in the grip of a scorching panic as my conscious mind flailed to concoct a narrative to make sense of it. I immediately deduced that IRA men had targeted Daddy and set off a bomb outside our house. The blasted-through window had given them access and they would be inside any minute with guns to finish the job. I sprang across the living room and burst into the kitchen, quickly realising that there was no point in fleeing through the back door if we were surrounded. I figured that my best option was to hide. Mummy kept the pedal bin in a small gap in the corner of the lower kitchen cabinets. I pushed it out of the way and climbed into the space, ears ringing and terror pulsing through my body. It felt as though the sonorous boom had shaken my very fillings loose, which was the least of my problems because here was Martin, crying (I deduced from his face, he sounded a hundred miles away) and trying to be with the person he loved the most in the world, in this too small hidey-hole. My first instinct was to push him back out for fear he would give my position away. That probably wasn't my finest moment to date, and I envy anyone able to continue in the smug assumption of selfless bravery in a situation of life-threatening peril. You weren't there, man.

Mummy appeared at the entrance to my top-secret location - where there definitely wasn't room for all three of us – but I could read her lips and she reassured me it was okay. She coaxed me out, much against my better judgement, and sat us at the kitchen table as she hurriedly made some hot, sweet tea for the shock. Gradually, my hearing returned, and I wept out the tension of the preceding minutes.

"It's okay, love. Have a wee sip of tea."
"Are they trying to get Daddy?"
"No, love! That bomb was in the Army Estate."
"How do you know?"
"The police were looking for the bomb when I was coming back from the garage. They told me to get home quickly."

I sat for a moment, trying to process that Mummy had almost been caught up in a bomb, having left the house at my behest. She had somehow narrowly avoided it and arrived home just in time to close the venetians and save Martin and I from being peppered with sharp glass. Daddy shook his head gravely.

"Them policemen out looking for bombs in the dark. They're some men."
"When I was coming up the Cutts, one of them was going down into the undergrowth, and I heard him say, 'If this goes off, I'm going up with it.'"
"Evil bastards, giving a warning and not saying where they've planted it."

I was a Free School Meals kid, ferried off to the regimented dining hall while the lunchbox kids sat with friends in our warm, carpeted classroom. They swapped items from what seemed to me to be very exciting selections. It looked like a party. Most of my lunchtime was spent lining up to be served by ladies in string caps and aprons, before bolting the food to get out and play. Chocolate Cracknel appeared on the menu rotation once each month and was one of the few perks. On those days, all bets were off. The dessert sat all delicious and chewy, while I horsed my main course with scant regard to flavour taste or etiquette.

One Chocolate Cracknel Day, my friends and I were nailing down plans for the playground, and I excitedly hoovered my first course, keen to get to dessert and with my one good eye on the spare, leftover cracknels at the dinner hatch. I masticated those mouthfuls with the same alacrity I had applied to the dinner. My friends laughed - I must have looked ridiculous. My mirthful audience stalled me not one iota, although I hoped they'd get over it and shift their attention elsewhere so that I could be left in peace with the finest dessert in existence. Instead, they took turns imitating my mastication, frenetic squirrel impressions.

"She looks like she's storing nuts for winter!"
"She looks like a beaver gnawing a log!"

I had no doubt they were correct. Further jolly impressions accompanied my second cracknel, after which we hurried outside to salvage the last few minutes of playtime. When the bell rang, we ran to the line and stood in customary solemnity as the teachers scrutinised our orderliness. The silence gave me space to process how my friends had laughed at me - not with friendly laughter but mocking laughter. My thoughts spiralled.

They don't like me. Nobody really likes me. They laughed at me because I look silly when I eat. If they tell everyone else, they will all watch me eat and laugh at me every day. I will never get peace to eat again. I will never get peace to enjoy Chocolate Cracknel again.

By the time we took our seats in the classroom, my eyes were brimming with hot tears that threatened to overspill. I didn't want anyone to see me crying and announce it for the edification of all, so I bent under the table as if to retrieve something from my bag. It wasn't a great plan. There's only so long you can pretend to be poking around in your bag before someone notices and loudly wonders if you are ever coming up again. The musings of a concerned few drew further attention and before I knew it, other heads popped below the desk to investigate and make the gleeful broadcast.

"*Peggy is CRYING! She's CRYING!*"

Mr Vance was quick to respond.

"*Peggy, are you okay?*"

"*Yes.*"

"*Will you come out and tell me what happened?*"

"*No, thank you.*"

His silence told me that my polite but firm refusal had him bamboozled, and I felt sorry for that, but the prospect of twenty-five pairs of eyes, twenty-six including Mr Vance, scrutinising my soggy bake, mouth downturned in sorrow made me stay hidden. What forced me out was the realisation that I couldn't stay under there indefinitely, doing my work, then making up a bed and sleeping there under a desk in the P6 classroom. I hastily formulated Plan B.

"Mr. Vance?"

"Yes, Peggy?"

"May I go to the toilet, please?"

"Yes, you may."

I fled the room, face downcast with embarrassment, to a cubicle where I could reside instead. It offered more privacy than under the desk and had obvious toilet amenities that the classroom lacked. I cried all my tears out sitting on the toilet and when sanity returned, I washed my face in a sink and steadied myself for returning to the classroom, hoping to steal in like a mouse - a mouse which had not just been crying, because there was nothing to see here so, please everybody, just move along. I sheepishly opened the door to the classroom, whereupon twenty-five pairs of eyes fixed upon me. (Mr Vance had the decency to be getting on with something at his desk). The atmosphere was tense, indicating that something had transpired in my absence. I noticed my playmates weeping at their desks and our other twenty-three classmates looked a little shell-shocked. After school, Julie told me that Mr Vance had conducted a witch hunt and loudly ripped through my friends upon discovering their laughter to be the source of my upset.

I felt dreadful. My tears had not been directly proportional to their actions, but to my very delicate sense of self-worth. At various points, I had been mocked for my glasses, for the way I had to clear my throat before speaking (I had almost perpetual catarrh from the smoke at home), for my clothes smelling of cigarettes, for the way I wore my socks up to hide my leg hair instead of rolled down like the other smooth-legged girls, because I had been warned that nice girls don't shave their legs - and a plethora of other small matters that marked me out as different. Mr Vance seemed to know I was an underdog and levelled the playing field for me like an angry bulldozer. From that day on, I was seldom lampooned.

Mr Vance continued to supply the compassion and connection I needed to thrive. I had grown in confidence and began to wonder if I might pass the test and therefore be eligible for a non-fee-paying place in a Grammar School.

Mummy lit the fire and drew the curtains and I watched Daddy lower himself into the chair by the window that Martin and I begrudgingly vacated after the funnies were over. He lit his post-dinner cigarette, took a long drag and puffed out a plume of billowy blue smoke that hung like cobwebs before slowly dissipating. Martin hopped up onto the sofa beside me and snuggled in.

"Daddy?"

"What?"

"If I pass the Eleven Plus, can I go to a Grammar School?"

He licked his lips, buying himself time to think.

"What about Laurelhill? They have a new computer suite with all new equipment."

"I don't want to go to a secondary. I want to go to a Grammar."

"Well, if you work hard and pass, then we will talk about it then."

"I will work hard. Can I have a tutor?"

"There's no money for a tutor."

"Julie has a tutor! And some others too."

The main criticism levelled at the system was elitism. A high proportion of children who passed the test were middle-class, with a high likelihood of parental academic support and, much to my chagrin, money for tutors.

"If you get into a Grammar School, it has to be on your own steam. What's the point in a tutor getting you in, then you can't cope with the work? No. No tutors."

"But that's not fair. Other people are getting help and I'm not."

He held his empty hands out.

"Peggy, we don't have money for tutors."

The thought of being a Grammar pupil gave me the white light feeling; I simply had to get a place, so I knuckled down hard in school. On the day of the tests, I stilled my nerves, read and re-read each question and did every calculation twice. I aligned myself with the energy I imagined a Grammar pupil possessed: diligent, careful, assured. I had listened to Daddy lament his poor education and restricted opportunities often enough to know the importance of a good school.

After we sat the tests, the rigours of the academic syllabus gave way to a more enjoyable routine of project work and school trips. The P7 London trip was the highlight of the social calendar; children excitedly planned who to share a room with and the teachers doubled up as acting parents and tour guides. Once again, I was to be conspicuous as the only pupil not attending.

Most years yielded at least one child who stayed home rather than leave their parents for a week however my issue was not clinginess but a lack of finances. My classmate's curiosity was piqued.

"Are you too scared to be away from your mummy for a week?"
"No."
"Why aren't you coming to London, then?"
There was no way round it. I had to declare us poor.
"We haven't the money to pay for it."
"Sure, we have until Easter to pay it off! You can pay it off weekly!"

I didn't have the details – or the heart – to explain how our tight budget simply didn't allow it. All I could do was repeat that we didn't have enough money for it, in the hope of shutting down the excruciating inquiries.

I was glad to see the back of everyone for that week; the excited build-up in the preceding weeks had me feeling alienated and lonely. Mr Vance set me the task of producing a project on a topic of my choice and kindly said he very much looked forward to seeing my work upon his return. Earnest little berk that I was, I took him at his word and launched myself into researching and collating information, borrowing books from the library and producing two projects that week - one on Gandhi and one on Shakespeare. In hindsight, I understand that project work was intended to merely keep the pupil ticking over: it would be unethical to leave one child unable to engage in an education of sorts during term time while others were availing of an educational trip, and yet it would be unfair to leave monotonous, but potentially more useful worksheets (and a jip to have to mark them). Nevertheless, Mr Vance kindly read my work and wrote very encouraging and pleasant comments in the margins - all the more generous given that my work was thinly veiled plagiarism of said library books.

Shorter, more local residential trips were planned for later in the year yet, despite being much less expensive than London, my parents were unable to provide funds. I didn't mind quite so much; I wouldn't be conspicuous in my poverty because only a handful of children went at a time.

Mr Vance sent a note requesting to speak to my parents in a private meeting. Despite being a six-foot ex-boxer, something of the working-class cap-doffer persisted in Daddy, who dressed in his best funeral suit and buffed his shoes. Mummy gave her face a good wash and lacquered her hair in place; clean, tidy and no-nonsense. He greeted them with a friendly, professional handshake and gestured towards the two pupil seats arranged by his desk.

"Please, have a seat. Thank you for coming in."

"It's a pleasure to meet you, Sir."

"And you, Mr Bell. You have a bright daughter."

"She does her best, Sir. I make sure of it."

"Indeed, you do. Now I have asked you to meet with me this afternoon in regard to an opportunity for Peggy."

Daddy nodded.

"We have a surplus in the budget for exactly this kind of thing; I am hoping that we can fund a place so she can attend the trip to Castlewellan."

Daddy nodded, needing more time to process this information. He fumbled for the right words that expressed his concerns.

"Is it... charity?"

"Oh my, no. As I say, there is a budgetary surplus that we must spend by the close of the academic year. It's a funding issue - we need to spend it otherwise we will be allocated a smaller budget next year. If anything, it helps us, to be frank."

Daddy nodded, only partly convinced.

"If you are sure that it is, as you say, a budgetary surplus, and not charity, I don't see why not."

"Can I confirm her place with you, then?"

"Yes Sir. That's very kind of you, Sir."

"It is a pleasure. Thank you for coming in."

My parents chose always to live within our means - *never a borrower nor a lender be*. Charity triggered the shame of

Daddy's boyhood. Mr Vance was a politician to convince them to avail of such a fund, if indeed it even existed. For all I know, he could have funded my place directly from his own pocket. I had a wonderful couple of days away and loved, for once, being the same as everybody else.

∞∞∞

Each year, Mummy attended the Teacher interviews alone, but during P6 and P7 Daddy was keen to join her and avail of the opportunity to spend a few minutes with the man under whose tutelage I thrived, the man who had succeeded in blazing the fire within me that Daddy had toiled so tirelessly to spark. Suited, booted and groomed, he looked immaculate; freshly shaved and still-black hair combed neatly in a side part, for a meeting of equals. Daddy listened respectfully to Mr Vance's assessment of my performance during the year and thanked him profusely for everything he had done for me, deploying a firm handshake and affectionate shoulder pat to convey the strength of his gratitude

Our last day in Pond Park Primary was Mr Vance's too; he had been offered the post of Vice Principal in another school. I felt sad because in coming years I wouldn't even be able to visit him in our old classroom. As was customary, the school leavers asked teachers to sign their names or write a little note of farewell in a keepsake book. One teacher drew a cartoon duck and wrote, *'I hope you shine in your new school.'* Numerous others wrote variations on best of luck with flamboyant signatures. I was keen to see what Mr Vance would write for me. When the time came, he simply wrote, *'Now nobody will shout PEGGY! at you!'* - in reference to our morning roll call tradition. It felt a little anticlimactic.

Mr Vance stood to give a small speech of thanks and farewell in our final assembly. There he stood, tall in his immaculate suit with that tidy moustache and projecting his familiar baritone. I recalled the forbidding authority figure he was before we got to know him and felt honoured to have come to know the very best of him.

"Just like the Primary Sevens, I too must say goodbye today with great gratitude for the wonderful times I have had here over these past years, but though I am leaving, I wish to leave behind something which I hope will continue to encourage the considerable talent found here at Pond Park Primary."

He turned and lifted a large trophy from the table behind him.

"This trophy is to be awarded each year to a pupil who demonstrates notable talent, effort or achievement in their areas of specialism. It is my great honour today, to award it to a pupil who is a talented and prolific poet, and whose work I have enjoyed over these past few years."

My heart started to hammer. Surely, he wasn't talking about me? I realised it wasn't just me with these suspicions as I became subjected to a barrage of pokes and whispers.

"It is my great pleasure to present this trophy - the first name to be engraved on this trophy of outstanding achievement – to my now former pupil – Peggy Bell. Peggy, come up and receive your trophy!"

I was pushed to my feet and made my way to the front of the hall on shaking legs as two hundred pairs of hands clapped, and two hundred pairs of eyes took in my stunned, blushing face. The trophy was huge.

He shook my hand and sent me off into the world with a souvenir of his high regard for me and a reminder that my talent existed, that I was worthwhile. Over the course of two years, Mr Vance championed me, encouraged me, defended me and as his final act as a staff member, celebrated me. Without his dedication to foster my academic progress and self-esteem, I probably wouldn't have passed the transfer test to be offered a place in a Grammar School, a move which itself opened many subsequent doors. His explicit appreciation of my writing convinced me that I had something worthwhile to say and a talent for expression, which sowed seeds of self-belief. The litany of events that had to happen to lead me from a broken family in Tate's Avenue to his classroom in Lisburn were many, and yet, I can't imagine that anyone else could have accessed those parts of me that needed unlocking. And just like that, our contract was complete.

We were dismissed from Assembly, said our last farewells and departed Pond Park forever. I raced home, buoyant and eager to show the trophy to my parents. As I opened our gate, I remembered his note. *Now there will be no-one to shout PEGGY! at you* - these words now rang with sorrowful sentiment. My eyes stung with tears. The world was going to be a very different place without Mr Vance. I wondered if anyone would ever care enough to shout *PEGGY!* again.

Eleven

This grammar school you want to go to - things will be more expensive. Money'll be tight."

My stomach roiled with nerves as I understood this to be an opener to a discussion about big school. Daddy looked around for his lighter, a sign that I had his attention for the duration of a feg. He found it nestled on a shelf in the oval alcove by the fireplace, beside the main photograph of Billy, aged seven, smiling shyly at the camera, a blush on his tan face, chocolate hair and eyes, overly colourised from the black and white original. The flame hissed to life and as his head bowed over his first inhalation, I scurried over to the rocking chair by the window and arranged myself, back straight, hands folded demurely in my lap; an officious little twerp ready to ace this interview.

I was surprised to discover that my desire to attend a Grammar was being met with resistance. Daddy had long lamented that Jeanette had thrown the transfer test so that she could go to the secondary with her friends - a wasted opportunity and tutoring money down the drain.

"It's a religious school, Daddy, founded by Quakers. I got a book out of the library about Quakers, if you want to read it."

He nodded.

"We will have to go without some things to pay the fees."

He wasn't saying no, but my heart sank as I realised that if I got my wish, we would be worse off. I thought of Mummy counting out the coins in her purse for milk that would need to stretch until Thursday. I thought of the value pack biscuits we got for a wee something sweet with a cuppa and realised with a stab of horror that there were no cheaper treats and this might be the first extravagance to go.

"*You could give up smoking...*" I suggested tentatively.

Every budget day, when the chancellor announced higher taxation for cigarettes from the television, gloom mingled with the smoke clouds floating in the living room. Mummy appeared like an apparition at the doorway.

"*That's enough of that. It's our one vice! You'd know all about it if we were out drinking the money!*"

Daddy waved her away with a dismissive flick of his hand and she begrudgingly retreated, mumbling under her breath. We locked eyes, Daddy and me. I missed biscuits already.

"*Cigarettes are very expensive…*"

"*That's enough, nai.*"

I had an arsenal of anti-smoking logic - destroying your lungs was an affront to God, it left a smell on clothes, it was expensive, there was a high biscuit to cigarette ratio. Daddy simply wanted to hear that I would justify the coming financial strain by working hard at school.

Julie and I started Friends together the following September. Traditionally, school uniforms were purchased in August, as close as possible to the new school year in order to mitigate the disaster of a last-minute growth spurt. The shop with the greatest stock of Grammar uniforms was at the top of Bow Street, Lisburn's main pedestrian shopping precinct. Market Square was located here, so called because for centuries it had been the site of – wait for it – a market. It had been an epicentre for trade and in the 1800s the site of public hangings of Irish rebels.

Daddy had joined us for the shopping trip, keen to oversee the purchase of the correct items. Mummy's penchant for bargains meant that he couldn't entirely trust her not to get derailed. The shop was having a sale on Friends' boys' blazers; they were half the price of the girls'. The blazers were ostensibly the same except that the buttons were stitched on opposite sides. As we stood in the shop waiting for an attendant to become free, it became apparent that parents were happy to send their daughters to Friends in boys' blazers, and in sizes larger than required in order to get as much use as possible. Finally, it was our turn.

"We'll be needing a full Friends' uniform for this one."

He gestured in my direction and though his tone was casual, my trained ear detected undertones of pride. The assistant had clearly been run off her feet in the preterm rush, nonetheless her tired eyes lit up as she shared what she believed to be good news.

"Our boys' blazers are half price at the moment, so we can save you a few pounds. It all adds up, doesn't it?"

Despite the fact that we had watched all the previous customers avail of this offer, Daddy detected pity. Scarred by a childhood of being noticeably poor in ill-fitting hand-me-downs, he was versed in the language of apparel and didn't want me to be marked out as someone whose parents couldn't afford the requisite item. Martin was getting a bit fussy from all the waiting, and kids acting up in public stressed him out almost as much as this subtext laden interaction. He was brusque.

"*No. We'll take the girls' one.*"

"*Are you sure? What size is she? Let me see…there is a difference of almost thirty pounds in that size of blazer. Are you sure?*"

The furrow between Daddy's eyebrows was deepening. When he spoke, his voice was quiet, but stern, the familiar tone of warning that this was the final word.

"*Yes. The girl's blazer.*"

"*If, you're sure. You might want to try the boy's blazer on? Then you can see for yourself that the difference between the two is barely noticeable…no? Okay. What size are you thinking?*"

She whipped out a measuring tape and flung it around my chest then along my arms.

"*I'd say she's a 26, so to allow for -*"

"*We will take a 26.*"

"*Are you sure you don't want a 28, or 30? They grow fast at this stage!*"

The fact that every dick and his dog was high tailing it out of there with a boy blazer was moot. I grew worried about being the only girl wearing an appropriately sized girls' blazer, while everyone else enjoyed the norm of a boxy blazer with rolled up sleeves.

"Daddy, Julie is getting a boy's blazer, I can get one too. And a bigger one will last longer."

It was a rookie mistake to appeal to his common sense, which had flown the coop taking with it any chance I had of blending in.

"I don't care! No child of mine is getting sent to that school in half-price clothes."

"But Daddy..."

He fixed me with *The Look*, which conveyed that a cuff round the ear could be on the cards, right here in the middle of the shop, in front of potential classmates and their well-heeled parents. We were somehow at odds despite our identical desires to fit in and, to keep our heads below the parapet.

Having no experience of Grammar schools, Daddy assumed that this step up in the world was a considerable one. I was a female version of Pip from Great Expectations, and he proved a very determined Magwitch. We made our way down the gentle decline of Bow Street, past the sport shop where future classmates were merrily choosing neon hued backpacks, until we came to a pokey little shop, so unobtrusive in its plainness that I had never noticed it in all the Saturdays I visited town. The little bell jingled as the door opened, a quaint indulgence rather than a necessity given the bang and creak of the jolt required to dislodge it from the worn frame. If the door situation hadn't tipped me off, the smell of tobacco and dust put paid to any notions I had of purchasing anything capable of catapulting me up the social ladder. Besides shiny wooden pipes and handcrafted wallets, they sold leather satchels. In a pointless gesture of indulgence, Daddy magnanimously allowed me to take my pick from a colourway that ranged from brown all the way through to darker brown (black was off the table). I thought a small to medium sized one would best suit my needs, but Daddy anticipated my porting a volume of books equivalent to the library of Alexandria, so we went for the most capacious one that wouldn't have looked out of place on Jeff Capes' larger brother. *Tonight, Matthew, I'll be a five-year-old heading off to Eton in the 1800s.*

Uniform is intended to democratise the educational setting, but indicators of social strata can be invented easily enough. The differences were subtle but spoke volumes. I wore a correctly fitting girl's blazer, with the less popular green shirt and socks (pulled up) with brown leather shoes. It was cool to wear the overlarge boy blazer, the standard white shirts and socks (pushed down) with black leather shoes. My neat little cardigan juxtaposed others' baggy jumpers. My A-line skirt below the knee could not be rolled up in the same way that the more popular straight skirts could. Other pupils swung a sports bag over one shoulder, with a nonchalance I could only dream of.

Nothing I could do made my satchel remotely acceptable, short of setting it on fire.

The main building of Friends' School was beautiful. A sweeping driveway revealed a three-storey redbrick facade with two door arches and curved bay windows. A sympathetic two-storey extension jutted to the left, connecting this imposing building to the numerous add-ons since its inception in the late 1700s. I had the sense that these structures had been the site of much becoming and felt privileged that I could unfold in such a place. I was so keen to fit in and do well.

We were a class full of strangers with big school nerves in an overwhelmingly large and maze-like campus. On the very first day, our teacher briefly left our classroom to speak to a colleague in the corridor, and instead of braying across the room or nipping over to another table for a quick hello as we might have done in primary school, we all sat in awkward silence. The apprehension didn't last long. My unusual bag served a useful purpose as a topic of conversation for hitherto unacquainted classmates to bond in shared horror. Emboldened by numbers, some began fielding direct questions.

"Why have you got a satchel?"

I tried to palm the blame off on Daddy, but this only added another layer to my strangeness. My anxiety at being singled out for unwanted attention gave way to a sinking feeling; it was happening again. Coming to Friends wasn't going to be a fresh start on a level footing. It was to be another environment where I was different and ridiculous. This time though, there would be no Mr Vance to act as buffer or balm.

Julie and I were equally nervous to be starting a new school and stuck to each other closely. On a few occasions, classmates mixed us up and called me Julie. For the second time in my life how I wished to be Julie, whose parents didn't insist on a correctly-fitting blazer, a skirt no higher than the knee, a bag from Goodnight Mr Tom, a French plait and rules against shaving legs like a wanton woman - the very reason I was content to wear socks up instead of down like everyone else. The satchel merely served as an opener, and I was answerable for further oddities.

"Why are you wearing your socks up?"
"Did you ask your mum to do your hair like that?"
Some kinder but no less intrusive classmates offered advice - earnest little faces, eyes wide with helpfulness.
"Just roll your socks down! Just roll the top of your skirt up!"

Rolling my socks down would reveal downy hair that was guaranteed to invite further unwelcome advice about shaving, and if I raised the hem of that skirt I was risking creating a parachute and one good gust would have given me sufficient lift to float me over to the hockey pitches. I was more afraid that Daddy would find out I had chosen to display my legs. Besides, it was too late - I was already the figure of fun and my differences had dehumanised me.

I refined my accent to that of my classmates, but just like the blazer, the satchel, the socks, it was all theatre and I felt like a fraud. I shrunk as I had watched my parents do when they were around anyone that wasn't working class. Their example overruled any desire on either of our parts for me to be worthy. It wasn't long before the humiliation of being an oddity was joined with its old bedfellow, shame at being poor.

Geography was taught in the farthest flung porta cabins, known as the Huts. We loitered outside until Miss Hillis invited us to mount the rickety steps, covered in chicken wire for torque on icy days. We left muddy footprints as we walked across the lino to sit at tables of two, alphabetised and in pairs, the better for the teacher to learn our names and for controlling the class - as you were statistically unlikely to be sitting with your friend for a chat. One of our first lessons was about primary, secondary and tertiary employment - primary being manual labour, secondary, production and tertiary the provision of services. We took turns to stand and declare in which sector our parents worked, beginning with those whose surname began with A. I sat, sweating, heart hammering, as my contemporaries announced, doctor – tertiary, solicitor – tertiary, teacher – tertiary, company director – tertiary. To my great relief, the bell went before it was my turn. I assumed that we would resume the lesson the following week and loitered, packing my bag slowly so that I could speak to the teacher out of earshot.

"Miss Hillis?"

"Hmmm?"

She looked around as if surprised that the room hadn't emptied. My heart thumped as I tried to figure out how to say the thing that I usually went to great lengths to hide.

"It's just…my Daddy doesn't work."

She seemed to understand my subtext – don't make me stand up and tell everyone – and she scrambled to think of something to say to ease my blushing discomfort.

"Well, what about your Mum?"

Perhaps she assumed that I was in a househusband / working wife situation and was embarrassed about the gender roles. I started to feel sick.

"Mummy doesn't work either. She…looks after Daddy. He's…disabled."

"I see. Did they ever work?"

She was trying to help me, but all she was doing was handing me a spade to dig myself a deeper hole of shame.

"Yes. Daddy was a stager in the shipyards."

"And so, which category was that?"

"Primary."

I felt like I had turned myself in - the primary offspring hidden amid the sea of tertiary offspring. The jig is up - I don't belong here. I'm a fraud.

"Well done. That's your turn over. Off you go."

She was kind, having seen my discomfort, but I suspected my classmates would have been a great deal less-so. Clues abounded, if it was an episode of Treasure Hunt, Anneka Rice would have directed the camera away from her arse to shout STOP THE CLOCK within seconds -

my address, the smoke from home that clung to my uniform, which now mingled with the smell of pubescent body odour. I had no antiperspirant for two reasons: it was a luxury item that we couldn't afford it and besides, I wasn't to smell like a whore's bedroom. My parents were in receipt of social security payments, disability benefit and child benefit, and that only stretched so far when it came to feeding us, clothing us and paying for the numerous additional costs of having a child at a Grammar school. There was the expensive uniform, sports equipment, fees for music tuition and a wholly unnecessary Gabardine trench coat for the winter – because an expensive, warm new coat meant you were well looked after. After the fegs, of course.

    I felt hopeless. I have always moved so conspicuously through life that I suspected the relief of anonymity was never part of my plan. This inability to blend in or belong meant I couldn't build my self-esteem on the shifting sands of others' approval, as young adults tend to. I was given the opportunity to build true self-esteem that comes from withstanding disapproval.

    Julie's mum collected us from school and ferried us up the road to be home for shortly after four. I threw my satchel over my shoulders and tramped the two-minute walk to the bottom of her street, through the Hole in the Hedge and across the strip of green to my back gate. For once, I couldn't see Mummy at the kitchen window, where I usually caught her eye and prompted a cheery wave. I vaulted the gate (I could never be bothered to open it -

jiggling the rusted, squeaking bar lock across and then back again) and opened the back door, listening carefully for signs of life. I stopped cold when I heard a strangled cry from upstairs. It was Daddy.

 I tiptoed through the kitchen, padded over the carpeted living room and eased the door open on to the front hall. He shrieked, a high sharp sound that pierced me with icy horror. I called upstairs.
"Hello?"
Mummy shouted down.
"Peggy, your daddy's back's away."
I wasn't sure what to do with this information. I left the door slightly ajar in case instructions were issued and sat in his chair, knees pulled to my chest, listening. My stockinged feet agitated the weft of the grey velveteen. Mummy's voice carried, imploring.
"Ben, just get back into bed. I can bring you a bottle to go in."
"No, Gloria…aaaaa!"

 He wailed again. Every muscle in my body tensed as I imagined him in excruciating pain. The familiar creaks on the landing floorboards under the thin carpet told me that he had become stranded at the middle of three doors - the hot press between our bedrooms. He sounded like a trapped animal, as though the slightest movement was agony. I realised that I was also whimpering when I put my hands over my ears and was glad that the echo of my own voice drowned out the sound of his. I took my hands away in the hope that his pain had relented but the screams kept coming, then a worse sound: my daddy crying. He sounded like a lost child, sobbing, wailing in pain and desperation. I put my hands hard over my ears and cried, too.

Panic made Mummy abrupt.

"*That's it, Ben, I'm phoning the doctor. This is too much.*"

Daddy hated doctors. Over the course of his adult life, he had seen too many of them, examining him to establish whether he was fit for work, looking at him with suspicion, implying that he was overplaying his injury to sit at home collecting disability money. I knew by her tone that this was not the first time she had suggested a doctor that day, and now she would broker no argument. All the same, she paused a beat, knowing that she needed a tacit agreement from Daddy, broken and distraught as he was, because even in this state he would not be overruled and emasculated. There were a few seconds of silence, perhaps he nodded faintly, or flicked a finger in a gesture of dismissal, unable to meet her eye or look up lest it send another jolt down his back.

Her footsteps trilled down the stairs and our eyes met as she rounded the doorway to get to the little phone table beside the door.

"*He's in a bad way.*"

I nodded an acknowledgment, dumbstruck with worry and continued clenching and unclenching my toes, scritch-scratching. She lifted the receiver and automatically dialled the number, too familiar from the repeat prescriptions ordered over the years.

"Hello? This is Mrs Bell - we need a doctor here as soon as possible. It's my husband, he has a chronic back injury and is in a bad way with the pain."

Soothing, sympathetic tones came muffled from the earpiece; professional, caring but unruffled.

She scurried back upstairs leaving me alone once more. I hugged my knees and felt stress-sweat grow cold on my shirt. Wailing resumed as she guided him back to bed, ready for the doctor. I clamped the heels of my hands hard over my ears and rubbed back and forth, for white noise to drown all else out, and prayed hard; *"please God, make it stop, take his pain away, please God, make the doctor come quickly."* But it wasn't stopping, and the doctor was taking too long and soon I was sobbing in desperation, my prayers wordless, rocking and crying, my heart upstairs.

The click of the gate-latch had Mummy at the front door before the doctor had even closed the gate after himself. She flung it wide and shouted – *he's up here!* – and bounded back up the stairs to stand sentry. The doctor's shadow passed behind me and he trudged up the stairs, a caricature of flapping coat and weighty doctor's bag. Mummy remembered herself, remembered her manners, or simply understood that the quality of care her husband would receive might depend upon how well she upheld social niceties.

"Thank you for coming, Doctor."

His calm, low voice barely carried as I strained to listen. There was no mistaking the rich, confident tones and accent of someone who did not grow up around here. The conversational tenor was that of *what seems to be the problem?* – as if the crying ex-boxer, grey with agony, wasn't indication enough. The examination was a duet of high-pitched cries and the doctor's monotonous baritone narration. Mummy's voice was the only clear one, reproachful.

"Now do you see how bad he gets? You need to write this down. The amount of times doctors – not you, doctor – other doctors have said he's fit for work! How is this fit for work?"

Low murmurs of inferred assent.

"Then making him jump through hoops for his DLA - get on this treadmill, bend over, and the next thing his back is away and he's in bed for a week, sick with the pain of it! Sometimes all he has to do is cough and that's him seized up and on painkillers."

Daddy interjected weakly.

"Gloria…"

Mummy paused a beat but had her final word.

"Doctor, there has to be an end to it. Look at him."

A few minutes later, the doctor was scurrying out to his car, having left a prescription for stronger painkillers (despite the fact that his usual ones were so strong that they ripped at his stomach lining) and vague promises to specify the extent of Daddy's pain in his file. It was cold comfort that this bout of incapacitation might stave off further scrutiny at the Health Centre to see if he was putting it on for the Disability Living Allowance.

Examining our respective miseries - not fitting in at school versus this life-altering, excruciating back injury - my lot paled in comparison. It was another thing to add to my list of worries and woes that was mine, and mine alone.

Twelve

When I was twelve, Mummy decided to have The Talk. I was listening to Atlantic 252 on the radio in my room when there was a formal little knock at the door, the politeness of which was soon undermined by her entering without invitation. That knock wasn't so much a question as a statement of intent.

"*Peggy?*"

"*Yes, Mummy?*"

"*It's time for us to have a wee talk.*"

I scrutinised her expression for signs that I was in trouble before a sickening realisation hit. My mummy, this tiny wee Christian lady who used a safety pin for modesty in blouses that didn't fasten to her throat, was about to regale me with her version of the Sex Talk. I couldn't decide what was worse; witnessing her verbal gymnastics to avoid explicit detail while shame hung in the air like an accusation, or explicit detail.

"*I want to tell you something that I told Jeanette at your age.*"

I could feel my treacherous cheeks hitting a reddener and hoped fervently she deduced it was from embarrassment rather than guilt.

"Ack, Mummy, there's no need; sure, they cover all that in school."

"Just you sit yourself down."

I steeled myself but needn't have bothered. She looked at me intently and spoke with unnecessary crossness.

"Keep your head up and your skirt down. Do you hear me, wee girl?"

"Yes, Mummy."

"Do you understand me?"

"I do, I do!"

Well, if I understood anything, it was that I had just dodged a bullet. If Mummy started banging on about the mechanics of sex, I'd boke so hard my eyeballs would hit the carpet. Though I was affronted by her irritated tones, I was relieved it was over so quickly.

Not long after that close shave of narrowly avoiding redecorating the floor, Daddy delivered a diatribe on the same topic. He had a horror of anything like that. If kissing happened on a TV show, he coughed and hastily located the remote to change the channel until the worst was over. It was a Saturday afternoon and we sat waiting for dinner as a film droned on. Daddy lit a cigarette, took a puff and slowly exhaled.

"Peggy."

"Yes?"

"I want you to listen carefully. You ready?"

I nodded.

"Imagine a basket of apples for sale; shiny, fresh, crisp. Now imagine if someone was to take a bite out of one and throw it back into the basket. There it sits, mouldering, festering, rotting. Would anyone passing that basket choose this particular apple to buy?"

I shook my head.

"Why not?"

His eyes bored into me as he waited for a response.

"Because someone had already taken a bite?"

He looked like he was unsure if I was being deliberately obtuse, or if I too was utilising the safety of metaphor.

"Yes - because someone has already sampled it, and the sampling has made it rotten. Why would anyone want a brown, smelly, maggoty apple, when there were fresh ones to be had? A disgusting, dirty aul' apple with someone's germs on it?"

I nodded, slightly dumbfounded.

"Do you understand me?"

He had hit the point so hard that I suspected even six-year-old Martin understood him. Even when trying to be subtle, he was never one for delicacy, and it would be a while before I would enjoy an apple with anything approaching enthusiasm.

My sex talks were limited to abstinence lectures. My parents had grown up in the time of keep yourself for your husband, when it was generally acccpted that girls put themselves in danger by abdicating their responsibility not to get raped by dressing or acting provocatively, and rapists were not held accountable for being yoked to the power of suggestion. Any progress since then is debatable. The media normalises misogyny - policing women as they navigate the elusive fine line between prude and slut, undermining autonomy with thorough critiques of attractiveness, hair removal, shape, size, sexual expression.

Some might say things are worse - the joyful abandon of sixties' free love and seventies' rollicking full-bushed porn have been superseded by baby-women - shaved, bleached, plucked, waxed, plumped and immobilised, literal objects, homogenised and infantilised. I already knew it was the responsibility of a female not to be raped, rather than the responsibility of a male not to rape.

This was a comparatively simpler time before internet dating and internet porn, before blink evaluations deemed people fuckable or unfuckable by a swipe left or right, before a proliferation of too accessible internet pornography portrayed sex as a mechanistic event where girls merely facilitate male pleasure, the glorified cum shot showing men not having sex with women but having sex at them.

Daddy's head might have exploded had he known what lay in store for society in the coming decades. He saw himself as the only buffer between his vulnerable daughter and a world that wanted to do harm, a world that closed in on innocence and reputation. Boys were not allowed to call to the door. If one did, Daddy's eyes narrowed in scrutiny. *"What kind of a girl has wee lads calling to the door? Why are they calling for YOU?"*

My honest response - that I was required to make up the numbers for whatever game was happening on the green - was met with suspicious silence, as if it was just a matter of time before his surveillance would yield unfavourable results.

When I picked out a pair of cream leggings from a box of hand-me-downs, they were immediately vetoed. *"Those things show the whole shape of you. Bad men will look at you."*

The message was everywhere, in implicit and explicit form. It was my job to not make bad men think bad things.

He didn't condone victim-blaming or absolving sexually aggressive men of culpability. He acknowledged the cultural narrative and short-cut to a fast and effective way to keep his daughter safe. He wanted me to be invisible. I understood his concerns, but the whiff of suspicion wounded me, the implication that it was only a matter of time before I fucked up. I wondered about the how and when of my imminent mistake but couldn't picture anything plausible.

The Twelfth of July is a Northern Irish public holiday commemorating the Battle of the Boyne - a key moment in the Protestant Ascendency when the Protestant William of Orange defeated the Catholic James II in 1690. The popularised and oversimplified historical narrative omitted unhelpful details (such as the fact that Prince William of Orange had the support and funding of the Pope and much of his army was made up of Catholic mercenaries) in favour of a romanticised version of a beloved King Billy, defeater of Catholics. These politics of separation had calcified with the help of Protestant evangelical firebrand, Reverend Ian Paisley, whose vocal opposition to Catholicism and the Civil Rights movement played no small part in fomenting hatred and polarisation. His rhetoric of gruff defiance - *Never, Never, Never!* and *Ulster Says No* (to the Anglo-Irish Agreement) had a simplistic appeal to Loyalists. He stoked fear of Loyalist disenfranchisement and hatred of Catholics, who he said *breed like rabbits and multiply like vermin*, while alleging that Catholic priests handed out submachine guns to parishioners.

The rhetoric of disempowerment found its target in generations of loyalists herded in housing estates, wrestling with unemployment, poor educational support and barely addressed mental health issues. Politicians roused sectarian feelings in the poor of both sides, ensuring they remained entrenched and embittered against them'uns with whom, in fact, they had much more in common. All the while this ruling elite took a wage and gave every impression of wanting change for the better. It's a tale as old as time - imply responsibility for poverty to another group of poor people (the Catholics, the Protestants, the Muslims, the immigrants, the refugees, the dole spongers) and let them fight it out while the middle classes are kept just comfortable enough not to want to rock the boat and the wealth is siphoned ever upwards.

British flags and bunting were hung from lampposts and porches, kerbs were painted red, white and blue, flute bands practised, and bonfires were built in preparation for the Glorious Twelfth, the social event of the season in Loyalist estates province-wide. My Grammar school friends, and indeed the people in the nice private houses on the main road didn't seem to be as bothered about tribalism as we were in the estates. It looked to me like triumphal loyalism was the remit of the Protestant poor.

    A bonfire was built on our green in the weeks preceding the holiday and consisted of old wood and furniture - mattresses and sofas - built around a central stabilising structure of pallets and tyres. Knowledge of bonfire construction was passed on down through overlapping generations, year after year. My friends and I sat on the grass or perched on low garden walls to watch the bigger boys arrange items in feats of engineering far beyond their education, while the younger boys fetched and ferried, heavy-browed with the gravity of the task. They made a den inside the construction, where they smoked cigarettes and drank tins of beer on discarded settees and mattresses. One day as we walked around it looking skywards at the dizzying height, my friend Mandy punctured her foot on a rusty nail protruding from a wood plank and ended up the unhappy recipient of a tetanus shot.

    The lighting of the bonfire took place on the Eleventh night amid drinking, dancing and sometimes debauchery. The windows of the houses flanking the green became scorched and blackened. The year that the heat from the fire shattered windows heralded the end of the Ballymacash Park bonfire. Thereafter, residents made their way over to the larger green in the main Ballymacash

Estate for revelry around a much bigger bonfire than we were accustomed to.

Our estate was buzzing with excitement, but while my friends' parents were getting the drink in and sorting new outfits for their kids, my Daddy seemed oblivious. I approached him with weak hope.

"Daddy, can we go to the bonfire this year?"

"No. I can't be annoyed with all that nonsense."

"But everybody is going!"

He shook his head dismissively.

"Load o' aul' shite."

I tried to appeal to his political sensibilities.

"But it's our culture!"

"Drinking and carrying on like eejits isn't our culture."

He was deliberately missing the point. After a few moments of silence which conveyed that I had relented, he spoke.

"You can go over until the fire's lit, then your Mummy will be over to take you home."

I squeaked with excitement.

"Now, listen - you've to stay with your friends. No dandering off on your own, and no going off with anyone."

"Yes, Daddy."

"And no boys. You hear me, wee girl?"

"Yes. No boys."

I pondered the statement I had just made and realised there might be obstacles to committing to my word.

"Daddy?"

"What, love?"

I was unsure how to explain how boys were fairly unavoidable - given that they made up approximately 50% of the populace - without giving the impression that I fully intended to fraternise.

"*What if Rachel and Carol talk to boys from their school?*"

He turned in his chair, angling himself towards me in a familiar way.

"*Peggy.*"

He paused for a moment, choosing his words carefully.

"*Do you know what happens to wee girls that talk to boys?*"

I gazed back in the full understanding that the question was rhetorical.

"*They get a reputation.*"

I wanted to point out the fallacies in his assertion, but if I canvassed too enthusiastically for platonic friendship, there was every chance that permission to attend the bonfire would be withdrawn.

"*I don't think Carol or Rachel have reputations.*"

"*I don't care about Carol or Rachel. I care about you. You don't know what wee lads are like.*"

I kept my features neutral in case a micro-expression suggested the contrary.

"*When I was a wee lad, there was a wee girl let boys look up her skirt. Do you know what we called her?*"

I shook my head.

"*Nelly No-Knickers.*"

I was curious to know if her name had actually been Nelly, or if this was simply an alliterative moniker, but I knew this was very much beside the point. Nelly No-Knickers was a one-dimensional cautionary tale.

"*That was her name for years. Her card was marked. Do you think anybody wanted to marry Nelly No-Knickers?*"

It was not the time to quip, *Maybe, depending on what they saw up her skirt.*

"*No.*"

"*Exactly. And do you know what happened to wee girls that went with boys? Do you think wee lads don't talk? Nobody wants to marry a girl that's been all round the place. Do you know how many wee girls I saw that got caught out?*"

It was a familiar euphemism. Pregnant was a dirty word. His lip had curled back in disgust.

"*Wee girls that could'a made something of their lives. That was it; their whole lives - ruined.*"

I nodded to show I understood.

He took a breath and his countenance softened.

"*I don't want that for you, love. You think I'm being too strict, but I'm just doing my job. I'm your father. I'm strict with you to keep you safe. It's because I love you.*"

I must have visibly flinched with surprise at those three words.

"*Do you think because I don't say it all the time that I don't love you?*"

I gazed back, unsure how to respond. I knew I was loved but I didn't always feel loved. My silence was an entreaty to hear anything that might help this abstract love to bed down in my heart.

"You see these ones - Yanks - blethering on, all sickly sweet," – and here, he used an American accent and a sing-song voice – *"Love youuu…- slabbering on every five minutes about how they love you, the postman, the shop assistant, somebody they met once for five minutes… fuckin' bastards."*
Mummy chimed in.
"Ben!"
"Well. They are."
He lit a cigarette as he gathered himself.
"What I'm saying is, the more you say a thing, the less it means."
I nodded in earnest agreement, in eager acceptance of this love that I needed like air and sustenance.
"Oh - and when you're over at the bonfire, stay away from the bushes."

I was definitely up for a party, but I wasn't sure how I felt about the political divisions that the Twelfth had come to represent. It was easy to preach about the happenstance of birth location when discussing Muslims or Buddhists but considering the possibility of being born into a Republican community and being raised a Catholic filled me with discomfort. One the one hand, I tried to reassure myself that in such a situation I would educate myself about both religions and default to Protestantism, because the Bible explicitly warns against idolatry, but on the other hand I knew that if I was raised Catholic, I was more likely to denounce Protestants as heathens. I simply wanted to be the 'me' that existed beneath and beyond the mutable confines of nationality or race, but our violent

175

history had muddied the water. My mother's cousin was a prison guard who had been shot on his own doorstep and the IRA had planted several bombs that, but for chance, could have decimated our family. Surely, though, if I had been born to the other community, that family would just have easily been subjected to loyalist paramilitary violence.

We met at Carol's house to drink weak Buck's Fizz. Rachel was almost beside herself with excitement.
"Do you think it will get us drunk?"
I was nervous.
"Not if we don't drink very much."
"I'm gonna drink loads!" she announced.
Fortunately, the glasses were small, and it was disgusting. Taste buds destroyed and a gut full of bubbles, off we went down the road with our arms linked doing the Monkees walk and singing the Sash.
"It is old but it is beautiful, and the colours they are fine
It was worn at Derry, Aughrim, Enniskillen and the Boyne
Sure, my father wore it in his youth, the grand old days of yore,
And it's on the Twelfth, I love to wear the Sash my father wore."

We weren't sure of the lyrics, and substituted Derriaghy (just outside Lisburn) for Derry, Aughrim, and the grand old days of yore became the grand old days of York. I was a bit confused about York being involved in a Northern Irish battle, but in fairness, King Billy was Dutch so I supposed anything was possible.

We traversed the graffiti emblazoned underpass into Ballymacash Estate. The bonfire towered in the centre of a large green, taller than any Ballymacash Park bonfire. A poor sound system blasted muffled music, and everyone had a drink in their hand as they danced or loitered around the behemoth. A smaller fire had been lit, a mini bonfire for the little ones whose bedtimes were well before midnight. Woodsmoke drifted as the sky darkened. Bigger boys and girls kissed or let their hands rest in the other's jeans pocket, giving me a sick twist of anxiety. I side-eyed the bushes, half-expecting to see eyes looking back; an opportunistic paedo or rapist festooned with twigs for camouflage, waiting to pick us off if we became separated from each other. I cleaved to my chums like a limpet. A few boys from Rachel's class came over to demonstrate their drunkenness with exaggerated staggering and hawing Top Deck Shandy breaths in our faces. I could see immediately that the no boys rule was going to be a tricky road to traverse. They were everywhere, looking like normal human beings, rather than the calculating life-ruiners my dad warned me of. One was called Jimmy and had wavy hair parted in the middle, to his shoulders.

"*Fuck the Pope!*"

"*Yeooo!*"

I tried to join the conversation.

"*Did you know that King Billy had the support of the Pope?*"

"*Ballicks!*"

My talent for not fitting in was on-point. He dandered off to have a word with his friend, who then walked back towards me.

"*Here, will you meet my mate?*"

I looked at Carol.

"*Jimmy wants to meet you!*"

Rachel chimed in.

"*Go on, away and meet him.*"

I threw a cursory look around the crowd to see if Mummy was about, eavesdropping on this incriminating conversation, but she was nowhere to be seen. Rachel noticed my hesitation.

"*Peggy's frigid. Stop being frigid!*"

"*Are you frigid?*" inquired the friend.

"*No,*" I replied, unwilling to lay claim to this unpopular trait.

"*Good!*" announced Jimmy, who threw his arm proprietorially around my shoulder. I froze. Shrugging him off would be confirmation of my frigidity, which apparently was as frowned upon as Catholicism, and so I allowed him to use me as a leaning post while he played out the charade of drunkenness. Worry gnawed at my stomach. Every second that arm lay across my shoulders like lead was another second of opportunity for discovery. I stood bollard-still, karate chopping wandering hands like a coquettish Jackie Chan.

It wasn't long before Mummy bounded over to extricate me, having been utilising her diminutive stature to aid espionage.

"*You were told: no boys.*"

"*I didn't ask him to put his arm round me!*"

"*Come you on home with me. You were warned.*"

She steered me away from the crowds, towards home. When we were sufficiently out of earshot and eyeline, I began my appeal.

"*Mummy, I wasn't doing anything, he just wouldn't get off me.*"

"*You should have pushed him off. I saw you letting him put his arm around you.*"

I didn't know how to explain my situation. Explaining that I was avoiding accusations of frigidity was not going to help my case. Every step we took was another step closer to home, where Daddy would be waiting to hear whether I had behaved myself.

"*Mummy, don't tell Daddy.*"

"*I'm not keeping secrets from your daddy.*"

"*I didn't do anything.*"

"*I saw you with my own eyes!*"

"*Please, Mummy.*"

"*I'm not telling lies for you.*"

I knew there was no point in pleading, but nonetheless, every few minutes as we drew closer, another plea would escape me.

"*Mummy, please.*"

"*Give over.*"

"*Please don't!*"

"*Give my head peace.*"

It was futile. Mummy had been sent as emissary and her report would be completely factual, devoid of sympathy or nuance. That image of an arm draped across me spoke for itself. I had made my own bed.

As we came in through the back door, Daddy was waiting there in the kitchen. Mummy didn't beat about the bush.

"*A wee lad had his arm round her.*"

"*A what?*"

The angry tone confirmed that he had heard perfectly. She nodded grimly.

"*You were fucking warned! Get up them stairs 'til I get my belt.*"

"*Daddy, no!*"

"*Get UP!*" Spit had begun to gather and fleck at the corners of his lips.

"*Take your trousers off. And wash yourself! Gloria – go up there and make sure she washes herself before I get up there.*"

Confusion mingled with fear. This was a strange new punishment. Mummy looked off-balance but knew better than to argue. She pushed me up the stairs to the bathroom at the top.

"*Take your pants off and wash yourself. Then put them back on and go to your room.*"

"*Mummy, no!*"

"*Do as you're told. Hurry up. I've to make sure you do it.*"

I washed my private area with the door ajar so that Mummy could confirm that I was clean. It was humiliating. I cried from embarrassment. The implication that I was dirty was not lost on me. I was a rotten apple. Mummy oversaw me replace my pants, but not my trousers, so as not to impede the belt. I didn't stifle my cries when the belt hit me; my friends wouldn't hear me because they were still at the bonfire, dancing, cheering, maybe even under a boy's arm. Other girls could make mistakes, but not his girls. Not on his watch.

    He was keeping me safe because he loved me. But I didn't feel safe, and it didn't feel like love.

Thirteen

I entered my teens still preoccupied with spiritual questions. Why are we here? Are we finite, or infinite? If infinite, where were we before? Where do we go after? Is there a God? Eventually I had to concede that Christianity simply wasn't a good fit for me. It raised more questions than it answered. The Christian God was too slippy a character for my liking. There was the weird decision to take Billy to Heaven – that one had settled over me like fine asbestos dust. He'd winkled out the illusion of safety from my parents' hearts when he took Billy. He'd left them frightened husks, then threw me in to live with the fallout. I was cross with this God, the child-thief, the atrocities onlooker, the absentee landlord. I began to feel less afraid of a world where he was a construct than a world where he was real and sitting back, watching us suffer, a vicious child with a magnifying glass, lazily choosing random ants to fry.

I understood that religion had been assigned to me by the geographical location of my birth, and that there were other human beings as complex and searching as me, living in other countries, possibly also struggling, but from other paradigms. I researched the major world religions, looking for answers that resonated. If people smarter than me had already done the leg work, there was no point in reinventing the wheel.

Hinduism hit the dust fairly quickly. In sectarian Northern Ireland, Protestants had a deep suspicion of idolatry because of those Catholics with their rosaries and statues. Judaism wasn't working for me either - a vengeful Old Testament god and Messianic leanings sounded like Christians biding their time. Muslims referred to Mohammed as their Prophet, which sat better with me than Messiah, but the reverence to which he was referred made the Prophet / Messiah distinction potayto / potahto. Buddhism felt right. No god as such, an emphasis on living with kindness and respect and a belief in past lives. Reincarnation resonated with me; it explained my early penchant for knickerbockers, and goodness knows I needed an explanation for that particular proclivity. Evolving spiritually on a journey spanning many lives and experiences was more convincing than the three-score-years-and-ten - if you're lucky - to get it right or be forever damned. I quietly identified as a Buddhist; not that I ever told anyone. I kept my quick to blush face firmly below the parapet from everyone, except, Daddy. He was always the right person to explore ideas with and could always be found in his armchair.

Daddy was my sparring partner in philosophical debates. We spent long hours talking into the night about religion, politics, history, and current affairs. He was not a father who hugged, or kissed, or expressed affection with words, but the care he took to draw out my thoughts - like they were valuable nuggets of treasure to be mined, examined, and ruthlessly obliterated if not sound - was our path to closeness. In place of physical affection was a mingling of ideas. An innocuous question from me was enough to have him leaning forward in his chair by the window, reaching for the remote to turn off the TV and deliver his full attention. He was an attentive listener, a ferocious debater and a relentless opponent. He would begin at point A and remain steadfastly there as I tried to expose his logical fallacies, and he mine. Mummy and Martin registered our rising passions and stepped in to smooth things over with careful paraphrasing but they missed the point. It was exercise; muscle was being built; wits were being sharpened. Often, they simply relented and went to bed, leaving us to it, until inevitably I tired too and Daddy performed a victory lap soliloquy as I gazed at his face, which seemed to expand and contract as the fire flickered into ashes in the hearth.

"Maybe we need a wee trip to the library so you can read up a bit more."

Library visits took place on Thursday evenings, after dinner. Our closest library was in the local secondary school. On warmer nights we ambled the half a mile or so, but in the winter, we bundled up and hurried through the freezing dark, each orange streetlight making our shadows grow and fade, grow and fade on the narrow pavement. Daddy had a habit of frog marching us - me and Martin – to steer us across the roads. Sometimes his thick fingers dug in painfully - a reminder of how triggering it was for him to see his children near vehicles. Nevertheless, I looked forward to these moments of brief, intimate contact. He wasn't physically affectionate and those warm hands on my neck, and the concern it represented, was as good as a hug.

The library was a wide, low school building squatting boldly on the unfenced campus, straight lines on rolling fields, bordered by roads. The double doors cracked and whined open onto a tall, wide hall, the handrails of stone steps picked out in emerald green, basked in the weak glow of artificial overhead lighting. It smelled of dry, old books and dust burning on radiators. I was excited at the prospect of new books, new stories, new adventures. The librarian was visible through the door pane straight ahead, atop a swivel chair at the counter. We lined up and whispered our hushed thanks as she returned our library card holders and replaced the cards into the envelope glued to the first page of each book, fingers fluttering with the deftness of muscle memory. It was the same heavenly peace of the Donegall Road library; the hum of electric lights, low whispers and the occasional whirr as the microfiche machine sparked to life.

Children's books were to the right, and adult to the left. We took leave of each other with the understanding that we had twenty minutes to make our choices. Entertainment over education, I investigated the Pick a Path books section, walking my fingers over the spines to locate one I hadn't read. I loved these books for providing opportunities for consequence free decision making; the worst-case scenario was fucking up and having to skulk back to page forty-nine, and even then, nobody need ever know. I grabbed a Joan Lingard novel from her Across the Barricades series - would Catholic Kevin and Protestant Sadie's love be enough to overcome the impediment of the sectarian roots? Perhaps, it was fiction, after all - then nipped over to the Adult Non-fiction section to locate a book on world religions, and another on the paranormal, which I and my chums had recently become intrigued by.

Daddy was standing by the door ready to go after ten minutes. Mummy mimed sore back via wincing and tailbone rubbing. Lionel Blair missed a trick not getting her on Give Us a Clue. I checked out my books and sidled over.

"Y'alright, Daddy?"
"Aye, love, just a bit stiff, that's all."

He patted my shoulder in appreciation for the inquiry and turned away. He needed to focus everything he had on getting home. We left and matched our pace to his slow, deliberate steps, measured and considered, a study in mindfulness to appease the mercurial nerves of his spine. A gasp escaped him, and a moan, then he spoke through gritted teeth.

"It's all fucking uphill."
"Just take your Time, Ben."
"Yous go on Gloria. Take the kids on home."
"And leave you on your own?"

He was too deep in pain to answer.

"*I'll leave the kids back and then come back for you.*"

I didn't want to leave Daddy either.

"*I'll stay with Daddy, and you can take Martin on home.*"

Daddy put his hand on my shoulder in a gesture of gratitude, while leaning.

"*Yes, love. We will catch them up.*"

Mummy hurried off with Martin, shoulders scrunched up, a silhouette of stress. Daddy continued to lean his weight on my shoulder, his breath coming in gasps and blows. His pace slowed and eventually he could only manage tiny steps. He squeezed my shoulder at the top of the hill - a silent entreaty to stop - and rested himself on a garden wall with a grimace.

"*I can't go any further.*"

"*What will I do?*"

He thought for a minute.

"*Will I run to the house and order a taxi?*"

He shook his head.

"*I can't bend to get into a seat.*"

The prospect of him leaning his bulk on my shoulder for another quarter mile was overwhelming. He might have read my thoughts.

"*You will have to nip home and grab my crutches.*"

Two grey crutches stood propped in the corner of the kitchen for exactly this scenario. I ran home, called breathlessly that I was taking his crutches and ran back, hating the thought of him alone and in pain, hoping he hadn't tried to walk, fearing I would find him collapsed in the street, humiliated. Ultimately, he was right where I had left him, his face drawn, his eyes glassy, focus elsewhere, steeling himself. He wouldn't let me walk with him, sending me ahead so that he could make it up our street without the spectacle of my concern. As usual, it was weeks before he recovered sufficiently - physically and emotionally - to attempt to leave the house again.

My friends and I exhibited typical teenage curiosity about the paranormal. Hannah borrowed a library book about reading auras and we followed the step-by-step instructions to unlock this previously unheard-of skill, upturning palms and angling our hands inward so that each finger pointed towards its match on the other hand. We practised unfocusing our eyes as we gazed at the spaces between the untouching fingertips. As I gently swayed my hands - right hand up a centimetre, left hand down a centimetre, back and forth - it seemed as though little beams joined index to index, pinkie to pinkie and all the fingers in between. The beams came in and out of focus as my eyes readjusted and I imagined I could feel the energy, alive and elastic, a kind of bounce, the way magnets push back from each other when the polarities match.

We spent an afternoon taking turns to stand against a magnolia wall in Hannah's bedroom, while the rest of us squinted and stared. It was Julie's turn to stand when gradually, a faint fog seemed to emerge.

"*Not being funny, but do you see that?*"
It was a fuzzy outline, like when you stare at something bright for two long, and it leaves an impression on your eyes that you can see when you look elsewhere, except it was alive, like rippling air on a hot day and it didn't appear when I looked elsewhere.
"*I think so. Does she look a bit like the Ready Brek kid, but ghostly?*"
"*Yes!*"
It seemed to be that when our focus slid and became loose, a faint light became apparent. As we practised getting the focus right, faint colours appeared.
"*There's a patch of colour!*"
"*At her elbow?*"
"*YES!*"
"*What colour do you see?*"
"*Hmm…it's peachy, like somewhere between pink and orange!*"
"*Oh my god, I see it too!*"

Julie wasn't as enthused as we were.
"*Oh my god, what does it mean, what does it mean?*"
She looked like she thought her number was up. Hannah flicked through the library book and found the page she was looking for.
"*I think that colour means…healing?*"
"*Julie, lift your sleeve!*"
She hastily rolled it up to reveal some scarred skin.
"*That's where my eczema was, but the dry patch is clearing,*" she explained.

"Did we do that?! Or was it clearing up already?"
I wasn't sure I was ready for the responsibility of being a faith healer.
"I don't know!"
"Oh, Holy Hector! What else can you see?"

Julie was sent back to the wall for further scrutiny, but eye strain headaches loomed, so we called it a day, dizzy with our new discovery. If energy could be seen, hidden there in plain sight, then what else was there to discover? Seeing auras turned out to be a gateway skill. There was a dimension beyond what we could usually perceive, and we were eager to find out more.

The following weekend, we went round to Julie's to try out divination. We closed the curtains in case her mum spied through the window. It wasn't paranoia - she had previous. Years before, Julie and I were practising our fighting skills and refused to explain what all the noise was. Not long after, Margaret appeared at Julie's bedroom window with a watering can, under the pretence of watering a window basket.

Sunlight filtered through the drawn curtains, making the room warm and intimate. We sat on the carpet, Julie with her back braced against the door to foil any intrusions. She placed her necklace - a long string of fine multi-coloured beads - on the floor. We asked questions aloud and rolled a dice into this mystical O. When the two dice came to rest, we added the total and consulted the book for an answer which corresponded to the number. The answers were usually relevant to the questions we asked, and we began to get a sense that the responses to our queries weren't being randomly generated. Soon we were less curious about the answers we were soliciting and more curious about the entity providing them. It wasn't such a leap: I had a brother in spirit and memories of Reggie, my unmanifest friend. We were soon to discover that as the light exists, so does the dark. We had effectively seduced ourselves down a different line of enquiry more concurrent with the Ouija board. It wasn't long before we were addicted and thoroughly freaked out. Our dabbling descended from *"Does Gaffer fancy me?"* to *"Are you a good spirit?"* with alarming speed.

I began to wake in the night, convinced that I had been woken, or that someone or something was in my room, watching. I felt haunted. At fourteen years of age, I started skulking into my parents' bedroom to ask if I could sleep beside them. Daddy was unimpressed, and more than unimpressed – he was determined to dissuade these nocturnal visits given that sleep could be elusive enough if his back was bad and must not be jeopardised by some eejit carrying on like a child.

"You've been at a Ouija board or something. What are you, stupit? Well, if your bed rises up in the middle of the night, don't be coming in here looking for help! Now, away back to bed and give my head peace."

I hadn't even considered the possibility of spontaneously moving furniture until he suggested it. I returned to my bed to blink into the darkness, petrified, waiting to be catapulted across the room. I heard the hiss of a lighter as Daddy lit a cigarette, too annoyed to sleep now. I was only slightly sorry I'd bothered him, taking comfort that I wasn't the only one awake.

I stopped dabbling, but it seemed that this attunement to the sinister wasn't something I could shut off. I was in my room one night when I heard the back gate rattling, as though someone was shaking it while it was still bolted. I didn't want to be caught looking out, so I went downstairs to peep discreetly. It was twilight - the familiar twilight of my dreams, and I realised with a stab of panic that I was in a kind of waking dream, and far from my body upstairs. I raced back up the stairs to my room, to my body, as fast as I could. A song began, high pitched and eerie, as the gate-rattler walked slowly and deliberately, around our block of houses, high heels clicking. I sensed she was casting an enchantment and longed to be awake before she completed her circuit and unleashed goodness knows what. I had lowered myself back into my body and urged my leg to kick out, for the pain to shock me awake, but my body would not comply. When I came to, I was petrified and sweating, afraid to go back to sleep. Eventually sleep overcame me and when I woke, it was morning and the danger had passed.

I rushed to meet Julie for our usual walk to school so that I could tell her of this strange, lucid nightmare, but she interjected.

"*I have to go first. You are not going to believe this.*"

"*Okay, go.*"

"*So last night, I woke up and it was like, three in the morning. I could hear someone at the wall.*"

Julie's bedroom was at the front of her bungalow, beside the front door. The front garden was a ten-foot strip of grass, bordered by a low wall.

"*It was a woman's voice, she was muttering, singing and walking up and down; it sounded like she was just at the wall, but I wasn't about to get up and look, because I had this awful feeling she would be waiting, looking back.*"

"Oh my god, Julie..."

"*No — wait! I'm not finished! It sounded like she was getting closer; I could hear her heels clicking on the path outside, then...*"

Julie seemed to steel herself to say the words out loud.

"*She said in this really weird high-pitched voice, 'Ouija board!' and laughed this awful laugh. Like, she just kept laughing and it sounded like she was getting closer, and I knew that if I looked out she would be right there at my window.*"

"*Fuck.*"

"*Then she just click-clacked away into the distance. I swear, I didn't sleep the rest of the night.*"

I told her about my half-awake, half-asleep dream and we looked at each other aghast.

"*Fuck. That.*"

We swore never to mess about with divination ever again.

Fourteen

I lay on the pink rosebud's duvet cover of my younger days, bobbled rough with the wear of weekly washes. The room was south facing, and I pulled the floral-patterned curtains across to filter the harsh sunlight that blasted in and made sharp outlines of the window on the opposite wall, planning to lie down and read in soft, warm light, undistracted. I hadn't quite settled to read, enjoying the comparative calmness of the shade and the ambience of midsummer air pushing the curtains to and fro. I felt the coolness of the wall with my hand and traced the outlines of the embossed wallpaper, chosen by Mummy to hide the multitude of divots and cracks in the thin plaster of these council houses. When it was new, there were little hints of soft pink and beige in the pattern, but it had since been emulsioned and was a stark white. The paint on the foam outlines gave way when pressed.

I had barely begun to read when Daddy came in and sat on the bed. I was immediately thrown off-guard. Daddy visiting my room was fairly unheard of. I immediately knew something was wrong.

"*Peggy, I need to have a wee talk with you.*"

I froze, certain that I was about to hear something dreadful. My parents weren't in the habit of confiding in me. What little I knew of their troubles I had overheard or deduced. Telling me meant that there was a pending catastrophe that was beyond the remit of even my daddy.

"I went to the doctor to see about my sore throat, and I've got a wee bit of bad news. It's cancer."

My heart started thumping and anxiety seared through me. All those years of throwing whiskey down his gullet, of smoking packs of cigarettes each day had culminated in a tumour. We were never a family who could ever be straight with each other; emotional outpourings were unnecessary melodrama. I didn't know how to react without making him cross. I so badly needed to hear that he wasn't going to die but I could sense the strain under his formal demeanour and knew that asking was unfair and selfish. I began to cry. He pulled me into his warm chest and wrapped his thick arms around me as my tears soaked into his grey woollen jumper. All I could manage was to plead quietly between sobs.

"Don't go."

He made no promises, instead he said, for the first time;

"I love you."

I had yearned for those words for years, and here they finally were, sounding like a goodbye. Be careful what you wish for. I buried my face in his chest and stayed there a while, enveloped. My daddy. My daddy. He drew my face up and spoke gently, the words caught in his throat.

"I hafta have treatment to fight it, kid, so I'll be staying in hospital for a wee while."

Hope, but no promises. It was all I could do to nod as I tried to pull myself together to remedy the fact that my tears had upset him, too. He left the room and I sat trying to process this information. What if he died? I'd be fatherless; rudderless. For a second, I glimpsed a life where I wasn't controlled or on a warning and it felt briefly like a silver lining. On the tail of this thought came a weight of guilt. I was the kind of person who would rejoice in my own father dying if it meant I could hang out with my friends more. I was selfish and despicable.

He went to stay at Belvoir Hospital and had to be quarantined there for weeks at a time and allowed home for only a few days between treatments. On those days he smelt strange and had very little patience. We were glad to have him home but had no understanding of the consideration needed for someone fighting for their life. How could we? I approached him on tenterhooks for permission to go and hang out with my school friends who lived across town. He was physically and emotionally depleted and didn't have the energy to ask the pertinent questions of who, and where, and what time. The best he could manage in order to shut down the conversation and be left in peace to recuperate was a sharp no. On other days, my queries made him snap; he was a wounded lion, roaring and bristling, enraged at his vulnerability. He mostly lay in bed upstairs, dozing on and off. The skin on his throat where the treatment had focused was red and parched, his were eyes rheumy and his face mottled grey and yellow. The room smelled of sour breath and burnt plastic.

"Daddy, everyone is heading to Lauren's house on Friday, can I go too?"

"No."

"But...everybody's going. Please?"

"Will you fuck off and give my head peace? I'm not well! I told you already, no."

When he shouted, his breath smelled of harsh chemicals, melted plastic and decay. His features were taut; eyes narrowed, lips curled, teeth bared, spitting in rage - a mask of hatred. He just wanted to be left alone.

I had had it to the back teeth of having a too-strict father. My friends' dads were affable and genial, providing lifts or opening their homes to us. It felt as though my dad was hell bent on ensuring my misery. For reasons that I couldn't fathom, he wasn't on my side; we were locked in polarity. My unhappiness expressed itself in eye rolls, sighs and sarcasm. He responded to the perceived disrespect by thumping or grounding me, and on it continued, a self-perpetuating cycle. My friends were able to simply go about their lives with parental approval being the rule rather than the exception. Regarding my social life, I had two choices: wait until I was eighteen or lie and sneak to engineer one. Eighteen was too long a way off yet choosing to deliberately mislead Daddy had high stakes. I was already being punished when my unhappiness leaked out as surliness and could only imagine the fresh hell that would be unleashed at outright defiance. Regardless, I chose the path of the liar and sneak.

One Friday I was grounded yet again for goodness knows what and desperately wanted to go out with my friends that evening. They were meeting in a park in Lambeg for the weekly highlight of our social calendar: loitering, adjacent to boys from another school. I was done with missing out on the fun and only hearing about it second-hand in school the following Monday. I needed a plan.

It was a cold day. Julie, Melanie, Lauren and myself had finished lunch and congregated by the radiator at the bottom floor of the West Wing, a glass fronted, 70s brutalist, three storey add-on at the far end of the school. We warmed our bums on the radiator, hoping to evade unfeeling lunchtime supervisors who would certainly evict us to the freezing outside for fresh air. The carpeted rubber-bottomed mat was for wiping dirty shoes, but the friction of frantic feet wiping built a charge of static which often culminated in snaps of electricity detonating on the next person you touched. We huddled together and toasted our bottoms, hunched slightly so as not to blister our bare calves on the hot metal.

"What's the plan for tonight?"

"Lauren's for half six, then a dander to the wall?"

The wall was the outer perimeter of a church, running parallel to a road. Across the road was a garage, where we often bought provisions for the evening, Skittles, Jelly Tots, Spicy Bikers. I sighed.

"I'm grounded."
"Again?"
"Yup."

They knew better than to ask why. My answers were always unsatisfactory because I usually avoided this conversation. Sometimes the reason I was grounded was something as minor as 'giving cheek' and having to explain the unfairness of home was more than I could bear.

"I have an idea, though. I could say that Cubs is on."

I knew the only way I would be permitted to leave the house was if I had a non-social engagement, so telling Daddy that I was needed to supervise the cub-scout troop I had been assigned for my Duke of Edinburgh Award community service was the perfect subterfuge.

"Worth a rattle!"
"Hurray! Full squad!"

Julie had been surreptitiously rubbing her shoes on the mat and celebrated my fool-proof plan by poking me with a crack of static. The ensuing hubbub drew a prowling supervisor who gleefully evicted us into the fresh air.

The Cubs subterfuge worked, and I had myself a wonderful time idling in proximity to the local boys, who were comparatively much more attractive to us than the boys from our own school, chiefly because their school had not adopted the 'above the collar' hair policy that ours did. Consequently, their grunge uniform of flowing locks, plaid shirts and DM boots were an arresting contrast to our usual fayre of boys with short back and sides, middle-parted floppy hair, who looked like they'd be more at home doing the running man for N-Trance than brooding in Seattle.

We sat on the wall in the creeping darkness, bathed in the romantic glow of orange streetlamps, wearing tasselled tunics and skirts, reeking of Dewberry perfume oil from the Body Shop and laughing far too enthusiastically in the vicinity of our quarry. One of them (who knows which - they all looked so similar) made an announcement in our general direction.

"We are heading to Lambeg Park."

Well, this was as good as a handwritten invitation. We hopped off the wall and tracked them to the park, keeping a coy ten feet behind.

Fresh joy abounded at the park, for as we rounded the corner, there sat Gordon Savage with a battery-operated keyboard resting on his knees as he sat cross-legged on a park bench, his long hair covering most of his face and a protruding cigarette tip occasionally glowing red; a Poundstretcher Slash, but it was more than enough for us.

This evening of titillation might have been the perfect crime had I covered my tracks, instead of writing a letter to a friend in Belfast, which detailed the specifics of my crime. I had discarded the first draft in my paper bin; a sloppy move. In truth, I simply didn't anticipate Mummy rifling through my bin. This letter not only described my exploits in minute detail, but also referred to a mutual friend of ours as a slut. Worse, having recently watched Top Gun, I had been musing upon the scene of Goose and his wife, where she demanded, "Take me to bed or lose me forever," and had written this on a different piece of paper, several times. I don't remember why I wrote it repeatedly; I could have been savouring the drama of the scene or trying out handwriting styles. In any case, it wasn't a message I was hoping to convey to any specific person. If I was trying to entice someone into a liaison, surely, I'd have observed the formalities by beginning with the traditional 'Dear whoever,' and constructing a convincing argument rather than pummelling them into submission with repetition. Regardless, these pieces of paper exposed me as the liar and sneak that I was, while a suspiciously minded reader might deduce that I had intentions to become - or already was - a rotten apple.

On the day these items were discovered I returned home from school at around four o'clock as usual. I opened the unlocked back door and walked into a tense silence. I knew something was off immediately. Mummy stood primed in the kitchen and issued instructions to come in, while Daddy sat in the living room, a festering fury. I froze, knowing instantly that coming in was not in my best interests. Mummy darted behind me and locked the back door. It was at this point I noticed the two leather skipping ropes hanging limply off the coat hooks. Simultaneously, I felt a rush of screeching alarm and stomach-sinking doom. I was ushered into the living room, to answer to Daddy, who could barely contain his rage and hissed tightly through his clenched jaw. *"What's this?"*

He waved the letter in my face. He knew what it was as well as I did. His expression conveyed disgust, hatred. To him, disobedience was a choice to forfeit his love. I had no idea how to react; nothing I could say or do would circumvent what was coming. I was a mouse being pawed at; attack was imminent. I started to cry, fearful tears. Daddy instructed Mummy to bring in the leather skipping ropes. She acquiesced and retreated to the kitchen, closing the door between herself and us. He threw the letter at me.

"Read it out loud."

"Please, no. You've read it already."

"Fucking read it. Now."

I blanched at the thought of speaking aloud the words I had written. I was saturated with shame, afraid to disobey but afraid to obey - hearing it out loud would only fan the flames of his rage.

"You are a sleekit wee bastard," he said, through gritted teeth, as foam appeared in the corners of his mouth.

It was a savage beating. He lashed the thin leather ropes with all his might. The living room was a cell I could not escape, the soft sofas and chairs upon which we watched evening TV boundaried the room and it was on these that I flinched and cowered, soon discovering that when I tried to shield my exposed legs from the leather, it would land on my equally vulnerable arms. Pain made the screams insuppressible, and I watched as bright blue bruise streaks blossomed where the strap cracked. At one point the whip hit my hand, causing the glass on my watch face to smash. Somehow amid the panic and horror, I found space to feel sad - it had been my Christmas present. I had wanted a keepsake for Christmas. I pored over the display in H Samuels and chose the watch I imagined they would choose for me, a slim brown strap and cream face, inlaid with gold Roman numerals – not too expensive, but pricey enough to be meaningful. I chose the conservative, antiquated style because I knew they would like it, and hoped that someday they too would claim it as a special gift just for me, colluding in the sentimentality. In that moment, I realised I had lost not only a watch, but everything that I wished it to represent. I wanted special things to testify that I was worth special things, but the glass face had been smashed to smithereens.

Time is elastic; pain takes a pinpoint of time and magnifies, distorts and stretches it. No sooner had I mourned my watch, glass obliterated by an abrupt crack of leather, than I felt a sharp pain in the upper knuckle of my first finger; the lash that had taken my watch had also hit my finger, and it looked distorted, swollen and discoloured. I thought it had broken. I screamed in desperation.

"My finger is broken!"

I held it towards him, hoping that a broken bone would break the spell of his rage trance. It didn't. My mind was sharp with fear and some twisted logic dictated that if my broken body didn't concern him, perhaps a broken watch would.

"*You've smashed the watch! There's broken glass!*"

He had no intentions of stopping.

"*It doesn't give a fuck!*"

His rage was so far gone that he was having difficulty speaking coherently. His words were jumble of *'It doesn't matter'* and *'I don't give a fuck.'* In a way, *'It doesn't give a fuck,'* was an appropriate summation. When the red mist descended, he became It, and It really didn't give a single fuck.

He exhausted himself thrashing the ropes down. Out of breath, he leaned into my face and gasped, spitting saliva and hatred in my face.

"*I'm going to get a drink of water. When I get back, I'm going to fucking kill you.*"

He stormed into the kitchen, gasping for breath. I heard the tap turn on and water gushing into the sink. I pictured him leaning as he coughed and haughed phlegm onto the cold metal.

On the whole, *I'm going to fucking kill you* is seldom intended or taken literally. From a vantage point of many years later, I'd wager he didn't have plans to actually murder me. Nonetheless, I was almost insensible with terror, pain and the promise of more pain and something inside me silently screamed to run. I had never tried to escape a beating before. I endured them and wished for better days, but I had nowhere else to go; running just meant postponing the pain while creating another situation to be beaten for. This logic which I had formerly availed of had flown the coop, I was in a primal fight or flight state. I imagined him leaning on the metal sink to catch his breath, water splashing hard into the basin as he waited for it to cool sufficiently to drink, to splash his face. I was on the sofa, legs drawn up, pushing my back into the cushion as though, if I just pushed back hard enough, I might will myself through the wall into another room, or a different dimension. I knew for certain that there was no miracle coming and I had to save myself. Time did the elastic thing once more - all moments became Now.

I bolt towards the door of the living room and fumble with its slide lock, praying the splashing water covers the sound of sliding metal. The front door has two locks to contend with, and all the while I expect a hand to pull me back. I'm fumbling, fumbling frantically, as quietly as I can with these sore fingers. The door is open and I'm out. Fuck! He could be behind me! I run. I run across the garden into the street. Everything looks brighter than it should. I run down the street. I am running as fast as I can. I can't afford the time to look over my shoulder to see if I am being followed. My legs are bruised up and I'm certain people are looking; people who will look at my legs in horror and tell others, people who can tell Daddy which direction I have run, if he isn't already millimetres behind me. There are two children chalking the footpath; I leap over them and their game; swerving would cost precious seconds that I don't have to waste. I run to the main road, and it occurs to me that he might've gotten into the car and that running towards the main road would be to run towards him. I see a lady who has left the shop and is about to get into her car. She looks at me with confusion; I must look frantic, perhaps she sees my bruises. She is my one hope of escape.

"Please help me! He is coming after me!"

She hesitates only briefly.

"Get into the car."

I get into the passenger side and crouch in the foot-well, hiding, in case he is just rounding the corner that brings us into view.

"Please drive! Please drive, quickly!"

I'm too afraid to even put my fingers to the manual door lock in case I give myself away. I am certain that he is seconds from opening the door and dragging me out.

Though they are fewer and further between, I still get nightmares along the theme of being chased by a man who wants to hurt me. I dream in an eternal twilight. As light dissipates and darkness descends, I realise I am prey. I try to hide, but he always seems to gravitate to where I am. He knows where to find me. If I hide in a locked shed, pressing myself against a far wall, he will stab at me through the wood. Even in the dreams where I can fly, he is just below, reaching up and I have to use every ounce of strength I have to propel myself up and out of reach, always mere millimetres from being caught. In dreams where I can fly high and beyond reach there is a terrible price to pay - it is too high and I am afraid, more visible than ever, exposed and terrified in a navy and orange sky, with nowhere safe to go, suspended and alone.

The lady revved the engine as she started the car, understandably skittish with a terrified stowaway cowering in the passenger foot-well and the threat of an assailant looming.

"Who did this to you?"

Answering this filled me with shame.

"My daddy."

I felt conflicted. He wasn't an unhinged monster who assaulted people out of the blue, I had very much brought this on myself, and I didn't want to suggest a different narrative that shifted the blame wholly onto him when I knew myself to be guilty.

"I made him angry. I…I disobeyed him."

"I'm sure you didn't deserve this."

That was very much a matter of opinion, and I knew someone who would vehemently disagree. I stayed crouched, curled away from her, unsure of how to reply. Culpability and justice were a Gordian knot that I was not equal to untangling while my mind was filled with panic static.

Instead, I tried to focus on where we were going, using the lurches to left and right, slowing and accelerating as a guide, as I was still too afraid to raise my head to where it might be visible. We turned sharply left and up onto a steep incline when the car stopped abruptly, her driveway. I finally looked up and searched her face. She looked alarmed.

"*Have we been followed?*"

"*No, I don't think so.*"

"*Should I get out?*"

I wasn't sure if I was asking if it was safe to get out or where I should go next, still stuck in that eternal now moment of panic, where the future is an unknown and every decision was critical, where the smallest mistake could cement disaster.

"*Come into the house. It's okay.*"

I could not stop scanning for danger.

"*Can you open the door first, then I can run in?*"

I was still waiting for the hand on my shoulder, pulling me back. She nodded.

I glanced up gingerly to watch. Her house was a detached bungalow on a leafy side street that I recognised, one that branched off the main road that led me to school each day. The exterior was a patchwork of brown brick and white painted plaster work, private houses, not a council one. Mature shrubs bordered a small patch of lawn. She stepped up into a sheltered porch and turned her key in the lock.

I sprinted inside and helped her close the door behind me. There we stood in her hall, looking at each other in this strange reality. I searched the face of this fifty-ish, nice lady – nice in the way that Mummy said it, to refer to the pleasantness of those lucky few whom hardship hadn't made prickly or brittle, those with fewer impediments to happiness, who went to church to thank

God for their lives, rather than beg for mercy. She looked back at me, a frantic stranger, incongruent in her hall with the smoothly plastered cream walls - no need for the embossed patterned wallpaper here - lined with framed photographs; happy people surveying the good furniture and soft taupe carpet. I stood there, bruised and skittish, like a bad plot twist, and felt bad that I had made myself her problem. She gestured to a doorway on the left.

"Come into the sitting room. Sit down."

I sidled in, keeping my eyes on the window. The sofa backed onto it, and even in the supposed safety of her living room I watched for Daddy, waiting to be discovered. I'm not sure how much time passed before I finally understood that I would not be found. Only then did tears begin to force their way out. Years of crying quietly so as not to aggravate already fractious situations had bestowed me with a cry that was noiseless and did not distort my features. I realised how odd I must have looked as I stared off into the middle distance, blank faced, tears streaming, racked with hiccoughs that spasmed periodically. Eventually, the lady spoke.

"Do you have any family you could stay with?"

This question wounded me on two fronts, though she hadn't intended it that way, I felt like a burden she hadn't asked for, a nuisance. And worse, a family member would deliver me back. Who would stand against Big Ben? And wasn't this how things were done in Belfast? The one thing I was certain of was that I could not go back.

"Do you want to phone the police?"

I really couldn't see how that would help the situation. I was already in trouble for running; I couldn't imagine what would happen if I got the police involved. I shook my head.

"*Are there any friends you could stay with?*"

No. I was too ashamed to let anyone know how bad things were.

"*Do you belong to a church?*"

It was the first suggestion that held any possibility. I told her about The Salvation Army, from years ago, but the ministers change every few years and the new minister wouldn't know me. I didn't feel I could ask him for help; lack of attendance made me feel that I hadn't earned it, and anyway, hadn't I turned my back on the idea of God?

She went to the hall and began to make phone calls. As I waited in the nice living room, I glanced around. More photographs, overlapping frames of smiles and hugs, some aged, sunlight faded. I tracked the life of a daughter, a pig-tailed toddler, schoolkid, university graduate and many happy moments in between. She was so loved. Something resentful and ugly rose up in me; she wasn't even that pretty and that hadn't diminished her lovability at all. I felt sickened at myself for such an uncharitable thought. This mother had taken me in without question and here I sat, an imposter in her home thinking ugly thoughts.

She returned with news - the new Salvation Army officer was expecting me, and she would drop me to his house. I felt so ashamed; the shame of being beaten mingled unpleasantly with the shame of needing help that I felt I didn't deserve. I don't remember much about the drive to his house. I don't know if I crouched as we passed my street, or spoke, or if I had stopped hiccoughing by then. I only remember arriving at the familiar house at the back right of the cul-de-sac, a house I had visited many times before as the guest of former ministers, happy times, having tea between services at the Citadel, or waiting for a lift to work in the Salvation Army shop in town, sorting and pricing clothes. Though I had doubts about the dogma, I had loved being part of this happy church family. There was ignominy in this homecoming, like an enemy captive paraded in a Roman triumph.

The house looked the same but felt entirely different. Despite my history here, I was very much in the house of a stranger. He was kind. Having no other option, I relented and allowed him to phone social services. Someone arrived to examine the wounds on my arms, legs, back and buttocks, turning me this way and that, pausing to map them on a piece of paper. I'm not sure if it was a doctor or policeman, I wasn't paying much attention to the outer trappings of my reality because I was watching an inner dialogue between the part of me that berated my disloyalty and the part that insisted, I had no real choice, a cyclical conversation that came between tidal waves of numbness. I stared off into the distance, sometimes the hiccoughing would start again, and I would be self-conscious for a spell, wondering how long I had been spasmodically gasping. I wondered if I looked like a crazy person and realised that crazy people who acted this way weren't blissfully absent from reality but too consumed by their own horror for their appearance to register as a pressing concern.

By nightfall a social worker arrived, and I felt relieved, finally someone whose job it was to take responsibility for me, someone I wasn't imposing upon. I allowed myself to look at her face; to connect and to be two humans interacting rather than a problem surrounded by place keepers and box tickers.

"Okay. Do you want to go home?"

Her business-like manner landed like a slap. Self-preservation adrenalin rose once more, and suddenly I was one hundred percent back in the room, fighting my corner. I was stung; surely this was the one person who should be on my side, protecting me?

"I can't go home – he will beat me for running away!"

"I have spoken with your parents, and they have given assurances that there will be no further physical punishment."

I knew that going back was not a good idea. Beatings were only one way of expressing anger, which would only have been exacerbated by my escape and whistleblowing. After an evening of being emotionally disconnected from everyone, of refusing tea and being gingerly prodded and poked like a specimen, I switched on again. I was not going back. I was hurt. Had she seen me? Why on earth would you deliver a child back to a home where these sorts of injuries had been sustained? Perhaps it had been a routine question, but it made me feel like a fraud; as if I'd overreacted by running away or was deliberately playing-up the trouble I'd be in so that I could sustain the drama. I decided that the issue was not up for debate.

"I'm not going back."

"Are you sure? They can't hurt you."

"No."

She sighed.

"Okay, then. I need to make a phone call to the home to see if they have space for you."

What would happen if they didn't? I felt like an imposition again; she evidently hoped she could just dump me off at home and get on with her evening, but instead there were phone calls to be made and more people to inconvenience on my behalf. The lady had left me with the minister, who looked like he was ready for his bed by then, and the social worker was unable to leave him in peace until she had somewhere to ferry me off to. I withdrew again, a statue on the sofa, sorry to be inconveniencing people, ashamed of my predicament. I silently comforted myself with the mantra, *I'm not going back, I'm not going back.*

She took to me a short-stay Children's Home called Glenmore House, a large, detached property set in its own grounds, broad and imposing, with tall sash windows looking out over the lawns. The porch was lit, as was a window to the left of the porch. A driveway curved towards the entrance, where three steps led to a tall, wide door. A kind faced social worker met us there and whispered a greeting, subtly alluding to the quiet required at this late hour.

"Come in. My name is Cathy. Everyone is in bed, but I will take you on a quick tour before I show you your room."

I liked her much more than the previous social worker, she had assumed responsibility for me without question and was volunteering to give me my bearings without any prompting, as if reassuring me mattered, as if I might be here long enough for this information to be pertinent. She was plain, mousy hair in wispy layers, as though a short style had grown out. She wore no makeup, and her eyes were the colour of pond water; the upper lashes grew downwards and made me think of a donkey. Her natural, unadorned appearance was comforting; Mummy never wore make-up either which, over time, caused me to associate plainness with maternal qualities, as though taking care of yourself and taking care of others were mutually exclusive.

It became apparent as I followed her into the hallway that the well-lit window to the left of the porch belonged to a reception room. A large desk dominated, circled by padded metal chairs, two in front, one behind; reminiscent of parent-teacher meetings. Locked filing cabinets lined the walls.

"This is the office, and over there is a sitting room."

She gestured to a closed door opposite the office, at the other side of the hallway. She made no moves to open the door, instead walking down the long hallway, looking over her shoulder as an entreaty to follow her. There was a staircase to the right with a thick wooden handrail and a bulbous newel post cap, shiny and worn from decades of use. As we passed to the left of the stairs, she pointed left to another door.

"TV room."

I nodded as we passed. At the bottom of the corridor was a small area, about the size of a boot room, with a bench and public telephone fixed to the wall. A door to the right led to a dining room with long tables in rows and what looked like plastic-seated metal school chairs. This room was the thoroughfare leading to the kitchen, a large room lined with stainless steel cupboards, ovens, an island and an enormous fridge. I wondered how many people such a large kitchen catered for.

"Dining room and kitchen. This is where you come in the morning for your breakfast."

I nodded again, unsure of how to respond.

"Okay, now I will take you up to your room. Make sure to be quiet as everyone is sleeping."

We retraced our steps out through the dining room, down the shadowy corridor and up the stairs. At the top of the stairs was a small square landing, and four further stairs to the left leading to a door. Through the door, another landing, with a small staircase on each side; a boys' wing and a girls' wing. The girls' wing had a sizeable landing with four doors, two on each side. She pointed to the first on the left and whispered.

"Bathroom."

We entered the room opposite the bathroom, the first on the right. Cathy turned on a bedside lamp and I saw three single beds, two flanking a tall narrow window opposite, occupied by girls deep in sleep. She indicated to the empty bed adjacent to the doorway we stood in. I was relieved to see a night-dress folded atop it.

"*This can be your bed for tonight - you might not be here for long. Sleep tight! I will see you in the morning.*"

What did she mean? Was I to be moved to another room? Another home? Sent home? I was too exhausted to ask and didn't want to cause trouble, so I simply slipped into the nightie and climbed into the strange bed, where I lay worrying in the darkness. I had a bed for the night at least, and I was determined not to return home, so I put off worrying about that and fretted instead over a more immediate concern. I was to attend school in the morning and my legs were a mess. The jig would be up unless I acquired a pair of green school tights to wear instead of the socks I was in.

Fifteen

The light from the landing gave the door by my bed an amber outline. The tall window opposite was a long rectangle of grey between the two other beds. I slept fitfully; exhaustion overcame me in bursts. Each time I woke, alarm set in as I remembered where I was, and why. I redirected my worry towards the tights conundrum. I couldn't wear my school socks to school with my legs bruised and shops selling tights would not be open until ten minutes after I was required to be in class. The weak dawn sunlight illuminated emergency exit steps outside the window, their cold, flat metal a jarring contrast to the deep architrave around the Victorian window frame.

Morning came. The girls in the other beds sat up bleary eyed, smiling gingerly, unsure as to what reception this newcomer would give. I returned a weak smile.

"*What time did you arrive?*"

"*After 12, I think.*"

The one on the left rubbed sleep from her eyes. She was about my age. Her black hair was coarse, cut into a layered bob with a fringe at the front. Bits were sticking out. Her cheeks were pink. She pushed her fringe out of her eyes to reveal sparse black eyebrows, each hair of which seemed to grow straight up. I wondered if she had trained them to look like that by brushing them up, or if that was just the way they had grown. She yawned vociferously and fixed her eyes on me once more.

"What's your name?"

"Peggy."

I hoped she wouldn't be so crass as to ask why I was there; besides I hadn't been there long enough to establish what we were allowed to know of each other and what secrets we had to keep. The other girl was strikingly pretty. She stretched luxuriantly and then ran her fingers through her light brown hair, scraping it into a crude ponytail. She looked a bit older, more worldly. She looked like someone who would keep up with fashion and music while the other one looked like she'd just arrived from 1930.

"I'm Jane. This is Anne."

I smiled my hello as our bedroom door opened. The lady from last night breezed in, Cathy with the donkey eyelashes.

"Morning, girls! Oh, I see you've all met, that's good! Will you bring Peggy down with you to breakfast when you are all washed and dressed? Chop! See you downstairs at eight, yes?"

She was about to leave without waiting for an answer but swung round with another thought.

"Oh - Peggy - I have a prescription for you. One minute..."

The spring-loaded door swung closed after her, puffing bacon smell into the room. A few seconds later she was back with a Pharmacy paper bag. She sat on my bed, positioning herself so that I was out of view from the others, who, from the dead silence I assumed were straining to hear. She leaned in to whisper and I could smell her light, floral perfume and coffee breath.

"*It's just some Sudocrem for your bruises.*"

I thought of my striped, spackled legs.

"*Would there be any tights I could wear to school? I only have socks.*"

She thought for a moment.

"*'I think we have some black in the lost property. Would those do?*"

"*Not really. The uniform is green tights.*"

"*Perhaps they would do, until you got to school, and you could borrow some until we could get yours for you?*"

I considered this. I didn't want to borrow from anyone because I'd need to explain why I needed tights in Spring and why I didn't have access to my own tights, but there didn't seem to be another option.

"*There's a phone downstairs if you want to call a friend?*"

I nodded.

"*It's a payphone but I can give you 10p.*"

She patted my hand and leapt up from the bed.

"*Right! Come on, girls, up and at 'em!*"

I followed my roommates into the bathroom on the other side of the landing. The walls were tiled to halfway up, above which was painted plaster in soft pink. A row of sinks stood beneath the frosted window. There was a door to the left of the sinks, closed and locked, from which came the faint sound of water running. Jane shouted against the door jamb.

"*Donna! Are you in there having a bath?!*"

"*I'll be out in a minute!*"

"*I need the toilet!*"

"*Go downstairs!*"

Jane grunted in exasperation and muttered to no one in particular.

"*Every bloody morning…*"

I cleaned my face and teeth, matching my pace to hers, rather than Anne's, whose haircut led me to suspect that she wasn't the full shilling. Back in the bedroom, I slipped out of my borrowed floral nighty and quickly into my uniform, hoping that no one was watching. A voluminous pair of pants had been left on my bed, presumably Cathy had left me fresh underwear for the day. I tried not to think about whether they had been someone else's at one point.

I trotted after Jane, down the four or five swirly-carpeted stairs to the small, shared landing. Two boys were racing down their own stairs opposite, laughing and pushing each other playfully in a race to get to breakfast.

"*Watch it!*"

Jane held back as they charged past, through the door and down the main stairs that led to the hallway. It looked different in daylight; the shadowy, forbidding hall of the night before was bright and grand; light flooded in from the tall porch double doors flanked by tall side windows, and from the broad, deep architrave doorways of the rooms either side. The thick mahogany handrail shone with smoothness from the friction of countless hands. Bacon and egg smell and chatter came from the far end of the corridor beside the stairs. The payphone was where I had remembered it, just outside the dining room. I lifted the clunky receiver and held it to my ear. The mouthpiece smelled like the breath of too many strangers and plastic. I held my breath and slid the ten pence piece into the machine, causing the loud dial tone to cut out in silent anticipation of my dialling. I knew Lauren's number by heart. Her phone was answered in three rings.

"Hello, can I speak to Lauren, please?"

Her mum sounded forced cheerful, the sound of someone trying to keep their good humour in the morning rush.

"Hold on a moment."

Lauren's voice was quizzical.

"Hello?"

"Lauren, it's me - Peggy! I don't have long. Could you do me a favour? Could I borrow a pair of your school tights today? I can explain when I see you."

"Emm...yes, no worries."

"Will you meet me in the West Wing toilets before the bell rings?"

"Yeah, no probs. Are you okay?"

"Yes, I'm grand. Just....I'll talk to you then."

"Okay. See you soon."

Breakfast passed in a haze of confusion; the faces of strange children of all ages, cereal bowls that were too shallow, thick utilitarian cutlery that reminded me of school, chairs scraping back and forth, room temperature milk with a faint tang from having sat out on the long tables. I ate some scrambled egg and carved the fat from the undercooked bacon, leaving most of it. A taxi arrived to take some of us to our respective schools across town. Donna and skinny, fair-haired Jamie to one secondary, cheeky-faced, black haired Lewis to another. Lewis was loud and attention-seeking, and I had been warned that he was a compulsive liar. He informed the driver with gleeful sarcasm,

"*Fancy pants here needs to be dropped off at Friends', isn't that right, your Majesty?*"

"*Is that right, love?*"

"*Yes, please.*"

"*Ooh la!*" added Lewis, who hadn't got the laugh he was aiming for. The driver smiled at me in the rear-view mirror.

"*So, you're smart then?*"

I was used to getting ribbed about going to a Grammar from my Ballymacash friends, the apparently good-humoured joshing that somehow always had a sneer attached - that snobby school, aul' Brain of Britain. I shrugged, unsure of whether I was being set up to be exposed as thinking a lot of myself, or whether he was just being friendly.

"Wee smart hole," added Lewis, unhelpfully.

Donna kindly changed the subject and they chattered away light-heartedly until I was dropped off at the gates. I cut across the grass to get to the West Wing so that as few people as possible might notice the black tights.

I waited in a toilet cubicle, the chill in the spring morning air made worse by tiles that held the cold from the night before.

"Peggy?"

Lauren unzipped her bag as I exited the stall, looking curiously at my black tights.

"What's the craic?"

"Don't tell anyone, yet. My Daddy beat me yesterday. I need the tights to cover my legs."

"Jesus! Is it bad?"

I sat on the toilet seat and unpeeled the black tights. My legs were a patchwork of blue, green, purple bruises and white Sudocrem.

"Fucking hell!"

"I know. Don't say anything, okay?"

She nodded. When I had straightened myself after pulling on her green tights, she pulled me into a big hug.

She, along with our other friends, knew Daddy was strict owing to the frequent groundings that meant I couldn't join them for various activities. This was the first they knew that he used physical punishment. Inside, I felt deep shame about the way I was parented and really didn't want anyone to know. Now that ship had sailed, shame came from other sources too; shame that perhaps I was at fault, because I knew the rules and consequences and had chosen not to toe the line, shame that I had whistle-blown, that we were in this situation because I didn't just take my oil.

Despite vacillating between deep relief and deep guilt, Glenmore House turned out to be somewhere I could be more myself. Although I knew that my upbringing wasn't typical of my friendship group, my time at Glenmore threw my home life into very sharp relief. The staff worked in shifts, changed regularly and cared for us with a light touch. I spoke frequently with them and much to my surprise and joy, they seemed to find me interesting and likeable. Several commented on how mature I was for my age, but what passed as maturity was actually trauma, I was pleasant to be around so that I would not be rejected as an inconvenience. I was well behaved because I had never been given any other choice. My school reports described me as pleasant and conscientious, but what it meant was that I was convenient. Underlying my good behaviour was a terror of disapproval and the cost of being acceptable was my mental health. That said, although I was more myself here, I still wasn't sure who that was because a lifetime of trying to be good meant that I hadn't had the opportunity to know myself underneath the act.

I loved Glenmore. I saw my friends as much as I liked, without interrogation or reproach. We were even given pocket money, calculated according to age. Having received a pound a week at home, I was delighted to receive over three pounds a week at Glenmore, which skyrocketed to almost four pounds on my fifteenth birthday. After school, I went to Superdrug and bought the most pungent peach scented deodorant I could find, and a Rimmel lipstick in Coffee Shimmer. I learned a new normal, the normal that most other children experienced, of being accepted rather than scrutinised, being trusted to navigate my own path without expectation of disaster. I got myself a boyfriend. I made up for lost time and changed boyfriends on a fortnightly basis. On some level, the frequent rotation may have been to circumvent a relationship developing to a point of sexual contact. I was conditioned to fear becoming a rotten apple.

Life as a teenager has a wide dynamic range, the highs are stratospheric, the lows crushing. This new situation sent me swinging wildly, giddy from freedom and approval but devastated to have broken my family. Daddy refused to visit me, but Mummy came once a week for the visitation hour, held in the fine drawing room at the front of the house. Tall ceilinged, the wallpaper had a faded pastel stripe. The walls were unadorned except for one large painting, popular in a bygone era, of a smocked child crying against a wall, accompanied by a glossy coated collie. The room was furnished similarly sparsely; a mid-century wooden framed sofa, upholstered in stiff, embroidered fabric depicting pastoral scenes, two matching chairs, a Hi-Fi system on a unit set into a recess by the unused fireplace. I perched at the bay window, leaning my chin on my arms on the back of the chair, watching for the taxi to ferry Mummy up the wide, curving drive, turning quickly to sit upright when I saw her coming, as if I hadn't been waiting or wondering. A staff member in the office heard the car and opened the front door, then the drawing room door to usher her in, voice bright with false cheer.

"Here she is! I'm just in the office if you need me. Would you like a cup of tea?"

Mummy walked slowly into the room, face grim with indignity.

"No thank you."

She took in the scale of the room briefly as she crossed the room to sit, not in the adjacent chair but further away from me, on the sofa.

"Well?"

She looked at me intently, as though she had obliged me in my request for a meeting and was keen to get to the point. Her walls were up, holding back a torrent of anger that threatened to breach the flinty defences.

"Just so you know, there's now a Protection Order on Martin."

"What does that mean?"

"It means that he could be taken away from us!"

Her voice shook with accusation and rage.

"Because of you!"

I felt my brows contract in confusion, in anger.

"But...surely if you don't hit him, he'll be allowed to stay with you, right?"

I wasn't trying to be argumentative, but suddenly we were back in our usual dynamic; tone-policing, implications. After weeks of decompressing at Glenmore, I was back in the old, familiar territory of choosing my words carefully, saying my piece with the concentration needed to dismantle a bomb.
"We wouldn't have to worry if you hadn't put us in this situation!"
"It was what Daddy did."
"It was YOU. You knew the consequences for your behaviour."

We sat in silence for a few minutes, working from two different paradigms, realising the futility of trying to convert the other. I used my thumbnail to push back my cuticles. To look at her would be to see the reproach in her eyes, the absence of love, maternal warmth extruded, possibly never to return. I felt her eyes boring into me. If I look up, it might look like defiance, if I don't look up, it might look like dismissal. Feeling the strain of the silence, I looked up. Evidently, she was waiting for this, to tell me to my face, to drink in whatever effect she hoped her words would have. Brown eyes that used to be kind.
"Your Daddy had to go to court."
I held her gaze, unsure of what she wanted.
"What happened?"
"What happened? He had to stand there while they listed off his criminal record dating back to the fifties! Pages of it. They made him sound like a bad man. It was humiliating."
The cognitive dissonance was in equal parts astonishing and hurtful. I hated hearing that they believed that

culpability for his shame lay with me for whistleblowing rather than him for having committed the offences in the first place.

"I had to bring my bus fare, in case they took him to prison then and there!"

Adding that she could have lost her ride home really chafed. *Gosh, I'm sorry that Daddy being made accountable for my brutal assault may have caused you the inconvenience of having a ten-minute bus journey. If I'd have known that someday me avoiding a beating was going to lead to you having to avail of public transport, I would have taken my chances with the skipping rope, your fucking Majesty,* was what I did not say, because I had one parent left who cared enough to visit. In the end, he was given a two-year suspended sentence, but it was made clear that, given his history of assaults, he would have gone to prison had he not been receiving treatment for cancer at the time of sentencing.

Daddy's disability wasn't the impediment it was intended to be. Billy's death had made him regret his harsh words and punishments, but non-violent parenting was beyond his understanding. He had no one to model his behaviour after, no example of how to raise children effectively while sparing the rod.

Life will speak to you in a whisper, and if you don't listen, it will shout. When I ran, it set off a chain of events that culminated in a suspended sentence. The threat of jail time compelled him to relinquish force, not just because he wanted to, like after Billy died, but now because he had to.

Once upon a time, he wouldn't have given a fuck to be threatened with jail time, but at this point in his life, he had committed to being a parent first and foremost and his sense of self was inextricably tied to being a present, motivated father. I'm certain he thought that I could pretty much go fuck myself at this point, the disloyal daughter who seemed hell bent on pissing educational opportunities up the wall in favour of boys and moral decrepitude, but Martin was eight, and his champ, his buddy, his pal. He couldn't backslide into the oblivion of fuck you, like the bad old days. God had given him a son, after everything.

There were two me's at Glenmore, one giddy with joy to be living in an environment where I was liked for myself and the other despondent for being a whistle-blowing piece of shit. I vacillated between relief and deep self-loathing. If I wasn't in the drawing room, listening to tapes on the ancient music system or laughing with friends, I could be found lying on my bed trying to cry out the weight in my chest. I came to dinner downcast, and Derek - a dark humoured hippy social worker - expressed his bemusement. It was always good to see Derek on the rotation, who treated us like human beings, flawed and ridiculous as we all are, rather than a set of behaviours to be monitored or fixed. Just as plants thrive when being transplanted with slipshod care rather than over delicacy, his dealings with us were the kind of casual we needed.

"*Dear god, you were in great form earlier! Manic depressive, or what?*"

I shrugged. I was still thinking my sad thoughts from upstairs, about karma and reincarnation, and whether pain in this life was a result of a previous life's misdeeds.

"Derek, do you believe in reincarnation?"

He paused, looked thoughtfully into the middle distance, and swept a rogue strand of hair behind his ear. I readied myself for something profound.

"Nah. I've enough problems in this life without worrying about what's happened in another one."

He smiled at his own flippancy, then added, *"You think too much."*

Not one to miss an opportunity, Lewis took a break from teaching adorable four-year-old Luke swear words, to pipe up, *"That's because of that snobby school! She's a smarty-pants."*

Cathy swept into the dining room, having caught the tail-end of the conversation.

"Peggy has maturity, something you could do with, Lewis."

"Ooooob!"

A cheer went up, to acknowledge the burn.

"I believe in reincarnation!" announced Lewis, keen to move the topic along.

"I know, you were Baron Von Munchausen in a previous life."

We looked at him blankly.

"Spoofed a lot."

We laughed while Lewis flailed to regain control of the narrative.

"Nah, I was KING Von Munchausen!"

Derek shook his head and laughed.

"I'm gonna start calling you Eleven-arife."

"What's that mean?"

"It means, if I say I've been to Tenerife, you'll tell me you've been to Eleven-arife."

"Doesn't have much of a ring to it," huffed Lewis.

"Anyway," continued Derek, turning back to me. "I've got something to wipe the sour look off your bake. I brought you a tape with some decent music for you to listen to, instead of your aul' whiny music."

"Alright, Grandad."

He produced a tape from his pocket.

"Get your lug holes round that."

"Who on earth are the Sultans of Ping?"

Derek shook his head in mock disappointment at our parody of horror.

"Your ma's a horn!" exclaimed Luke, as Lewis looked proudly on.

My roommate Jane turned out to be something of an enigma. She was two years older than me and sometimes disappeared for days at a time, only to reappear eventually, making vague allusions to a boyfriend, tired and hungover. She self-harmed and when I first saw her bandaged arm, I could not fathom why anyone would choose to hurt themselves like that. Surely life was painful enough without adding to it? It seemed taboo to ask her directly about it, and besides, I hadn't warmed to her sufficiently to justify inquiring from a sense of friendly concern. On the days when Jane returned, or had been returned from one of her sabbaticals, I kept a friendly distance. Before lights out, we sat up in our respective beds in the sedate glow of lamp light, Anne updating her diary, me reading a book, and Jane brushing her long hair, or filing her nails, strips of bandage peeping from the cuffs of her pyjama top.

Across the landing, the bedroom beside the bathroom belonged to Donna and her little sister, Michelle. Donna was instantly likeable in that way that people who find something to like in everyone are. She laughed frequently and loudly, her face flushed pink at the slightest provocation and she wore round glasses for her significant short-sightedness. Donna was very protective of Michelle, who was seven and looked like a little doll, with bright blue eyes and porcelain skin. Michelle cleaved to the safety of her big sister, who mothered her, coddling and fussing over her with pride and affection. She watched the world from under Donna's wing, rarely talking, just absorbing the world with a serious little face.

Although we went to different schools, we caught the same bus to Glenmore each afternoon, then off to our respective rooms to complete homework before dinner. As Donna removed her blazer on our landing, I noticed a tell-tale rag of bandage flopping from her jumper sleeve.

"Donna! Did you…?"

She saw my eyes fixed on her cuff and rolled back her sleeve to reveal her bandaged forearm.

"It's just a few scratches."

"But why would you do that?" I asked, bemused and saddened.

"It's hard to explain…"

"Try."

She pulled her sleeve down and motioned me into her room. It was smaller than mine, but warmer and cheerier from a south facing vantage. She pulled a curtain halfway across the window to shield her bed from the harsh rays of the afternoon sun and sat down, patting the mattress beside her in invitation.

"*It's strange...*" she began, choosing her words carefully. "*When I get sad and it feels like too much, cutting myself kind of...eases the sadness. It's like it leaks out with the blood.*"

"*Is it not sore, though?*"

"*It is. But not in a bad way. I mean, it takes my mind off the things I was sad about.*"

"*Ack Donna. I hate to think of you hurting yourself like that.*"

She smiled a sad smile, conveying that she forgave me for not understanding.

"*At the very least, if you feel like doing that again, come and find me instead.*"

She nodded noncommittally.

I sat at the desk in the bedroom, pen poised over my English essay, my stare unfocused. All the hard things I had wanted to say to Mummy swirled around in my head, mingling with all the hard things I knew she wanted to say to me. I had brought that beating on myself. I had made myself look like a victim and Daddy was paying the price, as well as potentially Martin. Daddy was a disciplinarian because he loved us and wanted to keep us safe, but now he didn't even want to look at me. I felt worthless, unlovable. My chest tightened and I felt my throat strain with the ache of suppressed crying. I imagined Mummy seeing me and saying, mocking and disgusted, *are you gonna squeeze out some crocodile tears?* and Daddy, intolerant of the reproach he felt from a crying child, *fuck up with that noise!* Their voices had internalised and somewhere along the way I had lost the ability to let loose and cry. The bad feelings just stayed in my chest as the backing track played on a loop; waterworks, gurny gub. *Shut up crying or I'll give you something to cry about.* Emotional pain was threatening to engulf me and I didn't know if it would ever subside. I thought of Donna and her bad feelings leaking out with the blood and wondered if it would work for me, too. At any rate, I hated myself enough to punish myself; inflicting some deserved pain might lead to the respite of atonement.

I knew that Donna kept her razors in her bedside drawer and had finished her homework and gone downstairs to the TV room with Michelle. I opened my door a crack and listened; silence - I was alone. Hastily, I located one of her stash and stealthed to the little bathroom, locking the door behind me. I looked at myself in the mirror above the sink, unsure of how to proceed. I unwrapped the razor from its sheath and pushed the blade against my thumb, gently, testing the edge. Sharp as a scalpel, it left a thin line. I moved it to my wrist and pressed down until the skin stung and gave way. Little beads of blood bubbled in a neat line. My scientific observation was that I was only adding sharp physical pain to the weight of emotional distress, and I wondered if I was doing it wrong, or maybe if it just wasn't going to work for me. I persevered out of desperation to feel some kind of relief. I wasn't planning on dying, so the task became an absorbing investigation, carving carefully around my blue veins, wondering how quickly I would bleed out if one accidentally got nicked. I slid the blade across my skin and a deeper incision appeared, warm blood barely had time to bead before it ran in rivulets into the sink, where it dripped, these little splats of red, a testament to my unhappiness. At first, the immediacy of the sharp slices was a vehicle to transcend the mire of my misery – it was a different kind of pain, and let's face it, a change can be as good as a rest. The sharp stings brought tears to my eyes, and with each incision I said aloud my bad thoughts that just earlier had weighed on me when I was unable to cry. I attached my sad feelings to the tears of physical pain, tears that were somehow permitted in a way that emotional tears were not. Watching the blood flow was soothing and despair slowly ebbed from me through those little red rivers. There were other cutting sessions that were transcendent; the task of cutting - just enough, of watching slices open and bleed and eventually begin to clot was mesmeric. That little room became a sanctuary of release. I thought the bad thoughts, hurt myself and leaked tears and blood until I felt numb and spent.

    Doing these things was never a suicide attempt or cry for help. Frankly, the thought of anyone finding out that I was hacking away at myself like some kind of lunatic was excruciating. I wrote no letters of goodbye and did not hang around by the blood spackled sink hoping to be caught. If anything, I was ashamed to be such a cliché of teen angst. These little sessions were for me alone, infrequent and relatively quick - perhaps twenty minutes or so of excavating my pain, with tears and blood splashing into the sink then ten minutes in the trance of relief, hugging my knees on the cold tiles, wedged beside the locked door, half listening for footsteps. Then I'd come to, hastily clean up and depart, relieved to have gotten away with it.

But, discovered I was. It was a warm May afternoon and I had gotten caught up in the bloodletting, of watching in satisfaction as blood pooled in the sink. The door was knocked, loudly and urgently.

"Peggy - is that you in there?"

It was Donna, sounding worried.

"Yes - I'll just be a minute!"

Fuck. I ran the taps and wet some toilet paper, dabbing frantically at the tiles and taps shelf as my handiwork swirled down the plughole.

"Are you hurting yourself?"

Her tone was not confidential but alarmed. Her voice was too loud, as if it was less a question for me, and more of an announcement to anyone within earshot.

"Shut up! No! Just give me a minute!"

She was projecting. Her cutting was a cry for help, a declaration of her unhappiness, so she assumed mine was too and was alerting others in an attempt to secure concern on my behalf. I didn't want concern. My whole jig was being unproblematic, mature, smart.

Brenda was on duty that day. She reminded me of Sandi Toksvig - middle-aged, short-statured, hair clipped and utilitarian. She was no-nonsense and when she said encouraging things to me, *"I can hear from the way that you speak that you are a bright girl,"* I knew that she meant it and wasn't just soft-soaping me in the way that some of the social workers did. Brenda finding out about my silly little habit compounded my sense of shame, because her good opinion mattered to me. Her voice was authoritative.
"Open this door now."
I lobbed the soggy pink tissue into the toilet and slid the lock back. Her eyes darted around the freshly wiped porcelain and back to me.
"Let me see your arms."

There was no point in delaying the inevitable and playing innocent would only diminish me further in her already lowered opinion. I held out my right arm, palm upward and she pushed back my sleeve gingerly, where a length of toilet roll had been folded and placed, blood binding it to the skin and soaking through in a dark circle. She lifted the crude pad gently and sucked air through her teeth in a wince.
"Oh, for goodness sake! Why would you do this to yourself?"
I heard the emphasis linger on the you. By this point the other girls were trying to see round her, eager to get a look. I tried to distance myself from the act.

"I don't know. I wasn't thinking. I was just trying it out."
"Well. We will have to go to hospital. Get your coat."
"They aren't that deep!"
"It doesn't matter. It is protocol."

A & E was excruciating. Triage cleaned me up then I sat on a plastic seat in the yellow glare for hours, tell-tale bandages wrapped thickly round my wrist, waiting to be seen by a psychologist before I could be discharged, while people whose eyes I avoided trotted in and out.

In the end, the psychologist meeting was quick and perfunctory; a side room, a young-ish girl with a tick sheet. *Do you have suicidal ideation? How frequently do you self-harm?* Quantifying my unhappiness on an arbitrary scale. She seemed tired, or disillusioned, perhaps both, more concerned with the paper exercise than with me. I don't know what I was expecting, but on some level, I must have been hoping for compassion, or something closer to human connection, to have felt such a sense of anti-climax.

I realised that these innocuous sheets of paper might be a permanent fixture in my medical history - that I wasn't here for help, but to be profiled, boxed and labelled, my card marked, perhaps for life. I gave all the 'right' answers in order to minimise the incident; it was 'just' a cry for help, I was a silly little girl who was trying to elicit sympathy. It seemed darkly funny to me that a genuine suicide attempt would draw attention that the victim so desperately wanted to avoid, while a 'cry for help' would not be dignified with the compassion the act was intended to elicit. My commitment to cutting extinguished from embarrassment and that was the end of that.

One evening after tea, Jane, Donna and myself were parked in front of the television. Jane and Donna flopped on the sofa and I, a parody of boredom, slunk so low on the adjacent seat as to be almost on the floor. Jane suddenly sounded bright.

"I have an idea. Have you ever done a Ouija board?"

Donna and I exchanged glances of excited apprehension.

"No! Have you?"

"Yes! It's so freaky!"

Donna's cheeks grew pink with excitement.

"Did you make contact with someone from the other side?" She began to fan herself in a familiar gesture. *"Oh my god, I'm taking a reddener here!"*

Jane continued as if the matter was settled and not still at the stage of debate.

"Right! Donna, grab a glass from the kitchen and meet us in our room. Not one of those plastic ones."

She confided seriously, as if she was an authority on the matter,

"The glass needs to break at the end, otherwise the spirit will stay."

Upstairs, Jane sat gravely at the desk, wrote the letters of the alphabet and the words yes and no onto a page, and showed us how to rest our fingers on top of the glass. The situation called for ambience, so we turned off the overhead light to rely solely on the soft glow of my bedside lamp. Giggling from nerves and feeling faintly ridiculous, Donna asked, *"Is anybody there?"* which was so reminiscent of an advert that featured a seance, that I imagined a Toffee Crisp appearing in mid-air and went giddy.

"Shhh! Concentrate!" instructed Jane. With some difficulty, we slowed our breathing and approached the activity with the solemnity it deserved. After some minutes, the glass jerked, but I was sure it was Jane trying to get a rise out of us.

"Stop moving the glass, Jane!"

"I'm not!"

"Is there anybody there?"

Donna was stifling a giggle when suddenly the glass lurched. It couldn't have been Jane as it slipped from beneath her stationary finger. In that exact moment, the bedside lamp flickered, plunging the room into temporary blackness. I felt a pain shoot up my arm, starting in my finger that touched the glass and ending as a stabbing sensation in my shoulder blade. In a flash, we ran out of the bedroom, tumbling past each other, screaming in terror, thundering down the stairs. My left arm had gone numb and limp. Cathy's head popped round the doorway of the office.

"What is happening out there?"

"Nothing!" we announced as one, glad to be downstairs, relieved to see an adult. We skulked back to the TV room, where we at wide-eyed and incredulous.

"What the fuck happened?"

"Did the lamp flicker?"

"A pain hit me in the shoulder! My arm feels weak."
Donna began to whimper. Jane was having none of it.
"Stop that! You'll give us away!"
Donna bit her lip and tried to stifle her sobs. Jane reflected,
"Oh, fuck. The glass. We haven't broken it. If it's still upright, the spirit is trapped in there and we can break the glass to get rid of it. But if the glass fell over, the spirit will be free."
It sounded ridiculous that the spirit world abided by such arbitrary rules, but within the confines of our ludicrous evening, also entirely plausible. She looked at each of us intently in turn.
"We will have to get that glass."
"I'm not going up there!"
Jane rolled her eyes as if we were being childish, as though her reason for not volunteering was something less juvenile than abject terror, then her eyes widened with a happy realisation.
"Anne!"

Poor, unsuspecting Anne was summoned and dispatched upstairs with specific instructions to retrieve the glass, but first observe whether it was upright. She scrutinised us to determine if it was a trap, lowering her barcode eyebrows in suspicion.
"Look, just do it, I'll give you fifty pee!"
We sat in strained silence, listening to Anne trot upstairs, pause, then trot back down, our eyes fixed on the doorway.
"Well?"

"It was knocked over."

"Fuck."

Donna began to cry again, horrified by the prospect of living in a haunted house of her own making, and sobbed intermittently for the rest of the evening. We vowed never to do anything like that again.

That night, on the cusp of sleep, drifting from conscious thought to dream imagery, I felt a pressure on my chest and a sound filled my head, white noise, buzzing like static from a detuned radio. I knew I wasn't dreaming because I was still very much conscious. I tried to move and found that I could not. My arms and legs would not do my bidding; I was pinned, frozen and terrified. Out of the buzzing came indistinct voices, sounding like snatches of muffled conversations behind closed pub doors. The voices grew louder as the radio static subsided, as if those pub doors had swung open. The snatches of different dialogues came closer, seeming to seek me out, gliding ever closer with malicious intention.

Cunt.

You fucking cunt.

Dirty, rotten bastard.

My heart hammered as I tried desperately to move, once again willing myself to kick out at the wall so that pain could jar me out of this in-between hell, but the only thing I seemed to be able to control was my breathing. I panted in the hope that someone would hear me, realise I was in distress, and shake me out of it. No one did. The paralysis subsided too slowly, like contracted muscles gradually relaxing, starting from my chest and emanating outwards to my fingertips until I found myself awake, alarmed, pulse racing and wet with sweat. Was I being tortured by entities, or was it just a physiological manifestation of stress? I could never say for sure, but I felt haunted.

My social worker was called Peter. He had overlarge glasses, curly greying hair and an English accent and made valiant efforts to broach the schism between myself and my parents by discussing the situation patiently with each party separately. Eventually he was satisfied enough with his diplomatic efforts to deem it time for a meeting with both parties together, with Peter acting as both translator and mediator. The meeting was to take place at the house in Ballymacash.

Mummy opened the door for us to enter, lowering her eyes as she stood aside to admit us. Daddy sat in his chair, his back to us, not bothering to look around. It was an affront to tolerate - in his own home - a discussion where my perspective could be given parity with his. It felt strange to walk back through the front door that I had burst from just two months before. Everything looked the same, wood surfaces polished to a shine, grey suite of furniture, everything seeming a little drab in the north-facing gloom. Smoke smell. Martin was out, I assumed he had been sent out to play so as to avoid this further unpleasantness I was foisting on them. Suddenly, choosing a seat felt political. Choosing the sofa was to sit beside Peter, which may give the impression of us against them. I lowered myself onto the seat by the telephone table, the site of my watch smashing. The last time I was on this chair, I was curled into a ball, my arms wrapped around my legs, begging for mercy. Sitting here meant I was just out of Daddy's line of vision, something that I suspected we both would prefer, and yet, I was sure he was taking it as a sign of disrespect, just as my sitting on the sofa could be taken as brazen.

  Peter wittered on through some preliminaries and advised us of his intention to refer to his notes and take further notes. He attempted to stimulate discussion with a scientific assertion that I knew would be taken as thinly veiled criticism.

"Studies show that the most effective way to teach a child is to allow them to learn from their own mistakes."

Daddy turned his head to fix Peter with a look of warning, as if Peter had just tried to land a punch.

"That sounds irresponsible. A good parent intervenes to prevent consequences."

Peter was conciliatory,

"Yes, our instinct as parents is to protect our children, to stop them from getting hurt if it can be avoided. But if we step in every time, how will they ever learn to protect themselves?"

"Hold on a minute. So, you're telling me I have to stand by while my child experiences the painful consequences of bad decision making?"

"That's the idea, within reason, of course."

"So, I just watch while she throws away her education, gets into trouble with wee lads, demeans herself? And how many bad decisions do I have to observe, doing nothing, before I can step in and say enough's enough? When she's pregnant? When she's fucked her exams? When?"

"Well…we learn from our mistakes. All of us. It's how we grow to understand our boundaries and what is best for us."

"When? When am I allowed to say stop? Don't give me this airy-fairy sociology waffle. Tell me."

Peter paused to consider his words carefully, realising he was being put on the spot.

"You have to give them enough rope to hang themselves, I suppose."

Daddy was incensed.

"I was given enough rope to hang myself and look how that turned out! Nobody gave a fuck!"

I saw the angry wee boy he had been. Smart, but not supported in his education. Shoes flapping, hand-me-down jacket too tight under the arms, learning to box so that he would be less vulnerable. To him, love was intervention, protecting your children before the world could hurt them. Parenting is reactionary. People acknowledge their own wounds and vow that their own children will not have to suffer them. As Larkin said, *'they fuck you up, your mum and dad,'* more importantly acknowledging they were fucked up in their turn by fools in old style coats and hats. Daddy's lived experience, though subjective, felt like truth, and to him, truth was fixed and immutable; anything else was lies. As we all are wont to do, he consistently mistook his feelings for objective logic, for rationality. He believed himself infallible.

"Give her enough rope to hang herself. Fuck me."

He shook his head at this stupidity.

That phrase shut down any possibility of understanding between Daddy and Peter, and Daddy felt confirmed as the only sane voice in a world of idiots. As we got up to leave, Mummy grabbed my arm with the bandaged wrist.

"What's this?"

She knew exactly what it was. The staff had been legally obliged to inform her.

"I cut my arm."

"What are you doing that for?"

"I just did it. I might be depressed."

"Depressed?!" she exclaimed; her voice suddenly shrill.

"Don't be so stupit."

I pulled my arm away and walked to Peter's car, stung and enraged.

I arrived back at Glenmore primed to report the goings-on to Donna, who I knew would be ready with some gratifying eye-rolls for these adults who complicated everything, but in my brief absence, she had received some news that had rattled her. She sat hunched on the drawing room sofa, sensible Brenda's arm round her shoulder as she wept into a sodden tissue.

"Here's your chum to give you a hug, Donna."

Donna looked up as Brenda stood to give me her place beside my pink, wet-cheeked friend. She gave me one of those it's for the best half smiles, and patted my arm as she passed, as if tapping me in, *tag - you're it*, and closed the door gently behind her, leaving us alone.

"Donna, what happened?"

"Michelle...she's...going to a foster home."

"Without you?"

Donna nodded and sobbed, bent under the weight of her grief.

"The foster parents don't want a teenager. Just Michelle. They are fostering but plan to adopt her."

I imagined a childless couple meeting quiet, pretty little Michelle and planning their picture-perfect life. A life without the imposition of a teenager. Michelle was to be a clean slate without Donna.

"They live by the sea. The social worker says that they are really nice people and will take good care of her."

Her faux cheer made me think of wartime mothers of evacuees, sending their kids to strangers in the countryside, imagining an idyll to dull the keen pain of loss. Getting to the sea was two hours of public transport. As if she had followed my thoughts, she said,

"I can visit her."

"Are they really going to split you up?"

Something inside Donna broke and fresh waves of tears spilled down her cheeks.

"Ack, Peggy! Look at me, then look at her! Who would want me?"

All the logical reasons for preferring a child to a teenager would not make the situation any less personal. She wasn't wanted, and after today she would have to put on a brave face and reassure her sister who looked to her for guidance, the little human she had effectively raised, that it was all for the best.

Sixteen

Peter sat in the drawing room with a thick folder on his knees and battered briefcase by his feet, eyes round with earnestness. Some of the boys were playing football on the grass outside, shouting and laughing, their boisterousness unbridled.

"As you know, Peggy, Glenmore is a short-stay home. It has been three months now, and we have to come to a decision about where you will live after this."

"What are my options?"

"Well, Terrace Hill is the longer-term home, in Belfast."

"How would I get to school?"

"Bus, I expect. Or, well...you can return home to your family if you wish."

I looked at my boots. The laces on my left DM boot were loose and about to slip the knot. Peter countered my silent evasiveness.

"They want you to come home."

I knew this to be true. My parents wanted me back, not as a prodigal daughter to be cherished anew, but to draw a line under this whole embarrassing episode.

"Your father isn't allowed to hurt you. The suspended sentence means he will go to prison if he does."

I pictured living at home again and realised that violence was the only metric by which my quality of life would be measured and anything less tangible than bruises was moot. Daddy hadn't had a road to Damascus moment. He was still a strict father, who had merely forfeited one weapon of control. I anticipated more grounding, shouting and stonewalling. Going home meant my uniform and hair stinking of smoke again, my social life policed, Coffee Shimmer lipstick in the bin. But what if he really wanted me? What if he loved me? Liked me? Wouldn't that be something? Wouldn't that be the thing that made my list of cons disappear? Peter's owl eyes were burning a hole in me, so I looked up and shrugged apologetically.

"You don't have to decide today."

"But I've been here for three months."

"Well, about that. Your dad says he will pay for you to go to America and stay with your sister over the summer. You could take those two months to decide where you want to live when you come back."

∞∞∞

"Oh my god, look at you!"

Jeanette rushed towards me in the too-bright lights of the bustling Dallas Fort Worth airport and enveloped me in a tight, perfumed hug. I could hear her breathing hitch in my ear, overcome with happiness. My big sister was as stunning as ever; the bleached buzz cut which might lessen the attractiveness of most other people only served to emphasize her lovely face - round chocolate eyes set in the symmetry of high cheekbones and perfect jawline. She looked like a beautiful meerkat. She stepped back to take me all in, beaming with affection, and as I noticed her floral babydoll dress and biker boots, it came back in a rush how she was always effortlessly cool.

She lived on the ground floor of a duplex, across the road from the hairdressing salon where she worked as a stylist. The front door opened onto a shared hallway papered in a grey-green damask that belied the modern apartment beyond. Her own door led directly into the large living room with polished wooden floorboards and polar white walls. To the back right was an open kitchen, while a doorway to the left led to the bathroom and bedroom; white fixtures, white bedding, white curtains, white everything. She set my luggage upright against the bedroom wall and took my face in her hands.

"Ah, sweetheart! You've grown up so much!"

Her large brown eyes searched my face and she smiled and tucked a strand of hair behind my ear. I tried to imagine what differences she saw when she looked at me; perhaps familiar features set in a face devoid of the soft roundness of childhood. My hair had darkened to brown, and I no longer wore glasses, but my trademark fringe was still there, hiding thick eyebrows.

"I'm so glad you're here! Are you hungry? Let's go for lunch. But first, we need to drop by my work. I've talked about you non-stop and now everybody's dying to meet you."

Toni and Guy were one unit of many in a long, squat cream monolith of commerce, encircled by widely delineated parking bays, merely a two-minute walk from the duplex. Dry heat and exhaust smell assaulted my senses as unfamiliar cars stopped for us to traverse the crosswalk. The oppressive Texas sun had baked the grass beyond to a brittle, dull sand colour under the relentlessly blue sky. By the time we arrived at the building, I had a sweat on.

"*Here we go!*" sang Jeanette, voice bright with anticipation. The automatic doors whooshed open; the blast of chilled air was a welcome relief.

"*Oh, my goodness, is this your sister?*"

A beaming receptionist hurried out from behind the counter, trim and lithe, with immaculate make-up and glossy dark hair. She pulled me into a tight hug.

"*Oh, honey, you are beautiful!*"

I wasn't sure what to say, because - particularly when juxtaposed with this enthusiastic glamazon - I most certainly was not. I must have looked as flummoxed as I felt as I scrambled to find words to deflect this compliment, which is the appropriate Northern Irish response to praise, warranted or otherwise. Jeanette came to my immediate rescue with a too-wide smile.

"*Thank you!*" she exclaimed, demonstrating the appropriate response. I smiled weakly as Jeanette looped her arm through mine and guided me to the left of the reception, which opened up onto a massive salon with rows of occupied black leather chairs. Every stylist somehow conveyed a sense of personal style despite the requirement of an all-black uniform; these were edgy, cool, classy, chic people, selling the dream that you too could look this beautiful. There was a frenzy of activity; washing, colouring, cutting, drying, foils in, foils out, towels on, towels off, all against a backdrop of animated interaction, exaggerated visual communication to circumvent the impediment of the constant white noise of hairdryers, exaggerated laughter, scandalised from titbits of outrageous gossip, hyper-focus at the crucial stages of a cut. Jeanette guided me around the salon, her colleagues taking turns to down tools and bestow warm, enthusiastic welcomes.

"Welcome to Dallas!" exclaimed a random client, unselfconsciously interjecting. *"What are your plans while you're here? I'd love to take you out! Oh, you are DARLING!"*

I stammered and blushed my thanks. Having completed the circuit, Jeanette announced our intention to go to lunch and we took our leave. I fixed a smile and spoke through my teeth like a ventriloquist.

"Jeanette, that person isn't really going to take me out, are they?"
"Fuck, no. That's just something people say."
Why anyone would go to the trouble of making me feel uncomfortable was boggling.

I found Dallas overwhelming. Wide streets, block after block of shops and businesses, sprawling malls, towering skyscrapers, a spaghetti of freeways and tollways. So many people, some with cowboy hats and boots, or white socks with sandals, people of every colour, so many accents. The city had an abundance of large fronted white mansions set amidst shady trees, where the flag rippled over sprinkler-maintained lush lawns. Not more than a minute down the road, black people sat on dusty stoops of dilapidated houses, eyeing us warily from behind chain fences.

I wanted to be like Jeanette, pretty, cool, unruffled. I pushed my trademark fringe out of my eyes and tweezed my Michael Heseltine eyebrows to thin lines of surprise. I sat as a hair model for Jeanette's stylist friend, who transformed my shoulder length brown hair into a sassy copper shag.

Soon, my two-month hiatus from real life was coming to a close. We sat eating takeaway pizza from the box, aware that our remaining time together was short. Jeanette spoke in a light, too casual tone.

"So, where do you think you'll live when you go home?"

I screened for underlying reproach and gauged none.

"I really don't know. Honestly, there are pros and cons to both."

She rolled her eyes, a parody of exasperation for my reputation to analyse rather than feel. Jeanette was a go-getter who unapologetically followed her bliss.

"You think too much. What do you really want? What would make your heart happy?"

"I don't think it's that simple."

"But what if it was? What would that look like?"

I dared to state the yearnings of my own heart.

"If Daddy just...relaxed...and I could come home and we could be...a normal family, I guess."

"Normal how?"

"I want to be like everyone else; go to school, stay out late from time to time and for it not to be a huge deal."

It sounded petulant that this could be my biggest gripe and the reason I had almost destroyed our lives.

"I just wish he wasn't so strict."

"You think you got it bad? You don't know the half of it. Every Monday morning, me and my friends would be in the school toilets, comparing bruises from the da's coming home drunk at the weekend."

I felt a flicker of envy that she had friends with whom she could normalise beatings, instead of carrying the shame of it alone, then had a wave of self-disgust. My sister was sharing the pain of her past and I was centring on myself. Here was someone who had been parented in much the same way as I had, by the same people and I still somehow managed to feel alone. It felt like ingratitude, managing to reframe my parents scrimping to afford me with educational and social advantages as an impediment, and yet, it was painful to not belong in any camp but my own.

"He was worse with me. Last year he told me that he knew you went out drinking with your mates and he didn't stop you. He caught me drinking once at your age and do you know what he did? He filled a bath with cold water, chucked me in, grabbed my hair and held my head under the tap."

"Fuck."

She grabbed another slice and cradled it, gaze unfocussed.

"Look, I can't tell you what to do. It's your decision, sweetheart."

"Maybe I should just go home. He can't hit me anymore. Besides, it'll be easier to get to school than if I had to get two buses from Belfast."

She nodded; her mouth set in a grim line of agreement.

"Do you want to tell them, or will I?"

My retort was quick as a whip.

"You."

Somehow, over the past few months, we had become strangers and the thought of speaking directly to my own parents filled me with trepidation.

My red shag and pencil thin eyebrows meant that my own parents looked past me in the arrivals lounge. It was a symphony of awkwardness. I tentatively reintroduced myself - *It's me!* - unsure as to whether their coolness was shock at my appearance or grim acceptance of my return to the fold. The passing of six months had made us strangers, with the exception of Martin, who was giddy with excitement.

"Howdy pardner!"

What was funnier than that parodied Texan greeting was the thought that he had probably been rehearsing it for the whole hour's drive to the airport, and I laughed with relief for this one glorious constant - Martin was a tit. Daddy took my luggage, a normal event for any other family except ours, where I took it is a proprietary sign. I heard the voices of friends, family, social workers saying you think too much, and realised that I did with good reason. When the stakes are rejection or estrangement, you soon become attuned to all communication, spoken and unspoken, analysing interactions like your safety depends upon it.

"Go on up 'til you see your room."

I looked at Mummy quickly, her earnest eyes flicking to the landing, as if I'd forgotten where the bedrooms were. Her eyes were bright with impatience.

"Go on!"

She followed me up the stairs.

"Not the wee room!" she exclaimed, keen to reveal the surprise. *"The big back room."*

As kids, Martin and I had shared this room after Jeanette left, then I had moved to the box room for privacy. In this new chapter of our lives, the box room was to be Martin's bedroom and this larger, south facing bedroom, mine. Mummy watched my face for a reaction as I took in a new double bed, centred on the wall, flanked by bedside tables and a desk opposite. There was fresh new wallpaper on the walls, a hardwearing super fresco with a subtle rose-tinted pattern, and a floral print bed set.

    I took it as evidence that I was wanted, perhaps even forgiven for my infraction and felt heartened. It was an ostentatious display of something, yet unease crept in. This was not a room for self-expression, it conveyed who they wanted me to be. It wasn't a room for posters blue-tacked to the wall, or friends to visit. Our love languages were still at odds, theirs was money spent, mine was

acceptance, and neither could appreciate the mother tongue of the other. I wasn't being accepted, there would be no leeway. I was being given a second chance to be who they wanted me to be, and the pressure was on to get it right this time. Mummy stood waiting for a reaction.
"It's lovely."
Daddy and Martin mounted the stairs, laughing and shushing each other, some shared joke between them.
"Martin has something for you."
He held out a sheet of lined A4 bearing his handwriting.
"It's a contract!" he blurted out, giggling.
I looked between their faces, confused. Daddy was bright with merriment.
"Read it!"
It was a facsimile of a legally binding document, one which I was to sign, agreeing that I would pay Martin a nominal amount for the rent of this - his - room. There were stipulations about room upkeep, details of late fees, couched in faux legal jargon that was beyond nine-year old Martin. I imagined them together, composing it in cahoots, laughing. On one hand, it might have been that the only way Daddy could distract from the awkwardness of my return - with an attempt at humour to break the ice with this skit, but I felt like the butt of the joke. I stood in the floral palace made for some other girl I didn't want to be, and forced a smile as I signed, playing along with the jape where I was renting my place in their lives, committing to sleep in a borrowed space.

I pushed down my ungrateful feelings. The week before school started back, we went on a day trip to Bangor. We never had family holidays, the lack of money a convenient subterfuge for other inhibiting factors, the stress of planning, the changeability of weather, Daddy's back. Too much could go wrong, it was too much trouble. The only day trips we had were when Aunt Janet, or Jeanette was visiting, and there was an assumed obligation to show them a good time. It felt awkward at first, the four of us self-conscious amongst the crowds of easy day trippers, unsure of how to be on holiday without the focus of a Dallas expat to please. It was a warm, balmy day and children in shorts darted from here to there, too excited to keep pace with their families.

Daddy became loud and jovial.

"Will we get a poke? Who wants a poke?"

Ice-cream was the first box to tick on a day trip.

"Yes, please! Can mine have a flake?"

We found an ice-cream van.

"Four ninety-nines!"

Eventually we were caught up in the forced merriment. Daddy pretended he had no cash, comically confiding that Mummy was withholding his pocket money, and Mummy fished the purse out of her worn leather shoulder bag, feigning frustration.

"Watch out for the moths!" laughed Daddy, *"Here she is, the last of the big spenders!"*

Mummy started to redden as she counted out her shrapnel. Daddy was performing for anyone within earshot, ribbing his wife, basking in indulgent smiles of passers-by.

"*Stop it you!*" she muttered, looking tinier than ever bent over her purse, forcing a smile.

"*She'd hear a fiver hitting the carpet, that one!*"

Martin was in fits of laughter, Daddy in full caper mode was a thing to behold. We had barely licked our ice-creams when Daddy suggested the next activity.

"*Come on we'll go on the swans!*"

These pedalos seated four for an embarrassing twenty minutes of bobbing around on an outdoor pool, trying to avoid other swans. Ours was called Penelope. We took turns pedalling and steering, laughing at our ineptitude, looking ridiculous in the too-big neon life jackets. It felt good, this easy way of being.

When we disembarked, Mummy needed a cup of tea to settle her vertigo, so we lined up at the cafe, scrutinising the menu as we waited our turn. Daddy feigned scandal.

"*£1.50 for a cup of tea?!*" Sure, you could buy a whole box of 80 teabags for that! Good ones, too, not the rubbish."

Mummy warmed to the topic.

"*Look at that - £2.50 for a sandwich! Two rounds o' bread and a bit of ham? I could buy a loaf and a packet of ham for that! Have enough sandwiches for a week!*"

"Go on buy me a sandwich, I'm starving," teased Martin.

"*Get away o' that. D'ya think I'm Rockerfeller?*"

The queue moved at a snail's pace. As we loitered, it became apparent that someone had passed the most noxious of farts, a nostril burner, and worse, a lingerer. Soon, people were sheepishly looking around to see who could possibly emit such a stench, setting aside the well-known tenet of *'he who smelt it dealt it'* out of genuine concern - whoever did that must be at death's very door, or at least, gravely ill. As people glanced around in silent interrogation, Mummy had the misfortune to lock eyes with a man just ahead in the queue and panicked. She had the kind of guilty conscience that forced confessions or denials from her, she moved through the world in a constant state of apologetic explanation. Her eyes grew wide, and she showed her palms in a gesture of honesty.
"It wasn't me! I'm not from round here!"
Daddy looked at her and shook his head in mock disappointment. *"Trust you."*
Not only was her protest suspicious, but she had just cast aspersions on the locals.

It was the beginning of a new school year, and I was thoroughly glad to be with my friends after a summer of missing them. Clare had created a comic strip called a Day in the Life of Peggy, which lampooned my foibles, one panel of which illustrated a typical school morning meeting, wherein my speech bubble issued a cantankerous *fuck off* to my smiling chums. Although it usually took me a while to pull round in the mornings, that first morning of fifth year was one of unbridled joy. I felt at home again in the easy company of my friends.

I had some trepidation that my altered appearance would draw unwanted attention from others, those who had long mocked my appearance, that I smelled of smoke and sweat. As predicted, the snides honed in on me without hesitation. Waiting in line outside classrooms,

"She was a model? Maybe for men with white sticks."

Stares. Smirks. Derisive snorts. Vicious laughter. I bore it stoically until midday in RE.

My name was called during rollcall, and a prominent snide muttered,

"The model! I hope my boyfriend doesn't dump me for her."

I had finally had enough. When you live your whole life in one extreme, as I had, trying to avoid attention, playing small so as not to be noticed, there will come a point when the pendulum will swing the other way because you have a finite number of fucks to give, and once they are gone, that's it. When the bell rang for lunch that day, I was, to all intents and purposes, fuckless. Fuck-free. I had undergone a fuckectomy. I watched Chuckles, matched the pace of packing my bag to hers and caught her at the door. My heart was thumping, not with the usual anxiety, but with rage.

"What's your problem?"

She ignored me, conveying that I was once again too beneath her to acknowledge, but I suspected that she wasn't brave enough to mouth off unless in the safety of a teacher-supervised classroom. It was an epiphany to realise that my victimhood could only be perpetrated with my complicity. I pressed on, keeping up with her as she hurried across the tarmac towards the locker room.

"*What's your problem?*"

"*I don't know what you're talking about.*"

"*The model comments.*"

"*That wasn't me.*"

She looked at me, her face defiant, daring me to disagree. I kept at her all the way to the lockers, going in circles, until I was so exasperated all I could do was growl,

"*If you don't leave me alone, I'm going to punch you in your fucking face.*"

She looked at me with derision, but some of her self-assurance had left her.

"*You don't have it in you.*"

"*Fucking try me.*"

After that she kept her jibes to herself and limited expressions of her animosity to dirty looks. I had had it with being jeered at, I had had it with bearing it with dignity. I'd been a figure of fun for four years and the hopes I had of returning to school and blending in for once, hopes of being allowed to go about my business without attention or criticism were being sabotaged on the very first day. I hadn't wanted attention for my new look, but I was being treated as if I needed to be cut down to a size that the begrudgers felt more comfortable with. They needed me to play small because it's hardwired into human nature to have a whipping post, and if you can't point to one, there's a risk you might be filling the position yourself.

There was no real honeymoon period at home. I concluded that the refurbished room was more for the benefit of social services than me. In hindsight, maybe my parents really did intend to move on with a clean slate, but it seemed as though Daddy's heart had hardened against me. He had ticked off the boxes of parenthood: I was fed, sheltered and provided with a good education. I was an ingrate who kept a mental tally of sharp words and dismissals for evidence that I was not liked. He got up early to drive me to school, planning to drop me off early to miss the worst of the morning traffic. He snapped his usual commentary on my poor time keeping, as he stood, rattling his keys by the door, growing progressively redder in the face.

"Every fucking morning!"

To him, my chronic lack of punctuality was evidence of my disrespect for his time, and a lack of appreciation for the favour. These snapped reproaches set the tone in the car, where I gave myself a crick in the neck looking out the passenger window, too cross to so much as register him on my periphery as we accelerated and slowed in our lane.

"Does anyone even like you?"

It came out of the blue.

"What do you mean?"

"In school. Your school friends. You being a huffy wee bastard. How do they stick you?"

It felt like a slap, although I wasn't sure if it was meant to be, which was worse - the possibility that he wasn't saying it to wound, genuinely curious. I felt my throat grow tight and looked out at the passing houses, imagining families where children were liked by their parents as default. I glared.

"Why are you so mean?"

He turned from the road to look at me, his face filled with disgust.

"Me? What about you, dragging that sour bake everywhere you go, making your snippy wee remarks. I'm sure your friends don't even like you."

I focussed on sucking air steadily into my tight chest, eyes wide to drain tears back into my aching throat as I exhaled, for fear of being seen walking up the lane crying. I could be moody, sometimes grumpy, but I'd assumed the unconditional positive regard of my friends. I had barely accepted Daddy's disdain, the thought of theirs was too much to bear. I thought of the comic strip and wondered if it wasn't so much a friendly ribbing as a passive-aggressive critique. Perhaps I was just unlikeable.

We continued in the familiar dynamic where he policed my social life, an awkward dance where I would gauge his mood before asking if I could meet my friends at the favourite school haunt – a bar in Hillsborough, not daring to ask until I had dotted the Is and crossed the Ts on which parent was providing the lifts and the exclusively female friends group. Sometimes he refused for some trivial reason - I had homework to do, or I had given him cheek recently. On the nights that he granted permission, he would sometimes be found sitting in the dark in his chair by the window, the tip of his cigarette glowing red with each inhalation as he waited for my return.

"*Have you been drinking?*"

"*No, Daddy.*"

"*Come here 'til I smell your breath.*"

I would haw at his face, and sometimes he grabbed my hair and pulled my head back to get a better angle.

"*Breathe.*"

I pushed my breath out.

"*You fucking were, you lying bastard. Let me see your eyes.*"

"*What?*"

"*Look at me! Are you on something?*"

I opened my eyes wide and gazed at him. His eyes were narrow, searching for signs that weren't there. This was no guarantee that he wouldn't find any. He used the leverage my hair gave to cast me away from him, his disgust for me palpable.

"*Fuck away off to bed.*"

It felt unfair. Of course, I had been drinking, but two little bottles of cider was as much as I could afford on the wages from my Saturday job, and out of fear or respect, I drank them, got a buzz then made myself sick in the toilets to minimise any residual smell or effect, chewing gum on the way home. I wished he was more like Clare's dad, who picked us up with merry inquiries about our evening and kept a basin on hand for anyone who had overdone it. Instead, my daddy sat at home, brooding on a multitude of ways I could be morally compromising myself. I wasn't like the others; a kid learning how to navigate new situations, establishing the boundaries between fun and danger. I was his kid, for whom mistakes could be lethal. I was another Billy waiting to happen, and while Billy was an innocent, torn from him by a dreadful accident, I was wilfully courting danger. Once upon a time, Daddy's view of our relationship was lion and cub; he saw all of the things that could go wrong and kept me close. Now, he was a lion with his teeth extracted and saw his cub jeering at him holding a set of pliers. Ours was a schism that would not be broached.

My only option for Daddy-approved extra-curricular socialising was the Army Cadets, where the promise of drills and physical training could make me as disciplined and competent as any boy. It got me out of the house every Tuesday night from seven until nine to compete and socialise, so it was win-win. I was forbidden from hanging around at the end after we had changed back into our civvies: boys outnumbered girls by a considerable margin. Any time spent waiting for me was an affront, whether it was two minutes or twenty. One night I figured I may as well be hanged for a sheep as a lamb and pushed it further than was wise. When I came out for my lift, Daddy furiously revved the car and screeched off down the road, leaving me to take a forty-minute walk home, where every footstep brought me closer to another angry reception. Two cadet friends saw me standing under the amber streetlight, shocked and embarrassed.

"*You can't be walking home by yourself on a dark night. We'll walk you up the road.*"

It was a tender teenage notion of chivalry, but I found myself caught between a rock and a hard place, grateful for the offer, but worried in case Daddy decided to drive back down the road and saw me with two boys. He wouldn't see two concerned friends; he would see sharks circling willing bait. I felt torn between two sets of men who knew what was best for me.

When I reached home, the usually open back door was locked. I knocked. The key was turned but as I attempted to enter, I was shoved out again.

"*Fuck off. You're not staying here.*"

He had had enough. I was more hassle than I was worth. As I stood on the doorstep, I briefly considered bedding down in the bushes in the side garden, some primal part of me urging proximity to home, but was afraid of being chased by Daddy if he saw me, and besides, I might be seen by the neighbours, and my old companion, shame, wouldn't allow it. I suddenly grew attuned to the wind and light rain, and racked my brain for somewhere I could stay, unobserved, but sheltered from the weather. I went to the only place I could think of - the army park, where there was a little climbing frame with a roof on, long enough for me to lie down inside, if I bent my legs.

The wind whistled through the sides, which were suspended some three or four inches off the corrugated metal floor. I took my cadet uniform off the hanger and put it on over my clothes, but I was still cold. I put the black plastic bag which had covered the uniform over my clothes and breathed warm breaths into the space, but the moisture in my breath stuck to the bag and cooled, making my makeshift sleeping bag clammy-cold. I shivered throughout the night, drifting off from exhaustion for brief minutes before shaking awake. As soon as the blackness of night gave way to twilight, I got out and sat on a bench, for fear that anyone should see me bundled up in the climbing frame and realise my predicament. At 17, I was too old for the respite of a Children's Home and understood that the Housing Executive was the next option.

    I walked to the Housing Executive in town, glad of some movement to shift the stiffness in my muscles and ache in my bones. It was the same route I had walked to school each day, that busy main road lined with private houses, cars in the driveways, yet it was as if I was seeing it through new eyes as places where I could hunker down unseen for a night - a disused alley, thick shrubbery, a cul de sac of business premises that would be unpopulated after dark. There were several gardens where I could easily hide myself and be in comparative safety from the hypothetical bad men I had been taught to fear and who I now felt at the mercy of, but the thought of discovery by a homeowner, disgusted and outraged at my vagrancy filled me with shame.

    At the Housing Executive building, I took a number and waited, glad of the heating, hoping that I wouldn't be called for a while and that the cold in my bones would have a chance to dissipate.

"Come this way."

A tall, thin lady, middle-aged, wearing glasses and a forbidding demeanour showed me into a small interview room, taking the seat on the other side of a broad desk.

"My parents don't want me to live with them anymore."

"I see. What are their reasons?"

I felt foolish, recounting the events of the night before.

"Surely, they will have you back, though?"

"I don't think so. I don't want to go back, though."

"Well, unless your parents are willing to declare you homeless, there's nothing I can do for you."

"I think they would."

"Well, we would have to get them in to sign documents to that effect."

"Can I... phone them?"

She pushed the telephone across the table. I dialled, feeling blood pulsing in my neck.

"Hello? Don't hang up! I'm in the Housing Executive. They said that if you don't want me back you need to sign something to say that I am homeless."

They arrived fifteen minutes later.

"What do I need to sign?"

As the paper was proffered, Daddy reached for a pen.

"We've had enough. It's constant disrespect. Staying out late. Drinking. God knows what else."

The heat of hatred had been replaced by the cutting ice of indifference. Mummy signed too, his right-hand man, his sentinel. Their job done, they exited the room without a backwards glance, headed back to the peace of their warm front room. There was a hard lump in my throat as I understood that I was alone at seventeen, thoroughly, unmistakably unwanted.

The Housing Officer glossed over the awkwardness of the encounter by appraising me of my options.

"So, in order to put you on a housing list, you need to be working, or enrolled in a Youth Training Programme."

"I'm not sure I can do that. I'm doing my A Levels. I still go to school."

She shook her head.

"The only way you'll be entitled to housing is if you are in employment, or on a Training Programme."

Only kids whose parents loved them enough were able to do their A Levels. The system was a stacked deck.

"But...I want to go to University! I've done a year of study already; I just have one year of study left!"

She set her pen down and sat forward in her chair, lowering her voice to a confiding murmur.

"I can only help you within the confines of the law. You are only eligible to be housed if you are in employment or a work scheme."

"But..." I began. She cut me off.

"Or pregnant."

She fixed her eyes on mine, an intense gaze to convey the significance of her statement. Here was my Get Out of Jail Free card, except availing of it would send me down an entirely different path. The Housing Executive was unable to help me.

I walked back out onto the cold street, and having no destination, I was unsure whether to go left, back up the road I had come from, to the familiarity of a place I no longer belonged, or right, into the anonymity of the pedestrian town centre. The meeting had left me with a sense that my homeless status deemed me less than human. I was no longer a person with feelings, but a problem. I'd gone, cap in hand, dignity foregone, for something that should be accorded as a basic human right, and left feeling like an ingrate for not taking her advice on how to game the system.

I took a right and walked into town. It felt strange to be homeless. Here I was, amid the shoppers, masquerading as one of them, wandering aimlessly with nowhere to go. I thought of the homeless people I had seen over the years sitting on pavements and wondered at what stage you stop wandering about and sit down in grim acceptance. I remembered hearing people say *don't give them money, they'll only spend it on drink or drugs* and thought that if I was sitting in the freezing cold getting looked down upon, I'd be inclined numb myself with whatever came to hand, too.

Town was getting busier as the morning wore on. Some of the cafes had queues for tables, people happy to pay for a cup of tea and take the weight off their feet, unconcerned with the fact that they could buy eighty teabags for the same price. I imagined being a pregnant teen. Unsurprisingly, there hadn't been a proliferation of teen pregnancies at my school of well-heeled, well-prospected, middle-class students; it would be a salacious scandal. I imagined someone saying, *well, she was from that council estate* as if it was a fait accompli, an accepted norm for poor people, which absolutely was not the case. I thought of Joanne, who had become pregnant at fifteen, how she was no longer allowed to wear the attire of a Senior Soldier of the Salvation Army because her predicament had brought shame to the uniform.

Joanne! She had been given a house by the Housing Executive, a house that might even have a spare bedroom I could sleep in until I got myself sorted. I tracked her down and, much to my relief, she was happy to offer me her back bedroom. I lived with Joanne and her little daughter Carrie for the summer, leaving the house each morning to work in a department store in town and returning in the evening, grateful for the roof over my head.

Each day was another day closer to returning to school and, just like that summer at Jeanette's, I wished that I could live with normal parents like everyone else. My sleep paralysis returned. Every night as I drifted off, my body turned to lead as the static noise grew louder, bringing voices who muttered dark things, horrible things and wished me harm. I just wanted to go home, even if that home was a prison where I had day release for school. I just needed to get this year out of the way, and I could go to University and be free. I walked to the nearest pay phone and dialled home. Mummy answered in two rings; I imagined them moments before, Daddy sat reading his paper, Mummy her book.

"*Hello? It's me.*"

Her voice was cold.

"*What do you want?*"

"*I want to come home.*"

"*No.*"

"*Please! I don't want to be on my own.*"

"*You had your chance.*"

I started to cry.

"*I just want to do my A Levels!*"

There was silence at the other end, and I grew desperate, fearful that the receiver would be replaced.

"*Nobody loves you like your parents!*" I blurted out.

Saying those words stung, because nobody I knew had parents who loved them the way mine loved me, but I was desperate, worn down from unbelonging, from falling through the net of the welfare state, from borrowed space that I could not rely on. The line went dead. I dried my eyes, ashamed to be seen crying in the street. Determined that I hadn't lowered myself for nothing, I steeled myself and walked to their house.

    Mummy opened the door. Her countenance darkened when she found me on the doorstep and she moved to close it again, but I put my arm out to prevent it. Her eyes narrowed.

"*You're not getting in.*"

"*Mummy, please -* "

She shut in the door in my face.

I stood, bewildered.

A moment or two passed, then the door opened. Mummy glared at me from the hallway and a voice from the living room issued the command.

"*Get in here.*"

I scuttled inside, humiliated and hopeful, and stood in front of my daddy's chair, assuming that taking a seat might be too presumptuous. He lit a cigarette. He blew out the first puff in a long exhale, then pointed his finger at me.

"*You can come back on the condition that you do not put one toe out of line. You go to school; you come home and do your homework.*"

I capitulated, promising myself that I'd knuckle down, get my A Levels and go to university, where I could be free and, for the first time, on a level footing with everyone else. We didn't have to be friends. I had given up on the dream of being liked. I settled on being tolerated.

Seventeen

I was admitted to university in the same year that Martin started grammar school. As my baby brother followed in my footsteps to the posh school, I was continuing to push the family boundaries. My dreams of going off to university were hampered slightly by living at home but I was in.

Two buses transported me to Queen's, the first taking me into Lisburn town, and the second dropped me off in front of Methodist College, on the Lisburn Road, which ran parallel to University Street. A series of side streets connected the two roads, each with tall, terraced houses - former homes of the well-to-do, converted into student digs. Autumn sun filtered through the trees and dappled the path. Some windows had ragged net curtains, or displayed curled, faded posters, others had curtains still drawn, suggesting lazy mornings and hangovers. Occasionally, a large, paint-peeled front door was pulled shut behind a student hurrying with the sense of purpose of one who knows where they are going, dressed with a stylish insouciance I envied. I filed upstream with these natives, feeling like a tourist.

The famous Lanyon Building of Queen's University stood, imposing, impassive to the throngs that passed. Built in the early Victorian era, its Tudor-Gothic architectural detail echoed the medieval buildings of Oxford and Cambridge. A wealth of sculptural detail in buttresses and parapets overlaid the red brick and sandstone. Tall windows overlooked the lawns, hundreds of little panes set in a diamond lattice. Daddy's friend was proud to hold the contract for cleaning those windows and I could scarcely believe that soon I would be on the other side of them as an undergraduate.

I was ready to find my people. The Students Union building hosted Freshers Week, where an overwhelming number of clubs and societies set out tables and canvassed noisily for new blood. I joined RAG (Raise and Give), a group that raised money for charity in numerous unconventional ways - most notably Sponsored Pub Golf, or curating and selling PTQ, a publication which was prized for edgy and often smutty humour. The meetings were on weekdays, but the bulk of interaction was in the various bars dotted around the Union. The RAG students were fun and friendly, and I soon realised that the merriment was just beginning around 10pm, which was also the time I had to dash off to catch the last train home. I feared that my curfew would mean I'd fall out of what was only a tenuous loop and remain alone and friendless. Noticeboards around the Union bore countless adverts for housemates. Perusing these boards gave me butterflies, freedom and maybe friends, a myriad of opportunities on scraps of pinned paper.

"*I think I want to live in digs.*"

"*How are you going to afford digs?*"

I'd thought of that already and had decided I was going to get a Student Loan. I thought of Mummy's well-worn *never a borrower or a lender be* and imagined Daddy's more straightforward *fucking DEBT?!*

"*I will find a part-time job.*"

"*Then give your hard-earned money to a landlord to live in some shit hole? Sure, you'd be better off here, living rent-free.*"

A pause ensued, as we each silently considered how best to convince the other, but the time for debate had passed.

"*I've found a room in a house on Malone Avenue, just me and five other girls. It's only a hundred pounds a month.*"

I didn't mention that it was cheap because there was no central heating. The day I had viewed the room, I could see my own breath and it was only September. Jennifer, my cheerful new housemate explained that electric heaters started at ten pounds in Argos.

"*Well, you listen to me, wee girl, and listen well. Are you listening?*"

I nodded.

"*There are bad men in Belfast - .*"

I put my hand up to interject, to reassure him that I would be living with girls, that my life would consist of classes and meeting with friends who were kind and good, but he was undeterred.

"*You're not listening! I've done bad things. You hear me?*"

He watched my face for signs of understanding, his dark eyes narrowed. I noticed that his eyebrows had the odd fleck of grey that had also started appearing in the sides of his jet-black hair.

"*Yes, Daddy.*"

"*Do you understand what I'm saying? There are men in Belfast who would hurt you to get to me. Never - I mean never tell anybody who you are.*"

I wanted to pull at this thread, but equally, I understood that he had relented and wanted to get out of there as soon as possible, before he changed his mind.

"*If you get a taxi, get it in another name. Never use my name. Never mention my name to anybody. Do you get what I'm saying?*"

"*I do.*"

"*And get a lock on your bedroom door.*"

I climbed the stairs to pack a bag, less jubilant of my win than I'd hoped. My clean slate was already sullied. Yet again, I was moving forward with a sense of being different, of needing to conceal and hold back. I reassured myself with thoughts that I didn't want that old script anyway. I was free to write a new one.

I rented a room in the shared house - a tall mid terrace on Malone Avenue, damp and cold, but wonderfully, reassuringly mine. I bought a little space heater to thaw the bone-aching cold on winter nights. Sleep paralysis returned for a while. One night during an episode, a man had pulled a chair beside my bed and sat with his head in his hands, heavy with sorrow and devastation.

I acquired a boyfriend. Cathal was witty and kind and seemed sophisticated having just returned from a year studying in Austria. On the first night he stayed over, sleep eluded us as we sat up finding out everything we could about each other; our favourite books, food, places, our hometowns and schools, feeling the unparalleled joy of a budding romance. My head rested on his shoulder in the velvet dark, our fingers interlocked on his chest.

"*Siblings?*"

"*Two. Jeanette is thirteen years older than me and went to live in the States when I was six. Martin is twelve.*"

"*Twelve? Ah, he'll have had sex by now, for sure.*"

I laughed, scandalised.

"*Stop it! My baby brother will die a virgin!*"

As the words left me, I felt a strange, consuming certainty that this indeed would be the case and that I had predicted his early death. Panic began to rise and the dark suddenly seemed menacing. I scrambled up to a sitting position.

"*Cathal, turn on the light!*"

"*Jesus! Are you okay?*"

The small side lamp cast its light. For that moment in the dark, I had felt so haunted that I was just glad to be able to see my room, devoid of the apparitions I had sensed so profoundly.

"*Yes, I just...I had the most horrible feeling when I said that. As if...someone beyond was confirming that what I said was true... like some Ancient deity is looking down and saying Be careful what you wish for."*

He looked at me quizzically.

"I don't know, it doesn't make sense. I just felt sick when I heard those words."

"It's okay. Maybe you are over-tired. Let's get some shut eye, shall we?"

I nodded, slipping down into bed as he reached to turn off the light once more. I couldn't shake the sense of foreboding. It was as if the joy had been sucked from the room. Tiredness overcame me and as I drifted to that stage between wakefulness and sleep - the stage that sometimes-heralded sleep paralysis. I hated that suffocating terror. Suddenly, a skull hovered above me, caged in a pentagon, both glowing green.

"Turn on the light!"

Cathal lunged for the light and turned to find me wide-eyed, hugging my knees. Despite his reassurances, I couldn't shake the thought that I had been allowed to glimpse what those on the other side already knew. A skull meant death, but I couldn't understand the significance of a five-sided shape.

∞∞∞∞

Lectures, though few as an English undergrad, were daunting. The lecture halls had the typical tiered seating Hollywood leads you to expect, with the requisite lecturer dryly narrating notes from his presentation into a microphone. I scribbled away furiously, unsure of which parts were most pertinent, hoping things would be made clearer in tutorial groups and glad to scuttle off and decompress when the hour was up. Tutorials turned out to be worse, with none of the anonymity of a vast lecture hall. Instead, we were drilled for insights about the week's required reading - itself a challenge to acquire. Ultimately two or three people waxed lyrical about the information these books had yielded while the rest complained about how the texts had been checked out for the duration of time between the lecture and the tutorial. It was a baptism of fire. Grammar School had been a breeze - our education was spoon-fed, teachers predicted what kind of questions were likely to crop up in formal examinations and gave us templates of essay answers which we rote learned and regurgitated. It was a straightforward way to keep passing grades high for the league tables. Unfortunately, it was also a straightforward way of teaching someone what to think instead of how to think, to be a passive consumer instead of an inquiring mind. I had none of the tools required to thrive in this environment, all I had was this redundant spoon. I felt out of my depth and anxious. If they weren't going to tell us what was likely to come up on the exams or provide answer templates, how on earth was I supposed to pass the course?

    The RAG office was a kind of home from home. We hung out there between classes, scoffing sandwiches from the shop on the ground floor, finishing up essays for submission or just having the craic. It was a large, square room on the third floor of the Union, the huge windows overlooking the junction where the Malone Road converged with Stranmillis, at the entrance to the lush, leafy parks of the Botanic Gardens. Clunky staff room chairs lined the walls, their pads worn and frayed. The back wall was covered in photographs documenting the highs of RAG life; the annual trips to Gortin, laughing students fundraising in various stages of inebriation, a myriad of capers and shenanigans. The most recent picture was one of all of us, which had been taken for a newspaper; the current RAG administration including the latest recruits. I showed the newspaper cut-out to Daddy when I went home to visit. He located his glasses sitting on the table in his mucky corner and picked out people who caught his interest.

"*Who's that?*"

His voice had an accusing edge. I bent low, my head close to his, the familiar smell of laundry soap and musk, his breath sharp with the tang of a recently finished fag, as he scrutinised the image in the poor light afforded by the window.

"*That's Emma. She is super artistic.*"

"*And who's that?*"

"*Ian.*"

He muttered the names to himself; names that didn't indicate one tribe or another. His finger landed on a smiling girl in the front row, her thick dark hair parted in the middle.

"*And who's that fenian looking bastard?*"

"Daddy! That's Melanie! We went to school together; don't you recognise her?"

The reproach hung in the air, though whether for the slur or the failure to recognise my friend, I wasn't sure.

"She's a Presbyterian."

"She looks like Bernadette fucking Devlin."

"Ben!" admonished Mummy.

During the Troubles, Bernadette Devlin was a young Nationalist civil rights activist. When Daddy was interned in a loyalist wing of Long Kesh, she had been a leading spokesperson for interned IRA prisoners in the Nationalist wing, who demanded Special Category Status as political prisoners, objecting to being treated as common criminals. These prisoners garnered worldwide attention through blanket protests (wearing blankets to show their rejection of prison uniforms) and dirty protests (smearing excrement on the walls). Imprisoned IRA leaders had also called for the execution of police staff and Mummy's cousin, a quiet, mild mannered prison officer, was shot dead on his doorstep in front of his wife and young child. Daddy had seen too much to tolerate nuance. In his mind, there was Them'uns and Us'uns, and them'uns were fucking everywhere. In fairness to Daddy, Melanie and I were two out of the piddling four Protestants in RAG that year. Luckily, the popular adage that Catholics had eyes that were too close together didn't hold up, so he was not to know.

"Oh, for fuck sake!"

Melanie was exasperated when I told her about her recent appraisal as a 1970s Nationalist firebrand. I suggested that perhaps it was an upgrade from previous likenesses, certainly more flattering than the glossy maned Rasputin, a particular favourite of mine.

"What are you two laughing about?"

Melanie's playful outrage had carried and drawn the attention of our fellow RAG skivers.

"Nothing, don't mind us," I replied, unable to explain without outing my father as a bigot. I was glad of the distraction of Cormac, the Student Union President, who popped his head round the door to check if we were providing a cloak room for Shine (the student nightclub) for the coming weekend. Conor confirmed this, and before Cormac dashed off, quickly added,

"Are you actually going to remove the Irish language signs from the Union?"

Cormac exhaled slowly, considering his words carefully and spoke in a North Coast lilt unfamiliar to me.

"I think we have to. The review found that they made Unionist students uncomfortable."

"Fuck them! It's our language!"

"I know, and personally I agree with you. But I can't just do what I want. I'm here to represent all students, I have to act on the findings."

"They feel uncomfortable. Boo hoo! They need to wise the bap."

He shrugged apologetically as grumbles of dissatisfaction rose from all corners. I kept my mouth shut, once again finding myself in the no-man's land of unbelonging. I didn't consider myself to be Loyalist - allegiance to Orange and Green had long seemed reductive, but I had been raised in just such a tribal community. Those little signs dotted around the Union; unfamiliar words, unmistakably Irish with the fadas and the chunky Gaelic font - gave me a neon flash of panic. As a child, I saw such signs from a taxi that ferried us up 'the wrong road' after hospital ENT appointments, where Tricolour flags waved from posts and murals depicted IRA men armed to the teeth, faceless in balaclavas, while Mummy pinched me and curtly shook her head in a gesture to say nothing. As I grew up, I heard stories of people who had been murdered for being in the wrong area. There was an understanding that if you came to be in a Catholic area and you looked unfamiliar, you might be asked to recite the Rosary or speak Irish, and an inability to do either could result in a beating. Just like red and yellow are warnings in nature, Irish signs had come to mean danger to me.

  Nevertheless, I understood my friends' objections. The Nationalist cause was a romantic one - they had something worth fighting for: freedom from the colonial rule that oversaw genocide during the Irish Famine, freedom from continued occupation of the six counties. On the world stage, Loyalism roused no sentimentality, it was the noise and bluster of stand-offs, agitating to assert the right to march traditional routes through now Nationalist areas and clinging to the union with Britain like a battered wife using love as an excuse. Politics was complicated and muddied with violence. Cormac headed back to his office.

Old dreads of unbelonging set in. I was under orders not to talk about Daddy, but I wouldn't have anyway, because to do so was to align myself with poverty and bigotry. I connected with potential new friends on a very shallow level, ever treading the tightrope between saying enough to be considered part of the group but not so much that would engender rejection, which loomed, seemingly inevitable. I felt a visceral panic, but instead of flight or fight, I fawned. I had looked to my environment for cues of how to fit in for so long that I had missed the opportunity to find out who I was and what I enjoyed. I wanted to be like them and to be liked by them, but I was an interloper. Worse, because my worth was predicated on academic success, my inability to navigate this new environment had created the perfect storm for depression and anxiety.

Getting lit at the weekends was a superb distraction. I volunteered to help with the cloakroom at Shine, charging a pound to stash each coat on a rail in the back corner of the Mandela Hall while DJs played thumping techno to a gyrating, pulsating crowd. We put up a sign to indicate that the cloakroom was full and took turns guarding the coats to dance. I nipped to the bar to avail of some liquid confidence and returned with a vodka and coke.

"Do you want a pill?"

Ian's voice buzzed in my ear, shouting to be heard over the booming bass. I looked at him to ascertain that I had heard correctly, and he mimed putting something in his mouth.
"I've never done one before."
"Do you want to?"
I looked around at the sweaty masses, on a shared journey of the music that had got inside them. Even the briefest of interactions - sidling past to get to friends, accidentally bumping - had all the hallmarks of connection; eye contact, pressing handshakes, spontaneous hugs. Acceptance.
"Yes."

He glanced away furtively, then pressed a tablet into my palm with the surreptitiousness of passing a note in class.
"What do I do?" I shouted. *"Chew it?"*
He held out my glass.
"Nah, just neck it."
It reminded me of petrol: acrid, chemical. I drank deeply to calm my threatening gag reflex and looked out at the crowd. It looked like a stop motion movie under the staccato lights of the Mandela Hall.
"How long does it take to work?"
"Depends. Maybe half an hour."

I spent that half hour pondering how awful it would be to die from taking ecstasy for the first time, and how my parents' grief would be compounded with the shame of me being a junkie. I imagined being plastered over the front of the Daily Mail, another victim of illicit substances with an image of me unrecognisable from intubation, or perhaps a memorial photo from more innocent days. The tablet was disintegrating in my stomach and passing into my bloodstream; if I was going to have an allergic reaction, I had passed the point of no return. I could feel my heart rate speeding up, but whether from panic or drugs, I was unsure. I wanted to run.

"I need to get out of here!"

It was a tsunami of heat and sound. I felt swarmed by the vastness of the crowd, bulldozed by the relentless beats. If I died, no one would notice.

"It's okay, don't freak out - it's just kicking in."

"No, you don't understand! It's too crowded."

Ian grabbed for my hand.

"Come with me."

He guided me past the stage and to the double doors and indicated to the security staff that we needed to nip up to the RAG office. The doors closed behind us, muffling the music while the brutalist concrete walls offered cold relief from the mugginess of before. We climbed and turned, climbed and turned, up three floors. The exercise felt good and provided an outlet for the nervous energy that had built up. My muscles felt energised, and I thought of a cat stretching luxuriously after a long nap. The windows of the office looked out over the busy night, the lights of passing cars sending shadows stretching across the walls. I looked down into the street below and was pleasantly relieved to discover that I had no urge to test my flying skills. I was lucid and in control. Everything was okay - lovely, in fact. I gushed my gratitude to Ian, lovely Ian, wonderful Ian - and we glided down the cool, airy stairwell, where the thumping bass was already beating a tattoo in my heart.

Happy, excited butterflies flitted in my tummy. I pointed towards the toilets and Ian thumbsed-up me as I wove through groups of sweaty dancers chewing gum and huffing Vick's, wide eyes dilated and inky. Then came the Official Best Poop of My Entire Life, where somehow, I excavated insecurity and self-doubt with the contents of my bowels. The mirrors above the wall of sinks reflected frenetic activity under the glare of strip lights - girls reapplying makeup that had been sweated off, others buzzing with inquiries: *where did you get that top? You look beautiful! Can I borrow that lipstick? What's your name? You have the most gorgeous hair! Oh my god, you are so* LOVELY! There were compliments and hugs and plans to meet for a dance - *front left - by the stage!* At last, I was free from constraint and able to interact without fear of rejection. Catholics and Protestants came together effortlessly in that vast, dark room, where ecstasy bulldozed the barrier of religion and politics to ensure that our fractious history would not divide us. The harsh overhead lights came on in the early hours of the following morning, illuminating faces, pallid or flushed, wild-eyed, some lads bare-bellied and chanting: *One more tune! One more tune!*

Returning the coats was fun, so many people, such gratitude! - but also very challenging as my eyes weren't behaving. I held proffered coat tickets at arm's length, then up close, in futile attempts to read the number through eyes that seemed to flick rapidly from side to side every time I tried to focus. Occasionally, I saved time by asking someone else to tell me the number, which I would quietly chant in order to remember, but as I rifled through the ticketed hangers to find the correct one the numerical song in my head changed and I stood wearing the thousand-yard stare of a geriatric who forgot why they'd come into the room.

"House party off Botanic, you in?"

"James is having everyone back to his!"

Cloakroom finished and leftover coats bagged up for Lost Property, our footsteps echoed in the harshly lit, strangely empty corridors of the Union and we exited into the cool, darkness of University Road, excited for the next chapter of adventure. We traversed an undaunting Belfast in this slipstream of reality where strangers as bangled as ourselves stopped for friendly chats and the very idea that the Troubles happened was ludicrous.

James's was a typical student shit hole. The front door was ajar in a gesture of welcome to this tall, dilapidated house at the end of a seemingly endless street of terraces. The houses across the narrow road looked baldly back, a mirror of the same faded red brick and dusty porches, a filthy student land, devoid of rules or reproach. The smell hit me before I put my foot across the threshold; damp, mould, unmopped spills and smoke, both cigarette and hash. We climbed oddly steep stairs towards the sound of conversations and dance music. At the very top of the house, jutting jawed students milled about a small landing between a large bedroom and bathroom, drinking from cans. A cheer went up as we entered the room, the freshness of cold night air still clinging to us. The cheer was not the simple appreciation of the more the merrier, but one of recognition, that we had been missed, our arrival anticipated. I was heartened by this indication of belonging. Cheap side table lights and a lava lamp afforded the vague shapes of groups dotted on the manky threadbare carpet and the single bed against the wall. A desk in front of a small Victorian iron fireplace held massive decks and speakers. James's head was crooked to his shoulder to secure fat, spongy headphones and a roll-up hung from his mouth, features scrunched in concentration. Ian passed me a can and we found a spot on the floor. My heart continued to thump heavily in my chest, a reassuring beat that reminded me that I was gloriously alive.

Good to meet you! Where are you from? You've lovely eyes. What are you studying? Good night? Want a smoke of this? How do you know these ones? Want some gum?

The muscles in my jaw were flexing as I compulsively ground my teeth. So many new names, faces and conversations while we were all beautiful and interesting and forgiving. *Surely this easy connection, this generosity of kinships was the meaning of life?*

Somewhere along the way the insistent, enervating beats and shrill motifs had been replaced with something more mellow, melodies that lulled, that invoked images of soft clouds and sunsets. I felt a wave of nausea from all the swallowed air from hours of chewing gum. I took a swig of my can, except somehow it was down to the dregs, and someone had flicked ash into it. I wondered when I had finished it or whether I had been the one to use it as an ashtray.

"Where are you from again?"

The guy beside me had slipped back into sleep by the time I turned to answer, and I had a sense of deja vu. Daylight seeped through the curtain cracks, and I was stiff and cold. I sneaked out, waiting until I was outside to squeak my coat over my freezing, sweaty arms in the too-bright morning.

Soon, I was wishing the weekdays away to get to the weekend where I was free to be myself again. One tablet led to an effervescent, ringing high, but I wanted more. I told myself I was developing a tolerance for MDMA, which may have been true, but my real motivation for taking more was to get further away from old, cautious, frightened me, who seemed to loiter on the fringes of my consciousness, waiting to get a foothold again. She needed to fuck right off. It wasn't long before Suicide Tuesday became a thing, when the serotonin high of the weekend swung the other way as my brain traitorously sought to address the chemical imbalance. My weeks became a shambles; I was high on Friday and Saturday, slept through Sunday, hungover on Monday and endured Suicide Tuesday, which soon had the cheek to leach into Wednesday. Thursday though, was vicious. I felt like myself again, normal programming had resumed, and with it, a renewed itch to get away from myself, while the memory of the consequences of doing so was all too recent. On Thursday, I was clear headed enough to simultaneously hate old, insecure me and new fun me, who, in the attempt to escape old, me, was fucking things up royally. Pre-existing social anxiety and come-down torpor joined forces to ensure I skipped tutorials and lectures. I told myself that at some point before the exams, I'd have access to the reference books required and get caught up.

    I visited home, where the atmosphere had become altogether more pleasant in my absence. Daddy and Martin had just returned from a trip to Manchester, where my brother had trialled for Manchester United School of Excellence. If admitted, he would train there as he continued his schooling. It boded well for his much-wanted career in football. Daddy positively glowed as he recounted their trip.

"*And this one,*" he nodded towards Martin, who sat looking somewhat abashed on the sofa beside me, "*he's a defender but he takes the ball the whole way up the wing, beats every opponent and scores!*"

I gave Martin a look of happy incredulity.

"*Sounds like some pretty sweet moves you have going on there.*"

He shrugged and looked down, suppressing a modest smile. Daddy's tone became serious.

"*There'll be no more of that showboating, though, sure there won't?*"

It seemed he had celebrated his goal with some kind of dance move. The younger footballers were modelling this on the professional leagues, where many players patented post-goal celebrations: the Robot, the Caterpillar, knee slides, blowing kisses to the sky. His eyebrows lowered.

"*No, Daddy.*"

Martin looked embarrassed and I deduced that this conversation had played out before, perhaps Daddy had reprimanded him in front of his teammates and coaches. He wanted Martin's talent to stand out on its own merit. He didn't like a show-off. I changed the subject.

"*What was the hotel like?*"

"*Ah, kid, it was great, wasn't it? The food was lovely. We all ate together, the coaches and the wee bucks, we even got a look round Manchester.*"

"*And what did you think?*" I asked Martin.

"*Brilliant,*" he beamed.

"*And the other lads?*"

He nodded and smiled. He had found his tribe. I noticed how handsome he had become. His skin, ever-olive from days on the pitch, smooth upon his more defined brow, cheekbones and jawline. His dark eyes shone with excitement for the days to come. He was on the brink of manhood and success.

"*Ack, there was one wee buck I really felt for,*" continued Daddy. "*We were walking into town, and I heard some of the fellas giving him stick for wearing a past-season football top. He probably couldn't afford the new ones. I goes, Hold on! Let me see that top? Son, that's what they wore when they won the treble! You're wearing the best strip here!"*

He stood up for an underdog, because even as an adult, seeing a child being made to feel less-than was still too close to the bone. It was why he ran the boxing club, to be a mentor, an encourager, a builder-upper for the poor, overlooked, working-class boys who needed it, as he had.

Martin gingerly got up and sidled into the kitchen. I heard a dining chair scraping as he sat himself down and spoke to Mummy, who turned the little television down in response.

"What, son?"

"Will you tell me what Billy was like?"

I strained to hear, but Mummy spoke in that hushed, low voice, as if confiding secrets.

My merry-go-round of weekly chemical highs and lows continued, but though the highs were never as high as they once were, the lows were becoming crushing. Messing with my serotonin levels had provoked a chemical depression, which combined with a reactive depression in response to my stressful academic situation. I'd finally left home and was at a prestigious university, but a preoccupation with my past of poverty, ridicule and abuse, and anticipation a foreseeable of either constantly hiding this, or worse, being exposed - culminated in depression and anxiety so severe that I developed agoraphobia. Attending classes was an impossibility, as was maintaining any tenuous friendships I'd made in RAG. At this point I was having difficulty convincing myself to walk from my bedroom to the kitchen for food, or even go to the toilet for fear of bumping into a housemate and having to converse. Cathal, no stranger to dark days himself, brought me food and stayed with me often, but ultimately, he was no match for a darkness of this magnitude and wisely directed me to the doctor for antidepressants and to the student counsellor for talking therapy.

The student counsellors worked from offices on the third floor of the Union, accessible only by a remote set of stairs that was seldom used. I trudged the three flights and sat in the small reception room, rigid with worry. Soon, a pleasant lady in her sixties popped her head round the door and invited me in. Jennifer looked like a kindly grandmother with her short grey hair, soft cheeks and eyes that drank you in, searching for the unsaid. She arranged her cardigan round her shoulders and positioned a writing pad on her lap, then spoke in gentle tones.

"What brought you here today?"

I wasn't sure where to begin. I was unable to establish chronological causality and was heavy with shame for the massive clusterfuck I had manifested.

"I'm pretty sure I'm failing this year. I don't really understand how to do the work. I have stopped going to classes because I'm too scared to leave the house."

"Can you tell me a bit more about that?"

I took a deep breath to steel myself.

"I'm afraid all the time. I palpitate and sweat through tutorials and lectures. By the time I get home, I am exhausted."

"When was the first time you remember feeling that way?"

I thought for a moment and realised I couldn't identify a time when I didn't feel anxious in an education setting.

"I think I've always felt this way."

"What are you afraid of?"

"I'm afraid to speak in class in case I'm wrong, or sound stupid. In case I make a mistake."

"When you were a child, what happened when you made a mistake?"

I grimaced.

"What do your parents say about your difficulties?"

I had carried my worries alone for so long that this question felt irrelevant.

"I can't tell them. We aren't... close like that."

"Don't you have a good relationship?"

"It's okay, I guess. It hasn't always been okay, though."

"Can you tell me a bit more about that?"

She nodded and made notes throughout my potted history of all the things I had studiously avoided admitting in my attempts to fit in, to finally be someone else. Shame weary and pierced with sorrow, saying the stories aloud felt like extruding little daggers and being left with a mass of raw wounds. Speaking my truth confirmed my greatest fear, that I was damaged beyond redemption, and yet unburdening myself and finding this soft place to land felt like a long exhale.

By the time I availed of help in the form of medication and talking therapy, it was the end of first year and I had failed most classes. I was called to a Tribunal, a formality that preceded being kicked out of university. My diagnosis of depression was the extenuating circumstance that bought me another chance. It was a hard one to celebrate; I felt like I was playing the mental health card, downplaying the pivotal role I had in my own educational demise.

I started to keep a journal. It was gruelling to re-hash painful memories and try to make sense of my narrative. As I wrote, it became evident that I had internalised the punitive and intolerant voices of my childhood and had become my own harshest critic. As I lamented the stacked deck and felt rage and overwhelm at the issues I had yet to overcome, another little voice started to speak - a calmer one, who felt loving and wise.

"Yes, this is painful work, but these experiences and your example of overcoming them could be of use to others someday."

I felt a palpable shift, for a moment it felt as though I was suffused with white light and peace. My conditioned thoughts snapped me out of it.

"I'm a shambles," I thought. *"How on earth could I help anybody else?"*

No answer came so I lay back on my bed and tried hard to hear more, but that little voice had spoken its truth and didn't feel the need to expound. Instead, I closed my eyes and absorbed the calm and hope it had brought.

Jennifer explained that my flaws were the behaviours I adopted to survive my upbringing and offered a course of inner-child therapy, an exploration of my early years where I could access the vulnerable child and reframe the past. It sounded surprisingly out-there. I wondered if Jennifer had been a hippy-dippy flower child in the sixties and worked to keep my face neutral.

"*I have never heard of it.*"

"*Well, I suppose, in a nutshell, it's about becoming acquainted with the child you once were, giving her space to express her emotions her experiences. It could help you in understanding some of your adult feelings and behaviours.*"

I nodded. It didn't sound implausible.

"*Why don't we try it? For homework, I'd like you to write down your earliest memory in as much detail as you can remember and include how you felt at the time. Next week, when we discuss it, we might just be able to make some links with how you felt then, with now.*"

Back at my digs, pen and notebook at the ready, I plumped my pillow and settled my back into it, wondering which childhood anecdote to chronicle. The Milky bar beating felt a little too on-the-nose, like I was setting out my stall as a victim of abuse, working the shock factor, desperate for sympathy. I chewed on the pen lid, flipping through the Rolodex of memories, trying to select an appropriate one that held emotional resonance without too much drama. Eventually, I recounted Daddy returning drunk from the pub and me pulling the boots from his feet and how the air changed from playful to foreboding when I wasn't doing it fast enough. I flipped the bottom of the duvet up to warm my feet, feeling comfortable and safe as I pulled threads of memory - strained Mummy, buoyant Daddy, the emotional climate shifting like ripples in tides. My default had always been to remember events from a safe distance, unobtrusive like a film made remote by black and white, the sound turned down, yet imagining this little person so happy to see Daddy home, hoping for fun and trying so hard to please made me feel sad. I gazed out the window, trying to imagine what connections Jennifer might make from the child's emotions to the adult's behaviour. I felt anger at Daddy, and how our worlds revolved around the fallout from his desires and moods.

Ultimately, I never went back to therapy. In the course of that week, something happened that made it impossible.

Eighteen

Jeanette came home for Christmas with a round pregnancy bump and knockers the size of my head. It was the first time we had shared a Christmas as a family of five, and the house shook off its torpor to become lively and joyful. Mummy fussed around us, ferrying endless plates of food and cups of tea from the kitchen. Daddy was full of craic, reminiscing about the days when Jeanette was a kid; the tin bath by the fire, the freezing outdoor toilet, Jeanette fighting bouts with the boys at the club. Martin and I lay at opposite ends of the sofa and put the soles of our feet together, an old habit, pedalling lazily, listening to the stories absentmindedly. Our pedalling inevitably culminated in a red-faced battle of strength, concluded when a fart escaped, and laughter weakened us. Jeanette watched from the chair by the door, smiling affectionately, looking a little bit sad. I wondered if she felt left out. I wondered if she was remembering Billy.

Usually a teetotal house, Daddy declared he would bring drink into the house so that we could toast on Christmas Eve. Martin cheekily requested some tins of Harp, testing the boundaries as I had done at fourteen, too. He had grown into a likeable kid; friendly and funny, with a smile that would break hearts. Daddy hadn't taken a drink since the slip he had when I was seven and he came home from Belfast, drunk and furious. I had been playing with my friends in the street when we heard shouting and followed the sound to my house. When I went inside, Daddy sat quiet and menacing, an irritable lion ready to strike. The glass top on the coffee table he had made in prison was smashed and thick shards and glass dust peppered the surface and rug below. Mummy shook her head in a gesture of say nothing, a purple bruise blooming on her chin and lip. Fear forced my words out regardless; I needed to know what this meant.

"*Are you and Mummy getting a divorce?*"

He looked up from his drunken haze and fixed me with a loathsome glare.

"*Yes. I've met somebody else. Her name is Samantha.*"

When I looked at Mummy, she gave a quick shake of her head to say that it wasn't true. He was simply drunk and seeping with fuck you.

Despite this stinging memory, I optimistically believed that he could enjoy a drink without descending into seething pits of hatred. That was volatile, damaged Daddy from another era; the Daddy we had now was constant and had healed. I imagined a drink would make this version red cheeked, tipsy and jolly. Martin and I were two excited puppies, eager to crack the first can and get festivities underway. Mummy and Jeanette were less enthusiastic and seemed hell-bent on skipping the momentous occasion altogether. They stood at the sink muttering to each other like two massive buzzkills.

"*Lighten up!*"

Their faces were drawn with worry.

"*You don't remember what he's like with drink in him.*"

This comment irritated me beyond measure. It felt less like a statement of fact and more a reminder that I was a late recruit, born after their time of real hardship. Their exclusive club had Billy and I was a postscript in a life where things had happened. I bristled at the implication that I was naïve, and they were wise.

"*Oh, for goodness sake, it's just a few bevs, it's hardly a bender.*"

"*It doesn't need to be!*" exclaimed Mummy. "*Do you know, it just takes one drink?*"

She turned to Jeanette.

"*Do you remember wee Noleen's daddy was off the drink for years, and he just had that one wee drink?*"

Jeanette nodded sombrely.

"*He ended up a homeless drunk. He died on the street!*"

I thought they were being melodramatic. They didn't want to drink – Jeanette was pregnant, and Mummy never enjoyed a drink (she once told me that she got drunk too fast then spent the rest of the night vomiting) so I denoted sour grapes for the fun us drinkers were about to have. They loitered on the periphery as Martin, and I settled in for a night of mirth and mild inebriation. We sat at the dining table in the middle of the kitchen, while Daddy sat further away from us all in the corner, on the hard honey oak step stool that Mummy kept to reach the high cupboards. We were barely halfway down the first tin when Daddy had gulped down almost a third of a bottle of whiskey. We laughed, incredulously.

"*Flip sake, Daddy! Get it into ye!*"

He smiled, relishing our laughter, possibly buzzed from the hit of alcohol he hadn't availed of in thirteen years, but he didn't slow down. Within fifteen minutes the smile had slid away, and his chin was jutting. He pointed at us and flicked his finger down towards his feet, a gesture to sit nearby on the cold lino.

"*Sit down.*"

I could feel that Martin too had registered the tone of unequivocal command and we were both slightly unbalanced by it. We lowered ourselves obediently to the floor and waited to see what was next, glancing at each other in silent communication, wearing weak smiles. *This is still fun, right?*

He wanted to tell us stories of the old days. We were accustomed to dramatic re-enactments and well-timed punchlines; he was an accomplished storyteller and knew how to work an audience. Instead, his stories were one-way traffic, our enjoyment secondary to our rapt attention. He was slurring over words and losing his thread. Martin and I were giggling from nerves and embarrassment. Somewhere behind those shuttered off eyes, he registered that we were laughing at him.

"*What the fuck are you laughing at?*"

The whiplash change in mood was enough for Jeanette. She pushed herself up gingerly from her seat. Daddy registered this as an affront.

"Where the fuck are you going?"

"I'm tired. I need my bed. "

"FUCKING SIT DOWN!"

I remembered the charge in the air as I wrestled the boots from his tired feet as a child. Drunk Daddy turned into the worst version of himself. It seemed as though he was possessed; the light in his eyes dimmed, another entity surveyed us from his darkened visage - jagged, angry, spoiling for violence. It relished fear, it sought to dominate. For now, though, it let Jeanette leave, and made do with the two captives on the floor. He bored us rigid and eventually told us to fuck off to bed - we were shite company.

On Christmas Day, he nursed a spectacular hangover like a stoic. After a sedate Christmas dinner, we retired to the living room to graze and lounge as the telly droned in the background. I ripped into my selection box to discover that the fudge I had been saving had mysteriously disappeared. Mummy clocked my look of cross confusion.

"Who licked the cream o' your bun?"

That phrase had long annoyed me: the implication that my grievance was minor, and I was petulant. Both of which were maddeningly true in this instance.

"Someone -" I looked around accusingly, *"has stolen the fudge out of my selection box."*

"*Not me,*" confirmed Mummy, who I could be taken at her word. Falsehood sent her into a frenzy of panic and confession.

"*It wasn't me. Although, if it had've been, so what? I bought the bloody thing,*" grumped Daddy, irritated.

Jeanette shook her head, but I hadn't spent enough time in her company to build up a profile, so she was still firmly under suspicion. My eyes landed on Martin.

"*Why would I want your fudge when I've one of my own?*" he reasoned, before undermining himself with a burst of nervous laughter.

Then everybody laughed, because he was such a crap liar. I was incensed! My fudge, the fudge I had been saving, my favourite part of the selection box was gone, and they were all having a jolly good wheeze over that rapscallion and his adorable inability to deceive.

"*Give me your fudge, then,*" I insisted.

"*Piss off!*" he retorted.

"*Piss off?*" I repeated, incredulously.

"*I can't anyway, I ate that one, too!*"

Renewed peals of laughter.

"*It's only a fudge,*" added Mummy unhelpfully.

"*MY fudge!*" I insisted.

"*Grow up!*"

I launched myself off the sofa in barely contained fury to a chorus of groans and laughter, determined not to spend another second with these immoral shits. My decorum suffered only slightly as I landed an almighty thump on Martin's back and darted up the stairs like a scalded cat before he could catch me to retaliate. The next day, he headed off to Manchester for football training, and I refused to see him off, bolstered by a deep sense of injustice.

After Christmas, life returned to normal. Jeanette was back in the US, I went back to Uni digs, Martin was ferried to and from school and Tuesday football practice. By the time February half-term came, my resolve to be a good student meant I hadn't been home since Christmas.

∞∞∞

One Tuesday in February, they dropped Martin to the Grove Activity Centre for practice with Lisburn Youth. On the way home, they nipped into the garage to buy a couple of crème eggs to give him for a wee treat after football practice. The mobile phone rang.

"Ben? This is Billy, Martin's football coach. Listen, he's had a wee turn here, could you come back?"

"Yes, we are on our way."

Daddy dropped the crème eggs and relayed what the coach had said. As they hurried back to the car, Mummy speculated, grasping for an explanation. Martin had a form of epilepsy whereby he could have little seizures, but usually they were barely noticeable. He'd 'zone out' when watching television and wouldn't answer questions, as if he couldn't hear, or respond.

"Do you think it's his epilepsy? Maybe he has had a fit?"

"Maybe."
The five-minute journey felt endless.

When they got to the Grove, they found the practice hall cleared of players. Martin lay on the floor with medical staff surrounding him. A well-meaning coach grasped Mummy's arm as if to steer her away from her son. She had a flashback to being steered away from Billy at the hospital and resisted.
"Not this one," she said, pulling her arm away.
Martin lay unconscious and unresponsive. Alarmed, confused, only then did she allow herself to be escorted to a small room where she waited, terrified. Eventually a young doctor came to speak to her. His formality made her head spin. It was a rehearsed speech, poorly delivered from nerves.
"As you know, Martin suffered a fit this evening. There's no easy way to say this. He's dead."

Mummy heard a long wail, an animal noise. It went on for some time before she realised it was coming from her. Her son. Her boy. Her dear, strong boy. Vicious grief was back to rip her apart.

∞∞∞

My housemate, Catherine was still up when I waltzed in from seeing a band in town.
"Are you not in bed yet?"

Catherine worked nine to five hours in an office and was seldom seen downstairs after nine.

"Your Dad has phoned twice and said to phone him back as soon as you get in."

"Did you wait up to tell me that?" I asked, abashed.

I checked my watch. It was half ten. I knew from experience that they panicked if the phone rang after ten, assuming it would be bad news.

"It's late, I'll phone him in the morning."

Catherine exchanged glances with Ciara, another housemate.

"He sounded worried; you should phone him."

They seemed grave and determined, so I shrugged and dialled the number. Daddy picked up the phone after two rings.

"Did you want me to phone you?"

"Yes. Come on up home, love."

"Why? What's going on?"

"Come on home, love. I'll talk to you then. Get a taxi and come home."

I got off the phone and reported the conversation, bemused. Catherine offered to drive me home and I gratefully accepted.

In the car, nerves made me ramble. Maybe someone had died, I reasoned. I wouldn't entertain the thought of it being someone close, so I speculated on a range of possibilities, none from our nuclear family. I started to buckle under the strain of not knowing.

"Why can't he tell me on the phone?"

The twenty-minute journey was taking too long. The thought came like a gut punch. Martin.

"What if something has happened to Martin?"

I felt panic rise as Catherine and Ciara stared ahead, strangely evasive. I felt utterly alone and started to pray, at first muttering under my breath, eventually begging with increasing vociferous desperation.

"Please, please don't let anything have happened to Martin. Please. Let him be okay. Please keep him safe."

I leaned into the front of the car.

"Do you know if something has happened to Martin? For God's sake tell me, I'm going mad here."

They shook their heads, non-committal. It was too much. I sat back and endured the rest of the journey in terrified silence.

When the car pulled up outside the house, I leapt out and shouted over my shoulder that I would be back in a minute, still vainly hoping that whatever missive Daddy wished to impart in person wasn't cataclysmic, that I could return to my old life.

My knock was answered by my cousin, Gloria, who was red-eyed and shaking.

"Where's Martin?" I demanded.

She held a tissue to her face and stepped back to allow me through. I rushed past her into the crowded living room, where Mummy sat hunched and staring, surrounded by her sister and sisters- in- law.

"Where's Martin?"

Mummy couldn't or wouldn't hear me. One of my aunts started to cry. The living room door opened, and my Daddy called me through.

"*Come in here, Peggy.*"

I put my head down, suddenly self-conscious, and rushed to him.

"*Where's Martin?*"

My uncles lined the walls of the kitchen and huddled by the sink, looking down or looking away, affording a semblance of privacy in this horrible moment. Daddy's voice strained with suppressed emotion as he pulled me hard into his chest.

"*He's dead, love.*"

"*No, Daddy.*"

"*He's dead.*"

Over and over, I said no into his chest, a mantra of disbelief, willing it not to be so. He shook and held on tight.

I felt dizzy, as though the fabric of reality had ripped open and I was free-falling; down, down to this horrifying new land where Martin had been torn from the world. My brother being completely, irreversibly gone was too enormous a loss to comprehend, and my brain short circuited to rage. *Had someone hurt him? Deliberately taken him from us?* I wanted to channel this sickening adrenaline to exact revenge.

"*What happened?*"

Daddy stepped back and held my arms, as if understanding this impulse to lash out.

"They think it was a heart condition. The coroner will tell us when they know."

I nodded and pulled away, self-consciously bringing my hand up to chew on my thumbnail.

"I have to tell the girls I am staying here. They are waiting in the car."

He took in my chipped purple nails.

"You'll have to get that off for the funeral," he said, exerting a semblance of control in an uncontrollable situation. For the rest of the night, I bunched my hands into fists and quietly obsessed, in this room full of crying women, about how to get nail polish remover. It was easier than feeling anything else.

Mummy was broken. Her grief shrunk her. She sat grey and vacant while people trooped in and out of our house, acknowledging their sympathy with weak, unbelieving nods as she stared into the middle distance. Twice Daddy decided that it was all too much for her and made her eat sedatives to get her to sleep out the days. Twice she resisted, protesting through choking sobs that her grief was her own, all she had left of her son. When she relented and the medication took effect, we supported her as she stumbled and sobbed up the stairs to bed. She asked me to stay with her. I climbed in beside her and held her as she sighed and gasped into sleep, frail like an injured bird. It scared me to see her this way. I was afraid that Martin's death spelt the end of her.

"Mummy, don't give up."
"I sat with him in the ambulance. I held him as the heat left him."
"Mummy, I still need you."
"My first son died at seven. My second at fourteen. I was given twice as long with Martin as with Billy."
She looked at me intently.
"I always hated February and now I know why."
She turned her back and wept. I moved closer and curled my body around hers, cradling her as if on my knee.

Two days passed before they brought him home to us. Daddy ushered everyone into the kitchen, where we stood quietly, reverently, as the coffin was carried into the living room. Daddy said Mummy was to go in first to allow her time alone with her son. I watched shapes and movement through the frosted glass door. When the coffin lid was lifted, Mummy's silhouette backed away. We heard her strangled cries.
"That's not mine. That's not my son!"
She collapsed onto the sofa keening, then disappeared into herself once more, staring and gasping, remote and untouchable. We filed in, close family first. His skin was yellowish grey, and his lips pulled into a smirk. His fuzzy buzz cut, his dark eyebrows, long black lashes. It was Martin. But my brother, their son was gone.

Before they took their leave, one of the undertakers motioned for me to follow him outside. I weaved through mourners and met him on the back step, pulling the door behind me for privacy. He tilted his head confidentially towards mine, eyes intent, and spoke in a hushed undertone.

"Keep this away from your parents, in case it upsets them. Do you understand?"

Nodding I held out my hand.

He passed me a plastic shopping bag and nodded, patting me on the arm before he retreated to a waiting car. I took the bag to the shed and steeled myself to unpack the clothes Martin had been wearing when he died. I lifted his football shirt to my face and inhaled. Immediately I was transported to our shared childhood, squeezed side by side in the armchair by the window watching children's television, me and my little brother who smelled of green grass pitches and the faint musk of childhood exertion. I remembered how we stuffed ourselves into that chair for years, resisting separate seats, even when our hips grew wide and one of us had to sit at an angle. I sniffed the neckline, quick little whiffs, to eke out the experience of feeling close to him - the smell of contentment, of belonging, of home - knowing that it would soon dissipate and this portal of remembering would close. When I opened my eyes, I noticed that the front had been cut with scissors, the line jagged, implying haste. Dark red spots peppered the fabric, and I felt a dizzying horror. It was only then I realised that my mind had stopped the story of his death at the point of his collapse, an omission of kindness to circumvent the pain the undertaker had wished to spare my parents.

Those blood stains were part of a later narrative I had ignored, when medics had tried to save my brother, who I needed to believe had been dead before he hit the floor. I located my dad's friend, Sammy and asked him to take the bag away. I passed it gingerly like a loaded bomb.

Later that day, a journalist came, reluctant to impinge on our grief but hoping for something for the front pages. He didn't wish to intrude by coming into the house, so Daddy spoke to him on the back doorstep.

"I really appreciate your willingness to speak to me at this terrible time. Please accept my condolences."

"Thank you," replied Daddy, quiet and dignified.

"Could you tell me a little about his love of football?"

Daddy chose his words carefully and spoke in his formal accent, the one he used for teachers, or the minister.

"We were just back from trials at Manchester United School of Excellence. He was a great wee footballer, with a promising career ahead of him."

The man nodded sympathetically.

"Have the club gotten in touch with you?"

"Alex Ferguson phoned to express his sympathy. He remembered Martin well."

The journalist scratched into his notebook.

"I apologise in advance - I know this is hard to talk about, but I have to ask - have the coroners given a cause of death?"

"Cardiomyopathy. Enlarged heart causing Sudden Death Syndrome, the same condition that has taken so many young sportsmen."

"I'm so sorry."

Daddy nodded an acknowledgement. Such occasions called for dignity, tribute. Emotion could be so crass.

And yet, in the days to follow, Daddy cried. Again, it was a keening sound - he wasn't crying, the crying was too big to be contained and was forcing its way out. When the visitors left, as he sat in his chair by the window, my broad, strong daddy wept like a forlorn child. His buddy, his pal was gone. Comforting was an alien practice in our home. All I could do was avert my eyes while the sound tore through the room. That was it for therapy. I couldn't sneak off to bitch about my daddy who was broken and raw, hollowed by grief. The door to this kind of healing was firmly shut.

The coaches of Lisburn Youth gifted a framed orange jersey, embroidered with his name and those of his teammates. My parents mounted it on the wall of the living room, the number of his shirt emblazoned in the centre - a large, bold five. He was buried five rows back in Lisburn's Blaris Cemetery. If the vision of the skull inside the pentagon was a harbinger, it wasn't one I could have done anything with. It was a foreshadowing, nothing more. His departure was a foregone conclusion.

∞∞∞

Grief is tumultuous. At nights, I cried until sleep overtook me, but woke frequently with sleep's sweet fog still clinging, feeling all was well, until the dark, heavy feeling seeped back, and I realised gradually, crushingly, all over again that he had died. I wondered if this ebb and flow of grief was hardwired, if the brain was programmed to let us forget for a while, a merciful little reprieve from relentless anguish. It did not feel like a kindness, though, when grim reality dawned, and fresh horror stabbed. I lay in the dark, watching my life telescope out in front of me with no Martin by my side, no brother to share the burden of ageing parents, no uncle for my future children. The permanence of death was staggering. No matter how many times I woke from sleep, he remained horrifyingly dead.

The days leading up to the funeral were a pantomime of coping. Family and friends trudged in and out, and though I'd no doubt of their genuine shock and remorse, it felt unfair to have to show appreciation for their sympathy, to provide tea and navigate the unchartered waters of grief with an audience, when all I wanted to do was close the doors and hold him while I still had the chance. The night before the funeral I made my bed on the sofa by the coffin, where I lay gazing at the honey oak box with the too-shiny gold fleur-de-lys handles and whispered my love to the shell of my brother before sleep sneaked in to rob me of precious minutes.

The funeral itself had a sense of unreality. The limousine rounded the corner of the church he had been christened in fourteen years before, with the same trim lawns and sweep of driveway we had travelled on that happy day when hope had been restored with this much needed son. The entrance was swarmed with black clad mourners. His teammates formed an unofficial guard as the coffin was carried in, rows of broken-hearted boys in suits that somehow made them look older and younger than their years.

 The church was packed. Rows of people turned to look. Jeanette and I walked with our arms around Mummy, half supporting her as we made our way to the front pew. I kept my face a mask, eyes downcast, unable to make a spectacle of myself with tears. I squeezed Daddy's hand as he choked on near silent sobs. He squeezed back, hard. I didn't know if that squeeze meant he was taking comfort from me or trying to provide comfort, but this foreign togetherness was all that mattered.

 At the graveyard, as they began to lower him into the freshly dug earth, Mummy wailed, and her legs gave from under her. Jeanette and I held her up, but Daddy told us to take her to the limousine to be taken home. I felt cheated. There were friends throwing flowers on the coffin and if anyone should be able to do that, it was me. There was a dear friend who had travelled from London to offer condolences, one person I had wished to receive comfort from and I hadn't had the chance to see. I felt resentful of the instruction, resentful of Daddy pulling rank and giving orders when I too was bereaved. My resentment filled me with disgust. There was a hierarchy of grief, and mine was beneath that of my parents.

 We went home. I climbed the stairs to bed, too worn out to manage post-funeral tea and sympathy. He was gone and I was spent. Jeanette left to go back home to the States a few days later and I felt like an only child.

The last interaction I had with Martin was when I had hit him. Though a painful recollection, it was somehow fitting that after years of nipping, kicking, running off, farting on heads and so on, that our relationship be concluded with a heartfelt and well-aimed dig to the shoulder blade. What else could you do when the self-elected bane of your life nicks your fudge? A kinder, more dignified interaction might have made for a less embarrassing story, but it wouldn't have been right. We laughed harder together than we ever laughed with anyone else. We raged at each other, we huffed, we were protective, we had secret codes. Despite the pain of losing him, despite the pain of having to move forward without him, I had him for fourteen precious years that I wouldn't change for the world. Like Billy, his absence has moulded part of me, but his presence moulded me more. My parents did their best but ultimately, their love had long been conditional. Martin taught me all about unconditional love. That's the beauty of children, the spark of heaven still shines bright, and they love because they don't yet know any other way to be. Rules and conditions are an acquired language. To grow up with a sibling by my side was a blessing. If his presence taught me about unconditional love, his passing had fresh new lessons. Losing someone forces you to address big questions and the perspective that you choose sculpts you.

Billy's contract was seven years, Martin's fourteen. The lessons they imparted were sharp. After Martin died, Daddy told me that time was not a healer and that he had cried for Billy as recently as two weeks before we lost Martin. He missed his boy and mourned for the man he would have become. He regretted his harsh words and the tough love he had employed when Billy was still here. After Billy died, he forgot the truth that your children do not belong to you. He held us closer, protected us more and stifled us with defensive, fearful love. The short leash we were chained to was for nothing. Billy died of an avoidable accident, but Martin was stolen by a health condition, a ticking time bomb that counted down the hours until the lesson was to be repeated. Daddy was shown that trying to control the world was pointless. He finally understood that we are loaned to each other, and the job of a parent is not to mould, or push, or prevent. It is as simple and as difficult as unconditional love.

As for me, when Martin came to Earth he gave me two committed parents who were focused on their children and not their problems. He came and released Jeanette from her role of protector in a fractured family, enabling her to fulfil her dream of living in the States. His life gave our parents the gift of a son's love, his death, a reminder that tomorrow isn't promised and today is all we have.

Over the coming days, weeks, months, years, Daddy recounted anecdotes to re-acquaint himself with his lost son. He laughed, sighed and said, *"well, that was just*

Martin to a T." He missed him sorely and didn't know how else to express his longing for him. As he talked, Mummy would bow her head and shrink back into her chair, nodding occasionally from behind her defensive wall, her internal world shredded with pain. We cried alone.

Nineteen

I sat down on the chair by the kitchen and stared off into the middle distance. Mummy set Daddy's cup of tea on his table and retreated to the sofa with hers, each remote, lost in their own worlds. It had been a fortnight since Martin died, and the quiet of the house amplified his absence. The ticking clock seemed louder, being the only sound. Mummy came to, as if only just noticing me.
"You may get a move on if you don't want to miss your bus."
I bit my lip to hold back tears, but they were already leaking. The weight in my heart pushed out in shuddering gasps and sighs.
"I don't want to go," I admitted, breaking Daddy's trance.
"Why not?" he asked, as if he hadn't realised that my world had also been shattered.
"I'm...I'm too sad."

It was the first I had said it aloud. It sounded childish in its simplicity, but I couldn't add to their weight of grief with my own. To my mind, their grief trumped mine and to express my own heartache was somehow obnoxious. My role was to alleviate their suffering in any way I could. This way of thinking was not entirely selfless;

in fact, there was a selfish component; if I underplayed my wound, I could avoid dark and painful terrain. That morning, grief had butted in regardless. I covered my face as excavating sobs tore through me, chest sore from the long suppression and from the violence of the release. Mummy looked worried. Her hunched shoulders and concerned expression felt like a reproach.

"*I'm sorry. I'm just so sad.*"

It was a relief to finally say it, despite the taboo. Daddy reached for a cigarette, which I took as an encouraging sign that he was gearing up for a talk. Smoke curled and hung in little dissipating clouds.

"*You can't be dropping out because of this.*"

This. Martin's death.

"*I won't. I... just can't today. It's too much.*"

I desperately wanted to stay home near my parents, even if that meant having to hold my pain in. At least my sorrow could take shallow little breaths in the stillness of home. The world just seemed too much.

"*I promise I won't drop out. Please. I just need today.*"

"*You've worked hard to get to where you are. You can't throw it away.*"

"*I know, Daddy.*"

He nodded my reprieve and relief flooded through me as the familiar silence returned.

University attendance was as difficult as I had anticipated. I trudged to class, absorbed little and stifled the urge to cry. Waiting outside classrooms and lecture halls was the worst. I dreaded small talk, where a simple *how are you* was a ticking bomb. The alienation of lying was painful, admitting my heartbreak was worse. I attended a Classics lecture on Antigone - a tragedy wherein the eponymous heroine's brother dies. The lecturer expounded at length upon Antigone's lament that the death of her brother was worse than the death of a husband; a husband she could replace, but her parents were past child-bearing age and there would be no more brothers. I felt the familiar strain in my chest and throat and my heart raced with anxiety. The white lights of the classroom seemed brighter. I became hypervigilant - suddenly it seemed as though everyone was either stealing glances or studiously avoiding me. It may have been neither.

    The professor approached me after class as I hastily packed up my things, preparing to bolt for the door. *"I'm so sorry. In hindsight, it might have been better for you to miss this lecture."*
I gave a wan smile, unsure what to say. I didn't want to cause anyone discomfort with my vast, unpalatable pain. Having no words to offer in reply, I nodded and raced out, before her sympathy was my undoing.

    These spells of overwhelm were not infrequent. I was at the computer library typing up an essay when heart palpitations came, sudden and thumping. For one shrill, terrifying moment I feared that I too had cardiomyopathy and my heart was about to sputter to a stop. Keyboards clicked and pages rustled amid the low hum of electricity. I looked around at the rows of students in various degrees of boredom or concentration, oblivious to my emergency and felt torn between wanting to cry out for help and needing to remain inconspicuous. My symptoms were the consequence of having no outlet for grief. I was trying to contain the uncontainable as it threatened to burst out.

In the subsequent weeks, my parents developed new routines. Instead of driving Martin to school, they drove to the cemetery. Instead of preparing his meals, Mummy prepared floral arrangements to adorn his grave. Our phone calls became more frequent than the weekly check in of Before. Daddy used to offer a cursory, gruff hello before passing the phone to Mummy, but since Martin, his tone had softened. We let each other in.
"Y'alright, love?"
"Yes, Daddy. How are you?"
"Ah, we're okay. Your Mummy's made a nice arrangement for Martin for Easter Sunday. Are you coming up, love?"
"Yes, I'll be up."
"Good, kid. That's good. You okay to come to the grave with us?"
"Yes."
"Ah, lovely. Okay, kid. See you then."

It was my first visit, almost two months since we had laid Martin to rest in Blaris Cemetery. It seemed vaster than it had on that day, when everything and everyone seemed to converge on that six-foot abyss, but now I noticed the serene simplicity of the place. Neat rows of headstones lined the gently sloping lawns. Birds chirruped as they pecked and scratched the soil around freshly budding saplings. Clouds drifted lazily across the cold Spring sky. Daddy explained the location of the grave in relation to the metal gate through which we had entered, subtly coaching me on how to find it unaccompanied.

"*Count five rows back and there he is, the first plot. Five like the number on his football shirt.*"

I nodded and we walked slowly towards his resting place, where the three of us stared at the headstone wordlessly. Beloved son and brother. Called home. Mummy withdrew a cloth from her coat pocket and wiped around the already clean marble, then placed her hand on it, conveying her mother's love like a warm palm resting on a shoulder. Daddy's breath hitched. I took a step back to be closer to him and he put his arm around my shoulder. We stood there like sentries, lost in our own thoughts, never taking our eyes off the black stone. I wondered if this new closeness felt strange to him, too. Eventually Mummy kissed her fingers and tapped the marble, a full stop to her wordless love, and we turned and walked heavily up the path, back to the car.

It was only a five-minute drive to home, but it felt much longer as my lungs ached from tears I would not allow myself to shed. Home at last, I sat down on the sofa while Mummy went to make tea and Daddy lowered himself onto his chair. He muttered to himself, three-score years and ten, a mantra which reminded him that his earthly life was finite, and he'd soon be with his son.

I was flooded with a feeling of utter exhaustion and put my head down on the arm of the sofa for a moment. No sooner had my face touched the leather than a familiar feeling enveloped me – sleep paralysis. My body was immobile, but I was still very much awake and my ears were filled with a familiar radio static. Martin stood on the floor directly in front of where I had slumped. Behind him was an apex of light that came to a point where he stood, as if he was being beamed from everywhere beyond. A similar light radiated from him, too, a strange light that wasn't visual but emotional. It emanated perfect peace. My heart grew full with joy as I looked at him, his dark eyes crinkled by a radiant smile and that olive complexion from being out in all weathers, the sense of his physicality, his height, solidness, his Martin-ness. He saw me as clearly as I saw him, enjoying my surprise and excitement to see him.

"Hiya, big sis."

It was his voice, the exact tones and depth I knew so well, his specific accent – Lisburn with the occasional Belfast inflection. It was staggering. I hadn't realised I had missed his voice until I heard it so clearly.

"I'm doing fine here! Everything is great."

I couldn't speak, but my curiosity was conveyed through a kind of emotional telepathy.

"What's it like?"

"Never you mind, Nosy Parker! That's not what I'm here for."

He laughed. He was teasing me with the same old playfulness. Then he grew serious. I got the sense that I couldn't be trusted to stay receptive for long and that time was of the essence.

"*Look, I'm just here with a message. You can see how happy I am, can't you?*"

I felt the light around him pulse with contentment, safety, completeness. He knew I could sense it.

"*That. You have to tell Mummy and Daddy that. They need to know that I'm whole and happy.*"

"*I will.*"

"*You promise? They really need to know.*"

He conveyed how disconnected, how desolate they were, and a sense that these feelings were unnecessary.

I promised.

My exhaustion lifted as suddenly as it had come and I was wide awake in the same room he had just stood in, except now it felt heavier, darker without him and the light that carried him to me. The joy I had felt started to fade as I considered how to tell our parents. Would they be upset? Would they suspect me of cheapening his passing by inventing a fantastical tale to ease their suffering? Was that a genuine visitation or wish fulfilment from the deep suppurating grief following the cemetery? My happiness plummeted and once again I was locked inside a cage of my own making.

The dead were not so easily deterred.

A few weeks later I was curled up on the sofa watching a film with my latest boyfriend. We had pushed the sofa away from the wall and closer to the television, leaving a gap wide enough for my housemates to get through to the kitchen if they needed. As the film progressed, I grew steadily more attuned to a sensation of being watched and occasionally, at the edge of my vision, I registered movement behind us, and yet each time I turned my head, there was nothing and no one to see. Soon, Stuart noticed my odd behaviour.

"*Why do you keep looking behind you?*"
"*I keep thinking I see something.*"
"*Is it the light from the TV flickering on the wall?*"
"*Maybe. Yes, that's probably it.*"
I knew that this was not it. I had a strong sense of a tall, slim person standing off to the left, observing, biding their time.

Halfway through the film I needed the toilet, but the thought of going upstairs alone filled me with childish trepidation. I'm not sure what I thought would happen, but I didn't want to find out, either.
"*I need to nip to the loo.*"
Stuart nodded and paused the film.
"*Would you mind...waiting for me at the bottom of the stairs?*"
He looked at me quizzically.
"*Seeing things out of the corner of my eye has freaked me out.*"
I was embarrassed, but not so much so that I would brave the stairs alone. He laughed.
"*Go on, then.*"
We turned the lights on in the hall and top landing, and Stuart stood at the bottom stair, smiling wryly. As I

ascended and descended the stairs, I felt a presence following closely behind, just at my left shoulder.

After the film ended, we went to bed and I blethered on about anything and nothing for hours, knowing with absolute certainty that the moment I started to drift into sleep, someone would be there, waiting for me. By five in the morning, Stuart and I were both so thoroughly exhausted that sleep was an inevitability.
"If you hear me hyperventilating in my sleep, will you wake me up?"
He looked at me strangely.
"Why?"
I sighed, unable to put it off any longer.
"Well, sometimes I get sleep paralysis. It's like being half-awake and half-asleep, aware but unable to move. It's really scary. The only thing I can control is my breathing, so if I start to hyperventilate, I need you to nudge me awake."
"Okay."
"Promise?"
"Promise."

I closed my eyes and began to drift; immediately the same tall figure stood beside me, leaning over and peering into my face. Panicked, I pushed my breath out in short puffs and Stuart shook me awake.
"Are you okay?"
"Yes, I'm fine. Maybe I'll try to sleep on my other side."

I turned my back to where the figure had stood to my left and drifted off into sleep paralysis again. Even though they were now behind me, I could still feel their presence and attention, but having my back turned made me feel more vulnerable. I hyperventilated and was woken once more. At this point, I knew that I wasn't going to be left alone until whoever it was had said their piece. I turned onto my left side to face the figure and told Stuart not to wake me and to disregard any erratic breathing. I closed my eyes, and soon white noise filled my ears, and I couldn't move. I couldn't help but puff for help and regretted my former instruction to leave me be. The dark figure grew clearer - it was a tall, slim woman. I had never seen her before and yet she looked familiar...she looked like Mummy, and then I understood it was my maternal grandmother. She smiled gently and reached out the crook of her finger to brush my cheek.

"*You look so much like your mother.*"

I relaxed. We had never met, but I felt a familiarity, an affinity with her. Her next communication didn't come in words, she simply overlaid her emotions on mine. *Your mummy is so sad. My poor daughter. You have to ease her burden. You have to hold her broken parts together. Just love her. That's all you can do. Love her. I need you to love her.* And then she was gone, and I was awake. The sense that someone was there had lifted. The room felt empty, and I felt free. I rolled over and slept the sleep of the just.

Some days, I felt equal to the mammoth task of pushing down my pain to be of whatever solace I could to my parents, but on other days it was all too much. I wished I had been the one to die. I believed that my death would have been a blow, but much less so than Martin's; that losing a girl - this girl, fractious and troublesome - would have been less painful than the loss of this only son, this embodiment of pride and potential. If there was a God, he had slipped up by taking the wrong kid and yet again left me with the fallout. It was too hard, the stifling of my pain, the stifling of long held resentments as I tried to be there, to be enough, and knowing I never would be. I was grief stricken and traumatised and I wanted to die. On long, anguished nights I fantasised about ending my life only to be pulled back with the horrible image of my parents having to bury a third child. I couldn't do that to them. I wondered if it would be a kindness to somehow kill us all and have done with it.

As the months passed, my grief began to morph into something less unbearable. I had grown accustomed to the weight of it, the fresh wounds of grief had scabbed and scarred, and I was able to start considering my future without Martin's absence suffocating me. He was no longer here, but it started to come into greater focus that I was still very much here and needed to make urgent plans for after graduation.

I was working the Thursday night shift at Cafe Clementine with Frances. It was a slow night, so we polished cutlery and folded napkins to the dulcet tones of Nina Simone.

"How's teaching practice going?"

Frances smiled wryly.

"*I am teaching a ton of absolute berks.*"

"*You must feel right at home.*"

"*Ha! Actually, I do. The other day, a kid was nipping out to the toilet, and I said Hurry back! and he looked me dead in the eye and said - did you just say I have a hairy back? Complete eejits.*"

"*You seem fond of them.*"

"*Do you know what it is?*" She froze mid-polish to find the words. "*They are so likeable. Even the naughty ones. Especially the naughty ones. They are so...transparent. Open. I really feel like I can make a difference.*"

She gazed off for a moment, eyes shining.

"*Do I sound like a massive dick?*"

I went for the low-hanging fruit.

"*No more so than usual.*"

I felt a deep resonance with the way she spoke with such warmth and affection for her pupils. It ignited a spark of inspiration, and strangely, of recognition. An image of me teaching came unbidden, and with it, the ringing white light of inexplicable knowing, the familiarity of a recurring dream, or deja vu. I hastily dismissed it, however. The thought of being a focus of attention filled me with horror. Frances cast a cursory glance around the tables and resumed polishing.

"*What do you plan to do after Queen's?*"

"*I haven't a notion.*"

"*None at all?*"

"*Nope.*"

"You might want to address that. The closing dates for post-grad courses close soon, if you're planning on continuing study, that is."

Study was all I had known; I wasn't ready to catapult myself from the bosom of academia.

"How would I find out more about that?"

"Make an appointment with the Careers Office. And pull your finger out, you don't have long to submit applications."

My appointment fell on a bright Spring day, when the peeping heads of snowdrops and unfolding daffodils showed that Botanic Gardens was waking from its winter slumber. Sunlight glinted off the glass domed Botanical House and morning dew glistened on the grass. People walked the various paths winding through and around the gardens just a little slower than usual, as though newly awakened themselves, content to slow down and drink in the beauty of new beginnings. The office was on the Malone Road, a short distance from the main back gates of the gardens, a ground floor office in a tall, late Victorian terrace. Thick cornicing and picture rails gave clues that the room had been someone's parlour a long time ago, in an era before Queen's had crept, sprawling ever-outwards from the main Lanyon building. Now the room was fitted with cheap, thin carpet and the walls lined with floor to ceiling open metal stacks heaving with books and prospectuses from floor to ceiling. I gave my name and a young man invited me to sit on a rickety metal chair in front of his weathered desk.

I wasn't quite sure what to expect from this interview and wondered if he was trained to speculate on potential professions based on the educational profile of each client. I remembered the multiple choice test we took in school at age fourteen, all of us crammed into a technology suite, scratching our proclivities and aptitudes into small tightly packed boxes with a nubby little pencil, in gradients familiar from teen magazines: strongly agree to strongly disagree. A computer analysed our answer sheets and spat out predictions like an Oracle, a digital Russell Grant telling us what the future held. The pronouncement on me had been Sociologist, assuming third level education and Prison Officer without. I wasn't entirely sure what to make of that, and no follow-up was forthcoming, so eventually we all just shrugged it off like yesterday's horoscope and carried on with our default routine of cramming for tests. The Careers Officer was not much older than me, which I did not find reassuring. He settled himself onto his chair and steepled his fingers.

"*So!*" he declared, rather more loudly than necessary, "*What do you want to do?*"

The word want was jarring; this seemed to be the first educational juncture where my desires were relevant. So far, my educational journey had been largely dictated, the illusion of choice quickly evaporated when GCSE and A Level subjects had been predicated on what I had shown aptitude for rather than what I actually enjoyed. Perhaps teachers assumed a convenient correlation with the subjects you were good at and the subjects you liked, or maybe the more pertinent correlation was that of good grades and league tables position. We were on a conveyor belt; achieve these GCSEs, achieve these A Levels, achieve a university place. The next step had always been dictated, and too much 'help' had stunted my growth. At no point had I been trained in the essential skill of looking inward to establish something so frivolous as my own joy. Joy was moot, shoehorn in a hobby if you are one of those pleasure-seeking libertines, seemed to be the general consensus. I was as affronted as if I'd been asked to expose my body rather than my interests. I blinked and wondered if I had misheard *the question*.

"*Pardon?*"

"*What do you want to do? What career path can I advise you on?*"

"*I was hoping you could help me with that,*" I stammered, realising how pitiful I sounded.

He looked at me suspiciously.

"*You must have some idea of the general area you are hoping to work in?*"

Jesus. This guy was really making me work for it.

"*Well,*" I began, stalling for time, "*without postgraduate qualifications, my degree in English and Classical Civilisation qualifies me for a career in a call centre and not much else.*"

He nodded as if he understood and was mentally adding Career Advisor to the list of things a Humanities degree could lead to.

"*Any ideas of which post-grad courses you would like?*"

I considered the modules I had enjoyed as an undergraduate.

"Creative Writing?"

He seemed relieved to finally be able to scribble something on the page in front of him, and looked up expectantly, prompting a fresh wave of sweat as I cast about mentally for a second option. In my mind, I saw Frances laughing about her teaching practice and her new catchphrase - *Hairy back!* Immediately, my conditioned mind flagged up roadblocks - I'm not confident enough, I'm not middle class enough - but the idea of teaching sparked the white light feeling regardless. The air around me seemed to buzz and hum, and butterflies were freestyling in my tummy.

"Teaching."

From that moment, it was as though a switch had been flicked deep inside me. I was consumed with determination to train as a teacher. The Postgraduate Certificate in Education (PGCE) Primary course was in the University of Ulster, in Coleraine, and the odds were stacked against me. The year I applied, there were seven hundred applicants for the seventy available places. Undeterred, I reframed the odds by reminding myself that I only had to be in the top seventy. Surely, I would be one of the top seventy most determined? I studied the curriculum and rehearsed answers to interview questions into the mirror, over and over. I dyed my bleached hair a conservative brown and toned down my wardrobe. All I had to do was convince the interviewer that I was a teacher, and to achieve this, all I had to do was BE a teacher. Slipping into another persona was easy, I'd done it all my life. Disapproval had made me a chameleon. After years of lamenting my conspicuousness, I understood its gifts. The conspicuous have two choices; learn to blend into the surroundings or get used to being noticed. Both of these skills aided me in going forward, I morphed into a teacher and braced myself to stand in front of a class.

I began to observe teaching in my old primary school once a week, which necessitated going home more frequently than before, and sometimes even staying overnight. There was an ease between myself and my parents now. Martin's death brought us closer by bringing sharp perspective to our former grievances. One evening, Daddy took himself off to bed early, and Mummy and I found ourselves watching a television show about ghosts. The wind sucked flames up the chimney in hollow gusts and I reclined Daddy's chair and pulled a blanket over my knees. An eerie tune overlaid each interviewee's recount of spiritual visitations and the climax of each tale often punctuated with shrill stabs of music. It was grating on my nerves.

"The music is unnecessarily scary," I commented.

Mummy murmured in agreement.

"Surely if someone from the other side visits you, the point wouldn't be to scare you."

She murmured again, and I was reminded of playing charades as a child, the almost involuntary grunts of affirmation as someone was getting close.

I turned to look at her and she was sitting motionless, her eyes shining with secrets. I paused, choosing my words carefully. Mummy was a wee Christian lady and the Bible warned against consorting with such things.

"*I think I was visited.*"

She nodded and smiled.

"*I don't want to be disrespectful, but I think it was your Mummy.*"

"*What was she like?*"

"She looked like you, but taller. Dark hair. Gentle. She felt...very..."

Words were failing me, because it felt trite to say she was kind.

"*She was kind,*" said Mummy simply.

I nodded and my heart started to beat faster. I knew that now was the right time to tell her.

"*I'm pretty sure I saw Martin, too.*"

I searched her face for a sign that I should stop. It remained a mask, a gentle smile, that sense of already knowing what was coming.

"*Yes?*"

"*It was on Easter Sunday. He wanted you and Daddy to know that he is fine.*"

She smiled and nodded, an enigma to me. I had to ask.

"*Have you had any...visitations like that?*"

A curt nod let me know that she had, and that discussing it was not an option. I turned back to the television.

"*It's nice, isn't it, Mummy?*"

"*Yes, love,*" she answered quietly. "*It is.*"

I thought about the many times I had felt haunted in that strange land of fading consciousness and wondered if the dead find it easiest to communicate with the living when we are in that undistracted, receptive state. So many of my experiences had been terrifying and I wondered if negative energies found their way to me when I myself was in a dark place. These loving beings, my Granny Martha and Martin had found their way to me when I was suffused in grief, which I had come to realise is love in its rawest form. The others were drawn by my fear and pain.

I had two years of university left and knuckled down with a new determination to speak up if I found myself floundering. Martin's passing meant I was the sole focus of my parents and I desperately wanted to bring them whatever happiness I could. I endured lectures and classes - the anxiety had been marginally lessened by continuous exposure. My Classics teacher, Dr Sheehan was kind and cheerful. She seemed to genuinely enjoy her job and took great delight in exploring texts with us. She laughed unselfconsciously at her own nerdy Latin grammar jokes, made a point of including everyone in tutorial discussions and if someone seemed lost or unprepared, she explained patiently and moved on without a hint of reproach. She made herself available outside class hours to discuss progress with assignments and wanted us to love the Classics as much as succeed academically. She brought joy to learning and for the first time at Queen's, with her gentle guidance, I felt confident enough to tackle the material, speak up and engage. I achieved good marks in her courses, and had I achieved similar marks in the English component to my degree, I would have achieved a First. As it was, I narrowly missed out and left Queens with a 2.1. Another chapter was over.

Twenty

I always felt Queen's was at its most beautiful in graduation season. The summer sun warmed the earthy tones of brick and stone, and the trimmed lawns were lush and soft as carpet. The imposing symmetry of the Lanyon building, with its gothic architectural nod to the ancient universities provided a stirring backdrop for the proud parents celebrating graduates in timeless flapping midnight gowns and solemn mortar boards. I graduated on just such a cloudless, sunny day.

My parents bought new clothes for the occasion. Despite approaching 60 years of age, Daddy was still very much a handsome man, clean shaven with his short black hair combed to a neat wide side parting. His height and broad shoulders made him a formidable figure and he wore a suit well. Mummy was, in her words, clean and tidy, determined to draw no criticism for vulgarities of make-up or ostentatious attire. Both were socially anxious; Mummy remained quiet and watchful, while Daddy put on a pantomime of confidence, patting my shoulder with his big, heavy paws, smiling broadly and cracking jokes. This was gregarious Daddy who appeared at weddings, who performed for old acquaintances he happened upon in the street, and I suspected he would exhaust himself by noon. Stuart took photographs of the three of us for posterity, and then we went our separate ways to locate seats for the ceremony. When I approached the podium to receive my degree certificate, I searched the rows for their faces. There they sat in the comparative inconspicuousness of the back row, too shy to wave, reluctant to make a show of themselves in this historical place amongst these fine people. We met outside afterwards.

"Well done, kid!"

Daddy flung his arm around my shoulder and beamed around at the other families, circling their graduates and posing for photographs. Mummy looked up at him with wide eyed expectation and he cleared his throat.

"Right! I suppose we had better head home."

I looked from him to Mummy in confusion. Mummy nodded in enthusiastic support of this plan and smiled apologetically at me.

"It's your Daddy's back," she declared. *"It's starting to get sore."*

I felt a stab of disappointment. A sore back meant it was non-negotiable. You can't argue against a bad back.

"But...it's customary to go to lunch after graduation. The parents take their kid out to celebrate," I argued, plaintively.

Daddy lowered his head to confide.

"I can't sit in those hard dining chairs, love. Not for any length of time. It'll set my back off."

I nodded my resignation, knowing that the decision had been made long before this conversation.

"*Look -*" he added, more upbeat. "*Here's a few quid for you and Stuart to go to lunch.*"

He took a fat envelope from his breast pocket and forced it onto Stuart.

"*There's plenty there for a restaurant, and a bit more besides!*" he announced with a wink. "*You don't need us cramping your style.*"

He was pretending to do me a solid, these cool parents who let the kids get on with having fun. My heart plummeted, heavy with the weight of disappointment. I felt sorry for myself, short-changed at the last moment, my sense of abandonment made keener by the juxtaposition of the swathes of proud parents who surrounded our pathetic little group as we navigated this awkward goodbye. I felt sorry for my parents, for whom the idea of public dining in nice restaurants with nice people was so beyond their comfort level as to be untenable. My parents had dressed themselves in the best of clothes, polished their shoes up to a fine shine but couldn't buff off the feeling of being less than. I understood. Despite having attended the good school, the university, it clung to me regardless. I'd learnt it at my mother's knee.

    I felt the sting of their absence as Stuart and I ate the nice food amongst the nice families, trying not to think of how many week's groceries they could have bought with the cost of this meal, swallowing guilt and sadness while wondering if those at neighbouring tables thought I was an orphan, and whether it would be worse if they knew that my parents were alive but felt themselves too unsophisticated to eat in restaurants. Afterwards, I met my classmates at a bar and counted down the seconds until I could jettison the gown and go back to being inconspicuous in my unbelonging.

Having applied for both the Creative Writing Masters and the Postgraduate Certificate in Education, I was offered places for both. I opted for the teaching course, which seemed like the sensible choice in that it yielded an obvious career path. It became apparent, however, that a teaching qualification was not a passport to a job. It was particularly difficult to get a teaching position in Northern Ireland, as evidently most teachers stayed in their positions until retirement, and available posts were advertised with either very specific qualitative criteria (which suggested the likelihood that the job description may have been tailored to a particular candidate already known to the school), or quantitative criteria specifying several more years of experience than us newly qualified teachers could offer. The likelihood of getting an interview, much less a job, was slim, but once again, fate steered my path. A teacher at the school where I had completed a very successful teaching practice was married to a Principal of a different school that urgently needed a Primary Six teacher. It felt like serendipity. Primary Six was the year that Mr Vance showed me that a compassionate teacher could change a child's life.

It was a lovely little school, a wide low building, white with bright emerald framed windows and doors, on a plot of green. The double doors at the front led to a reception hall where the Secretary worked, sorting paperwork and fielding phone calls behind a sliding glass window. The Principal's Office was directly opposite the doors, central and important; here children hushed as they filed past the closed door, cajoled into respectful silence by their teachers. A corridor ran to the left, leading to rooms with various utility - the toilets, the library, the staffroom, ending in a gym that became the dinner hall at midday. The corridor to the right led to classrooms. A series of display boards punctuated the walls, lined with colourful paper that faded and curled as the months passed, festooned with jolly pieces of work or photographs of the children engaged in a variety of learning activities. Navigating the school was a journey of smells; coffee, toilets, the tang of break snacks, light perfume, a savoury lunch wafting up from the gym, cut grass and shafts of sunlight warming dusty textbooks piled on countertops.

My first-year teaching was a baptism of fire. The paperwork alone was a full-time job. Yearly planners had to break down into half-term planners, weekly planners, daily planners. On a normal day, each lesson had to have an explicit introduction, activity and summary session, with differentiation for ability groups within the class. Delivering lessons accounted for only a fraction of the job and I had to find time to understand the curriculum, prepare resources, then assess if learning had taken place. When I wasn't in school, I was at home marking, researching, planning or laminating. It was fast-paced, and

I worked hard to keep my stress levels in check in order to be the kind, benevolent carer they needed.

Despite the workload, I visited my parents frequently. They spent their days, much as they always had since I was six and Martin saved us - together at home, passing their days with a schedule of light meals and hourly news bulletins from the kitchen radio, Daddy eavesdropping from his chair by the window with his ashtray, book, notepad and cigarettes neatly arranged on his side table, Mummy ferrying cups of tea and doing housework.

Each visit, I parked at the side of their block, walked to the gate and stopped a moment to take in Daddy's profile at the window - glasses on, bent over a book. He heard the metal click of the catch on the gate and his outline turned to ascertain it was me. Only then did he set his reading aside to answer the door. Mummy was the designated door answerer unless I was calling, in which event he waved her away and hurried to receive me, while Mummy dashed off into the kitchen to put the kettle on. This flurry of activity was a choreography of excitement on an otherwise uneventful day. I was cherished, but I could only briefly bask in their adulation before a mixture of other emotions tainted my joy - pity that a flying visit from me was such a highlight, sorrow at the Martin shaped hole in our lives, suspicion that my acceptance was a making-do, that had he not died I'd have remained surplus to requirements. Most wearing of all was the effort it took to tamp down the resentment that this demonstrative love had not appeared during my childhood when I had most needed it.

I hated myself for these unbidden thoughts, but still they pushed in as Daddy held open the door that Mummy had been told to shut in my face when I begged to be allowed home at 17, the same door I had fumbled to unlock as white-hot panic overtook me during the beating at 14. I hated myself as these two broken, humbled humans looked to me for a silver lining, arms open, eager to love me. The sad fact was that my narrative had long since been laid down; I was unlovable. In my formative years, love had been conditional so I could not guarantee I would always meet the criteria. Now they meant for their love to bed down in me, but by then love was abstract and flighty, not concrete or dependable. I knew that they loved me, but niggling doubt remained that their love was a reflection of their need rather than of my lovability. I shapeshifted into the good daughter as the front door was flung wide.

Daddy greeted me with a big smile and exclaimed in tones reminiscent of Mr Vance's enthusiastic Peggyyy!
"Ack, kid! What about ye?"
He looked so happy; cheeks pink, dark eyes twinkling.
"Not too bad, Daddy," I smiled.
I followed him into the clinging smoke of the living room, aware of creeping resentment that I would have to wash the smell from my hair for work in the morning.
"Well? How were the kids today?"

"*Ah, grand,*" I replied, as I lowered myself onto the sofa by the electric fire, where glowing artificial coals brought cheer to an otherwise dull room.

Daddy's elation to have produced a teacher was palpable. His reverence for education endured. Most days he sat at his study desk for long afternoons poring over philosophy tomes or algebra textbooks, making notes in the margins or highlighting phrases with a fat yellow marker, smoke curling from the ashtray, his tea forgotten and mug rings branding the leather desktop. He might have made a great teacher himself, in another life where survival could be taken for granted, where opportunities had not been withheld. He lived vicariously through my tales of school.

"*How are they getting on with the practice papers?*"

Primary Six was the year that the kids were drilled for the Transfer Test.

"*Ack, some of them are getting tired. It's a lot for them.*"

"*You have a big responsibility up there at that school. If you get them kids through their qualifying, it could change the trajectory of their whole lives.*"

"*I know, Daddy.*"

"*Remember Mr Vance got you through it?*"

"*I do.*"

"*Great man, Mr Vance. Great man. Now you get to do for them what he did for you,*" he said, looking intently at me over the top of his glasses.

"*Anyway. Do you teach them algebra? The beauty - the logic! - of maths!*"

I smiled at his broad Belfast pronunciation. *Aljee-bra, Loh-jeek,* and the zeal in his eyes.

"*I've to stick to the planners, Daddy. They do it in Primary Seven*"

"*Ack,*" he lamented, a verbal shrug.

I smiled as I pictured how he imagined me as a teacher - some unlikely combination of Little House on the Prairie spinster with no curriculum but her own whims, and Euclid.

"*I didn't see them today. I was on a course earlier this week, about teaching children with dyslexia. It was very interesting.*"

A voice piped up from the kitchen over the white noise of the boiling kettle.

"*Oh? Dyslexia?*"

Daddy nodded his head towards the doorway.

"*Can't hear me shouting for a cup of tea, but she heard that.*"

Mummy shouted back.

"*What did you say?*"

"*Nothing.*"

"*Thought so.*"

He pulled his shoulders up and giggled silently, the picture of mischief, our wee joke.

Mummy appeared around the door with two steaming cups of tea.

"*Here y'are, love! D'ya want a couple of wee biscuits?*" she asked, eyes wide, cajoling.

"*Ack!*" Daddy interjected. "*Give my wee daughter the good treats from my secret hidey-hole!*"

"*I'm okay, Daddy,*" I laughed. He wiggled his eyebrows.

"*Sure, you don't want a wee Turkish Delight?*"

My favourite treat has been purchased and kept specifically for this moment, evidence that they thought of me when they went grocery shopping, that they looked forward to letting me know - through the medium of chocolate - that I was loved, because a lifetime of repression meant that they couldn't just say it.

"*Ooh, go on then,*" I relented.

He beamed and flicked his finger imperiously in the direction of the kitchen, sending Mummy to an old biscuit tin hidden behind porridge boxes.

She returned from the kitchen with her own tea and three Turkish Delights in her cardigan pocket. Mummy ate half of hers and folded the wrapper over the remaining half for later. I nibbled the chocolate off mine, deconstructing the slab to its component parts. Daddy ate his like a civilised human being.

"*So, what about this course, then?*" she prompted.

Mummy was undoubtedly dyslexic. Her abysmal spelling had been a longstanding family joke. One time, my parents had nipped out to the shop and locked the back door behind them. As I climbed in the kitchen window, I caught sight of the little whiteboard where she wrote her shopping list, saw that she had mis-spelled Oxo and took such a fit of giggles that I fell off the counter and nearly did myself a mischief. She had written *Okso*. I could imagine her defensiveness, *Never you worry what's on my board! I know what I mean!* It was only as I got older that I realised she was embarrassed, self-conscious about her difficulties, and our gentle mocking didn't land as the affectionate family banter we had intended.

"Yes, the basic message was that dyslexics process differently, so we as teachers have to amend our teaching to accommodate the different styles of learning."

Mummy looked triumphant.

"So that oul' bitch – godforgimme – Miss Smith was in the wrong?"

"To say the least."

Mummy's cheeks grew pink.

"She used to hit me when I got things wrong! She badgered me in front of all the other kids when I couldn't read a word, or spell a word, until everybody was laughing at me."

"That's horrendous, Mummy."

"I still have nightmares about that aul' bitch - godforgimme. But she was."

She had been terrorised into self-loathing and left with the hallmarks of PTSD - situational panic and nightmares.

"You can't terrorise a child into learning," I confirmed. Mummy nodded, ruffled but vindicated, then looked over at Daddy. *"See?"*

"Ack, that oul' bitch was a sadist. But you have to remember, someone with difficulties in reading can get a dislike for it, and that's when you have to keep them at it, or they'll never get it."

I realised this wasn't about Miss Smith anymore. Daddy was remembering how he had tried to help Mummy with her reading. He was remembering cracking Billy around the head during a reading homework when he decided his son wasn't trying hard enough. An image came to my mind of Daddy broken and weeping in his chair by the window after Martin died, lamenting, *I was too hard on yous*. At the time, I thought these words signalled the beginning of a new Daddy, but ultimately, he still had to find a way to live with himself in a world where it was too late to take it back, where apologies fell on the deaf ears of the dead. He would have no absolution but that which he could allow himself, and so absolve himself he did, because the alternative was relentless self-torment. He sunk into a reflective silence.

Mummy leaned in from her side of the sofa, her face earnest.

"Just be kind to them, won't you? Just one wee word from you could build them up or destroy their confidence."

"I know, Mummy."

"Kids are sensitive wee things. You're kind to them, aren't you?" she inquired nodding, willing it to be so.

I considered the question. I wanted to be kind, and for the most part I was, however, the reality of a classroom was such that in order to deliver a lesson effectively, to keep to a schedule and ensure that everyone was on task meant employing class management techniques. There was being an effective teacher and being a kind teacher, and on stressful days, I had to pick between the two. It was exhausting, but over the first few years, I learned to temper my perfectionism - the urge to demand unrelenting maximum effort - to allow the children to be children, rather than work-producing auto-bots. When the children felt liked, appreciated and seen, they cared enough about my good opinion to want to keep it.

Harder still than ensuring both happiness and productivity in the classroom, was my struggle with the teaching of Religious Education. Unlike the rest of the UK, Northern Ireland does not utilise the opportunity to teach children about the differing doctrines of major religions. Instead, Primary level RE focuses almost exclusively on Christianity. The curriculum is divided into three elements: The Revelation of God, The Christian Church and Morality. Essentially this means that from four years old, children are told about the Christian God, presupposing the existence of one, before they have even developed the reasoning faculties to question it. Christianity is not taught in the context of one amongst many religions, but in isolation. Thirdly, they are taught Morality almost exclusively through the medium of Bible stories, tacitly implying that Christians have the monopoly on moral fortitude. It is a conflation of spirituality and religion - essentially indoctrination. Furthermore, I felt resistant to facilitate Collective Worship. I saw no real opportunity for personal spiritual development through the veneration of a being, and from childhood experience, I knew it could lead to feelings of confusion and isolation.

I felt passionately that school should be a place to learn how to think, rather than what to think, and balked at the arrogance of an education system content to teach opinion as fact and killing inquiry at the root. Having to teach the NI Curriculum for RE posed an ethical quandary. I could keep my head below the parapet, silencing my concerns and performing the job I had been hired to do, but in so doing I would be inflicting the same harm that I had suffered as a child - the terror I felt when I could not assuage my doubt, the guilt of unbelief. However, I didn't wish to appear ungrateful for the opportunity which had been generously extended to me by beginning my teaching career with a list of grievances.

Fulfilling the requirements of the job and trying to adhere to my principles was a contortionist act. Instead of referencing God, I said the God that Christians believe in, which was the best I could do to open that little window for doubt just a crack. I used parables solely as stories to illustrate points of morality, so long as they didn't hinge on the existence of God. I took my turn at holding Assemblies but omitted the collective worship aspect by choosing non-religious songs and deliberately running out of time for the concluding prayer. Eventually, my Assemblies became entirely secular: I used my Assembly time to drum up enthusiasm for World Book Day, or to demonstrate Primary Six's learning on our topics (Vikings, the Rainforest, the Tudors). Sometimes I managed to entice a visiting speaker; an author or poet, for example. On one occasion, I secured a scientist to showcase some fun experiments. My pupils were lined up, ready to walk down the colourful corridor to the assembly hall. We waited patiently as other classes filed past our cheerful yellow doorway.

"What's the theme of today's Assembly?" asked a colleague.

"It's a Science Show," I replied.

A frisson of excitement ran through the passing children.

"And where," inquired another colleague, sounding piqued, *"is the collective worship aspect?"*

There was the charge of confrontation in the air. Pupils close enough to be eavesdropping gaped like bush babies, thirsty for more. Despite the spontaneity of the interaction, I got the sense that my aversion to Religious Education had been discussed. I felt ambushed.

"I don't do collective worship," I stated, blushing, heart pounding from the sudden shock of skirmish and from embarrassment at this public reckoning.

It felt like a slap. I had put such effort into balancing the requirements of the job with my principles, but it was never going to be good enough. No one can serve two masters (a wise Biblical epithet from the book of Matthew, which I am happy to quote, as it doesn't hinge on the existence of God). The effort I was going to was beginning to feel like more trouble than it was worth.

I discussed my dilemma with Melanie over a cup of tea.

"The worst part is…" I considered, *"that I'm expending a lot of energy trying to do the job without compromising my principles, but*

the effort is neither appreciated nor acknowledged. I mean, I don't want a medal or anything, but I'm really trying. I'm exhausted and frankly outraged that I'm in this position at all in this day and age."

"It sounds tough," she agreed, setting out some fun sized treats. I reached for one and peeled off the wrapper.

"I'm required to literally indoctrinate children."

She winced.

"Surely you can object on some grounds or other."

"Well, there's something called the Conscience Clause - which means that I can effectively withdraw from activities that violate my principles."

"That sounds straightforward enough. Why the hesitation?"

I sighed.

"Numerous reasons. It feels duplicitous to suddenly announce that I have issues with aspects of the role I accepted. Where were these principles when I agreed to take the job? And then, assuming I no longer teach RE, the policy states that pupils have a right to a religious education, so another teacher would have to do it. I will not be winning any popularity contests by shunting part of my workload onto a colleague."

Melanie nodded thoughtfully and got that faraway look she got when she was choosing her words carefully.

"Everything has a cost. You get to choose between prioritising your principles at the cost of the good opinion of your colleagues or prioritising an easy working relationship at the cost of your peace. Neither is an easy path, but whoever said life was easy? You get to choose which path to take, which one is the least bad option."

I wrote a letter explaining my intention to invoke the conscience clause, which was discussed and approved at the next Board of Governors meeting. In order to avoid inconveniencing a colleague with having to teach my class RE, I suggested that I could teach about the major world religions. I knew that the other teachers had been informed of this development, but no one asked me about it. The silence spoke volumes. Ours was a chatty staff, we popped in and out of each other's rooms, sometimes just to say hello, usually much more. Everyone was bound to be talking about it, just not to me.

It wasn't long before some made their disaffection with my position evident. One teacher made a huge fuss when I refused to shoe-horn a hymn into my Assembly. Later, a parent complained that I was indoctrinating their child by educating them on the basic tenets of Islam, as if I was trying to create a band of radical Muslims in Protestant Ulster. A different parent took issue with my teaching about Buddhism, worried that I was trying to encourage atheism.

My rejection of the status quo was seen as an affront. I felt alienated from my colleagues, back on the familiar ground of outsider and oddity. It was the price I willingly paid to maintain my integrity.

Twenty-One

After four years of teaching, a relentless little voice was leaving messages in my head letterbox. Over the years, I had come to realise that whoever this voice belonged to - whether it was my Higher Self, a guardian angel, God, a relative in Spirit, I knew their intent by the feelings they overlaid onto me. This messenger allowed me little flashes of possibility, of inspiration. It was light, breezy, the colour of joy. It asked me to release with gratitude this career that had given me the opportunity to develop both personal and professional fortitude and nudged me on to new horizons.

As my intuition urged me forward, fear restrained me. The fear I felt did not come from an external source, it was all me. My brain worked overtime throwing up worst case scenarios, telling me to stay small and still and safe from the danger of change. I ruminated on how this career was the culmination of every exam I had studied for, over many years, a lucky break that I was throwing away. I was 27, that fork-in-the-road age of now or never, when we either put down roots or move on to something new, the year of get married or break up, of shit or get off the pot. I had the vague notion that there was more inside me to be made manifest and I didn't want to wait until retirement to find out what that was. The thought of being 65 and still teaching, my song still inside me, unsung, was horrifying. I didn't even know what my song was, but I felt instinctively I had one locked away and I wasn't going to find the key by staying where I was. I felt young enough to start again but old enough that there was no time to waste.

Like Joan Didion, I don't know what I think until I write it down. I retired to bed, pulled the duvet up over my knees and wrote prolifically, at first great lists of pros and cons, ruminative paragraphs of what-ifs and even a couple of obituaries - one an account of an uninspiring life where I stayed teaching, the other a manifestation of all the wildest joy I could imagine for myself, which turned out was not that wild, but entirely different from the path I was on. The longer I wrote, the calmer I became, until I was in a receptive state, no longer marshalling thoughts, but channelling ideas from the white light, my friend of old. In that humming, sacred space, phrases and images floated through the thin veil from unmanifest to manifest. My head letterbox was wide open and every missive was a delicious little flash of a potential future where I brought my flawed self into the world instead of fitting a box, where I dressed for myself instead of for my job. I am most myself when I write, and as I daydreamed about spending my days writing, I remembered the Creative Writing Masters I had passed up three years before. Sure, and steady voices insisted that they had shown me all they could.

But when do we ever trust our own knowing straightaway? For some reason, I felt unqualified to be the sole executor of decisions regarding my own life and yearned to proffer the wheel to someone more enlightened, someone with more distance from the quandary I was in. Friends were no help – they simply reiterated what I already knew and had the same fear-based reluctance. I wished I had a friend with a more transcendent view, unsullied by fear. The problem was that there isn't a person alive who is thus unencumbered, but I suspected that a few dead ones might be. I went to a medium, and although I didn't realise it at the time, I was there not for insight but for permission.

I booked a session for both myself and Melanie. We drove down together, giddy and giggling with excitement.
"Oh, God, I really hope we don't end up laughing!"
"Oh, no! Why did you say that?!"

We had a longstanding history of never, ever being able to make eye contact in a sombre situation without setting each other off in fits of giggles. There had been numerous School Assemblies where we sat, shoulders shaking with silent mirth, discreetly wiping tears of laughter, faces turned away from each other to avoid catching a peripheral glance that could set us off again. There was the time we went to an Angel Meditation workshop and almost burst blood vessels trying to suppress our laughter while others were literally being moved to tears with the profundity of their experience. Or the time she showed up to give me a lift to a yoga class wearing heels, having forgotten her leisure wear. I lent her a pair of Converse, which looked ridiculous on her as her feet are many sizes smaller than mine. When we arrived at the class, it transpired that she had mistakenly booked us into a Yogi lecture, and we sat with six others having a live web chat with a Buddhist monk in India who expressed solemn truths while Melanie sat there looking like Sideshow Bob. When the guy closest to the screen started to snore, I felt Melanie tense against laughing and almost blacked out from holding my breath.

   I decided it might be a good idea to get all of our giddiness out before we arrived.

"Mel."

"Uh hmm?"

"Did you know I can drive with my eyes closed?"

"What?"

"Yeah. Watch this!"

I waited until she turned to look and closed my left eye which she could see from her position beside me in the passenger seat.

"Peggy! Don't!"

"It's okay, I'm really good at it. Am I closer to the kerb or the median line?"

"You're in the middle - but STOP IT!"

I carried on for a good thirty seconds throwing in the odd, *Am I doing okay?* as she lost her shit. When I revealed the joke, we both went into hysterics, but sadly, my plan backfired - if anything, I'd added fuel to the fire. When we eventually calmed down, Melanie grew pensive.

"I'm not sure I want her to read both of us together. What if she says something super private?"

"Like what?! Stop pretending you're this really intriguing, complex character!"

"But what if she says something really embarrassing? Or awful? Nah, I want to be taken separately."

"Well, you may tell her."

"You're brave, you do it."

"Nah, mate."

And on it went, back and forth until we stood on the doorstep of a tiny bungalow, touching cloth with trepidation. The door opened, and there stood a small, slight woman with red hair and fair skin. She looked very relaxed, almost dazed, but spoke very quickly, with an unusual brogue – a mid-Ulster accent with some words taking on a Lancashire inflection. She motioned us into her living room.

"Come in, pick a seat. Ooh, they've been at me all day, they have. Especially yours."

She pointed at me.

"Your granny has a lot to say. I won't hang about, let's get stuck in."

The living room had been decorated in a monochrome greyscale. It was minimalist and utilitarian, with a few cursive script wooden signs declaring Love and suchlike. A bookcase displayed a collection of faceless wooden angel vignettes, simple figures with whitewashed cloaks and wings; a mother and daughter, a couple, a young nuclear family. We lowered ourselves sheepishly onto the sofa and I felt a tell-tale rigidity from Melanie's arm as it brushed against mine. I was perfectly composed but that tiny muscle inflection was enough to tell me that I must not, under any circumstances, look at her face. Fortunately, the medium was paying us no attention whatsoever. In fact, as we both struggled to maintain composure, her head cocked to the left, and she looked down as if straining to hear. She murmured.

"Uh huh. Yes. Oh, really? Okay…"

I was intrigued at this pantomime of communication until she snapped her attention back to us two emotionally uncomfortable eejits on her sofa and said,

"They are telling me that you want to be taken separately. Is that right?"

Mirth fled the room and we gaped wordlessly, nodding.

"So, who is going first?"

Mel volunteered and was ushered into the kitchen, while I sat in the living room unsuccessfully straining to eavesdrop. I had to content myself with re-runs of Most Haunted which played on a low volume as the minutes dragged by. When Melanie eventually re-emerged, she was pink cheeked and dazed. I whispered,

"Was it good?"
She nodded, wide-eyed.
"She said to send you straight in."

Brilliant. The moment had arrived. I proceeded to the kitchen and sat down, desperately hoping some sympathetic spirit might have a better overview of my life and could tell me what the best path was.

"Okay, I have to tell you straight off that they are telling me that you will write the book. Are you a writer?"
"Well, no, but maybe someday…"
"You write it," she interjected. *"Is it a travel guide of some kind? It's something to do with a journey, a kind of guidebook. Are you much of a traveller?"*
"No, I'm really not."
She shrugged.
"You write the book. Like a handbook for a journey."
I nodded, uncertainly.
"This wee woman has had me tortured since this morning! She says she's your granny. Your mummy's mummy – M name…Mmmm – Martha, is it?"
It was.
"She has no back doors, this one. Very blunt and to the point. She has a good sense of humour – swears a bit, does your granny."
"I don't know. I never met her."

Was it okay to say that? Had I just given her carte blanche to make up anything, in the understanding that I would be unable to verify it? She looked at my face.

"You look like her. You have her cheeks – they go into wee apples when you smile. Your mummy, too. She is showing me your mummy when she was younger, always had her hair in a plait. Now she is showing me that she was very clean and tidy, always cleaning her surfaces. And proper, she is pulling her cardigan round her bosom. Okay, I feel it in my throat – did she die from throat cancer? Okay, that's her. Ah, she left your mummy young. And your mummy…uh oh. Okay, she doesn't like your daddy much. Says he was a bad boy? Was he in prison? Okay."

She broke off, understanding that she had given sufficient validation.

"She says you are here with a question."

This was it. I finally had the attention of someone whose perspective was transcendent, who could intuit what was for my highest good from a place of knowing. I steeled myself.

"Yes. I want to know if I should leave my job."

She cocked her head to the left and began to nod, evidently receiving my much-desired insight. My heart raced with anticipation.

"Uh huh. Yes. Okay. Uh huh. Well, that makes sense. Yes. Mmm hmm."

I held my breath.

"She says she knows but she won't tell you. You need to work it out for yourself. She's not allowed to tell you what to do. She's gloating a bit, actually. She says she knows what you do, but she won't say. She's laughing."

I felt deflated and a bit cross. I wondered if she had accessed my granny at all, or if she had just been cold reading me the whole time and held back from giving actual advice as if that was a step too far; even the unethical had to draw a line somewhere.

"*Your granny watches over you, you know.*"

Oh aye, here we go.

"*She says that when she is close by, you will know, because you will feel this —.*"

And she reached across the table and stroked my cheek with the crook of her finger, exactly as my granny had done that night, I felt haunted and she came to tell me to look after mummy. Goosebumps rose on my arms.

"*Okay, that's her away but there are other ones here waiting to give you a message. I am being told you are a bit psychic yourself, is that right?*"

I shrugged.

"*I suppose I might have had a few unusual experiences,*" I said, feeling somewhat abashed.

"*Well, there are a few spirit guides here — one is a big Red Indian— and I am being told that there is a book you need to read. Hold on, I have never heard of that one before. Give me it again? P... Newton...no – P. H. Newton. I don't know, they say I haven't read it, but you need to, it will put you on the right road. P. H. Newton — you may google it.*"

I scribbled the name on to the page I had brought for notes.

"*Do you have any other questions? They might not answer, but you might as well try.*"

I did. I had been waiting the whole time for my brother. I wasn't sure how to ask about him, without it seeming like a reproach: *I have this massive, gaping wound of grief that you haven't picked up on.*
I simply said, *"My brother."*
She smiled and pointed to my left shoulder.
"There's a young man stood there, smiling."
I felt cross again, surely if he was there, she would have mentioned it before. Was she saving face?
"He has such a great smile. He is looking a bit older than he was when he died...he is in his late teens here, but I am getting the sense that he died younger."
Desperation made me a cynic, it was too good to be true, so I focused on her vague description as evidence that she was guessing. I wanted more than vague descriptions. I wanted something that only I could know, like the exact way my granny touched my cheek with her finger.
"Why is he pointing to his shirt? Was he a mechanic?"

I was gutted. She was guessing professions now.
"No. He was a footballer."
"Ah. Okay, I thought he was a mechanic because there are spots all down the front of his shirt. I thought it was oil...He keeps pointing at it, though. It must be important. Does that mean anything to you?"

And there it was - the one thing that only I knew about - the shirt, speckled with blood that I had dispatched and never spoken of since. This image was so much more than confirmation that it was him, it was also confirmation that he had been with me when I opened that bag, that he existed to witness it after he died.

During the journey home, Melanie and I breathlessly discussed details of our readings before drifting into stunned wordlessness. The car hummed along the dual carriageway, monotonous but for the hypnotic rise and fall of electricity cables, measuring our journey back to tangible life.

As soon as I got home, I flicked open my laptop to search for the book by P. H. Newton, to no avail. I tried googling the name with words, such as psychic, spirituality and so on, until eventually I found Journey of Souls by Michael Newton, PhD. and felt certain this was it. I ordered the book and looked forward to it arriving. Before I closed the laptop, I felt a push to check the Queens website for details about the Creative Writing Masters course. The deadline for applying was imminent. Wavering between intuitive optimism and conditioned pessimism had given me emotional whiplash. Ultimately, I made the decision to trust the voice, the inspiration, the joy, because nothing good comes from decisions made out of fear. I hastily printed off an old piece of writing I had completed as an undergraduate and submitted it with my application. The universe had been poking me for months and I had responded in the nick of time.

∞∞∞

The book arrived a few days later. It consisted of numerous accounts, accessed via hypnosis, of the space between lives. Reading it was a staggering experience. It was as though someone had taken my own strange suspicions about the afterlife and had written them down. I had long suspected that we have multiple lifetimes to achieve spiritual evolution and that some obstacles and opportunities are predestined. Neither did I believe that we were judged by a vengeful deity but instead we delivered our own judgement in that space between lives, our true home, where the filter of earthly conditioning falls away and we see ourselves with clarity. I have recommended this book to many people, and it never fails to amuse me that it has not yet had the life-altering effect on a single other person that it had on me. I owe a debt of gratitude to whoever whispered the details into the medium's ear.

Even after all the magic of the previous few months (that sense of channelling when I was writing, and the many validations conveyed through the medium) I could not allow myself to believe. I had spent years decrying faith as a foolishness, because, by definition, faith is a belief without reason, and those who believe without reason cannot be convinced by reason. Faith had long seemed to me a wilful abdication of intellect, yet here I was on the verge of being hoisted by my own petard. Much as I wanted to, I could not allow myself the arrogance of the certainty of faith and wondered if Melanie had similar difficulties processing our shared foray into the beyond. We met in a coffee shop one evening the following week.

"Could it all be bullshit?"

Melanie ran her spoon over the pattern made by the frothed milk on her latte.

"How do you mean?"

"Well, Derren Brown can cold read people. That medium could have been reading our micro-expressions, feeling her way towards a recognisable description of a loved one."

"Well, yes, I suppose so. But what about how your granny touched your face? You have to admit, for her to describe the only contact you've ever had with your granny, that's something."

"Yeah, but perhaps all grannies do that. Maybe it isn't so unusual."

I looked around the cafe, feigning indifference, but desperately hoping that this small gap in our conversation would be enough for some insight to find its way through Melanie and to me, an insight that could banish my doubt and deliver certainty.

"What about Martin?" she offered. *"The shirt?"*

"Maybe once I'd confirmed I'd lost a brother, she realised that he died young and the young don't usually die of natural causes, so she hedged her bets on an accident."

"Okay…" said Melanie, settling into our familiar pattern of cross-examination, *"but you have to admit, that book she channelled has been a game changer for you. How would she have known?"*

"Maybe she didn't channel it. She could have been testing the waters when she suggested I was a bit psychic, then recommended a book that she knew about already. Telling me an approximation of the author's name gave credibility to her pantomime of channelling."

Melanie thought for a moment, chewing on her lip, before delivering the trump card.

"It felt real, though."

I nodded and drained the last of my tea.

"It did. But then, we wanted it to be. There's a chance that she earns a clean fortune cold-reading people. Maybe she doesn't even realise she is cold reading people, and we were so desperate to hear something validating that we subconsciously colluded in a delusion."

"Oh God..." she whined, *"we will never know for sure! Why do you have to think so much?"*

I threw my hands up in exasperation.

"Tell me about it."

Not long after, I received a letter offering me a place on the Creative Writing Masters course. I took it as a sign, choosing to trust the otherworldly guidance of the previous months, and in the words of Philip Larkin's Poetry of Departure, I chucked up everything and cleared off. I had no wage to rely on, didn't know where I was going to live or how I would manage to pay rent, but I had to find a way. I advertised my services as a private tutor, found a tiny, but newly renovated flat in an area I had always loved and began my new life. In the course of a few months, I had re-written my script. I was no longer a teacher, gathering dust until retirement but a budding writer with a terrifyingly clean slate.

Twenty-Two

Returning to full time education as a mature student at 27, I felt rather inclined to agree with the notion that youth is wasted on the young. I no longer felt like a fraud as I had as an undergraduate, suffocated by my sense of unbelonging. Having had some life experience and time, to figure out who I am and what I want meant that I was coming to education with intention and motivation. This time I embraced the joy of having days to learn and write. I relished listening to visiting authors read from their books in high ceilinged lecture halls and felt privileged to speak with them at the receptions in the Seamus Heaney Centre afterwards.

It turned out to be an exhilarating year, the first year in which I really felt I could be myself. Instead of trying to blend in, or get by, I danced to the beat of my own drum. I said what I thought without fear of judgement and dressed like I had rolled on the floor of a charity shop in the dark. My particular penchant was to wear dresses with wide-legged trousers underneath, allowing vast swathes of fabric to rustle and swish as I walked. I felt like a bad ass motherflipper, swanning up and down Botanic like the superstar of my own life. My style was striking enough to earn the admiration of a fellow postgraduate who penned a rather flattering poem about me. My acceptance of myself was contagious.

Having said that, not everyone was a fan. One day I was walking towards the City Centre wearing an ostentatious, oversized pair of sunglasses, thinking I looked pretty rock and roll. A car drove past, and its inhabitants jeered, *"Wearing sunglasses, are ye?"* - hooting with laughter at their remarkable understatement. It was a proud Belfast tradition, a carload of lads frightening the bejaysus out of unsuspecting bystanders with a well-timed heckle. Over the years, I have enjoyed witnessing the startle reflex of many a victim to the gulders of, *"Cycling, are ye?"* or *"Jogging, are ye?"* and my personal all-time favourite - a chap with neither getaway car nor companion, powerless to resist the urge of a jibe who bellowed, *"Learning, are ye?"* through the doors of the Seamus Heaney library, before legging it to the anonymity of the adjacent Botanic Gardens. I shook off the affront, and might have recovered my confidence, but minutes later a girl ran up to me, grabbed my arm and breathlessly demanded,

"Are you the City Beat Prize Pilot?"

As I looked at her in confusion, I had a dull recollection that City Beat, a local radio station often did giveaways and deduced that a Prize Pilot must be someone who hands out gifts wearing pilot goggles. I don't know which of us was more embarrassed. I retired those sunglasses. Belfast just wasn't ready for them.

I found a newly renovated second-floor one bedroom flat off Botanic, tiny and cosy as a turret, and spent hour after hour writing in glorious isolation. Of all the microcosm areas of Belfast, Botanic always seemed least sectarian, being equidistant from the loyalist Sandy Row and Donegall Pass areas and predominantly nationalist Ormeau Road. The proliferation of rental accommodation determined a greater than average quota of immigrants, giving it the potential to be a wonderful melting pot, an intimation that things could get better for all of us. On workshop days I walked five minutes up the ever-congested road lined with cafes, restaurants and well picked over charity and vintage shops. My classmates and I shared our work in those hallowed little rooms in the red-brick terrace on University Square, analysing and critiquing meaning and nuance, plot and theme - joy marred only occasionally by the awkwardness of having to face a classmate with whom a tipsy kiss had been shared at the last social. It was a giddy little return to youth, a last hurrah, and those of us who were repeat snog offenders coined the moniker Yardies, in recognition of our propensity to shit in our own backyards.

This was a one-year course and I needed to start making plans for what to do once it was over. Although the money was decent, I was averse to the idea of returning to teaching and considered applying for a PhD in order to buy myself three more years of self-indulgence. However, I couldn't shake the feeling that there was a missing jigsaw piece, a vital element to my moving forward that I had overlooked.

My mind kept returning to Journey of Souls. It had been gratifying to read a book where so many of the ideas expressed coincided with my own perspective regarding the idea that we set our spiritual intentions prior to undertaking a human life. Mostly, I envied how hypnotic regression yielded insight and meaning for each participant. I too wished for this clarity of purpose. However, each case study portrayed in the book did not have an eureka moment when they found the right career; their peace came from successfully fulfilling their contracts with other members of their soul group; their family and friends. Despite the need for an imminent decision regarding my next career move, I felt it more pressing to ascertain the overarching aims of my life, the broader and more elusive question - why are we here? It dawned on me that we are hoodwinked into conflating purpose and career, into seeing our worth as commensurate to our utility to a capitalist system. In a nutshell, it mattered less to me whether I was a teacher or an academic; I understood that the success of my life was to be measured by relationships. It was time to get clarity on the life objectives I had established before incarnating.

There were no official Life Between Lives hypnotherapists practising near me, so I endeavoured to find a past-life hypnotherapist who seemed open to the idea of facilitating a regression to the space between lives instead. I searched online and got a good feeling about a chap in North Belfast called Joe Boyle. When I phoned him and explained my aims, he seemed very receptive, so I made an appointment for the Saturday of the following week.

With effervescent excitement, I tapped his postcode into the sat nav and was directed to the bottleneck traffic at the bottom of West Belfast's Falls Road. Here, the city gateway was marked by the Rise Sculpture, an art installation forty metres tall, consisting of two skeleton spheres, the smaller inside the larger. The artist's intention was to represent a hopeful future for a new Belfast, rising like the sun and a halo to illuminate a new promising future. Sadly, this worthy concept didn't catch on, and instead, with typical Belfast humour, it soon came to be known as The Balls on the Falls, The Testes of the Westies, and most concise of all, The Westicles. Here, I miraculously navigated the confounding lanes and lights of the Broadway Roundabout to join the Westlink, where many a joyride had been cut short by police spike strips, past the Royal Hospital and the notorious Tricolour festooned Divis flats - a flashpoint area at the height of the Troubles. Driving away from the exhaust-stained greys of central Belfast, traffic eased, and wide roads unfurled into residential offshoots bordered by trees and parks. I pulled into a leafy side street of detached and semi-detached houses. This was affluent North Belfast, known for the proliferation of period homes within a manageable commute to the city centre, a stone's throw, but a world away.

I rang the bell and watched the light ripple and morph through the frosted pane of the half-glazed door as a tall, thin figure emerged from a back room. As the door opened, I was reassured to see a grandfatherly, white-bearded man, bald, eyes crinkled in a welcoming smile. He gestured me into the hallway and explained in the refined Belfast accent of the middle class (tinged with a lilt indicating he might hail from further afield) that our session was to take place in the first room on the left. It was a former parlour turned consulting room, the walls lined with bookcases groaning under the weight of numerous tomes, certainly gathered over many years. Two comfortably padded, green leather reclining chairs sat facing each other, the one in the bay window had a matching footstool. It was here Joe gestured for me to sit.

"Well, it's nice to meet you," he said warmly.

"And you! I've been looking forward to today."

"Indeed. It's an unusual one for me, you know. I've guided many past life regressions, but this is the first Between Lives regression, as you put it."

"Are you on board with the idea of such a place?"

"Oh, absolutely. I'm looking forward to seeing what we can unearth. On the phone, I asked you to compile a list of questions you wish to know the answers to, in order to keep us focused and on track. Do you have them with you?"

"I do."

I passed him a sheet of paper and he reached for his glasses. I was more excited than I had been when

visiting the medium, because this time I was to be the vessel through which the other side might be accessed. My aims were simple: I hoped to visit the space between lives in order to access my higher self and those of my family members in the hope of establishing what our soul contracts are - in other words, why we chose to incarnate together and what we hoped to learn from it. Joe pored over the page, occasionally seeking clarity or specificity. He was thorough and I felt reassured to note that he seemed keen to maximise the utility of our session. Once satisfied, he leaned back in his chair and smiled gently.
"Are you ready?"

I got myself comfortable and exhaled a long, calming breath. Joe guided me into a state of relaxation to facilitate the hoped-for journey to another realm. In my hypnotic state, I was only barely aware that my body lay on a green leather reclining chair opposite Joe in a book-lined room. Instead, my awareness was in a dark, velvety space accompanied by a spirit guide. He was a tall man in Native American dress wearing a large, unnerving mask crudely painted with a grotesque grin. At Joe's prompting, I asked him to remove the mask or tell me his name, both requests were gently but flatly denied. I knew this was his prerogative and felt safe with him, regardless of the mystery, knowing him to be an old friend who could see me more clearly than my layers of conditioning allowed me to see myself. His physical appearance was just an image I was being shown, but really, we were both disembodied energy, simultaneously everywhere, yet nowhere, floating through this dark tunnel towards another non-space. When we arrived, another image was imparted: he had delivered me to a campfire. Large boulders surrounded a crackling blaze. It was the twilight of so many of my dreams. My soul mates were there, recognisable to me by how they felt as I drew my attention to each of them in turn. These light beings took on the form I knew from this life, as they waited in the background, away from the fire, or sat close, watching the flames dance, both the living and the dead, co-existing in their purest form. Those who were still alive on earth were as present as those who had passed, a holograph, whole and no less real than their earthly counterpart. It was a meeting of our Higher Selves.

The following is a transcript of the recording, where Joe prompts me to ask questions which we had discussed before the session began. Each question is followed by a long pause and my answers were murmured as though talking in my sleep.

Joe: Can you ask your spirit guide and members of your soul group what your life's purpose is?
Me: I'm here to teach.
Joe: What kind of teaching are you here to do?
Me: Teaching through example. Teaching one on one. Teaching by sharing myself and relating. I'm a most effective teacher when I teach with kindness.
Joe: What kind of preparation do you need for this?
Me: I have it already.
(Joe knows I'm a primary school teacher).
Joe: So, a primary school teacher?

Me: For a while.

Joe: So, what other avenues should you explore?

Me: I need to develop my intuition and not second guess myself anymore.

Joe: Are there any other skills you need?

Me: I need to write.

Joe: What type of writing?

Me: Speaking from the heart.

Joe: Is there anything else you need to know about this path?

Me: Everything that I've been through so far has taught me something. The learning has occurred. I can stop feeling like something bad is about to happen. I just have to look at where I've been to see where I'm going.

Joe: Do you have anything else to ask the members of your soul group?

(In my mind, I move towards Daddy and silently ask why our relationship is so fraught).

Me: Daddy and I have experienced numerous lives together. I'm usually the parent. He always kicks against authority. In this life, we decided I would be the child and he the parent so that he didn't feel that I was dictating to him when I am trying to help him see a different perspective. We have had some success with this dynamic.

(I move towards Jeanette to ask if we have anything to learn from each other as siblings).

Me: With Jeanette, I always focus on how we are so different, but now I see that we are fundamentally very similar. We both have kindness and teaching ability. We both help people in a quiet way.

(I move towards Martin).

Me: Martin chose to be here for a short time. He had different functions for different family members. For me, his role was simple. His presence meant I didn't have to feel so lonely when I was growing up. His contract with our parents was more complex.

(I move towards Mummy).

Me: Mummy is hurt and fragile. She needs to be looked after. Granny is stepping forward to remind me that this is my job now. She says I need to be more open with her.

Joe: Is there anyone else there for you to communicate with?

Me: There are periphery members of this soul group, ones who have already passed. They are watching us with interest. This has been a tricky one for some of us. It has been...testing.

Joe: Are there any other members of this soul group who you haven't met in this lifetime yet?

Me: I have new teachers down the line; people who are proficient in their areas. They will encourage and strengthen me. They will teach with love.

I pause for a moment and continue.

Me: The writing isn't the primary thing at the minute, the primary thing is to hold on to this spiritual awareness and not be clouded by events or my mind.

Joe: Are there any steps you should take to enable this?

Me: Being open to spiritual guidance. I'll write my dreams into a dream diary and this will help me see the meaning of the dreams, some things will be obvious. Dreams enable two-way communication with the other members of the soul group.

Joe: I'm going to be quiet and let your experience of the space between lives unfold without my intervention.

In my mind, I stand quietly and wait. Martin moved closer.

Me: Martin's telling me he had joy in his life. I'm so hung up on the unfairness of him dying young and wondering if he was happy when he was here, but he's showing me an image of him playing football and feeling great satisfaction. He's telling me that his playing football was poetry in motion. I'm focusing too much on his utility as a tool for growth and forgetting who he actually was.

I approach Daddy's energy.

Me: I need to help Daddy make his last years productive ones, healing ones.

My consciousness reaches out towards Billy.

Me: Billy is more spiritually evolved than the rest of us. He is selfless and patient. When he was here, you could see the selflessness and patience in his eyes. Now he is in the space between lives, he is doing meaningful work.

I take my focus off the others and allow understanding to flow in.

Me: I need to stay open to other people and not hold myself back. There are people on earth who can provide an example of how to do that well. I need to be aware of energy exchanges and how I speak to people, how words can leave a mark on a person, how we get to choose the marks we leave on people with the words we select. In being open to others we should feel light, like going with the flow.

Joe: Any last messages before you go?

Me: I've to keep my eyes open. Opportunities that present themselves need to be taken. I am in tune enough to get a yes feeling but I have to stop letting my mind take over and talk myself out of things that will be beneficial. It's safe to be happy - I've been conditioned to be wary of happiness, as if it tempts fate. Life is just as simple as taking care of each other.

I see my granny stepping forward with a wry smile.

Me: Granny Martha says no more sneaky peeks, I can work things out for myself.

Joe: Thank the members of your soul group for meeting with you. I'm guiding you away from them and very soon I will count back from ten.

As Joe began to count back, I visualised myself imparting gratitude to each soul in turn, then descended through the black tunnel towards earth. I turned for one last glance, a final goodbye. Unexpectedly, my masked guide stepped forward and extracted a small ball of light from his chest. He threw it gently towards me and when it landed on my chest, I understood it to be a message, light packed with information, and I suddenly realised that he was Reggie, my childhood friend. This Native American guide showed me that his boy-self had joined me in my childhood to ease my loneliness and be the friend I lacked. Happy, incredulous tears sprung to my eyes and I was jolted back, thrilled and suddenly wide awake on a green recliner in a room full of books. That mask was intended to throw me off the scent to ensure that I would fail to recognise him and stay tranquil enough to access the beyond. I saw an image of the mask again some years later - it was that of a Native American medicine man.

Somehow, although it felt much shorter, I had been with Joe for almost three hours, by which time I had accrued multiple missed calls from an intrigued and increasingly impatient Melanie. I put on the hands free in the car and set out for home. She answered on the second ring and had no time for pleasantries.

"Well?"

I wasn't sure where to begin. The idea that I had accessed wisdom in the space between lives raised as many questions as it answered, so I simply relayed the narrative as reported to Joe.

"Peggy - that's amazing!"

"It is," I agreed, but she had picked up the hesitation in my voice.

"Oh no. You've rationalised it all away already, haven't you?"

"Not quite," I laughed. *"Well, kind of...it's just that-"*

"Just what? How can you challenge your own first-hand experience?"

"Well, everything that transpired during hypnosis was suspiciously in line with my spiritual views. Did my subconscious create a comfortable wee echo chamber?"

Quick as a whip, she flashed back.

"You've never talked about Martin having been happy, in fact, I remember you being upset that he was snatched away before he got a chance to enjoy his life."

"So did I invent the delusion of him having been fulfilled so that I can feel better about him having died young?"

"Okay, but you have to admit that the Native American sending his child self to be your imaginary friend came out of left field. You said that it shocked you."

"It really did. That ball of light and the sudden understanding - it felt like it came from outside of me."

"See?"

We shared silence as I left the motorway and I unplugged the sat nav as I flowed into the familiar roads of South Belfast.

"What are you thinking?" Mel prompted.

"Only that...it's interesting that I would tell myself that it isn't tempting fate to be happy."

"You've grown up with parents who wear their pain as a talisman, it's no wonder you think that way."

"Agreed. But how can the mind who cleaves to that belief for safety be the same mind that rejects it?"

"You said it already, it felt like the insight was coming from someone else. Not you."

"But it's so fantastical! And I can't prove it was real!"

Melanie laughed.

"Remember when Harry asks Dumbledore if their meeting in the 'beyond' at King's Cross Station was real, or all in his head?"

I laughed too and quoted the relevant line.

"Of course, it's happening inside your head, Harry, but why on earth should that mean it's not real?"

"Nerrrrrd!"

As the academic year drew to a close, I applied to do a PhD in Creative Writing, mainly because teaching felt like a step backwards, a return to an old life I had outgrown. I assumed I was a shoo-in: my marks were good, and my proposal was tight - I ran it past the Head of the School of English and had the enthusiastic support of two faculty members who proposed and seconded it. However, my rejection letter arrived on the Tuesday of the week that the PhD proposals were being considered. I had somehow been rejected on the basis of the course being oversubscribed - before they had even looked at all of the applications. It later transpired that some panel members objected to my theme, *A Critical Analysis of the Portrayal of the Loyalist in Northern Irish fiction,* feeling it to be distasteful to their Irish Nationalist sensibilities. I initially felt furious that such bigotry was permitted, but that quiet, insistent voice told me that it was not my path. The PhD route might have been enjoyable, and I could have written fairly well, but I still lacked something worth saying. My ideas weren't lean enough yet. It was such an unlikely curveball that after I had recovered from shock and anger, I had to concede that maybe I hadn't learned everything I needed to from teaching after all. The doors to Queens were firmly shut and I reluctantly, begrudgingly went back to teaching.

Twenty-Three

A year away from the coalface had made me judgemental. I had forgotten how difficult it was to undertake the immense workload of teaching while keeping stress levels in check sufficiently in order to stay kind. Hard as it had been in my first four years of teaching, a number of changes had occurred while I was a student gallivanting around Belfast which meant that my workload had ramped up considerably.

Firstly, the 11 Plus transfer test (the test which I had passed under the tutelage of Mr Vance in Primary 6) was being scrapped. The newly appointed Sinn Fein Minister for Education argued that it branded the majority of children failures at age 11 and unfairly discriminated against children from poorer backgrounds. Unionist DUP and UUP politicians fought robustly to maintain the system, reasoning that academic selection promoted social mobility and asserting that it would be replaced by a more unfair system of selection. The polarised parties were long embittered adversaries, each determined to thwart the plans of the other, making a political football of the test. The local news stations provided regular bulletins and newspapers printed opinion pieces for and against this new development. Staff rooms were awash with uncertainty and parents inquired nervously at the gates: what will happen to our kids? What measures will replace the 11 Plus?

New admissions criteria would ultimately replace academic selection. Catchment area was key, but those in receipt of free school meals were to take precedence. Working parents panicked that their children would be disadvantaged by this and house prices near Grammar schools began to sky-rocket. Grammar Schools responded by joining forces to provide their own academic selection test. Two organisations were birthed: the PPTC (Post-Primary Transfer Consortium) who provided the GL (General Learning) test for Catholic Grammar schools and the AQE (Association for Quality Assessment) who provided the CEA (Common Entrance Exam) for Protestant Grammar schools. This effectively privatised the 11 Plus and meant that parents would have to pay for their children to sit the AQE test. Although the specifications were ostensibly the same as for the 11 Plus, Science had been jettisoned, meaning there was no buffer for weakness in either English or Maths. Furthermore, the tests were in two different formats: question and answer format for AQE and multiple choice for GL. Worse still, those eleven-year-olds who had to hedge their bets and apply to both Catholic and Protestant Grammar schools found themselves having to attend two unfamiliar test centres to sit five tests in two different formats.

My own experience of the 11 Plus meant that I was still very much pro academic selection. Under the new guidelines, I would have gained admission to a Grammar School by being in receipt of free school meals, but I infinitely preferred the narrative of having achieved a Grammar School place on merit instead of charity. I recalled the abject horror of my eleven-year-old self in Miss Hillis's class when faced with the humiliating prospect of being exposed as poor. Furthermore, I felt doubtful that the standard of teaching at the Grammars would have remained high had there been a long academic tail for teachers to cater for. I had achieved my place on merit and had received an appropriately high standard of tutelage. It did not sit well that a change to the system could rob my pupils of the same opportunity.

It seemed to me that the test was a symptom of a broken system, rather than the cause of it; that the central issue was the emphasis placed on academic talents to the detriment of other types of intelligence. As the Einstein meme illustrates, *"Everybody is a genius, but if you judge a fish by its ability to climb a tree, it will live its whole life believing that it is stupid."* The solution was not to chop down the tree, but to provide mediums within which other talents could manifest and succeed. To me, getting rid of the 11 Plus was like throwing the baby out with the bathwater.

My musings were moot. The Board of Education was rolling out the New Curriculum and threatened disciplinary measures for schools which insisted on preparing their pupils for the 'breakaway test'. Schools which adhered to the new guidance risked unhappy parents withdrawing their children to be enrolled in schools covertly preparing pupils, and fewer pupils meant less funding. Primary school principals found themselves between a rock and a hard place. Like many of the Primary 6 teachers in Northern Ireland, I undertook the mammoth task of delivering the New Curriculum while still teaching English and Maths to test standard. In addition to this incredibly tight class schedule, I also provided two hours per week of unpaid, extra-curricular whole class AQE tuition.

Teachers had to attend training courses to familiarise themselves with the New Curriculum, which saw major revisions to the existing one in terms of structure, content and delivery. It was a lot. Our planners had to be overhauled to reflect these changes and set out in a new format. Two new elements of the curriculum were incorporated into our planning: Personal Development and Mutual Understanding (PDMU) and Thinking Skills and Personal Capabilities. Classroom Management became more collaborative; teachers were responsible for making learning objectives explicit and pupils used these learning objectives as a basis for establishing the success criteria for each piece of their work. Marking was to be more reflective: we were to employ the system of two stars and a wish, highlighting two aspects of the work that was done well and an area for improvement - ideally related to the success criteria.

And, as if all of this wasn't enough, we heard that we were to have a school inspection, news which sent the whole staff into a flurry of activity as we frantically set about putting the new guidance in place. My perfectionistic tendencies were put to good use as I amended my planners and classroom accordingly. Inspection week was showtime. I was able to demonstrate our class familiarity with the New Curriculum as the pupils were well versed in establishing the success criteria of each lesson, and also in self and peer evaluation - that is to say, coming up with two stars and a wish for their completed work. After Inspection Week, our Principal told us that a couple of us had received Outstanding and I was certain I was one of them. In fairness, I'm sure every one of us believed we were the recipient of the Outstanding report - we had all exhausted ourselves preparing for the inspection and each of us did a little smug squirm upon hearing the news. Mr Taylor was right to keep the names to himself.

At this point, I was beginning to have a real sense of pride in my work. Not only had I taken on the responsibility to deliver both the New Curriculum and transfer test preparation, but I had also navigated an inspection in which I was certain I had excelled. My organisational skills were commented upon; my classroom was always tidy, everything was neatly labelled and organised - a place for everything and everything in its place, as Mummy would have said. Even my store was orderly, with uniformly labelled tubs and box files in coordinating colours. Occasionally, Mr Taylor brought a visiting colleague in to marvel at this exemplary depository. With so much to keep on top of and so little time to think, it was no wonder that my sense of self was increasingly linked to my career performance. However, having an external source of self-esteem is a dangerous thing, as I was soon to discover.

There was vagueness around whether the standardised test scores dictated pupil grades, or whether these grades could be amended (upward or downward) at the discretion of the teacher - if the pupil's test performance was at odds with performance observed throughout the year, for example. This leeway unnerved me. It was theoretically possible to issue flattering grades arbitrarily, which could make subsequent grades, from teachers who allocated grades according to test scores only, look like pupil regression. Parents who noted a fall in grades would naturally assume failure on the part of the teacher to elicit the best from their child. I brought the matter to Mr Taylor, who held a staff meeting to ensure everyone was singing from the same hymn sheet when it came to grading. My ego needed parents to know exactly how much progress their children achieved under my tutelage.

I took pride in bringing the pupils on. Each year I combed through results to ensure that each child had either maintained or progressed throughout their year with me. My effectiveness as a teacher directly correlated with pupil progress and I was determined not to suffer any blows to my reputation.

I couldn't deliver results if the children weren't engaged, and the fastest way to ensure that was by utilising a reward system. Each pupil had a star chart on which I recorded their stars for work that was correct on the first try. Twenty stars earned a homework voucher, which was an exemption from one night of written homework. Those who cared not one jot for homework vouchers could be motivated through Star Teams - the team which accrued the most stars over the week were awarded a Trophy and sweets. In short; those whose reputations could not be held hostage by the individual reward system might be more amenable to peer pressure. I was training the children to be extrinsically motivated, to learn not for the intrinsic joy of it, but for the external reward. This is standard practice, formalised in any school's Positive Behaviour Policy, so on paper I was ticking the boxes for an effective class management system which aimed to generate improved results. I buried the niggle that I was enacting the very dynamic that had caused so much pain to me in my young life - that of trading a child's obedience for approval. Just as I had, these children had to lose parts of themselves to be celebrated. Their acceptability was blatantly conditional, hinged on something other than a genuine appreciation of the unique talents, skills and attributes that made up who they were. It was a normalised practice in education, to employ behavioural techniques, as if we have in our charge Skinner's rats, or Pavlov's dogs, rather than complex human beings. The children had become results fodder, a means to an end. Having been a child who had suffered at the mercy of this paradigm, I was now the one inflicting it.

My classroom became increasingly regimented. It was second nature to me, having grown up with a focus on academics and strict scheduling. My organisational skills were spilling over into all areas; not only did I have the meticulous store and classroom of a psychopath, I was also able to marshal the children with similar effectiveness. My pupils moved silently through the corridors under the ever-present threat of losing a star or suffering the humiliation of being demoted to the back of the line, past the scrutinising eyes of their classmates. Toilet visits were to be made during breaks, so as not to impede the schedule. I brought a whistle out when I was on morning duty or break duty so that, after the bell had gone, I could toot a shrill reminder to the children to stop their games and conversations and walk quietly to their line. Once a colleague commented on my ability to marshal the pupils so effectively and I bitterly replied that I would have been an asset in Nazi Germany - words intended to sting, a kind of cry for help, a plea to witness what I had become. In allowing myself to prioritise behavioural outcomes over the welfare of each child, I had sacrificed my humanity. Most of all, I hated how I was perpetrating the damaging practices of my childhood instead of being the cycle breaker.

In my first stint of teaching, I had encouraged and appreciated each child solely for who they were and on those last days each June, many would hug me or cry because our time together had ended. Some even said that I was their favourite teacher. Those days were gone. My childhood had been one of *'it's for your own good'* and *'you'll thank me for it later'* and here I was subjecting children to exactly that, despite knowing from personal experience that the damage incurred from being conditionally valued was too high a price to pay for 'success' on paper.

On April 1st I decided to play an April fool's joke on the kids, as I had in previous years. They came in after the morning bell and set out their pencil cases ready for the day.

"Okay, everybody. There will be no PE this morning, because I was marking your work from yesterday and the results were so atrocious that I think it best that we just do it again."

The children looked at me, searchingly, to ascertain if I was serious. Some, but not many, questioned the pronouncement.

"No way! It's a joke! She's joking!"

"I assure you; I am not. Some of you must not have been reading the questions carefully or trying hard at all."

An uncertain silence descended. I then took out a whiteboard on which I had written the words April Fools! There were a few relieved sighs but nothing like the uproarious laughter I had enjoyed in previous years, chiefly because the humour of this joke resided in the premise that repeating work was ludicrous, except now, with the kind of teacher I had become, this was no longer implausible; it was exactly the kind of thing a results driven, strict and inflexible teacher might do. Joking about poor results – which I had trained them to perceive as the most important aspect of their school experience - was tasteless at least, vicious at worst. Put simply, I hadn't put the work into our relationships to have earned the gift of their friendship.

  The low point was yet to come. One day, a genuinely lovely boy, who always did his best, wet himself in my classroom rather than ask to go to the toilet. I wouldn't have said no had he asked to leave the classroom, but the prospect of my displeasure, the possibility of being asked if he had gone at break-time, loaded with the weight of my suspicion and disapproval was too much for this sensitive child to bear. Later, so as not to interrupt the flow of a lesson introduction, I ignored a girl with her hand up. She subsequently vomited at her table and when the child sitting beside the puker complained that some splashes had landed on his side of the desk, I impatiently told him to grab a paper towel. I had sacrificed their dignity as humans, ignored their vulnerability as children. It was my rock bottom.

  I nipped in to see my parents on the way home from work, feeling utterly deflated. Daddy spotted me as he sat in his usual spot by the window, and I watched his outline get up and make for the door.

"*Y'alright, kid?*"

"*Busted, Daddy.*"

He called back into the house.

"*Gloria, make Peggy a wee cuppa.*"

"*Oh hiya, love! I'll just put the kettle on here.*"

"*Tough day at work?*" inquired Daddy, with all the joviality of a man who didn't know he had Himmler for a daughter.

"*Not great.*"

"*Sure, there's always tomorrow!*" he quipped.

I wanted him to put the defibrillator away, so I just came out with it.

"*A child pissed himself in class today rather than asking me to go to the toilet.*"

He winced and sucked air in through his teeth.

"*It was my fault. It's like Checkpoint Charlie trying to get past me to the loo. He was too afraid to ask.*"

I was handing myself in to my parents in the childish hope of an absolution that I couldn't give myself.

Mummy came in from the kitchen.

"*In years to come, those children may not remember what you taught them, but they'll remember how you made them feel.*"

"*Sure, stick the boot in.*"

"*Well, am I wrong? I still have nightmares about that aul' bitch, Miss Smith.*"

"*She knows, Gloria. Away and get my wee chocolate bars from the hidey-hole.*"

Daddy sensed the depth of my self-recrimination and was utterly sympathetic. I wondered if it pained him to see me in pain, whether he now cared more about my feelings than my transgressions. I wondered if he recognised this despondency caused by hurting children, and to pardon me was to pardon himself. I wished we could talk freely about it, but the past was locked up. I wondered if my strictness and inflexibility subconsciously mirrored his, to force him to see it for what it was.

I could sense him searching my face until our eyes locked. He smiled sympathetically, a funeral-smile.

"*Be alright, kid. You can always do better tomorrow.*"

But doing better tomorrow didn't erase the damage of the past. I funeral-smiled back.

"*Where's the good chocolate treats, Gloria?*"

"*Sure, I don't know where you've hid them!*"

"*Aye, right enough,*" he said, and hoisted himself out of his chair.

"*I'm not sure I remember myself,*" he muttered as he passed the sofa.

Mummy leaned in conspiratorially as he rustled around in the kitchen.

"*He's forgetting loads this weather. I think it might be the Aul' Timers.*"

"*Do you mean Alzheimer's?*"

"*Sure, that's what I said. He's got terrible absent minded, and he gets muddled. The other day in Tesco's he was standing there saying, 'Gloria, get us one of them there record things.' He couldn't think of the word. It's happening more and more.*"

I listened to the cupboard doors open and close as Daddy struggled to outwit the confectionary-hoarding mastermind of the previous week.

"*What was he after? Pizza?*"

"*It was!*"

Daddy came back in, bearing treats.

"*What are yous laughing at?*"

"*Oh, nothing. Just saying to Peggy that you're punchie.*"

He rolled his eyes and lobbed our chocolate bars over from his chair. He looked old. His eyes looked tired. His cheeks had hollowed, and red spider veins criss-crossed his once sharp cheekbones.

"So, what happened in school that has you so upset?" asked Mummy.

Daddy interjected, keen to save me from having to revisit my shame.

"She's alright, Gloria, she'll have a better day tomorrow."

Mummy's lips pursed in a too-familiar way, as if she was physically restraining the words escaping.

"Mummy, it's just...there's so much to do, so much to get through. Especially this year. And I want them to do well."

"Of course, you do, love. Like what Mr Vance did for you."

"It's not that, though. It's me, I feel like the whole system is geared to prioritise academic results over their mental health and emotional welfare."

"Yes, but you're making sure that they get their qualifications. That's the best thing you can do for them. You are doing a good job."

"It depends on what criteria you measure by. Our school system seems to be the one profession where practice is not based on current research. We start them too young. We test too much. We use behavioural techniques that backfire in the long term. I might be doing a good job in terms of demonstrating pupil progress for end of year results, but at what cost?"

"But Peggy - if you get them through this year, help them get their 11 Plus, they get to Grammar school, like you did. And look at you now - a teacher!"

"I don't know, Daddy. I'm not sure it's a fair test."

"Whaddya mean? Sure, you did the graft and got there on your own steam! We couldn't afford to get you tutored like the rest of them, and you still did it."

"I don't think I believe in that bootstraps theory anymore. I had support. You helped me with my homework. You kept my nose to the grindstone. If you hadn't done that, would I have passed? Is it fair on kids with alcoholic parents? Kids from families where generational unemployment is the norm? For an immigrant kid for whom English is a second language? I don't believe the transfer system is a meritocracy at all when there is a raft of other factors that affect the outcome."

"Don't bite the hand that fed you, love. And don't begrudge others the same chance you had."

"I don't, Daddy. I've just come to realise how detrimental it all is. The 11 Plus. The reward systems. The constant testing. All of it. The gap between what we know is good for kids and what we do is widening, and I'm a cog in the system. I hate it."

"So, what? Are you gonna leave teaching?"

He said it as though the very idea was ludicrous. Nipping off for a year to do a Masters was one thing, but to be disenchanted with a permanent post in a school, to walk away from such a respectable career was beyond credibility.

I shrugged.

"Leave a regular wage - a good wage? And to do what?"

I saw his panic rise at the idea of me losing my financial security. He'd been poor and had done everything he could think of to ensure that I wouldn't have to endure it.

"I don't know. I know I can be an effective teacher. But when I think of teaching school subjects with the aim of testing, it leaves me feeling cold."

"So, what do you want to teach?"

"I don't know how I could make it happen, but I want to teach people how to manage their mental health."

"Oh, aye. Well, do you know what's good for your mental health?"

"What?"

"Having a good job so you know where your next meal is coming from."

"Ack, Daddy. I'm in that classroom day in and day out with those kids delivering an academic curriculum. But what about resilience? Self-esteem? Confidence? Surely, those are as important to success, if not more so?"

"Could you not do that as well? What about that PDMU you said was in the new curriculum?"

"Lip service. The school system is the problem. You can't heal in the same environment that made you sick."

The school year was coming to a close, forcing me to make a decision: stay safe and manage my dissatisfaction or move on. The relentless little voice was back, urging me onward, giving me little glimpses of a future where I taught something worthwhile and - crucially - helped people. I no longer wanted to be a cog in a machine that prioritised data over self-esteem.

Twenty-Four

Just as it had when I was 27, everything was shifting. The sense of there being something else that I should be doing had returned. I visited Joe Boyle, feeling intuitively that he was the person to mull things over with. Once again, I found myself on that green leather recliner, digging deep with Joe.

"I guess I'm here because I'm wondering how to incorporate into my life the insights, I received in the between lives regression. The idea of teaching and helping people heal really resonated with me. I've been thinking about Life Coaching but am aware of the irony."

"Irony?"

I laughed.

"My life is a shambles!"

"How so?"

I took a deep breath.

"I feel emotionally damaged. I have a lifetime of unresolved issues plus an ocean of un-cried tears for Martin. Who in their right mind would take guidance from me?"

Joe smiled sympathetically and simply said,

"How do you think the rest of us got into helping others? Once you have overcome adversity, you have acquired the tools to do so and can share them."

With that one beautiful notion, he helped me see my struggles as essential to the path I'd chosen and had benevolently included me in the 'us' of helpers. We shared a peaceful silence; I basked in the idea of being a helper while Joe had a faraway look that I knew well - slightly tuned out, focused elsewhere. It was the look of the Head Letterbox.

"I wonder, though..." he added, pensively, *"whether qualifying as a life coach would be enough to bring you a client base? It might be better to qualify as a Cognitive Behavioural Therapist first. It's a more widely recognised qualification."*

Just like that, fate used Joe to lead me to a door I hadn't even known existed.

A few days after our session, I received an envelope through the post, containing compliments slip on which he had simply written:

Peggy – two thoughts:
1. Find the thing that makes your heart sing,
2. Find a way to get people to pay you to do it.

I was struck with the white light feeling again. It was time to train as a CBT therapist.

In what was becoming a pattern, I marvelled to Melanie about how this new path felt right, waxing lyrical on the white light feeling, how Joe's inspired guidance had steered my path and feeling safe in the knowledge that I'd be admitted because it was meant to be. Melanie smiled, nodded, did a bit of research on my behalf and phoned to inform me that I had under a week to submit an application. If Joe was my conduit to the other side, Melanie was my spiritual P.A. These invisible hands steered me through Joe and Melanie, and I sensed the rolling of invisible eyes, too.

It transpired that being eligible to apply for a place on the CBT course was conditional upon having a patient base at your place of work. In other words, had I not returned to teaching, this avenue would not have been open to me. Returning to school had not only drummed home the flaws in the system, something that my heart put a pin in for later but had also enabled this next essential move. Strangely, the following year, the criteria for admission to the CBT course became more stringent – teaching did not guarantee a client base and I would not have been eligible to apply. The window that the universe had briefly opened once again firmly shut.

The Social Sciences Building was on the outskirts of campus, a new-build red brick building situated at the leafier end of University Street. A tea and sandwiches reception was held for the new Social Studies postgraduate students in a large room on the first floor. Nervous postgraduates and inquisitive lecturers bustled and rearranged in tenuous groups getting to know each other. I introduced myself to a few adjacent students, but none were on my course. My eye kept being drawn to a girl on the other side of the room who seemed to glow as if under a spotlight of familiar white light. She had thick blonde hair, sparkling blue eyes and pink cheeks, flushed with excitement. I felt such a pull towards her that only social propriety prevented me from elbowing people out of the way to get to her. Eventually our paths crossed as we each introduced ourselves to the course convener, who was only too happy to palm us off onto each other before being hit with a new wave of enthusiastic newcomers. Her name was Jill. She worked with cancer patients and their families for a cancer charity and I could well imagine her warmth bringing comfort and solace to families in crisis. As the event came to a close, we swapped numbers and parted with a rather shy nice to meet you, when, as we later reminisced, what we really wanted to do was leap for joy. She was sweet and kind and good. I guess she thought I was alright too, because we loved each other immediately.

The course was intense. We learned the basics of CBT (how current problems can be broken down and understood in terms of our negative thoughts, feelings and behaviours) and explored the treatment models for depression and anxiety disorders. This highly structured approach to diagnosis and treatment was reassuring and I eagerly anticipated applying this evidence-based practice with clients. However, learning about the numerous mental health disorders led inescapably to self-examination. Many dropped out of the course in those early weeks - it's heavy work, learning how to pick through the contents of the human mind without holding up a mirror to yourself and finding that filtered version of yourself labelled and doomed. By the end of one particularly arduous day examining childhood predictors for poor mental health, I was on the ropes, reeling from the stats. I felt tainted and exposed, irreparably damaged. I wanted to go home and crawl under the duvet but instead I turned to whisper to Jill.

"I don't suppose you could come to Common Grounds for half an hour after class?"

"Sure."

When the lecture finished, we pulled on our coats and headed across to the café. I felt my throat tighten.

"Jill, this is all feeling too close to home."

Her face softened with concern.

"I'm sure. But you can do this. You're strong."

"I hate that word. It reminds me of living in Glenmore and being told I was strong, when actually I was just too afraid to admit how desperate I was, because I didn't want to be troublesome."

"Ah, love. I know how you feel. But I really think that if you look at what you've been through, we could find a lot of evidence to support my assertion."

Her therapeutic terminology made me laugh.

"You're going to be an excellent therapist."

She smiled.

"You are strong," she reiterated.

"I'm not. If this course has taught me anything, it is that the numbness and suppression that comes with trauma is misinterpreted as strength. I haven't dealt with anything; I have simply locked off the wounded part of myself."

"Okay, maybe strong is not the right word. Resilient? You are resilient. We can only develop resilience through enduring hardship."

"I'm not sure I've endured anything. I think I dissociate. You are giving me far too much credit."

We unpeeled our layers of bags, coats and scarves in the welcome warmth of our usual corner and ordered some herbal tea, wisely eschewing coffee, or as I called it, Anxiety Water.
"Look. You will be a great therapist. I know it."
"I don't know, Jill. Can I really be a therapist when I'm such a work in progress myself?"
"I imagine your experiences make you more empathetic. People relate to authenticity. Getting yourself through this crisis will make you a better therapist."
Her logic was infallible, but I simply couldn't imagine feeling different to the way I did in that moment - defective, broken, certainly not equal to the task of helping anyone.
"If you want to help others, you have to help yourself."
I looked at her wry smile. She knew she had me.
"Isn't it weird that I can be motivated to go to therapy so that someday I can help people I have never even met before, but I am less inclined to go if it only helps me?"
"Yeah, you might want to start with that."
We laughed together, a relief, like breaking waves.
"It's time to do the work?"
"It's time to do the work."

I decided to undergo CBT therapy with the best therapist I could find, knowing that I would be resolving outstanding issues while learning first-hand how an excellent CBT therapist operates. Sylvia came highly recommended. She had a vast wealth of qualifications, a mane of fiery red hair and a forthright gaze. She was warm and personable but took no prisoners. Upon discovering I was a CBT student, she assigned homework to write my own case formulation, an exercise that helped me understand my issues in a pared down format, while honing my professional skills. I was being simultaneously healed and unofficially coached by the one of the best therapists Northern Ireland had to offer. The assessment and diagnostics indicated that I had PTSD, as evidenced by the flashbacks, nightmares and dissociative feelings I had around the incident when I had run away from the beating at fourteen. I explained to Sylvia that I was so divorced from my own experience and feelings that I found it difficult to cry, how I don't even blink away tears as I once might have, but could somehow suck tears back into the ducts, swallowing them down at the exact moment I notice the sensation - that peculiar little stinging rush of lurching lacrimal fluid, that little stab in the gut as emotions try to make themselves manifest. I explained how I go numb, reprimand myself - *enough of this silliness, no need to make a spectacle*. I explain how the transit between sad me and intolerant me always gives me pause when I notice it, and then I'm outside of the experience, observing, marvelling that it has happened again. I admit that it's probably better to be meta-me, watching and judging from a safe distance.

This is dissociating, and like any pathology it serves a useful function of self-protection.

Sylvia suggested EMDR (Eye Movement Desensitisation and Reprocessing) - a system whereby the nervous system is stimulated in various sensory ways while the patient rewrites the narrative of the trauma.

In our first session of EMDR, Sylvia read the notes of my verbal account aloud while I sat on the sofa opposite wearing headphones and holding small paddles in the palms of my hands. As she read each paragraph, the headphones beeped and the paddles buzzed intermittently at alternate sides, thereby creating bilateral brain stimulation intended to help me process the memories.

New emotions and recollections bubbled up from the mire of the recovered memories. Sylvia recounted the afternoon I sat on the sofa of the car-lady, feeling burdensome and inconvenient, a pitiful peculiarity with striped legs, staring blankly as she phoned the minister to take me off her hands. I felt ridiculous all over again as I sat on Sylvia's sofa with tears welling up and – at last - pouring down my cheeks. I cried in the same strange way I did that day, expressionless with held breath, silence punctuated by deep, gasping hiccups, coming in spasmodic jumps and judders, my body at the mercy of a pain that would not be restrained. I wasn't sure if I was reliving that cry or crying anew at the fresh memory of it, but a more pressing question arose – at what point did I lose this skill for weeping freely? It was a strange sensation, reliving that corruption of crying, as though there were two of me - one crying and the other marvelling. A memory reared suddenly - I was looking at a photograph of the lady's daughter and had the unworthy thought - *Why is she so loved? She is not even pretty* - and was consumed with fresh stabs of shame that I should be so hateful. Each successive session, Sylvia added the fresh memories and insights of the previous, until I was able to unstick myself from that frozen moment, peel back the layers and bring new understanding. It surprised me that of all the aspects my subconscious could have repressed, memories of violence remained and this fleeting little thought - *why is she loved?* was too much to bear. I came to realise that it was symptomatic of my worst core belief - that I was bad, unworthy - and it was too painful to tolerate. With a mixture of EMDR and CBT, I came to unravel long bedded down ideas about my worth, likeability and lovability and began to unpick the hold of the past.

Undergoing this process made me my own first client and a more effective therapist. Daddy's parenting flaws forged a strength in me in two ways: our complicated past resulted in a genuine empathy for my clients, and having grown up mentally sparring with an argumentative, give-not-an-inch, perpetually correct opponent was excellent preparation for being a CBT therapist. Daddy had many strong opinions about politics, religion and philosophy, and over the years, we had many ferocious debates, taking opposing sides sometimes just for the enjoyment of it rather than defending any genuine principle. We loved punching holes in the other's arguments. Daddy is one of the most stubborn opponents I have ever faced, and through our debates, I learned to listen and reframe, feint and parry, retreat and counter. He gave me skills and strengths, because of, or in spite of, the things he gave me to overcome.

I grew to really love working with CBT clients. It was so rewarding to deconstruct unhelpful thoughts, assumptions and beliefs and watch as each person grew in understanding and competence. I began to keep a notebook by my bed as ideas and inspiration floated to me in the stillness of night. It was a kind of homecoming, this work, and I never really switched off, or wanted to.

Having become firm friends, Jill and I committed to doing peer supervision for each other, meeting up every fortnight to discuss our respective clients and offer insight or resources where possible. She laughed freely and often, irrepressible giggles and great cackles of mirth. She was thoughtful and kind; a bestower of food, flowers and thoughtful conversation. She'd gift things that she happened upon that made her think of you. She was a sincere ally and as a result had amassed a host of friends from every season of her life, similarly genuine souls who she was always keen to introduce to each other. I teased her from time to time about her frequent refrain - *You must meet my lovely friend, such and such!* At first, I mocked this perceived generosity, surely not all of these as yet unmet friends could be principally described as lovely. When I met them later, this was exactly the case, these birds of a feather had flocked to Jill as one of their own. I began to refer to her as my lovely friend Jill, got caught up in her loveliness and subsequently liked myself more when we were together. She built you up if you were struggling, not with platitudes but with considered and sincere thoughts. She was a checker-in and a go-the extra-miler. This was part of the reason that becoming a CBT therapist was such a good fit for her. Acquiring this training gave her a platform and framework which enabled her to help, soothe and uplift with greater efficacy.

She lived in an apartment in a newly refurbished Linen Mill in the Ardoyne, a traditionally Nationalist (read - predominantly Catholic) working class area of Belfast, made notorious for numerous incidents of violence and unrest throughout the Troubles, and in our own recent history, for the Holy Cross dispute, which gained the area notoriety. The Holy Cross Girls' School was located in the loyalist neighbourhood of Upper Ardoyne, where rumours had spread that school runs were being used as intelligence gathering details for the IRA. In their ire, loyalist protestors heatedly blockaded the route and prevented the children from gaining access to the school. Footage of frightened children being rushed past heckling; enraged loyalists had been beamed worldwide. In short, sectarianism ran deep here, and on the various occasions when I drove to Jill's apartment – happily located behind high fences and access granted remotely via electronic gate key – I routinely gave myself a good scare pondering upon what might happen if my car broke down before I reached the safety of the building. In the event of being accosted as an unfamiliar face, I had several Catholic identifiers in my arsenal:

- Nationalism 101 – if asked to list the six counties, remember to say Derry, not Londonderry;
- Be able to recite the Catholic prayers, The Hail Mary, Glory Be and Our Father, the last - critically without the *For thine is the Kingdom* etc addendum which can trip up the unwary Protestant. Thankfully these were taught to me in my Glenmore Children's Home days during the brief stay of a St. Louise's pupil;
- Speak Irish. Any fool knows the Sinn Fein war cry of Tiocfaidh ar la (Gaelic for Our Day will Come, referring to the hope for a United Ireland), but my penchant for short, dark, handsome Catholics throughout University had yielded a rudimentary smattering of words – I could count to ten and recite In Ainm an Athar, Agus An Mhic, Agus Spioraid Naiomh (in the name of the Father, the Son and the Holy Spirit).

I sat-navved my way through the strange streets revising these potentially life-saving recitations, understanding that being asked questions about these three very specific areas was unlikely at best, and ultimately if the car gave up, I was fucked. I somehow hit the red light at the entrance to the Ardoyne on every journey and only then realised my car was unlocked, but I'd be unable to lock it at that point, lest the tell-tale click gave me away as a nervous interloper. I subsequently endured the yawning countdown to an amber light, with all the apparent nonchalance of an Ardoyne Catholic. A lifetime of conditioning of partisan politics, of them'uns and us'uns had run deep, and despite fraternising, and more than fraternising, with a great deal of Catholics throughout my tertiary level education, I was still waiting for a bad one, an embittered one, a paramilitary one to spot me, drag me into the back room of a social club and demonstrate what happens to Protestants who wander into the wrong area. I wouldn't be the first. In these horrible meanderings of my imagination I did not survive to tell the tale, but the part that stung most was the thought of my daddy muttering, *"What are ye, stupit?"* to my stupid corpse.

Such was my love for Jill that I would endure this mental torture in order to hang out at hers. She, of course, had no such misgivings, having been raised in a middle-class family with experiences a world apart from those of my own. Once the electronic gates clanged shut behind my car, I was relieved sufficiently to take a moment to admire the beautiful ex-linen factory converted to accommodation, an imposing five storey brick behemoth with regular rows of tall glass windows which looked out onto the estate beyond. It spoke to me of a simpler time, that of my grandparents in the early 1900s, when Belfast led the world in linen production and our product was used in Royal households in England and beyond in

Europe. For the most part, women worked in the mills, donning aprons and securing their hair in caps to work long hours in the damp, amid the constant clank and swoosh of the heddles and shuttle. They were colloquially known as Millie's, a term which has since become a sneer at poverty and coarse manners, but in those far off days, Millie was a term of pride, a moniker denoting a hard worker. It was also a time before the Troubles, before politics created a schism between the working classes of both religions. Well, that was then and this was now. I positioned my keys between my knuckles for the journey to the doors, and kept them there in the lift, because you never know the minute that a Catholic might jump out and ask a specifically Nationalist general knowledge question that wasn't on my limited list.

Finally, I arrived at Jill's door, where she was already waiting. We hugged warmly and I shuffled into the safety of her apartment, relieved to be free of the burden of my overactive imagination.

"*Hello, my love! These are for you!*"

She took the little bunch of short stemmed roses, deep pink, with a happy exclamation.

"*Oh! My favourite colour – thank you so much! Let me take your coat.*"

Jill had started the lovely tradition of gifting a small bunch of flowers each time we met and I truly loved it. She hung my coat up and ushered me past the corridor which led to the two bedrooms and bathroom, and into the living quarters.

It was spectacular. The developer had retained the original features of the mill - vast swathes of exposed brick, high ceilings, curved walls and tall windows that allowed light to flood in. Plastered walls were painted crisp white and long linen curtains hung from plain poles and gathered modestly with jute rope tie backs. To the right was a simple fitted kitchen, made homely with the accoutrements of tea and coffee, then centred on the middle window was a glossy, sixties style round white dining table. As she decanted and refilled a vase with water for the flowers, I took in the latest chalked etchings on the little blackboard that hung by the table. It was a sketch of a girl turned away from the artist, hair falling in a curtain which partially hid her face. She seemed to be looking down, perhaps reading a book, and the graceful posture looked familiar.

"Jill – is this you?"

"Yes!"

"Oh, my word! Who drew it?"

She told me the name of a chap who she had gone on a handful of dates with, who had grabbed the board and sketched her in a quiet moment.

"Flip sake. What is it with you? Remember that guy bought you a guitar so that he could spend time teaching you how to play it? Now this! Well, I once inspired poetry, so…"

"No! How wonderful!"

"Well, in fairness, the words thunder-thighed were used."

She threw her head back and laughed. That was the thing about Jill. She wasn't ostentatious, at first glance she was proper and pleasant, a good girl from a nice family, but beyond the decency and polish, her essence was poetry. She was a trained dancer, but the lessons had merely been a conduit for a grace that was already her own. Once you saw her, really saw her, she was mesmeric, and I wasn't remotely surprised she had inspired art.

The walls furthest from the windows of the open plan room were lined with high bookcases which provided a colourful and textural backdrop to a squashy, cream corner sofa, lit warmly with an arc overreach floor lamp and the vanilla scented tea-lights which littered the coffee table. It was here we frequently lounged, feet up, under blankets, providing peer supervision for one another (an aggrandised term for discussing our respective clients and asking, *What the fuck will I do with this one?)* and often culminating in a good catch up with each other, cackling over wine or commiserating with cake.

That evening, we sat drinking herbal tea and nibbling on buns, having provided a cursory analysis of each other's caseloads. It was getting late, and the orange streetlamps bathed the rows of houses beyond in a sepia haze. I wheeled back to a topic of earlier, a client of mine who had admitted to suicidal ideation.

"I mean, I totally get it. I know how it feels to just want out. To be done."

"You do?"

Jill's blue eyes filled with sympathy that somehow, I didn't feel was warranted. To lighten the mood, I was flippant.

"*Yep. I mean, I'm still here, so obviously I didn't go through with anything.*"

She laughed, to be kind more than anything, and twisted her thick, golden hair back into a French roll before she pressed on.

"*So, I see! When was that?*"

"*When I was a student. Martin had died, I still didn't know what I was going to do with my life. Poor self-esteem, probable depression.*"

"*And so, did you try to kill yourself?*"

"*Well, no. I had a plan, but I never attempted it.*"

"*What was your plan?*"

I paused for a bit, knowing how ridiculous I was about to sound.

"*Carbon monoxide poisoning.*"

"*Carbon…so what were you going to do?*"

"*Oh, God. Don't laugh. So, I didn't want to go on, but I knew I couldn't put my parents through losing another child. So…I imagined I could get all three of us to somehow share a room with a faulty heater, and…you know, drift off into unconsciousness together.*"

"*Where were you going to get a faulty heater from?*"

The tension broke and we cackled.

"*Jesus, I don't know! I just knew I wanted to be gone and didn't want my folks to suffer. It was the kindest way I could think of.*"

"*A murder – suicide?*"

"*Obvs. Nothing says love like a wee murder-suicide. You know me, always thinking of others.*"

There was a little pause as we mulled. Jill was still curious.

"*So, why didn't you go through with it?*"

"*Other than the Judeo-Christian tenet of Thou Shalt Not Kill?*"

"*Obvs.*"

"*Well, for one thing, it would be a pretty shit thing to do to Jeanette. Mostly though, I'm pretty sure reincarnation is a thing, and if you crap out on this life, it won't be long before you're back on a new assignment to learn the lessons you tried to circumvent with suicide.*"

"*Ah. I see where you are coming from.*"

"*And here's the thing; I suspected that I'd already done all the hard bits - childhood, adolescence, bereavement and so on. I really didn't fancy ending it if death was just a reset button and I would have to do it all again. So here I am.*"

Her pink cheeks appled into a warm smile.

"*Well, I'm glad you are still here.*"

"*Me too, chum,*" I agreed, as I shared a blanket on a squashy sofa, drinking tea with one of the best humans I knew.

I took the natural break in the conversation for a toilet break. We had been talking for hours and the tea had fairly run through me. As I nipped out, I caught sight of myself in her hall mirror and was struck by how dull I looked in comparison to the radiant face I'd been gazing at for hours. My bleached hair was dulled with dark roots, my skin sallow, my eyes dark, and my expression ever on the continuum between pensive and Resting Bitch Face. I'm not being down on myself; the fact was that Jill was luminescent and most people looked drab by comparison.

After I helped her tidy the tea things, we checked our diaries for the next possible meet up, and, crucially, I remembered to click the internal locks in the car before leaving the comparative safety of the car park.

CBT was fascinating. Case formulations appealed greatly to my love of organisation - to reduce a person's mental issues onto an A4 page of Negative Automatic Thoughts, Maladaptive Assumptions and Negative Core Beliefs was gratifying. To then use this blueprint to systematically undermine the unhelpful ideas and replace them with helpful ones felt like alchemy. Addressing case formulations was gratifying work. Understanding how you got to be in the pickle you currently find yourself through examining the effects of biology, environment (early experiences, and the roles that family, friends, society place upon us - and we upon ourselves) is the first step towards liberation, towards seeing without the hindrance of the veil of perspective that conditioning has placed upon us. I treated clients by following the treatment models for each disorder, undermining maladaptive assumptions and filling the void left behind with more helpful and realistic ones. Through helping others, I helped myself; each journey of healing yielded insights that I wouldn't have otherwise come by. It reminded me of Reiki; as I channelled healing for others, I absorbed some healing myself. As I explored whether life was worthwhile with suicidal clients, I affirmed that my life was worthwhile too. People honoured me by breaking open before me, they blessed me with their vulnerability. Saving them meant I saved me too.

I began to notice themes emerge as I treated clients. One interesting theme was Obsessive Compulsive Disorder (OCD) flare ups caused by learning about the popular New Age philosophy, the Law of Attraction with its well-known tenet of Ask, Believe and Receive - ask the universe for exactly what you want, believe that it is possible and get ready to receive it. Clients were presenting with anxiety caused by unpleasant, intrusive thoughts that they worried were going to come true, that the Universe had taken a snapshot of their thoughts and had set about manifesting them. This fear of bringing unpleasant events into being by simply having a thought heightened their anxiety, which brought more intrusive thoughts – in a nutshell, the vicious cycle of OCD. I explained that the Ask, Believe and Receive maxim had missed one less sexy but very essential element: Ask, Believe, Work Your Ass off and Receive. None of the things they envisioned would come to pass without intention to make it so, and the intention needed to be followed up by very real, physical efforts to ensure manifestation. It wasn't a magic trick. We explored the idea that Ask, Believe, Work Your Ass off and Receive was not necessarily plausible either, given the existence of privilege (the absence of impediment foisted on ethnicity, gender, social background, education and, wealth).

A notable pattern emerged. Clients presenting with OCD tended to come from a Catholic background, while most Social Anxiety clients tended to have Protestant beginnings. It made sense that the ritualization of Catholicism (assuaging negative feelings or mitigating negative actions by engaging in confession and repetitive prayers) could easily lead to OCD. I wondered if the differences in the church experiences accounted for Social Anxiety Disorder to foment amongst Protestants, because while Catholics seemed to have a strong sense of community and could rock up to mass wearing jeans, Protestants (concerned with respectability and judgement - and therefore predictably scandalized by the very thought of wearing jeans to church) tended to dress in their Sunday best. This external locus for self-esteem (viewing yourself through the lens of how others perceive you) was fertile ground for Social Anxiety.

A large proportion of my Generalised Anxiety Disorder clients were females in their mid-twenties. Time and again I met with women who (unlike men) had to navigate balancing a career with a ticking biological clock, or new mothers who had to return to work too soon (or wanted to stay home but couldn't afford to), or mothers balancing responsibilities at work with the lion's share of childcare. Their mental health issues stemmed from the misunderstanding that there was something fundamentally wrong with them rather than the demands society placed on them. They were having normal and natural reactions to their situations, yet these reactions were being pathologized. In the 1950s most salaries were based on the expectation that each employee needed a salary that was sufficient to support a spouse and children, buy a house and have enough to manage living costs. By contrast nowadays, the higher cost of living demanded two working parents and childcare was juggled or outsourced.

I was reminded of the maxim *'If a flower doesn't bloom, you don't blame the flower, you change the environment'*. These women weren't in need of fixing; society was. I felt strongly that we need to address these social issues rather than dismiss those suffering from them as being mentally disordered.

Just as I had with school, I was discovering that the system was flawed and damaging. It left me in a personal quandary. A healer who takes your money but does nothing to change the system that maintains your oppression is simply capitalising off your pain. It wasn't enough to shrug and help a client work out a routine to tolerate the unfairness. I wanted to buck the system. Just like I had wanted to buck the system of teaching religion in schools, and in fact, the school system altogether. It was becoming a pattern.

My disillusionment with CBT had begun. Though this kind of therapy was incredibly valuable in terms of understanding the mind, I wondered if it was also limiting. An A4 case formulation wasn't enough to encapsulate the complexity of mine or anyone else's being. In fact, such a narrow perspective could paint a bleak picture. In my case, I had many of the predictors for poor mental health outcomes - poverty, abuse, bereavement, insecure attachment - factors that could doom me to a lifetime of needing to re-programme. For me, bringing in the spiritual context, the *why are we here?* had freed me from resentment by reminding me that I had elected to work through these issues. I wasn't just a victim of environment or biology - of happenstance - but a spiritual warrior. This transcendent perspective was vital in helping me see that these impediments had afforded me skill sets, empathy and grit which were all essential to my path of helping people to self-actualise. I felt strongly that other people would benefit from a spiritual context, too.

But was this spiritual bypassing? Explaining away perceived unfairness with an arrogant *It was meant to be?* I wasn't sure, but I knew that seeing a person as the sum total of their damage was limiting. I believed a spiritual context to be transformative.

I have a compulsion to pull at threads. I was sure that this unravelling would lead me somewhere, but I didn't know where yet.

Twenty-Five

Between teaching, and taking CBT clients, tutoring kids and meeting my CBT supervisor, I didn't have much time, much less energy for socialising, so Jill and I were conducting our relationship via telephone and text. It was over the phone she told me about meeting someone new, moving in with him, and shortly afterwards needing to move out again as it wasn't working. I came round to help her pack up and when I arrived, we had a long hug and she wept. As we sat on the sofa, I looked around at the home she had tried to create with him. It had her signature all over it; candles, blankets, art, but there was something missing, a tangible void, a black hole that had sucked the warmth out of her well-intentioned homemaking, the insidious coldness of a fire cooled to ashes.

"I'm doing the right thing, I know I am."

"You are. You haven't sounded happy in a long time."

Life had become so busy for me that I hadn't even seen Jill and her estranged beau together, but I was well acquainted with their difficulties from our phone chats. It was a no-fault mismatch and she had anxiously agonised over whether it was wiser to try harder or let go.

"I heard Karen from our course is pregnant. And here I am, starting from scratch again."
"Oh, for fuck sake. Is it wrong to want to punch pregnant people in their stupid pregnant faces?"
She giggled at my irreverence.
"I'm fairly sure it's frowned upon."

It was a theme we had returned to many times; the ticking of our biological clocks, which boomed like Lambeg drums. I was marginally less stressed, being halfway up a ladder, I wanted to climb, if it isn't too rude to refer to my boyfriend Phil as a ladder, but here was poor Jill with disenchanting ladders and disappointing disembarks. She was heartbroken at wasted dreams and wasted time, and her hope was beginning to wane.

We stuffed her things into black bin liners.
"You have some amount of baggage," I quipped, after stuffing another and knotting the top.
She had decided to fill the bags with whatever was to hand, and sort later. She arched an eyebrow.
"You'll be okay."
"I hope so. I can't even face work at the moment."
"Well, that's unsurprising."
"No, it's not just – this…"
She gestured to her life being packed into bags.
"It's the work itself. It's too much at the minute."

I could well imagine it would be. A key part of Jill's job was to facilitate respite weekends for families being

ripped apart by dying children or dying parents, to help them make memories before the inevitable happened.
"It is emotionally exhausting. I can't leave it at the door."
"I honestly have no idea how you do it."

I honestly didn't. To me, death was silent misery behind closed doors, a wound to be hidden. Perhaps because I had been made to patch myself up and forge on, I had never truly spent enough time with it, which at best, left me feeling unqualified to comfort others, and at worst, too terrified to confront the uncharted waters of my own pain. Jill could emote or simply sit with devastation in a way that I had never learned to. She took her responsibility seriously, providing steadfast care while families were eviscerated over and over, and all the while her friends started families of their own and pursued careers that didn't chip away at them.

I was on my way to visit my parents one afternoon after work when Jill rang my mobile. I pulled up outside their house and answered.
"Hello!"
"Hello, dear! Do you have a minute to talk?"
This was a figure of speech; Jill and I were incapable of speaking for only a minute, when sixty would do. I pulled my knees up to sit cross-legged and settled into my seat. She sounded excited and I imagined her smiling, rosy cheeked.
"Of course! How's it going?"

"Good, I think! Actually, I have a bit of news. I applied for a job at the Priory."
"THE Priory?!"
"Yes! I thought it was a bit beyond me to be honest, but Brendan said I absolutely must. He's such a pet. He has such faith in my therapist abilities and said this would be a great way to prove to myself that I can do it."

Brendan was her supervisor. Although other CBT supervisors were available in Belfast, Jill chose to travel hours away to Derry to meet with Brendan because he was funny, smart and genuine - a true kindred spirit. He knew, as I did, that she was a thoughtful, effective therapist. He too, recognised that they were cut from the same cloth.
"A behavioural experiment, then?"
"Of sorts! Wait for the best bit, though."
"What's the best bit?"
"I've just been offered an interview!"
"Oh. My. Word. That's brilliant! How are you feeling?"
"Oh God - flattered, nervous, excited, terrified! I'm all over the place!"
"When is the interview, then?"
"I have to go to London next week."
I squeaked with excitement, knowing that this opportunity might be a turning point for the better.
"I can't think of anyone better for the Priory."
"You're being kind. My own mental health has hardly been exemplary lately. I'm probably in worse shape than the patients."
"Hmm. Why does that sound familiar?"

She laughed.

"And do you remember what you said to me? When you've lived it, you know. Overcoming hardship makes you a better therapist."

"That's what Brendan said."

"Well, then. Brendan must be almost as wise as me."

Jill wanted to feel exhilarated at the prospect of a fresh start, but the hooked burrs of worry stuck fast, and depression continued to hold her in its vice-like grip. She pushed herself on with monumental effort, travelling to London and acing the interview, but still the darkness did not abate. On the railway platform of the return journey, she found herself imagining throwing herself under a train, yearning for the relief of nothingness, an escape from the relentlessness of this consuming despondency.

She moved to a one-bed apartment at the opposite side of Belfast. We kept up our phone communication and made plans to meet several times - excited, upbeat plans for lunch in a new vegan restaurant, or an old favourite - but each time she cancelled hours before, to give herself a reprieve from her anticipatory anxiety, or because she simply didn't have the energy to groom. I offered to take her for coffee at a café a few minutes' walk from her apartment and she reluctantly agreed.

I was taken aback by how frail and gaunt she looked when she answered the door. She had lost a lot of weight due to lack of appetite and wasn't wearing make-up - gorgeous Jill who was seldom seen without a cheery fuchsia lip. I felt triggered. This image of decline was all too familiar, and I felt a consuming need for her to save herself to know that I could save myself too, if depression struck. In that moment, I knee-jerked into a bootstrap's mentality, to the tough love of my childhood.

"Hi, chum! Are you ready to go, or do you want to smear on some lipstick for a bit of colour?"

We both heard it - the reproach, the lack of sympathy, the underlying unhappiness unacknowledged. My ludicrous notion that depression can be scolded away.

"Sorry - I look awful, don't I?"

"No, you look fine, I just thought you might like to. Don't worry! Let's go, I'm ready for a cuppa."

We started down the road, uncharacteristically not arm in arm, as we often had before, buffered by the depression that I resented and that she didn't ask for. She was my friend, not my client, and paradoxically this qualified her for less empathy, not more. I loved her and she was like family to me, but unfortunately for her my experience of family was conditional love and coercion. We walked along the pavement of a road with overtaking lanes. Cars roared by or idled loudly at traffic lights. We had to raise our voices to be heard, a factor which didn't help my tone.

"Jill, you are a CBT therapist. You have a wealth of techniques and knowledge at your disposal."

"I've tried everything, I really have. I even started going to a church down the road, in the hope of that helping."

"And is it?" I asked, genuinely interested.

"Kind of. Not really."

We walked along in awkward silence for a few beats.

"You can reason yourself out of this. You have leaned into the perspective that you are flawed and helpless. Convince yourself of a different perspective."

"But what's the point? If it's simply a matter of choosing a different perspective, then I am just deluding myself."

We entered the cafe and sat at a free table by the window overlooking the constant traffic and asked for two herbal teas.

"Jill, that's what we do as therapists. We take our clients, identify their unhelpful ideas and convince them of something more helpful. We steer them."

"I know, but that bothers me. When we guide them to another perspective, aren't we just patching them up for another day?"

"Exactly. It's all bullshit. All perspectives are bullshit. Who in the hell knows what is true? We just know that the ones we convince ourselves of become true for us. So, choose one that works for you."

"Base your life on a delusion?"

"That's what we all do. We just don't know we do. And it's okay. The end justifies the means, I guess."

Jill swilled her teabag around then dropped it on the saucer.

"Look, you don't understand. You are resilient. You had the opportunity to develop resilience because you had difficulties to overcome when you were young. I didn't have that. I never developed resilience."

I raised my eyebrows.

"I know it sounds ridiculous - poor me and my lovely parents and my lovely childhood. But I'm not resilient! I don't bounce back from things."

"Are you kidding me? Well, why don't you find a homeless person and tell them how lucky they are to be getting the opportunity to develop resilience?"

It landed like a slap. Jill was trying hard to unburden herself of her most difficult ideas and I was reacting instead of listening. As a therapist, I would have taken time to explore it, unpick it. I would have reminded her of the many examples of her resilience. Instead, because I loved her, I chose to fight, which only left her feeling more alone.

Understandably, she shut down and we continued sipping our herbal tea and engaged in awkward small talk punctuated by frustrated, helpless silence.

A few weeks passed, in which time I continued to check in, but eventually Jill stopped returning my texts. Her mum, Ruth, phoned me with an appeal to visit Jill, who had since moved home. Ruth had tried everything to help her and was running out of ideas.

Just show up at the door anytime; she won't be happy to see you because she'd rather be alone, but I'll make sure she won't turn you away.

I assured her I would. A week went by, then two, then more. As each new week began, I tried to work out when I could make the journey to Jill, between working at school and taking kids for after school tuition and seeing CBT clients. One week, I had a Monday evening free. I thought about visiting Jill, but imagined myself scolding her, my frustration with her doing more harm than good. I decided to stay home and recharge for the busy week ahead.

I took my Monday evening for myself. I had chosen to relax, but thoughts of Jill filled my head. I wondered when I would feel equal to seeing her, equal to overcoming my anger, equal to choosing compassion. The next day, I arrived home, frazzled from a long drive after work, ready to kick my shoes off and lie down for a few minutes. The phone rang but it was a number I didn't recognise. I deliberated. I didn't have the reserves to speak kindly to a telesales worker, so taking the call was to risk being snappy and feeling guilty for the rest of the evening. Something made me answer. An English accent.

"Hello, Peggy?"

"Yes," I replied cautiously.

"This is Rachel."

A friend of Jill's. We had met once, on a night out, drinking and dancing.

"I'm sorry to have to call you. Are you sitting down?"

Am I sitting down? Oh fuck. Fuck. Ringing in my ears. A pit in my stomach. The sensation of falling.

"I am now. What is it?"

"Peggy, Jill died last night."

"No!"

"She died. I'm so sorry."

I felt off balance. She wasn't here anymore and nothing I could do would change that. It was too late. Time had marched on.

"What happened?"

"Peggy, are you sitting down?"

"I am. What happened?"

"She lay down in front of a train. I'm so sorry."

Rachel dissolved into sobs. I went numb. I couldn't reconcile my gentle friend with the violence of such an act. It didn't feel real. Rachel loved her as much as I did, and so I switched my attention to that.

"Oh Rachel, I'm sorry. Are you okay?"

"I can't stop crying. I can't believe it."

I'm still free-falling and trying to get a foothold in anything normal.

"When is the funeral? Where? Shall we car-share?"

Back on the steady land of facts and the illusion of control. Back to nail polish remover because once again, reality is too much.

Grief lay like a boulder on my chest while I itched with what-ifs… What if I had visited the night before, instead of talking myself out of it yet again – would she still be here? Would I have found the right combination of words to keep her here? Would she have left us regardless? Or worse, would she have died with my recriminations buzzing in her ear? Would I have given her a face-full of ill-grace hours before she carried out her plan? Would I have felt it was my fault? When she moved out of her apartment, if I had offered for her to stay with me, instead of moving home, could I have helped her back to health, or would I have failed spectacularly as she chose to go whilst under my care, or deficit of care? What if I had said the right thing, done the right thing, been kinder, more understanding, more available, less selfish, impatient, cross, intolerant. Would that have made a difference?

Somewhere in our caveman brain, rumination runs deep. Self-recrimination is seductive – the idea that if we choose to see ourselves as instrumental in the disaster, we can take steps to prevent it from happening ever again and keep ourselves safe from experiencing this pain. But she was irrevocably gone. These what-ifs were like a tic - uncontrollable and pointless, because it didn't matter a damn now. I'm sure we all did it - her family, her friends, colleagues, acquaintances, exploring what-ifs to support the desperate illusion that we are in control, that we can ride the tides of life instead of being buffeted about on treacherous, merciless waters - each studying, dissecting, looking back for that small window of opportunity where we could have changed the trajectory of history. Can it work that way? Are we influential beings with a blank page, unfolding our own stories, wielding our free will? Or are we overpowered by fate? Each perspective is as terrifying as the other. Either I contributed to her death, or I had no power to stop it; either way madness lay. So, we muddled on, each bestowing the kindness of *don't blame yourself* on each other while doing exactly that to ourselves.

That afternoon was spent in shock. I cancelled the tutoring appointment, phoning my little charge's mother (already parked outside the house) and dissolving into tears as I heard myself say the words – my friend is dead. I felt reproach in those words spoken aloud, like a declaration of failure. I told an unbelieving Phil and spent the rest of the evening leaking tears, staring at nothing, or arguing with Phil who patiently allowed each thought space and each emotion to unfold. *How could she do this to her parents? How will they ever move on from this? Could I have done more to help her?*

I phoned Daddy, knowing he was my safe space, my soft place to land, as a child looks to a parent, throwing my heartache at him as a desperate entreaty to fix it somehow. He heard the shake in my voice as I unburdened myself and sighed as I broke and sobbed.

"*Ah, love. Ah, darling,*" he crooned.

He was finally the Daddy I had always wanted, one that radiated love and empathy. When had this changed? Surely it was all Martin. His birth gave me a conscious daddy and his death had given me a softer one. Daddy's raison d'etre was still to Protect and Fix, but now he could do it gently, without rushing in and dictating. He left space for me to talk.

"*Daddy, I knew she was depressed, and I didn't visit her. I could have done something.*"

I dissolved into sobs again. It was the hot thought, as we call it in CBT, the one that triggers the tears in the root of the issue. I had failed her, and she was dead.

"*Sweetheart, you listen to me. Are you listening?*"
"*Yes, Daddy.*"
"*Let me tell you a wee story, okay, love? Okay. Years ago, when I was a young man, a fella came up to me when I was doing the doors at the bar. Now, I didn't know him really well, but I knew him from seeing him about, you know? And he says to me, he says, Ben, will you give me my lift? And I'm not sure what he's asking, so I says, what are you talking about? And he says, my last lift, Ben, will you give me my lift? Peggy, he was asking me to carry his coffin. I says to him, aye, I'll give you your last lift, son, no bother. I thought it was just talk, maybe he was drunk, feeling maudlin. Peggy, he went home and killed himself. Now, he was practically telling me that he was going to do it and I didn't catch it. Now, I'm going to ask you a question. Are you ready, kid?*"
"*Yes, Daddy.*"
"*Was it my fault that man died?*"
He knew he could rely on my logic and compassion in evaluating the culpability of others, if not my own. Daddy didn't soft-soap, he met me where I was. Without having studied it, he was using the CBT technique of highlighting a Double Standard. He had me.
"*No, Daddy.*"
"*No, love. This terrible, awful thing has happened, but it wasn't your fault any more than that man's death was mine. You remember that, now, won't you? It isn't your fault, love.*"
"*Okay, Daddy.*"
"*There's nothing you can do. Be gentle with yourself. Tell Phil to make you a cup of tea. Go easy on yourself, sweetheart.*"

It was hard, but I tried - not for myself, but for my daddy who I knew was hurting because I was.

That night, I slept fitfully, with the familiar feeling of emerging from the torpor of sleep with a nagging sense of something being wrong, then remembering, then tears, then troubled sleep, on a loop. The morning came and I lay in a delta state, exhausted, solemn, open. Jill filled my thoughts and my heart.

Where are you? How are you? Are you at peace? Has the weight of pain lifted? Has it been replaced by the pain of knowing what you've left behind? Can you hear us? Feel us? You are so loved.

I alternated between bouts of nauseating grief and receptivity. I woke early the next morning and cried in a way I hadn't in years, excavating the anguish and leaving space for something else to take its place. I grew still and felt attuned to her. My questions hung in the air, as real as anything else, floating with me in an energetic space. I sensed her, but my conditioned mind, my judgemental mind tried to coax me away with criticism and condemnation: how arrogant to imagine that she'd be here with you, of all people, when her parents ache for her? But there she was, and I knew, who better? This isn't my first rodeo. Thoughts arrived in my Head Letterbox that I knew were meant for Jill's parents. She couldn't deliver them directly because they were too distraught and overwhelmed to receive it. I wrote them down, these words that manifested from the ether. Jill, gentle as ever, but insistent. *Tell them what I meant to you.* And I promised I would. I was no stranger to the grieving parent. Greater love, greater devastation does not exist. I lay there as day dawned, my questions hanging in the air, answers landing softly as sorrow weaved with love.

∞∞∞

Dear David and Ruth,

I am so sorry for your loss. As you have no doubt discovered, words are inadequate in capturing the magnitude of what Jill meant to us, but in this letter, I wish to try to explain what she meant to me. In the days following the tragedy, beyond the pain and the shock, I had little whisperings of truth, and one which repeated in the days leading up to Friday was a passage from Charlotte's Web by E.B. White, in which Charlotte the spider broaches the subject of her impending death with her loving little friend, Wilbur.

"You have been my friend," replied Charlotte. "That in itself is a tremendous thing. I wove my webs for you because I like you. After all, what's a life, anyway? We're born, we live a little while, we die...by helping you, perhaps I was trying to lift up my life a trifle. Heaven knows, anyone's life can stand a little of that."

In my relationship with Jill, we would take turns being Charlotte; she lifted up my life in allowing me to try to help her, and in helping me so many times with her unconditional and consistent love, perhaps I lifted up her life a trifle, too.

It's difficult to express what Jill meant to me and who she is without it becoming a list of adjectives. That she was so elegant and profound in her love of her friends and family is well known, yet something which can only truly be understood in our own hearts.

I recall the first time I met Jill. She was across the room during our Postgraduate Induction Afternoon in the Social Sciences Postgraduate Common Room. I spotted her very early and remember thinking how radiant she looked; so lovely and friendly with those big blue eyes and wee pink cheeks! Not one to miss out, I made a beeline for her during the reception and asked her which course she was doing (as it was a reception for all PG Social Sciences courses). I remember my heart literally leapt when she said she was doing the same course as me, and we swapped numbers and immediately became firm friends, even swapping texts before the term started, getting enthused about furnishing our new pencil cases, of all things! On the first day, we went to lunch together, as we did every day after. God, I love her.

As I'm sure Jill told you, my brother died some years ago. I remember explaining my journey of grief to Jill. My bottom line is now for Jill as it was then for Martin; her all too brief presence in my life has affected me positively and moulded my very self in ways that I would not forego to circumvent the pain of losing her. She was my friend and she lifted up my life more than just a trifle.

I am sure you have heard it many times, because it was true and widely known that Jill loved you both so dearly. She spoke of you often, and always with affection and great respect for the kind and loving human beings you clearly are. Her own qualities of kindness and loving friendship are a testament to you both; she enriched so many lives, and not least mine.

My heartfelt sympathy and love go to you both at this painful time. There are no words, but these, for now, will have to suffice.

Lots of love to you,
Peggy

The day of the funeral was a strange one. Her dear mum had requested that we all wear Jill's favourite colour – fuchsia pink – in honour of her. I couldn't bring myself to. Something of the shame of purple nail polish still lingered and I opted for a pale pink, safer, less ostentatious. As I blow dried my hair, I saw Jill in my reflection - her pink cheeks, two little apples sitting under her shining eyes. I dismissed the thought as fanciful. Of course, I saw Jill, she was all I had thought about for days.

The church was predictably packed, with faces both familiar and unfamiliar, swathes of hot pink and smatterings of unique fashion pieces connected with Jill - gifted items, garments bought on shared trips to London or beyond. Jill's body rested in a biodegradable coffin at the front, beyond reach. Her sweet little hands, once warm, her arms and legs that once danced, making her masses of blonde hair swish as she whirled, laughing, as she expressed music with her being like it was no great thing, this grace that most could never dream of. She was really gone.

After the service, her mum approached her friends and gifted each of us a piece of Jill's jewellery, something to remember her by. She gave me a set of earrings and a necklace that I felt I scarcely deserved. Did everyone feel that way? Something to remind us of her, as if we would ever need reminding, and something to be worn as we went on without her - never meant to be part of a shrine.

Jill's lovely friend Cathy offered to host after the funeral. We drank wine, talked of Jill, laughed and cried. I took a moment for myself in the bathroom to smooth my hair and once more saw Jill in my reflection. It was ridiculous - Jill was honey blonde, blue-eyed, cherub-faced. I remembered the day I caught my reflection in her apartment and was jarred by the dull comparison to her face, but again, in Cathy's bathroom, she was somehow there.

Jill's mum took time to speak to each of us kindly, warmly. Jill was her double, shining eyes, sweet smiling, pretty. My heart pined when I noticed her hands. Jill's hands.

Her daughter's passing had eviscerated her, but somehow, she allowed it to strengthen her grace. Jill's mum, who was been subjected to such pain, chose to remain soft. I wondered if it was not our successes, but our response to defeat that defines us. I hope to be half the woman Jill's mother is, but more, I pray I never have to be.

Jill's dad sat on a sofa and spoke quietly to those who sat nearby, treading water, grateful for Cathy's kindness in hosting, but biding his time to go home and come undone. I tried to catch his eye, to impart a fraction of the warmth I felt for him, this broken parent I was all too familiar with. He would hold my gaze for a second, nod, smile and look away.

Some weeks after the funeral, I arranged to meet with Jill's parents in 'our' - mine and Jill's – favourite café. Her mum (like Jill) was all chat, interest, empathy and encouragement. She admitted to being a chatterbox and announced she would leave to let David have a chance to

get a word in edgewise. We were just two, a little awkward without the lubricant of Ruth's easy friendliness. My heart ached for him, and I wished so fervently to be able to administer some kind of balm. He hesitated, then spoke.
"I'm sorry I didn't speak to you after the funeral."
"Gosh, not at all, you had enough people to get through."
"Well, it wasn't that."
He paused.
"You really reminded me of Jill that day. Even now – those wee pink cheeks... Does that sound strange?"
"It really doesn't," I replied.

Unshed tears shone in his eyes as he haltingly recounted stories of his younger daughter. An ex-teacher at her primary school, he lamented not having her in his class as he had done for his older daughter, and grieved seeing her through his classroom window, little shy Jill, wandering around the playground alone. His heart ached at the memory of things he wished he had done differently, had he ever thought their time would be so short. He began sentences too painful to finish.
"I should have insisted she was in my class... I could be strict..."
"You know she thought the world of both of you? Both of you. And she knew you loved her. And she loved you deeply."

His heart was broken with the remorse of the bereaved parent, pain I'd seen before. He was the father who loved viscerally, consumed with fear that it hadn't been felt, pinned by the full stop of death. Our conversation was a small bloodletting.

When we parted, he smiled and put his hand to my face.

"Those wee cheeks," he said, and seemed to marvel.

Was she overlaying her energy onto mine, or had grief and longing forced us to see what wasn't there?

Death. It keeps coming up. I mean, none of us get out of here alive, but when someone has had a good innings, we become circumspect and can avoid the tough questions. I never had that choice. I grew up in the shadow of dead brothers, then my dear sweet friend sought out death's kiss. When the young die, questions come unbidden. It has been in my path to ask questions about death, and answers keep coming. These lives we have, some brief, contain lessons. Sometimes we learn, sometimes we present the lesson to others. Now it was my turn for a painful lesson - it is always better to be kind than to be right. I wish I had made a peaceful little blanket fort for us to exist in until her depression passed. Instead, I was too rigid to admit that depression doesn't discriminate according to how knowledgeable you are on the subject. I underestimated the stranglehold it had on her. I should have been the soft place to land that she needed and deserved.

Jill, I love you. I miss you. I hope we meet again - on the other side, or on this one, in Earth's school room, where I promise – I PROMISE to be kind.

Twenty-Six

Phil and I decided the time was right to start a family of our own. I desperately wanted the baby to be a boy, another Martin to fill the void that he left in our family and in our hearts. Underneath the longing for Martin, however, lay a tangled web of internalised misogyny from the messages I'd received in childhood - that girls are more troublesome than boys. There was a massive cognitive dissonance between my understanding of the value of women, learned in feminist studies at University, and how little worth I felt I had as a girl. There was a gulf between intellectually understanding that my programming was faulty and the lived experience of having had parents who feared for me in a way they never did for Martin.

My preference for a boy left me in a Catch-22; living with the legacy of dead sons had given me an irrational fear that I carried a curse. I wanted a boy, but I did not want the pain of my parents. I quietly fretted and wished away the weeks until we could have a gender scan, so that I could know which scenario to prepare myself for. At sixteen weeks, the baby's legs were crossed. Again, at eighteen weeks. At twenty weeks, still firmly shut.

Maternal stress can affect the unborn child, causing changes in the brain and heightening cortisol levels, at least in the short term. The last thing I wanted was for this baby to intuit, inherit or absorb any of my anxiety so I focused on self-care. I ate nutritious food, took supplements and listened to relaxation MP3s every morning and night. I briefly considered talking therapy, but by then had realized it had limited efficacy for me. My programming to be a good girl - fast learning, untroublesome - tempted me to misrepresent myself and imply more progress and healing than I had achieved so I could give the therapist an easy win. On reflection, these were the very issues I should have been overtly working on in therapy, but I had shot myself in the foot so many times with exactly those bullets of self-sabotage that I saw myself as a lost cause.

Instead, I met with a Bodytalk practitioner. Bodytalk is a system by which a therapist facilitates synchronization of the body's energy fields, thereby enabling the body to heal and fix itself. If I had stored trauma, then Bodytalk could rebalance my energy. Most pertinently, I couldn't throw a Bodytalk session. The treatment rooms were situated in a business park in the country. The unit was a long, cold corridor with doors leading to small therapy rooms. A little Scottish woman, smiling and chittering pleasantries, beckoned me to her room which thankfully had a heater blasting warm air. Her name was Leslie. She invited me to sit on a chair by her small desk against the wall, facing the treatment bed and asked questions to fill out my treatment form. She reminded me of the medium in the way she flitted between chatter and reflection. She gestured to my bump.

"Do you know what you're having?"

"No — every time I have a scan, the legs are up. This baby is giving nothing away."

She invited me to get comfortable on the treatment bed, positioning pillows beneath my neck and knees, tucking me in with a warm, fleece blanket. As I relaxed, she sat by the bed with her right index and middle finger resting on the inside of my right elbow. From time to time her fingers would press and tap gently in a kind of unintelligible Morse code. She was interviewing my body and every so often she would take her hand away and write feverishly on a notepad. It seemed reassuringly like intuitive work. Leslie giggled every now and then, as though she was part of a delightful conversation.

"This baby is deliberately hiding its gender to protect you from your feelings. It feels like it will make you sad either way. You would be disappointed with a girl, and a boy will make you fearful. This wee baby loves you so much that it will hide who it is until it is sure you will be okay with the answer."

If this was true, this poor child wasn't even born and already it was feeling the weight of my issues. When I got home, I lay on the bed and held my growing abdomen and promised the baby that I would love it, no matter what. I couldn't allow my child to shoulder the burden of my fear. I had to ensure this soul came into the world with as clean a slate as I could offer. It was one thing to go through life acknowledging my issues like some kind of shit trophy when the only person I was hurting was myself but realising that staying stuck hurt my child was enough to make me commit to change. I womanned up. I leaned into being a mother, committed to my responsibilities to nurture, to keep my love strong but light, without the burden of expectation, and chose to deprive my conditioning of oxygen in the hope that it would wither and turn to dust.

Phil and I presented for yet another gender scan at twenty-two weeks. I hoped the baby had heard my commitments to love a little girl and make sure she grew up knowing she was worthwhile, to love a little boy and allow him to live a life unimpeded by my fear of death. I lay on the reclining bed and didn't have long to wait. The scan showed three little lines between the legs - I was having a girl. In the first few moments, I felt sad, but then realised that this sadness was for my parents. There would be no boy child to love in their old age. As those shadows cleared, I realised that I was not sad for me. In fact, I was a little bit excited. The excitement popped its head above the parapet, looking around to check if it was okay to come out. I looked at Phil.
"A…daughter?!"

He nodded back, watching for my response. I thought of my friends who were close to their mums and realised that if I played my cards right, I could have that too - a happy mother-daughter relationship, going through life with my girl. In that moment, I was giddy with the possibility of giving her the one thing I had felt I had lacked; loving her while she unfolds into her own image, and not mine. As we drove home, we imagined all the things she could do - she might want to travel, maybe she would sing. As we allowed ourselves tentatively, to explore these happy visions of a future of helping a human self-actualise, something deeper was happening inside me. I was suffused with deep joy, grateful that she had chosen me.

When we arrived home, my pregnant bladder forced me to beat a hasty path to the toilet. As I washed my hands, I looked at my face in the mirror and smiled. A girl! Then a second, more familiar thought. You look awful. I scrutinised myself. My smile faded - probably just as well, because I don't have a cute smile - my cheeks look fat, and I get deep marionette lines either side of my mouth. My hair had gone limp and because we internalise the voices of our childhood, I thought *rats' tails*. I was tired and needed to take out my lenses, but that would mean spending the rest of the evening being a speccy four-eyes. I started to spiral. *What if she looks like me? What if she has my stupid squint, my dark eyes hidden behind glasses, unbiddable hair? What if she is not pretty?*

I hoped she would look like Phil - light eyes, good bones, great smile, thick dark hair - but I knew that even if she was a goddamn supermodel, it wouldn't prevent her from absorbing my insecurities. She would learn a girl's worth by watching me and the example I provided would determine her susceptibility to eventual media-bombardment that a woman's worth is directly proportional to her fuckability. Not on my watch.

I thought of this girl and wished for her all the things I wished for my young self: confidence, self-esteem, a soft place to land when the world inevitably made you feel less-than. The best way to bestow these gifts was to embody them, as humans are hardwired to model their behaviour on those around them. In this way, my daughter was the catalyst for me to love myself, because the only way to save her was to save myself, and the best way to love her was to love myself and be seen doing it. I remembered the between lives regression with Joe Boyle.

"Are there any other members of this soul group who you haven't met in this lifetime yet?"

"I have new teachers down the line; people who are proficient in their areas. They will encourage and strengthen me. They will teach with love."

This kid was teaching me, and she wasn't even born yet.

I phoned Melanie.

"Well, we finally found out the gender today!"

"At last! Okay, so I'm guessing it is a boy because you sound excited?"

"It is a girl!"

"Oh my God – that's brilliant! Hold on – do you think it's brilliant? Are you okay with it?"

And I spilled out all my thoughts to my best friend, who was shocked, but delighted to hear of my breakneck speed epiphany.

Twenty-Seven

If my parents were sad that they weren't going to have a grandson, they did not let me know. Their consistent refrain was, *as long as it's healthy.*

For the most part, we muddled along well, my parents and I, under the shadow of an unspoken agreement that the friction of my juvenile years was never mentioned. When Daddy phoned, he would shout merrily into the receiver, *Peggy! It's me, your handsome daddy!* and peppered his chat with terms of endearment - sweetheart, my darling, wee love, kid – words that enveloped me with warmth and made my heart swell, words I wished I had heard with such frequency and abandon as a child, when they were held back, when conditional love waited to see how I would turn out, whether I would prove myself deserving. But now I was loved, and I beat down creeping resentments like whack-a-moles so as not to rock the boat. I wanted to be the good girl, not the troublesome one.

Ours had become a relationship of surface ease; we genuinely enjoyed each other's company. Perhaps this was normal, if such a thing exists, but I never took for granted that my worries were received with compassion and my stories with delight. I felt liked, which somehow felt as valuable, if not more so, than being loved. If love is a duty, then like is a choice. I had merit. We sat for hours (Daddy trying his very hardest not to reach for the cigarettes so I'd stay a little longer) and talked and talked - of serious things, of everyday things, of all the things - except that. I loved listening to Daddy's ridiculous tales from the old days, and he spun a yarn like no one else. *Here, did I ever tell you about the time I nearly broke out of jail?* or, pointing at Mummy - *Did I ever tell you about the time that wee woman jumped up on a pouffe and punched me in the face?* (The latter tale had us in kinks of laughter, but Mummy didn't join in, leaving me to suspect that she had indeed punched him in the face and still felt he had deserved it.) Right into my 30s, he followed me out to the door with his *Cheerio! Drive safe, kid!* and forced a twenty-pound note into my hand - *There's something for a wee drink!* - answering my protestations with *Go on, sure it's just a wee score a quid! Take it and frig off!* One time, he stuffed something into my bag saying, *that'll get you a wee drink!* and after I protested, it turned out to be a teabag. I had the last laugh when he put himself into a coughing fit laughing at his own joke.

The only time I wasn't welcome at the house was when Manchester United was playing, and I was under strict instructions not to phone or visit during the hours of play. He had never been a football fan until Martin played, by which time he was in his fifties. Daddy followed the team faithfully after Martin died and I was never sure if Martin had ignited a love of the sport or if Daddy sat by the window staring at the screen and imagining what might have been.

One sunny afternoon, I deliberately phoned mid-game.

"*Hello, Mummy.? Can I speak with my daddy a minute?*"
"*The game's on, love.*"
"*Just for a wee minute.*"
"*Uhh...okay, love. Ben?*"
"*What?*"
"*It's Peggy.*"
A creak as he got out of his chair.
"*What is it, love? The game's on.*"
"*Sorry, Daddy. My cars broke down here.*"
I stifled laughs as I anticipated him going into a meltdown.
"*Where are you, love?*"
I invented a location that was far enough out that rescuing me would mean missing the game.
"*The back road to Finaghy, just past Lambeg.*"
"*I'm on my way.*"
"*What? No! Ah, for goodness sake! I was joking! I thought you'd go beserk because the game's on!*"
"*You're not broken down?*"
"*No! I'm having you on!*"
He laughed.
"*Frig off, well! The game's on! Eejit.*"
Click.

I sat for a while smiling to myself, because my Daddy would walk out on a long-anticipated match for me without a second thought or a cross word. Because this kindness was consistent so late in our relationship, I was constantly surprised to find myself loved. I still am, mostly.

Eventually, inevitably, the same whack-a-mole thoughts kept springing up until I got tired of bashing them down and began to wonder if their love for me was strong enough to withstand my ugly thoughts and feelings. I wondered if our relationship was still based on the shifting sands of my deserving, and if I would still be loved and liked if I wasn't 'good' and brought up the past. I wanted them to love me enough to be accountable. Stuffing my feelings down helped me maintain a relationship with my parents, while simultaneously undermining it.

Things were coming to a head.

Phil and I had moved to Seahill temporarily while our house was undergoing renovations which would not be finished until after the baby was born. We were half an hour's drive further out than the usual ten minutes away and Daddy refused to visit, claiming that he did not know the route (despite having a sat nav). Instead, they phoned frequently, sometimes daily.

It bothered me. I dislike talking on the telephone intensely. Maybe it was because our telephone had been kept in the living room so that my conversations could be monitored, and I'd be interrogated afterwards - *what did you mean when you said this?* Perhaps it was the weekly family phone call with Jeanette – the pressure of trying to consolidate our sisterly bond in a few minutes on a

Sunday, plagued with awkward transatlantic pauses impeding the flow, having to heavily curate my bulletin for the prying ears of my parents, or worse, having nothing to say as the expensive minutes ticked by. My hatred of the mobile phone was greater still - that tinny little ring of obnoxious interjection, a demand to stop whatever you were enjoying and attend to someone else's needs.

Unlike Jeanette, I wasn't thousands of miles across the Atlantic, so interrupting my day via mobile and refusing to visit was not cutting it. I'd give the curt responses of a passive-aggressive, surly teenager, then feel shit, then angry about feeling shit. Eventually, Daddy phoned and demanded,

"Stop hurting your mother by refusing to have a proper conversation on the phone."

Being chastised for not showing sweet-faced gratitude to receive a call I didn't want was the last straw. My underlying resentment towards my parents had limped on for long enough. This irritation, like a tickling cold sore, had begun to ache and was about to burst into a pustulating, swollen, deforming thing of ugliness.

Up until then, my refrain had been that I would not punish them for the pain I'd experienced growing up, because, in the Louise Hay parlance, they were doing the best they could do with what they had been taught as children. And it was true - they were literally two hurt and traumatised people who had reacted to a cruel world and cruel circumstances by keeping their children safe in the most effective way they knew how. But no matter how much I reinforced this notion, to myself or with friends or therapists (of whom by now there had been several) - anger and resentment continued to leak out the sides, and there was no platitudinous maxi pad big enough to contain it.

I decided to have The Talk. I stuck Louise Hay in a cupboard and committed to let my folks know that their best had been far from good enough. I couldn't forgive. I couldn't forget. As a baby grew in my belly, I thought of the kind of mother I wanted to be and felt cheated that I wasn't loved in that way. On a logical level I could accept that they were the products of their own difficult upbringings, then broken with loss, that their love was expressed by giving me every advantage they could in terms of education and opportunity, while fiercely guarding me from failure through bad choices. Only it didn't feel like love. My head could acknowledge their dedication, but my heart was hurt and wasn't healing. I remembered Daddy, worn out from grief, confiding *I made mistakes with you,* but it didn't feel real. I badly needed to hear that Daddy felt remorse for his mistakes and that I had deserved better. I phoned Jeanette to ascertain that she had heard him say it too, doubting my own ears and my own memory. I convinced myself that hearing these words from his lips once more would make my problems disappear, as if all the damage caused could be erased with words, like the breaking of a spell that would set me free.

Now I was the reactionary parent, and in processing my experience through this new lens, I was determined she would get the gentle handling I hadn't and would suffer none of my hurts. On some primal level, I had positioned myself between her and the world, a Mother, defensive and ready to attack, laser-focused on a singular point of threat: my parents.

I wished our family to be a clean slate as she joined us, free of the burden of the unsayable and unsaid, a family where children were not controlled by fear and adults didn't wait to see if you turned out well before loving you overtly.

I understood that for her to embody the empowerment I wished for her, I would have to model it. If she was to learn assertiveness and self-advocacy, I would need to live it.

This was how I rationalised confronting my parents, to myself, but it may just as easily have been prompted by a cocktail of hormones, or that little whisper which I didn't want to acknowledge but which came nonetheless - there was a new baby on the way, and sometimes the universe operates on a one-in, one-out basis. Two months before, Daddy had attended hospital for a scan for lung cancer, and although the results were clear, I felt this might be my last chance to say my piece. I had just under two weeks left before the baby was due, but instead of deep cleaning my house, I was deep cleaning my heart.

I sat at one end of the sofa while Mummy sat at the other. We both faced Daddy, sitting in his armchair by the window. I gathered up my courage and said a silent prayer that I could stay calm if things became heated.

"I have some things that I want to say. I need to clear the air before the baby arrives. I'm not trying to start a fight and I am not trying to hurt you. Can I speak honestly?"

"What's all this about?" snapped Mummy, turning to fix me with a warning glare.

Daddy, ever the warrior, afraid of nothing and no one, put one hand up to silence her while looking me dead in the eye.

"You can say whatever you want."

It wasn't permission so much as a challenge.

"You spoke to me the other day on the phone about why I have not been having conversations with Mummy when she calls. The truth is I'm feeling a bit annoyed. First of all, I don't like talking on the phone, which I've explained numerous times, but more than that, I feel like a phone-call is a bare minimum of effort. You can visit the graves several times a month but hopping in the car to give me ten minutes is too much effort and that really hurts."

"Okay. What else?"

In Daddy's boxing days, he had a very specific style. His back injury meant that he couldn't bob and weave; the usual dance and parry was necessarily absent. Instead, he stood rooted to the ground and took punches. He waited it out with his guard up. He let his opponents tire themselves out before making his move.

"Well, I'm having a baby. Are you going to discipline her the way you disciplined me if she puts a foot out of line?" I couldn't wait

for an answer because talking about hurt children had ignited a blaze inside me, *"- because you can't hit my child."*
He continued to hold my gaze, poker-faced.
"What else?"
I turned to Mummy and my heart really started to hammer.
"You. You have hurt me most of all. Daddy lashed out but you, you are my mummy. You never stopped him!"
"What was I meant to do?!" she exclaimed, shrill.
"Leave! You leave someone who hurts your children!"
Daddy interjected.
"It's not her fault. I'm the disciplinarian. And I wouldn't let her leave."
I took off on a tangent.
"Well, she left regardless of when we ended up at that Women's Refuge."
His lip curled in disgust.
"They were all at it, back then, leaving and fucking off to the Women's Refuge."

My eyebrows shot up in imperious shock that he chose to view my mother's response to physical, mental and emotional abuse as nothing more than taking part in a craze, centring himself as the abandoned spouse, the victim instead of the catalyst.

I felt myself getting tied up as I tried to elicit threads of reason, but it was no use. I returned to the solid ground of criticising Mummy.
"If Phil even so much as raised his hand to our baby, I would not only walk out, I would stab him on the way past."

"*What else?*" Daddy asked, drawing my attention from Mummy.

"*You were too vicious. That wasn't discipline. That was abuse.*"

"*It was discipline. You needed to be kept on the straight and narrow. I made sure you got an education. I got you to Grammar. I made sure you got your exams to get to University.*"

"*No, you didn't! I did those things! If anything, you held me back! Did you know that I had such low self-esteem in school that I was a rallying point for bullies? That I was such an insecure mess that I failed first year of Uni? Using violence to control children comes at too big a price. I'm damaged.*"

"*Look, that's how I was raised. That's how you discipline children in Sandy Row.*"

"*No, it's not. You went too far! You were up for serious assault after that beating. Have all the fathers in Sandy Row been up for serious assault for disciplining their kids?*"

I was on thin ice. Even though I felt I had made a salient point, I had just skimmed past the central issue upon which we differed. I resented the violence; he resented the whistleblowing. Kids in Sandy Row didn't end up in homes because they didn't run off and tout. They took their oil. He leaned towards me and lowered his voice, conspiratorially.

"*Do you know why you ended up in that home?*"

"*Because you went too far in beating the crap out of me?*"

"*It was because you were manipulative.*"

I reeled.

"*What?*"

"Your social worker said it. He said you were manipulative."
I flailed, trying to understand. Peter? That soft spoken, seemingly sensible man whose job had been to advocate - not just for me, but for the family as a whole - had placed the blame squarely with me?
"He said you had manipulated the judge."
"I never met the judge! How did I manipulate a judge I had never met to pass a two-year suspended sentence? This is nonsense. Now you are just making things up to get yourself off the hook."
"He said it."
Mummy chimed in.
"He did. And you were. You manipulated the whole situation."
"Oh, okay. This is pointless. If you are just going to talk nonsense...look. Long story short: you damaged me with your violence and your strictness. And I need to know that you won't hurt my kid."

Daddy sensed I had spent my blows. Each jab had landed, even the ones he had tried to dodge had glanced painfully - but no matter. He understood it was time to finish it and he was going for a knock-out.
"What are you here for? An apology? You won't get one. Don't bring her around if you don't trust us. Just fuck off. Away you go and don't come back."
"Ack, Daddy, don't be ridiculous."
"No. If we are so bad, why bring a child near us? Go on. You've said your piece."
Mummy stiffened on the sofa beside me.
"Ah, Ben, no..." she muttered quietly.

This little baby her arms had been aching for was nearly here, and suddenly it was getting pushed beyond her reach. It was a prospect too hard to bear. She started to cry.

"I will go. But let's remember that you chose this. Not me. You."

I walked out on trembling legs and drove home shaking with adrenaline from shock, from grief. When I eventually cried, it wasn't for me, because that part had been closed off for years. I cried for these two damaged, hurt people. I cried for Daddy who owned all his other fuckups but refused to believe that the one thing he thought he'd got right – me – was in fact one of his largest failures. I had taken away the one thing he liked about himself, the one thing he had been proud of, his legacy, the one bright light in a life suffused in loss and pain. I cried for Mummy, who only wanted to experience the unconditional love of a little baby once more in the winter years of what had been a truly horrendous life.

Perhaps it was a primal desperation not to be abandoned, perhaps it was a need to have logic marshal the disorder of emotional pain, but I reframed the purpose of the exercise. I wasn't chasing an apology, I was finally putting my side across and letting him know that his harsh treatment had harsh consequences upon my self-worth, and that I was no longer afraid to tiptoe around that. I had spoken up for myself, and that was enough.

Except it wasn't. His failure to acknowledge my wounds, his failure to take responsibility for his parenting choices ate at me. On reflection, it was naïve to expect a man with almost seventy years' experience of not bending the knee to suddenly proclaim *mea culpa*. To his mind, parenting us, keeping our noses to the grindstone and out of trouble was the one thing he could stand over. Hearing me tell him that my successes were despite him rather than because of him must have cut deeply. Worse, it was the last thing he could ever concede because it was the one thing, he liked himself for, and there I was, an ingrate, crowbarring it away from his tenuous grasp. Yes, an apology would've been a convenient shortcut to tying up the frayed ends of a complicated relationship and starting to move on, but life isn't like that. Perhaps it isn't meant to be. Forgiveness is easy if it's sought, but what if it isn't? It is one thing to give your benevolent pardon to someone who acknowledges a fault. It is quite another to dispense forgiveness when the perpetrator of the offence is looking you in the eye with a, cheerfully defiant and frustratingly familiar fuck you. That is where the lesson is: granting forgiveness when it is neither looked for nor perhaps even deserved. Therein lies the alchemy. It was essential to my growth that I forgive even when I deemed it unwarranted. Daddy was under orders from heaven to deny responsibility. It was how we had planned it to be and it could never be any other way. His steadfast denials of wrongdoing ensured my path had no shortcuts.

  I wrote a letter. In it I said my piece in the measured way that writing affords. I don't know if he ever read it. I planned on sneaking it quietly through the

letterbox and tiptoeing away, but I caught his eye from his chair at the window and he intercepted me at the door, inviting me in. Mummy was halfway down the stairs when she noticed me being ushered in. She stopped and narrowed her eyes.
"What are you doing back here?"
The six-foot boxer's four-foot eleven (and a half) bodyguard. Daddy put his hand up,
"Shh Gloria. Enough."
He sat on his chair and lit a cigarette, a sign of no concession. I sat on the sofa and pretended not to notice.
"Do you hear that?"
I listened but wasn't sure what I was supposed to be listening for.
"The cistern! Can you hear it?"
I strained to listen and heard a faint gurgling from upstairs.
"The Housing Executive was supposed to be out by now. We have been in all day waiting for the plumber."
"It'd put your head away," added Mummy.
"Imagine that filling up all day and all night! It's a nuisance."

And while they prattled on about their latest domestic disaster, our own recent one loomed unacknowledged, and between the lines of the chatter, Daddy was clearly insisting that the matter was closed.

When I got home later, Phil asked how things had gone.

"He saw me coming down the path and got to the door before I could post the letter and sneak away, and he opened the door and told me to come in."

"Did he read it?"

"No. He put it on his side table."

"What did he say about the other day?"

"Nothing. He and Mummy just talked about the issue they are having with their toilet. Every time it spontaneously flushed, they both went, 'Do you hear that?' and complained about how long it was taking to get a plumber out."

"Did YOU say anything about the other day?"

"Fuck, no."

He looked at me strangely.

"So, you sat around talking about the plumbing?"

I nodded.

"You lot are nuts."

"Sure, I know."

Daddy could help me through any trauma except the ones he had inflicted. Though I dreaded the day he would die, I felt that when he arrived at that space between lives, the scales would fall off his eyes and he would see without the filter of this painful life. In the meantime, the best we could do was work out a routine whereby neither of us triggered or became triggered by the other.

Two weeks after the altercation, my girl was born. My parents drove to the hospital and held her gently, gazing into her tiny face.

"I called her Sia Martha, Mummy. After you."

Martha was her middle name, after her own mother. Daddy smiled.

"Ah, wee Martha…"

When we got home, they visited every day, bringing a little something each time; food provisions, a hot water bottle with a pink fluffy cover to warm the Moses basket before I set her in, little clothes. Daddy would take five minutes to recover his breath from walking from the car. I held up a yellow T-shirt and shorts set.
"*These are for age three!*" I exclaimed.
Mummy rolled her eyes.
"*Your Daddy insisted on those.*"
"*They look cheerful!*" he replied.

I laughed and quietly hoped he'd be around long enough to see her wear it, ignoring the little voice that told me that he wouldn't.

Daddy was diagnosed with Stage 4 Lung Cancer when Sia was two weeks old. The scans he had two months before had been clear, but by the end of June there were large masses in both lungs. Some say cancer is a disease of resentment and part of me wondered if I had triggered or accelerated this physical illness with the emotional wounds I had inflicted. After all the things that hadn't killed him, there I was hidden in plain sight all this time, harbouring words that could undo him, his kryptonite. My forgiveness meant that he didn't have to do the hard work of forgiving himself. Withdrawing it proved fatal.

When I found out about his terminal diagnosis, I went to sit on the doorstep for some fresh air, and another thought kept repeating. This is it. Never again will we sit and talk into the wee hours, never again the familiar push and pull of debate, never again the tales of the old days, the patchwork of stories he was made up of would be unstitched and float away on the ether and everything he was to me would be beyond reach. My Daddy. Phil slipped his arm around my shoulder as I wept, big, broken, racking sobs. This was it. The clock was ticking.

After I dried my tears and steadied my breathing, I phoned Daddy.

"What do you need?"

I delivered prescriptions, accessed oxygen tanks and mediated with doctors. I threw Sia into a car seat and travelled to visit them every other day, because the guilt of neglecting this new little baby was eating at me. I would bring her up the stairs and lay her on his bed. He looked tired and drawn, but the light would come back into his eyes as he stroked her face and called her his wee Martha.

In that time, I was more daughter than mother. Perhaps I was more mother to him than little Sia, who spent too long in car seats and the bouncy chair or pram as I tried to ease the too-heavy burden for my parents. I was finding my feet as a mother at a time when being a good daughter was more important than ever. I advocated for Daddy with doctors and chemists, typed a list to help him keep on top of what medication he had to take, and when. I couldn't tell him I loved him because that isn't how we spoke to each other, but I could show him. He asked me to be present to meet the undertaker with him, so that we could plan his funeral. I held it together and I took notes. I spoke for daddy when his speech was laboured through the combination of Bell's palsy, painful mouth sores and breathlessness. Afterwards, I shook the undertaker's hand and showed him out, then nipped back upstairs to Daddy to ask if he was content with how the meeting had gone.

"Peggy, I need you to remember who I want for my last lift."

I swallowed and steeled myself to imagine in vivid technicolour the dreaded day when Daddy was gone.

"Okay."

"The nephews. I want Wee Hughie at the front. John, Tommy and Jimmy."

Even after Big Hughie had died, his namesake, who towered over the rest of us was still called Wee Hughie.

"Yes, Daddy."

"And Phil. I want Phil to give me my last lift. Okay?"

I nodded and tried to imagine Phil's face when I told him. His own father, who had died when Phil was 20, had been carried by pallbearers and cremated after a short ceremony and Phil had processed his loss alone afterwards, on a beach, watching a cold horizon as the waves crashed. I knew he would feel misplaced and conspicuous.

When Daddy was satisfied that his wishes for the final day had been articulated, he allowed himself to succumb to tiredness and I went downstairs to the sofa in the living room and broke down sobbing. Mummy sat beside me.

"What's wrong, love?"

I knew immediately that she was unsure as to why I had broken down so completely at that particular moment, perhaps suspicious I had heard something that she wasn't already privy to. I turned to her and gasped out,

"It's too hard. All of this. I don't want to do it. It's too much…"

She looked at me intently and I felt sure she was about to say something compassionate, comforting, maternal. I was in a terrified free-fall and needed a soft place to land.

"Well, Peggy…you'll have this to do twice."

I looked at her blank with confusion, so she spelled it out.

"You'll have to do it all again when I go."

She looked at me searchingly, perhaps wondering if her own passing would elicit the same visceral grief. I stopped crying in shock that this was the best she could come up with, then burst out laughing. That exchange typified our relationship. God love her, she didn't have a mummy after the age of fourteen, and before then, her poor mother was dying slowly, so maternal comfort wasn't something she'd had enough exposure to. She had accidentally stuck the boot in when I was down and all I could do was laugh - at her earnest expression, at how badly misjudged her timing was, and how after all this time I was still holding out for a completely different mother to the one I had. She looked a little hurt as I cackled like a lunatic at the prospect of her inevitable demise, but sometimes (and all too often) there are such complexities of emotion and situation that laughing is the only way to discharge the extraordinary tension. Gallows humour.

I was always relieved to get home to Phil each evening, to shrug off the mantle of Good Daughter and just be. Just as I had predicted, Phil looked faintly horrified when I relayed Daddy's wish that he carry the coffin.

"Are pallbearers not doing it?"

"No. It's a thing, getting to carry the coffin. Giving the last lift, they call it. He wants you and the nephews to do it."

"I thought you had tons of cousins!"

"I do, but he wants you. You're the father of his grandchildren. Of course, you made the cut."

Each night, I lay in the velvet darkness with Phil on one side and Sia in her cot at the other, my love for daughter and father weaving melodies in majors and minors. I held her soft little hand and watched her chest rise and fall and felt the unbreakable thread that tied my heart to Daddy.

Twenty-Eight

Daddy wanted to stay at home to die, but the pain was becoming too much and the medication he needed to ease it could only be administered in hospital. I made up a hospital bag with toiletries and pyjamas and asked him what books he wanted. He chose only one: The Consolation of Philosophy by Boethius, wherein Boethius reflects upon religious questions as he awaits trial and possible execution. Ultimately, Daddy was too addled with morphine to absorb so much as a sentence, but his heart and soul were so wedded to philosophy that it was to this that he cleaved as death's doorway loomed. Philosophy had been his friend as he tried to navigate his own path through a hard childhood, had kept him company in prison and had offered a raft when his children died. In some ways, these dead guys were more real to him than the living.

He weakly insisted that I didn't bring Sia to the hospital, that I stayed at home with her, away from germs, but when I came regardless, he didn't object. Being a terminal patient, he had been given a room to himself at the back of the ward. I made my way past rows of beds, weakly smiling a hello to the staff at the nurses' station, who nodded their acknowledgement in silent sympathy. The door opened onto a room only big enough for a bed with a locker at one side and chair at the other, but it was suffused with light from the large window, through which other hospital buildings stood impassive under vast swathes of cloud, drifting and dissipating in the August sun. Boethius lay on the tray, untouched beside a glass of water, beaded with drips as ice chips melted, and an opened bag of sour gummy sweets - aul' sour bakes my parents called them. Mummy gave him a sweet to take away the taste of the bitter medication, but he couldn't enjoy them for long before the sores in his mouth began to sting, and he would push it out with his tongue. I looked away, at the Boethius and it occurred to me that my father favoured Stoics, those who could show him how to withstand the very worst life had to offer.

His speech was barely coherent. The Bell's palsy made his speech slushy and the blisters and sores from the treatment made enunciation painful. I sat at the window by the bed. He reached out and felt around the bed and I realised with a jolt of gratitude that he was looking for my hand. His big paw enclosed mine and he squeezed. I hadn't held his hand since Martin's funeral, when I overruled my uncertainty of expressing affection and just grabbed his hand as he wept, feet away from his dead child. It was strange territory, this handholding, and I hyper focused on every micro-movement to decipher meaning. There was one prolonged squeeze, like our clasped palms could relay all of the words he had never been able to say, even before he had been rendered incomprehensible. I knew he was remorseful. He knew he was dying and nothing else mattered but the love he felt then - had always felt but showed in the wrong ways. He was no longer a towering, forbidding presence; he was the child and man to whom terrible things had happened, whose own soft underbelly had been pierced so frequently that he donned armour to protect himself and wore it for so long that he no longer could tell where he stopped, and the armour began. I squeezed back because I wanted him to feel heard and understood and held tears in because even then I wanted to be a good girl, and good girls don't make a fuss. I knew he was putting sentiments into that grasp. I will never know for sure what they were, but I know love was there, fierce love that mingled with other things, love that left the imprint of my ring as it dug into my finger, and other marks that don't fade - and if that isn't a metaphor for our relationship, I don't know what is.

    Jeanette had already booked to fly home for a fortnight over his 70th birthday and had rescheduled to arrive earlier - a couple of days after the shock diagnosis. Her presence eased the pressure I put on myself to run back and forth. She was able to provide lifts for Mummy to and from the hospital and to simply be there. As her departure date drew close, she agonised over whether to extend her ticket. I wanted her to stay for the entirely selfish reason of having a sister to share the burden of practical and emotional support, but she had a family in the States that needed her, too.

"Peggy, I watched Aunt Janet die and it took months."
"He could be like this for months?"
She nodded grimly.

We sat on hard plastic chairs in the hospital's bright entrance foyer, amid the tang of antiseptic and hopelessness. I wondered how somewhere so sedate could be the scene for so much heartbreak. Occasionally, a nurse drifted by on soft soled shoes.

"Maybe I'm not the right person to ask, Jeanette. The consultant might have better advice."

I didn't hold out much hope that he could bring much clarity to her decision making; everyone had been understandably vague about life expectancy. However, the doctor she spoke to was mercifully blunt about her options.

"Well, it depends on whether you want to stay for the end or return for a funeral."

∞∞∞

She stayed. Together we watched as he lay wasting, a colostomy bag with dark contents betraying his dehydration. Flesh wilted and greyed, bones protruded. His mouth stretched open as though stuck in a terrible yawn, as he tried to suck air into his reluctant, tumour ravaged lungs. We propped him up when he slumped sideways, trying hard not to wake him to this awful existence that you wouldn't inflict on an enemy. An animal would be euthanised long before this stage, because allowing it to suffer would be inhumane and yet, my father, and other fathers, mothers, sisters, brothers, sons, daughters are forced to starve to death, in pain and without dignity. My thoughts turned dark and cynical. I wondered if compassion came with a price tag - that a proliferation of maintenance drugs is more profitable than one lethal shot. I condemned our society that denies a comfortable passing as vicious and unethical.

Watching him die was simultaneously the most real and surreal experience. It was brutish and blunt, heavy as a boulder. We were pinned and made to watch. Lung cancer is a drawn out passing of starvation and suffocation. He lay gasping, wasting, sore and nauseous, and as terrified as we were horrified.

And yet, as death drew close, two worlds overlapped tangibly as Daddy saw past us in that hospital room and caught glimpses of another world. We watched, confused as he pushed himself up to near sitting and put his arms out in entreaty.

"Daddy, do you need the toilet?"

He feebly swatted us away, and held his thinned, sallow arms out towards the end of the bed.

"Billy, I'm coming."

He saw his boys, who had come to collect him and to distract him from his suffering. Could it be the morphine? On some level, we all felt they were there. Perhaps they had never really left and only now as he was on the cusp of going home was the veil thinned sufficiently to perceive it. Such suspicions are seldom voiced. They are too good to be true, too beautiful and powerful in situations of such ugliness and helplessness. We downplay our knowing, we say we are clutching at straws and who am I to witness miracles? But, at times such as these, who better? It's a mercy to the dying to be received and a kindness to the bereaved to witness it.

In that hospital room, as two worlds overlapped, death was held off at arms-length, while protocol dictated that every last ounce of dignity, pain and suffering was extracted. Societies are judged on how they treat their weakest and most vulnerable. Why mercy for animals, but not people? His jaws gaped an overlarge yawp, dry tongue exposed, discoloured teeth and gums, then a twitch, a reflexive jerking like a fish flopping and gasping for life. Only then would the nurses make him comfortable. Only then was he permitted to die, his horror mask burned into our memories - our Daddy, the warrior, the philosopher, flawed and magnificent, the first man I ever loved, drained to an emaciated husk. Even then, with so little of him left, I felt the air change when he finally let go. The room seemed empty, it echoed with his absence. He died just thirteen days over his three-score years and ten.

The minister asked me to write notes for the eulogy. It was hard, summing up a life, a person in a few paragraphs, and harder still to create a summation that encapsulated this giant. In the end, I stuck to anecdotes and facts: the most expensive snowball he was ever hit with, his dedication to our educations, light sketches that barely hinted at the complexity of a man who could be both loving and hateful, who pushed me to my best and my worst, this human who evolved, who realised too late and too close to the end about unconditional love.

His nephews and friends wanted the honour of giving him his last lift, and it was heartening to see them negotiate shifts from the house to the hearse, hearse to the church, church to the grave. Phil did the last lift, and as they walked him to his final resting place, his little namesake, my cousin Ben who has Downs Syndrome broke from the mourners to be a pallbearer too, shuffling himself between the men to lay his hand on the coffin, face solemn, honouring his Uncle Ben who loved him and showed him how to box in the old shed at the back, holding up boxing pads and cheering him on with enthusiastic praise, *That's it kid! Go on, champ!*

Phil came to stand with me as the coffin was lowered into the ground.
"I get it. The last lift thing. It was like carrying a fallen warrior home from battle. It felt like an honour."
I nodded.

Mummy bought a headstone for the grave that resembled Daddy: broad, solid, no-frills. It bore the inscription of the names of my father and brother Martin with their dates of passing, and a space for when she joined them. I have never been one for graves. To me, when body and soul have parted, a grave is just an unpleasant reminder of physical decay. To Mummy, a well-tended grave meant respect and ongoing affection. I took her to visit the grave and she wiped the headstone down, changed the flowers, planted a kiss on the cold marble and stood for a moment in silent communion. One day I was studying the dates on the headstone – distracting myself from emotion, and from worse realities six feet below, when I noticed that Daddy had died fourteen years and six months after Martin, who himself had died at age fourteen years and six months. I drew Mummy's attention to this remarkable symmetry.

"Fourteen years and six months with Martin, then fourteen years and six months without him."

She gasped her astonishment.

"Do you think if Daddy had known, he would've accepted the deal?"

We stood in silence for a while, both sure that like us, Daddy would not forego the precious time we spent together to circumvent the pain of loss.

That symmetry felt like a little foothold in the chaos of life.

A few days after Daddy's funeral, Mummy phoned me, very upset. Her voice was thick with suppressed sobs over a perceived slight - a suspicion that people hadn't given my Daddy the respect he had deserved at his passing.

"Do you want me to come up?"

"No, no, honestly. I'm fine, really. I just wanted to get it off my chest. Stay there now, don't be throwing Sia in the car."

When I got off the phone, I felt good about going to see her and heard Daddy urging me – *go see your mother* -

but with his broad Belfast accent - *your mo'er*. I threw together the baby supply bag and we set off.

When we arrived, Mummy was a little cross.
"Ack, ya didn't have to come up, I told ye!"
"Well, I wanted to."
And I really did, but she frowned at me regardless.
"Flip sake, Mummy, get out of the way and let me in!"
Her face softened as she took in Sia.
"Well, I'm never going to say no to this wee love, am I?"

We sat together on the sofa while she re-hashed her burden and cried once more. Sia kept straining away from me to get to her granny, so I set her on her knee. Mummy held her and let the tears fall. I noticed Sia behaving strangely. She put her forehead to her granny's forehead for a moment, then closed her eyes as though empathising, then she opened her eyes and looked over her little shoulder towards a lamp table. She kept doing it - a gentle forehead touch and a glance behind her.
"Peggy – look at what she's doing!"
"I know, I'm watching!"
"She's giving me comfort, the wee pet. She keeps touching her head to mine…"
"Yes, but look what she does in between times…"

Mummy looked puzzled, until she saw the pattern herself. Daddy's photo was on the lamp table. Sia kept touching foreheads and glancing at her Grandad. Mummy laughed through her tears in wonder.
"Oh, my gawd! Do you see her looking at your daddy?"

"*Sure's, I do! Sure, I was the one told you!*" I laughed.

Sia kept doing it until eventually Mummy's tears turned to incredulous laughter.

"*Okay, Ben, I get the message!*" she said.

Only then did little Sia stop.

As it turned out, Daddy stayed close. Mummy sensed him on numerous occasions. If our two worlds merge when we are relaxed, in the delta state, in sleep, then he visited her in her dreams where he simply held her close and enveloped her with a deep and comforting love.

He visited my dreams too. I could always sense the difference between ordinary dreams where the brain processes experiences (brain fart dreams, I call them) - and genuine visitations. For one thing, they feel entirely different. Brain fart dreams invoke a multitude of emotions, from heart-thumping nightmares to the pervading anxiety of a door-less toilet cubicle or being late for a school you left twenty years before. Visitations feel clean. There's a tangible sense of the person as you knew them and a message.

One dream afforded a little glimpse of the other side, and I was shown images of Daddy watching Martin play football. There was a sense of this being practice for Daddy, not Martin. In these dreams, he was permitted to watch his son without intervening, to enjoy him but not correct him. It felt like Daddy was learning the lessons he had skipped over in life - to allow, to observe, to absorb - but not intervene. I got the sense of Daddy's remorse - not because he was prevented from engaging with his son, but because he finally understood that his interventions had cost his son's flow. I felt no strong emotion about it, it was a simple lesson, unsullied by the taint of punishment we are so familiar with on earth, discipline in its truest sense - *to teach*. What surprised me about it was the lesson that this glimpse held for me. I had assumed that life was the school room, it hadn't occurred to me that lessons could also happen in the space between lives. Daddy was once again utilising his experience to teach me something, showing me yet another cautionary tale – *don't make the same mistakes I did* - our dynamic from the get-go.

In another dream he spoke to me from a photograph at the top of a dresser in our family living room. This photograph seemed to be a portal that allowed him to visit and check on us. In the dream, Mummy was unaware of the portal, and I wanted to show her, so she could have the comfort of knowing that he continued existing, just out of sight. I pressed him to tell me when he would return to visit again so that I could have Mummy ready and waiting.

"*Alright, alright! When else? Boxing Day!*"
"*Aye, okay Rocky! Be serious, Daddy, I mean a proper date.*"
"*Okay, kid. 29th February.*"

This answer satisfied me because it was an actual date with no joke attached, but when I woke, I laughed. It wasn't a leap year and he had picked the one day of the year that doesn't exist, except when we make a little space for it, from a place that we can't perceive, except when we afford a little space for it. I felt him laughing, too - because he'd got the better of me and was feeling smug as he sauntered away, the joker, the trickster, leaving our interaction one step ahead, his big thumbs pointing at his chest, declaring *I'M the Chief.*

He dropped by in more tangible ways, too. One day, Mummy missed him sorely and felt guided to go to his writing desk in the shed. She found his key hidden on the underside of the desktop and opened the drawer to find a copy of Desiderata lying, waiting to be discovered. It was exactly what she needed to read, and it soothed her aching heart. Another time, her doorbell started working after not working for months. Back when it still worked, it was set to a simple chime - a ding dong, but when it spontaneously started up it played a tune it wasn't set to - The Westminster Quarters, better known as the chimes of Big Ben. Twice this happened, but no one had pressed it - when she answered the door there was no one there. She checked the settings and it was still set to the basic ding dong. As she sat on the sofa, it chimed a third time and her heart leapt as she understood. It was Valentine's night and there was Big Ben.

Mummy and I talked about how nice it would be if she lived within walking distance, but as I looked for a house, every option turned out to be a dead end. I talked aloud to Daddy and my brothers: *Come on! Help me find somewhere close so that she can be part of our lives and I can take better care of her!* - but there was no answer, and as I searched around, nowhere was suitable. I told myself to trust and reminded myself of my belief that those on the other side have more transcendent views than my limited human understanding, but it was cold comfort. The silence felt like an affront and some days I berated myself for being delusional, for believing that death was a comma, instead of a full stop. No matter how many signs or confirmations that I've got over the years that life continues after death, I still invariably suffer from crises of faith when the answers don't come fast enough.

Twenty-Nine

When Sia was two, I became pregnant with a son and every day I imagined how happy Daddy would have been to have a boy in the family again. After I gave birth, my boy remained unnamed for days. I had received a name for him in a dream, but my heart wanted to call him after Daddy instead, an acknowledgement of what he meant to me. I hesitated, though, because I did not trust myself to not regret that decision on bad days when I feel weak and damaged, on days when I rage impotently at my dead father – *I am this way because of you! Your faults are now mine!* I wondered that perhaps I should give my son the clean slate of a new name and suspected I was never going to be big enough, strong enough, healed enough to overcome my resentment. I explained my dilemma to Melanie. She always disliked Daddy for the pain he caused me, and I expected her to cast her vote for any alternative name but his. However, she gave me an entirely unexpected response.

'Oh flip, that's a hard one to give advice on! But I will say that I got tingly goosebumps when I read Benjamin Philip. Rather than being backward looking I feel it could pay homage to the good parts of your dad, being safe in the knowledge that you are going to help this little

Benjamin be the man your dad would have wanted to be if his circumstances had been different.'

Those words landed straight in my heart. Not for the first time, Melanie, a clear vessel for spirit, was conveying exactly what I was too close to see. I called my boy Ben. Mummy cried happy tears when I told her. I think making her happy was a big part of why I chose this name. Unsurprisingly, however, I had many wobbles over my choice, and on bad days, when I was exhausted and cross with the children, I would snap at them, then feel resentful towards daddy for not being the cycle breaker, for giving me a stressful childhood like his own, for passing on his flaws and leaving it to me to be the one to break the cycle. I referred to this feeling as Ben remorse and swore that if it continued, I would change my son's name, with the caveat that I would saddle up and stop complaining if I hadn't changed it by the time he was one.

Ben was a darling of a child, content to be snuggled next to me in the baby carrier, or in bed. He had the advantage of being the second child, reaping the rewards of having an older sibling who facilitated my steep learning curve of motherhood.

Mummy visited us every week, arriving on the Monday, staying overnight and leaving just before lunchtime on a Tuesday. It was a lovely start to both of our weeks. Sia and her Granny orbited each other constantly. Mummy acquiesced on every request - to read a book, to play tea party, to sing, and when they tired of their play, Sia crawled into her lap and they rested together wearing matching faraway looks as each absorbed the other in quiet contentment, while I flitted around Ben and his myriad of toddler needs.

I had two healthy, happy children, a girl and a boy, a little pink peg and a little blue peg travelling in the backseat of my Game of Life car, literally living my childhood dream. I was grateful every day, but for someone like me who had grown up with the silent keening of child-loss as the background noise, there was a fine line between gratitude and a paralysing fear of loss.

Ben was so different to Sia, who loved nothing more than a book or a chat. He was walking at nine months old and climbing before then. She explored ideas and people; he explored the physical confines of the world. On one hand I was proud of this capable, determined child, but on the other, I was terrified. Billy had died in an accident, and I had grown up saturated in the devastation of his loss. My fear was not a subconscious one - if anything, I was super-conscious. I wore my paranoia as a talisman – so long as I was fearful of death, it would repay my respect by leaving my family untouched. To relax into loving without fear was complacency that would invite disaster. I had learned this from watching Mummy mourn and pray for our survival, never daring to be so bold as to pray for us to thrive. She lived in terror and so did I. I knew this kind of magical thinking was a feature of anxiety disorder, but the therapeutic model for OCD dictated abandoning my safety behaviour of hypervigilance, which felt too much like tempting fate.

My feelings about my parents were complex. I had long resented their overprotectiveness, but now I worried that my unwillingness to forgive them could bring on karmic retribution: if I didn't pardon their shortcomings as two traumatised humans, perhaps I would be forced out of my child bereavement-free ivory tower to understand their pain first-hand. The refrain of child death overlaid the staccato rhythm of my default anxiety until my head was a cacophony of impending doom.

An extensive collection of safety products - cupboard locks, stair gates, tables festooned with cushioned edges and corners did little to alleviate my worry. I watched Ben constantly, coiled like a spring, ready to rescue, catch or intervene before some dreadful happenstance took him away from me. The house seemed filled to the rafters with death traps, but outside was worse. On the way to the play park, I watched every passing car for signs that the driver was texting, or drunk, or mid-heart attack and about to mount the pavement and ram my child's pram. The park itself was hellish - there were too many dangers to keep on top of and I watched in terror as Ben tottered in front of swings, amidst bigger children charging about, on uneven ground. Each close call brought horrifying visions of his head smacking against unyielding concrete, smashing like soft fruit. One day we had been at the park mere minutes when he stumbled and I burst into tears from stretched nerves, snatched him up, secured him into the pram and called over my shoulder to Phil, *I can't do this!* - as I sped off to the comparative safety of home, where I at least had the privacy to watch him without having to pretend to be calm or sane.

Sia watched and learned. Together we played with one activity at a time to minimise trip hazards, then put it away safely before choosing another. I sidestepped Mummy's concerns that Sia's focus was being drawn more to tidying than to free play by justifying it as a Montessori practice. In reality, I was not teaching her responsibility for her toys, rather I was passing responsibility for my anxiety to her - and she, perspicacious soul, understood it as such. Eventually, she began to panic each time Ben approached her and scrambled to gather her things. She was more attuned to the emotional climate than to my unconvincing spin. I was passing on my wounds.

I knew I was failing her, but I didn't know what else to do to keep us safe. The faults I resented my parents for were now mine. I didn't want to be like them. I remember them justifying their overprotectiveness, their attunement to danger - *When you're a parent, you'll understand,* but they had meant that I would hit and scold - the brash frontline of poor parenting. Both of us had overlooked the insidious dangers and inevitable damage of a tense emotional climate. As trauma expert, Resmaa Menakem said, *trauma in a family, decontextualized over time, looks like a family trait.* The way we moved around our children - coiled to react, braced for danger - was simply generational trauma. Trauma can leave a chemical mark on genes, and environmental trauma hardwires us for stress, but whether the cause of our generational trauma had a physical or mental genesis was moot, the outcome was the same, a default parental terror.

I wanted to be better than this. Each week, I girded my loins to take Sia to a kid's art class - a little outing just for her that also helped alleviate my guilt about the stressful environment of home. We were running late on the last day of term and in my haste, I missed my turning for the car park and abandoned the car outside a church after the most cursory of searches for a No Parking sign. I pushed Ben's pram to the top of the steep hill, then put him into the baby carrier and held Sia's hand as we climbed three flights of stone steps to reach the class, silently thankful that this would be the last time, for a few weeks, that I would have to endure the intrusive visions of Sia falling, or me falling with Ben strapped to my chest. Class consisted of Sia painting while I watched Ben exploring, snatching him away from pointy corners and toxic substances and counting down the minutes until we could go home. When that time finally came around, my anxiety to get home was compounded by the thought that the car might have been clamped. I kept Ben in the baby carrier rather than waste precious minutes strapping him into the pram. Sia and I held hands and I pushed the pram with my free hand, and she held her art with hers. We were about a third of the way down the steep hill when Sia let out a cry - her art had blown from her little hand and was rolling and flipping into the road. That yelp spiked my panic, and the horrifying intrusion of her running into the road to retrieve it heightened it further. I held her hand more tightly and let go of the pram to reach into the gutter where the page fluttered. The pram rolled away, slowly at first, but it quickly gained momentum. I believed that Ben was in the pram, as he had been earlier - panic made me forget that he was strapped to my chest. As I watched it career down the hill, bouncing at every uneven paver, veering towards the road, I had a choice – hold on to Sia or get to the pram. I screamed for Sia to stay where she stood and sprinted off down the hill after the pram, which inched leftwards towards the road, barrelling towards a blind junction, urging myself to reach the pram before the myriad of tragic conclusions swirling in my head could be made reality, before the pram could be side-swept by a car, or hit head on, or catch on a stone and tip forward with enough velocity to kill. It rolled into the junction and I after it, with no regard for potential traffic. My left foot snagged on uneven tarmac and suddenly the moment stretched as I fell towards the jutting edge of the kerb and realised that Ben was on my front, and if the trajectory of my fall continued, his little head would hit that kerb with my full weight and velocity behind it. My mind screamed – *No! I don't want their path of dead children!* I thrust my left arm around him and my right out to stop our fall. My right hand crashed into the ground and skidded across the gravel, sending searing pain shooting through my wrist and elbow. My knees smacked into the tarmac. Ben's little head missed the kerb by millimetres but hit the road.

    I listened for his cry, but no cry came. I tried to move to see him, but my right arm couldn't bear weight and my left was under him, and I feared that shifting my position could be the very thing that kills him. *Was he dead? Had I killed my son? Had the fear I nursed since he was born been a premonition?* I needed help. A man was walking down the road further down on the opposite side, so I screamed. He did not respond. I screamed again. Nothing. Then I remembered Sia. I turned my head, and she stood on the path behind me, frozen in fear, her face a mask of horror as she watched her mother bleeding and screaming on the road on top of her baby brother, who wasn't making a sound.

A car stopped and a lady got out and raced to help us.

"My baby! Is he okay?"

"Hold on to me, I've got you."

She hoisted me up, I moved gingerly. She looked at my hand.

"Oh – you're bleeding!"

"Is he okay?"

Only then did she realise that I had a baby strapped to my front, and as she peered into the carrier, he began to cry. He must have been shocked. His head was grazed, but I couldn't rule out the possibility that he was concussed or briefly lost consciousness after impact.

"The baby is okay. Let me drive you to the hospital."

"No, it's okay. I can drive."

It was somehow important to me to be in control again - as though the wheel had been wrenched from my grip and I committed to never relinquish it ever again. The illusion of control was enough to enable me to limp on.

She helped me down the street and loaded us into my car – unclamped – a worry from those happier times, when the worst I might have had to deal with was mere inconvenience. She drove just ahead of me towards the hospital, and I followed, steering one-handed and checking Ben in the rear-view mirror while Sia cried fearful, traumatised tears.

Ben was fine. The collar of the carrier had saved him from worse injuries, and my bones were intact, just some ligament damage and superficial wounds. Poor Sia was traumatised. For weeks after, she recounted her perspective of what happened on the day that Mummy *"had jam on her hand"*. She enacted and re-enacted me falling down and screaming. I used my CBT training to help her finish the story, to help her past the terrifying part and incorporate our mercifully happy ending.

Mummy came from Lisburn to stay a few days to help me with the children. I had a sprained wrist and strained nerves and was glad of her quiet, gentle presence, and the warmth that beamed out of her when she was around my children. The pain and stress I felt made me short-tempered and I understood how Daddy's chronic back pain was fertile ground for ill-humour and impatience.

I cried for days. The what-ifs overwhelmed me, the myriad of worse ways this incident could have ended. I looked at Mummy and thanked whatever gods stepped in to ensure her path was not mine. It felt like too close a call and reinforced my belief that danger loomed at every corner, waiting to catch me out and rob me of this joy that I ill deserved; an ingrate, judging the very people whose path I couldn't and wouldn't walk.

Thirty

Mummy had to adjust to a new normal without Daddy. He had been the sun she orbited for all her adult life, and she had wanted nothing else. Now, untethered, unanchored, she tried to navigate the world without him. It was at this point the extent of her learned helplessness became apparent. They always left the house together, although they never went far. The graves and Tesco's were their only regular outings, always with Daddy driving, and only occasionally farther afield. Mummy had to relearn taking the bus, which on the face of it, sounds like a simple task, but she was almost seventy and it had been thirty years since she had last used public transport. She broke the overwhelming task into chunks. One day she studied the bus timetable and walked to the stop, across the green where Martin and I had played as children, through the hole in the hedge towards Julie's house to watch the bus arrive and leave. She walked back home and phoned me to relay this small victory breathless with exhilaration, genuinely proud of herself.

"I did it! I know it doesn't sound like much, but I was really dreading it. Do you think I'm daft?"

"Not at all, sure it's been years from you've got on a bus."

"But here - wait til you hear this! I felt sick with nerves leaving the house, but when I got to the green there was a massive magpie that just watched me, and I felt like it was your Daddy cheering me on. I sound daft now, don't I?"

"No, Mummy. You really don't. You're not saying he is a magpie! You're saying you feel him close, and the magpie is the sign that he's around. I get it."

"Sounds daft."

"I know, but sure."

"And I didn't bump into anybody I know, thank God! I'm not ready for people to ask me how I am, Peggy."

"You'll get there, Mummy."

She sighed.

"I'll get there."

Over the next few weeks, she followed her plan of gradual exposure. Mummy lived in perpetual terror of doing or saying the wrong thing. Before engaging in the most cursory of interactions, she made a mental checklist of all the ways she could fuck it up and make someone mad at her. This next step - actually getting on the bus - was a litany of logistics. She had to make sure she didn't make the driver cross, and this meant being mindful to stand in the right place, waving him down politely, having the correct change at the ready and pressing the bell to disembark in a timely manner. Then there was everyone else. It was one thing to break the news of Daddy's demise to someone at a bus stop - at least she could scurry off home and cry in privacy for the pity and embarrassment she had caused - but the prospect of such an interaction on a bus, trapped in a tin can full of eavesdropping strangers stealing glances at her misery was worse.

Eventually, she steeled herself to ride the bus to town and get another one back. Before long she was getting the bus to do her grocery shopping, navigating another logistical hurdle of not inconveniencing the driver or other passengers by being too slow when lugging her purchases up the steps of the bus. She bought herself a smart blue tartan shopping trolley with tri-wheels for steps, so that she could get her shopping up the steps in a timely fashion. It never ceased to amaze her how people, the bus driver included, happily insisted on lifting her trolley up the steps for her. To be in receipt of kindness never failed to surprise her.

One day we went grocery shopping together. I pushed the trolley, and she rested her hand on the bar like a child afraid to be separated. Her eyes darted here and there, hypervigilant, ready to swerve us out of the way of other customers. She sent me to the meat counter and later to the checkout with instructions to let the checkout lady know that my Daddy had died. She wanted to circumvent the possibility of being asked where the big man was - the other half of the double act, never seen apart. When I met her outside she was holding back tears.

"I hurt that woman's feelings by not telling her myself, but Peggy, I can't say the words out loud, I can't…"

She saw only that her message had made the checkout lady sad, not realising that this empathy was the highest of accolades. After that, she only went to the registers staffed by strangers.

My phone rang when I had just put Ben down for his nap.

"*Peggy, the strangest thing happened today!*"

"*What, Mummy?*"

"*I was at the supermarket putting my groceries on the conveyor belt and the girl on the till was getting annoyed with me that I wasn't putting my things on fast enough. But Peggy, I was out of breath and I'm seventy! I could feel the tears coming. It is the closest I have been to breaking point. It's hard enough without your Daddy.*"

I imagined myself nipping down to Lisburn Tesco's to punch a cashier.

"*But then…How do I say this without sounding stupit? Then a woman came to help me. She just put her hands on my shoulders and smiled at me. And it was the most beautiful smile I've ever seen! Then she loaded my shopping onto the belt and packed it up for me.*"

"*Did she work there?*"

"*No, love. You don't understand. I'm saying she was an angel.*"

I wasn't sure what to say so I said nothing.

"*See? It sounds stupit, but I know she was an angel. She said it with her eyes. All my upset just drained away when she touched me. It felt like love, and she filled me up with it. She didn't speak a word. Just smiled. She was there when I needed her, then she was gone.*"

"*Like, disappeared?*"

"*I don't know. She was there one minute and then she was gone.*"

I believed her.

This small event reassured Mummy that there were others looking out for her. I watched my previously fractured, fearful mummy, perpetually bowed under the weight of her vulnerability, change after this meeting. She was relieved, relaxed, reassured and more content in herself.

∞∞∞

Eventually she was able to get the bus to town and catch a connecting bus to Belfast to visit me.

Her progress wasn't linear. Setbacks occurred amongst these small victories, filling her with further reticence. The firsts were hard. I collected her and brought her to mine for Christmas, visiting the graves on the way. Routine was observed - she wiped the headstone down with a cloth, then stood a moment with her hand caressing the top, the cold marble a conduit for her love. After a few moments she patted it, whispered I love you and walked away, rigid with suppressed emotion. I could hear Daddy's voice and knew what I had to tell her.

"*Mummy?*"

"*Yes, love?*"

"*I don't know how many Christmases you'll do without Daddy, but I know this, when you meet him on the other side, he will be so proud of you for forging on and you know what he'll say?*"

"*What, love?*"

"*He will say - Well done, kid.*"

She smiled. We both felt he was close by saying exactly those words as she walked away from the love of her life to put on a brave face and do Christmas with her little granddaughter.

Mummy and I muddled along, forging a new relationship without Daddy to impede or encourage. Having been set adrift of belonging at such a young age, she had given him her heart and soul, grateful to be accepted and part of something. In a way, she provided the means for his salvation. Her vulnerability allowed the expression of the worst parts of himself - his urge to dominate and control - and because she would not save herself from him, he had to learn to manage himself, to find and express the best parts of himself while suppressing the very worst. It took too many years of drinking and lashing out, but eventually when he stopped (I don't think he had even exhausted himself; it took every ounce of his strength to choose another path) - he looked back and proclaimed he wished he had chosen to settle himself years before. Mummy saw him more comprehensively than I could, this man who had come a long way, who once drank and fought and raged at the death of his son, at his painful disability, at having to rely on benefits and upon doctors and their personal feelings about what constitutes being fit to work, this man who chose instead to sit in a chair by the window and be consumed instead with how to give their children every opportunity that he had been denied. At this point, I only saw a man who wouldn't say sorry. Her beatification of him grated on me and I frequently found my irritation hard to contain.

The news happened to be on as we played with Sia and Ben in the living room, a bulletin about a paedophile who had been permitted access to vulnerable minors. Mummy cradled Sia on her knee, incensed, brows lowered as she muttered her disgust and outrage, appealing to me to join her in this easy censure. I found it triggering that she would be so incensed at the failure to protect these children, conflating my experience of physical abuse at the hands of my disciplinarian father with that of these sexual abuse victims. How could she muster condemnation for one and practically canonise the other? Why sympathy for those children and not me?

Something intolerant and resentful in me began to stir. I have long had the reputation of being able to start a fight in an empty room. How did I open the family can of worms with only this starting point? With gymnastic mental dexterity, that's how. I said:

"*These headlines are so black and white. A person must not be given a global summation and utterly condemned when there are many other things this person may have achieved in life.*"

It's never about what it's about, and because I still needed so badly to have my pain acknowledged, I made this barely tenuous comparison. In trying to expose the logical fallacies of my mother's black and white thinking, I had represented myself as a molester apologist. It wasn't my finest oratorical debate.

"*What are you talking about? A paedophile is a paedophile.*"

"*Well, Daddy, for example. Someone he had hit might, in this way, justifiably write him off as nothing but a violent man.*"

That somebody was me. I was somebody; somebody who was deliberately comparing the love of her life to the worst kind of human.
"Your daddy did nothing but protect you from the world!"
"Ironic, considering the only person I needed protected from was him."
"How dare you talk about him like that! I won't allow it!"
"You are missing the point! All I am saying is that people do many things and writing them off with one label is reductive…"

But that wasn't all I was saying. It had leaked out the sides again, another admonishment signifying my need for an admission of culpability, an acknowledgement that I had been hard done by. I remembered the maxim: *he that cannot beat the horse, beats the saddle.* I was punishing her because I was still angry at Daddy.

She walked out of my house, caught the first bus home and refused to take my calls, hanging up every time I phoned. When she eventually took my call – a week later - both sides of the conversation were a torrent of profanity and frustration. Eventually, we just had to agree to disagree.

Mummy doted on both of my children, but at 72, just over two years after Daddy had died, her health had reached the stage of one thing after another. She had COPD, angina, diverticulitis, arthritis and fibromyalgia. Performing the simplest of tasks, such as getting dressed or running the hoover over the carpets was becoming increasingly more difficult and left her breathless and sore. She found the impending loss of independence hard to accept and pushed herself on despite the consequences. A new ailment presented itself; her right femur was becoming increasingly painful, and she began to walk with a limp to avoid bearing weight. Her GP put it down to a spreading arthritis and prescribed morphine patches to manage the pain in her femur, but the amount required to dampen the pain made her drowsy, and every day she had to choose between being barely conscious or being in agony. Her various health issues meant regular blood tests and eventually one showed slightly elevated CA125 markers, a potential indication of ovarian cancer. We both felt a little panicked and I was reluctant for either of us to have to endure an NHS waiting list, so I arranged a private appointment.

We attended the Ulster Clinic one evening. It was a calm, restful space set in a building on the leafy Malone Road. The consultant was warm and patient, nonetheless Mummy was nervous and looked to me for confirmation each time she answered his questions. She hesitated when asked how many children she had, and the doctor looked at her with curiosity at her difficulty with this seemingly simple question. This hadn't been a straightforward question since 1975. I interjected to save her from having to say the painful words out loud: four live births - two surviving, two passed. She visibly crumpled. Mummy carried the loss of her sons like a wound, covered up and held close, but every so often, circumstances colluded to force her to expose its perpetual rawness. She endured the pelvic examination as I bounced Ben in the baby-carrier on the other side of the curtain, anxiously eavesdropping. He had found a lump, perhaps only a polyp, but it required further scrutiny via an abdominal scan, and a chest scan too, just to be on the safe side. She asked the doctor to look at her leg, too – this strange, painful swelling on her femur. He recommended asking her GP for a letter of referral to be seen privately.

On the way back in the car, she vacillated between apologising for keeping Ben out past his bedtime and asking me to repeat what the doctor had said. Fear and lack of faith in herself made her forget the big words that she planned to write in her wee notebook once she got home - the book that kept her right because she didn't trust herself to remember anything correctly. Her dyslexia meant she had a poor working memory, but she also reminded us, *'I was dropped on my head as a baby, you know.'* As we pulled up to her house, I gave reassurances: other causes of lumps, encouraging statistics for ovarian cancer survival, *you're in the right hands, at least they are doing something about it now.* All the while, the unmistakable smell of hospitals filled my nose. The private clinic we had attended had not smelled of hospitals, so I knew it wasn't just the clinic clinging to my clothes. I asked Mummy, "*do you smell hospitals?*" just in case there was a smell, but she didn't. I knew that smell was for me alone and I what it meant.

I phoned her Health Centre to request a letter of referral to be seen privately, as the consultant had instructed. Her GP seemed a little defensive when I requested the letter, insisting that she had made two referrals to the hospital which had both come to nothing, abdicating responsibility, as if to imply that chasing it up on behalf of her patient was beyond her remit. Righteous indignation rose up and I had to bite down the urge to tell her she had a cheek taking a wage. I collected the GP's letter, sealed for a specialist's eyes only and ripped it open. Fury welled up as I read the words, *possible sarcoma?* – that obnoxious little question mark, planted there as evidence of reasonable doubt, that lack of certainty which left my mother in pain for a full year while cancer may have been colonising in her femur and beyond.

In the meantime, Mummy received a referral letter with accompanying pages detailing her medical history. She phoned me, distraught, her voice strained.

"*Peggy?*"

"*Are you okay, Mummy?*"

"*I'm okay. It's just…I got a referral letter with my medical history on it. And it says…in 1979…it says I had an attempted suicide – but it wasn't…*"

She couldn't speak for weeping.

"*It's okay, Mummy.*"

My ears started to ring. I refused to process what I was hearing. I only knew she needed support.

"*Peggy, I wouldn't have left you…*"

Suddenly I understood. She thought that if I knew what had happened, I would be upset with her – perhaps too upset to support her - her one support now Daddy was gone. She was fearful that this event of many years ago could come between us.

"Mummy, I know you wouldn't have."

This was a lie to reassure her, but my truth, I hoped, would be more so. I said,

"If I had been through what you had been through – god forbid – I wouldn't want to stay either. I don't know how you've done it. I don't and I never want to find out. I wouldn't blame you if you had wanted to go."

"I wouldn't have left you, love. I was so unhappy."

"I know, Mummy. I know. Mummy, what happened?"

"Ack. I took a load of aul' tablets. But it wasn't enough to finish me. I just wanted not to feel."

"Mummy, I get it. It's okay."

A fortnight later, she went to hospital for her scans, and a week later attended the results appointment alone, with reassurances that she would be fine, that she didn't want to upset Ben's routine. I sat, coiled to answer the phone, cursing myself when I missed the call while putting Ben down for a nap.

Mummy left a voicemail telling me she would phone me when she got home. I suspected that if it was good news, she'd have happily announced the all-clear regardless of being on public transport. The familiar feeling of dread set in as I waited.

I answered the phone on the first ring.

"Well?"

"It's cancer, love. The doctor said there's a tumour in one lung and spots on the other."

"Aw, no. Mummy. I'm sorry."

Familiar ground. My world is falling apart, but she is suffering more, so I put my feelings on hold to help her. Her voice cracked a bit.

"I had a feeling it wasn't good, but I wasn't expecting it to be in both."

"I want to come and see you."

"But the kids. You can't be messing them about."

"I'm not. Phil is here. I'm on my way."

The drive to Lisburn was my time. I cried big, childish sobs. My Mummy. My Mummy. The front door was unlocked when I arrived. I let myself in and found her sitting on her usual spot on the sofa. She saw that I had been crying and began to cry too.

"Oh, Mummy."

"Ah, love."

I sat next to her, and we cried together. When our tears abated, she looked at me kindly.

"Well, it's all one whether I stay or go. I have you here, and the boys waiting for me over there."

I wanted to be comforting, but grief made me petulant.

"It's not 'all one' to me! You have an eternity with them. I want you here with me."

"I know, love. I know."

I attended her oncology appointment with her. The waiting room was quiet, a mix of fear and resignation, each waiting to be summoned. A young-ish lady doctor called us and explained that although Mummy's lung cancer was Stage One, her pre-existing health conditions, age and frailty from weight loss meant that they could not put her under general anaesthetic to perform a biopsy. A palliative dose of radiotherapy was all they could offer. The prognosis was one year, maybe two. The treatment could potentially extend her life by approximately three months past what she would have had otherwise. She received six sessions over a fortnight and that was it. The countdown had begun.

I was afraid. I feared having to watch her waste as Daddy had wasted, to see her starve and gasp into a vicious and merciless death. Life had put her through enough. It was so unfair that this loomed, and so soon after having witnessed Daddy's diabolical demise. I feared Sia having to watch, then lose, her beloved granny who doted on her, who loved her with gentle fierceness, Sia's soft place to land when I was stressed and fractious like my daddy. I feared losing her before I had finally put on my big girl pants and forgiven her for grievances that she would never concede. Things became strained between us. I wanted her to come and live with us, but she was tied to her house, the symbol of her independence and the first, last and only place she and Daddy had relaxed into each other and loved softly. It was the place she'd brought Martin home to, the place Martin had left from to go to his final resting place, and every blessed moment in between when her boy needing her had soothed and rebuilt her.

"You are going to have to think about when would be a good time to come down and live with us."

"Peggy, I just like my own space. My own house. I'm happy here. I'll come down when I'm ready."

"But when will that be? Surely you should come down now, when you are feeling comparatively well and can enjoy spending time with me and the children."

"Don't pressure me, Peggy. I just don't want to be a burden. I want my own independence."

"When you stay in Lisburn, you ARE a burden. I've got two kids to ferry up and down the road to get to you. It's too much."

"Well, I'll just get a home-help then and you'll not need to come up and down," she snapped.

"So, what? You'll stay there until you need help, then you'll get home-helps and have no need to come to me? This is ridiculous. You are putting bricks and mortar above your own flesh and blood."

Several weeks went by, when she was too worn out from radiotherapy and pain to make the journey to me. I stayed in Bangor, making more of an issue of Ben's nap schedule than it was in an attempt to show that living with me would make both of our lives easier. Each phone call invariably culminated with me bludgeoning her with the phrase, *you are putting bricks and mortar above your own flesh and blood,* as I deliberately chose to view her reticence in the worst possible light. On the Thursday before her femur biopsy, which was scheduled for the following Monday, I smelled Daddy. It first happened when I was in bed, putting Ben down for a nap. I sniffed at the bedding, but it wasn't coming from there. It happened again later on the sofa. I smelled the cushions, my clothes, the children.

Nothing. I smelled it again in the side garden with nothing but fresh air around me, and a white feather floated down in front of where I stood. I put my hands up in surrender and said aloud,
"*Okay, Daddy, message received.*"

It was time to intervene and take care of her. Daddy was close by because time was running short. He was coming to guide her over.

She phoned me the following day, the Friday before her Monday biopsy. A palliative nurse was leaving a commode and perching stool for downstairs and asked to speak to me as Mummy's next of kin.
"*Hello?*"
"*Hello, I'm Dympna, from NI Hospice. I'm here with your mum and her oxygen levels are a bit low. We are off until Monday and I'd be worried about her getting worse over the weekend. Could you come and check on her tomorrow?*"
"*Of course. Thanks for your help.*"
I took Dympna's number and phoned her back when she had left Mummy.
"*Dympna, if it was your mother, would you be happy for her to be living on her own?*"
"*No pet. I'd be worried about her being on her own and taking a turn with those oxygen levels or having a fall with that leg.*"
I phoned Mummy, rage crying.
"*I'm just off the phone from Dympna who said that if you were her mum, she'd be worried about you having a fall. I'm demented here with worry. You are being selfish, and you need to just come down and stay with me. Enough is enough.*"

"Not this again. Peggy, I've told you, I'm not ready to -"
"I know. You love the house more than you love us."
"Stop it. I can't take this. I'm not well —"
"Then you need to be with me!"
"Oh, for goodness sake. Okay! Okay, I'll come to you. But I don't want to be there."
"Oh, I know you don't — you've made that clear. I'll come and get you tomorrow morning. You can pack tonight. Over-pack rather than under-pack."

When I collected her the following morning, she looked drawn and weak. I thought she'd be mutinous - cold and huffy from having to capitulate, but instead something had given.
"Peggy, I'm glad to see you. Last night I felt dreadful. I'm so grateful you've come for me."
"I just want to take care of you, is all. You're my mummy. You should be with me."
As we pulled up to my house, she looked relieved.
"I can't even find the words - I'm just so happy to be here."
It felt like a dream. She got into her pyjamas and blue spotty housecoat and lounged on the sofa, dozing on and off, content to be catered to. It was as if the weight of the decision had been lifted and there was nothing left to do but sleep off the exhaustion of deliberation.

I borrowed a wheelchair from my cousin to get her to and from the car for biopsy appointment, so that she didn't bear weight on that leg. We were friends, chatting in the car, an ease between us, as she accepted help that I had been spoiling to provide. Any tenseness had dissipated, and we were finally in it together because she had let me in. Sometimes accepting help is a greater blessing to the helper and I was grateful for the benediction. I assisted her in getting undressed and into the hospital gown and was taken aback by how thin she had become. It reminded me of holding her, a frail little bird after Martin died, and shocked me that she had withered further.

Now that the charade of coping had been dispensed with, she allowed me to witness the breathlessness caused by the effort of simply dressing and confided that it took her an hour to get ready each day, after which she spent the rest of the morning recovering. The cheerful nurses told me to pick her up late that afternoon and I left her, tiny and brave, in the bed. She never left my thoughts the whole day. I counted down the minutes to get her home. On the way to pick her up, my phone rang. A nurse explained that her oxygen levels were too low to release her and that she had been transferred to City Hospital. I returned home, packed her an overnight bag and delivered it to A & E, where she lay in a holding bay, breathless and sore. She was relieved to see me but looked uncomfortable and disturbed.

"*Peggy – when they put the needle in for the biopsy, I heard a crunch.*"

"*Oh no. Are you very sore?*"

She nodded, grimly.

"I'm not allowed to bear weight on it in case the bone fractures. I've to use the wheelchair."
She was put on a ward in the City Hospital. I phoned Jeanette.
"Should I come home? Do you think this is it?"
It was a question that I couldn't answer, but I remembered the words of Daddy's consultant.
"I don't know. I suppose it's like with Daddy - you have to decide whether to come home and spend time or come home for a funeral."

Jeanette was home within two days – on the Wednesday - and had a ticket to leave a month later. I picked her up from the airport and we drove straight to the hospital. On the way, I got Jeanette up to speed and mentioned Mummy's account of the medical records detailing the events of 1979.
"She was so upset, Jeanette. She kept saying she wouldn't have left me. I suppose she would've left a note if she was planning to go."
"She did leave a note. I remember it word for word."
My heart started thumping, but I tried to appear calm.
"Oh yeah? What did it say?"
"It was to Daddy. It said, I am going to be with Billy. Jeanette and Peggy are my gift to you. I love you."
"Oh."
"She took a load of pills then walked until she could walk no further and was found by a farmer who noticed that his cows were behaving strangely. They had formed a circle round something in his field. It was Mummy. She went to where she thought she wouldn't be found."
"Fuck."

Fuck indeed.

She would have left me. My head spun. I suspected it, but the confirmation hit me hard. Even then, I didn't blame her. I never understood how she managed to go on after Billy, but knowing that she didn't want to – well, I entirely understood that. As we drove along, my brain whirred in the spaces between conversations. When I was one, my mother had been so depressed that she tried to die. I had no doubt that she loved me. Mummy was warm, she fussed over me, handmade my clothes, sang me songs and kept me close, she lay with me until I went to sleep after our prayers - but though she loved me, I wasn't enough to make her want to stay. This must have been why poor Jeanette was running around making bottles at age thirteen and pushing her baby sister around in a pram.
"Daddy was furious with her."
I thought of the Daddy of my early years, barely managing his own grief, his default rage bubbling under the surface.
"I'm sure."
"When the ambulance brought her home afterwards, she locked all the doors to keep him out. He broke the window to get in. She ran upstairs and screamed for me to take you. He got her and dragged her down the stairs towards the broken window - dragged her by the hair – shouting - Do you want to fucking die? Come on, I'll cut your fucking throat for you!"
"Jesus."

If she had seen it, I had seen it. I thought, *This is why I am how I am. This is why I am hardwired for anxiety.* She wanted to die, and he wanted to kill her. I was one and this was my life - and I felt relief, because it made sense. I'm not defective - I'm hardwired to anxiety the way anyone who had been through such experiences would be. My stress responses were dysfunctional because my depressed and suicidal mother was not able to provide the consistent, nurturing care a child needs. This childhood experience would have literally impacted the biology of my brain, impacting how I would function for the rest of my life.

I thought of my poor Mummy, who at that point didn't have the strength to go on and still couldn't find a soft place to land. And Daddy, who didn't have the resources to save himself, never mind anyone else, who was so terrified by the prospect of having to be solely responsible for us that he might've done time to avoid it.

No wonder she had been so intolerant of my arm cutting episode. My claim to depression and self-harming actions must have triggered her. She knew what it was to be in the grips of a desperate depression, to long for the release of death. On one hand, she was incensed that I had tried to lay claim to an equivalent pain to hers. On the other, the thought of her daughter experiencing suicidal ideation was so abhorrent to her that she wished to shut it down immediately, via the short cut of shame.

We took her home from hospital that Friday, very much against hospital advice, and I signed her out with the full weight of responsibility that if something happened to her, it was entirely on me. I am my father's daughter - six foot and bulletproof - making questionable decisions with scant regard to anyone's opinion, if it falls under the category of looking after my own.

Thirty-One

A series of events took place that seemed to be evidence of something bigger steering us. After three years of hitting roadblocks while looking for somewhere nearby for Mummy to live, things moved fast.

She was taken into hospital on a Monday. On the Tuesday I discovered that the lady who lived in the apartment at the back of our house was moving out in two days. On Wednesday Jeanette came home. On Thursday we got the keys to the apartment and did a quick Ikea trip to get it furnished. I arranged for a hospital bed and stair lift to be delivered on the Friday morning. On Friday afternoon, we busted Mummy out of the hospital and brought her to her new home.

We secured her into the stair lift and excitedly followed its too-slow whirring trajectory up the stairs. Sia bartered for the next turn and the rest of us inched up the stairs, impatient to see her face as the apartment came into view.

"Oh, my gawd, it's lovely!"

She wore a face of genuine shock.

"Did you think I'd put you in a crack den?"

"No comment!" she answered, as she beckoned for someone to help her up for a closer inspection.

Light spilled from the south facing windows and skylights onto the shiny porcelain tiles of the open plan room. Mummy got herself steadied on the Zimmer-frame and shuffled into the room, gasping as she took in the white gloss kitchen. We had placed a cream sofa and beige armchair with footstool at the far end, opposite a tv unit and a glass dining table. We softened the neutral palette with pastel rugs, cushions and a gallery of family photos I had hastily printed off the day before. I never hung family photographs up, unwilling to saturate myself with everyday reminders of loss, or too-complicated relationships, but now the dead seemed more alive than ever. Instead of being a reminder of who was gone, these photographs were a celebration of who had been, and who might be waiting over this next horizon.

Jeanette stayed with her, lying on a blow-up mattress on the floor in case Mummy needed help in the night. Jeanette made her breakfast, I brought over lunch, we wheeled her over to my house for dinner and I went over last thing at night to have a cup of tea and rub ointment into the bedsore at the base of her spine that kept threatening to open since her hospital stay. Mummy arranged a care assistant to come every other day to help her shower and to ease our load. She shuffled to and from the toilet using her Zimmer-frame, sat in her chair with her sore leg elevated or dozed in her hospital bed. Sia and Ben visited to give her kisses and cuddles, while we took pleasure in waiting on her hand and foot. She soon grew accustomed to asking us to fetch things - a cup of tea, her tablets, her wee notebook - and rather enjoyed being addressed as Your Majesty. The framed photographs prompted reminiscing without the usual wincing caution. Mummy was getting amped up for the family reunion. She smiled at a picture of Daddy, a candid shot of him smiling, unaware he was being photographed.

"*Your Daddy was very gentle,*" she said, unselfconsciously.

"*Oh?*"

"*Very gentle. Remember that time I got dizzy painting high up and fell off the ladder?*"

I didn't. Now that her guard was down, she was talking freely about things she had probably hidden to circumvent worrying us.

"*When I came to, I was on the sofa, and he was kneeling down near my feet, holding my legs and just saying over and over, You are alright, love. I've got you, sweetheart.*"

"*Sounds like you scared the shite out of him.*"

"*I think I did, that day. But he was so gentle.*"

She gazed off in reverie. My eyes travelled over the other photographs resting on the shelves and landed on Martin, smiling his megawatt smile.

"*Mummy, d'ya remember the time Martin fell and split his eyebrow?*"

She winced and set her tea down on the side table.

"*Gawd, thon was terrible.*"

"*I know. Tell me this, though – why did you never punish me for letting him fall like that?*"

"*Whaddya mean?*"

"*I mean, when I was walking him along and let him go, and he fell, I never even got so much as a barge.*"

"*To tell you the truth, I didn't even know that was what happened 'til now.*"

Thirty odd years later and I'd reverse Columbo-ed myself. In asking this 'one last thing' I was exposed as the culprit.

"*Well, if you want to smack my arse now, you'll have to catch me first,*" I laughed.

She had finally let us in. Every day she smiled and said how content she was. Every night she said, "*I love you*" as we put her to bed. Perhaps she was relieved to get to the end of a rough shift, relieved to not have to wait for another disaster. Suddenly she was living in the present, savouring the day, sucking the marrow from every moment.

That said, it wasn't all roses. I found my responsibilities gruelling. Every day I promised myself I would cope better, try harder, but my fuse remained short and my ability to manage myself poor. The children were getting the worst of it: Ben, determined to be the first under two Parkour champion had my nerves in shreds and Sia would talk the hind leg off a donkey, leaving me no time to reboot. I was reaching breaking point too often - shouting, then dashing to the kitchen to recover myself, leaving two frightened children abandoned in the playroom. I knew first-hand how damaging a fractious parent could be to a child, from my own childhood, then reinforced throughout my CBT training and therapy. Mummy noticed how tightly wound I was.

"You've bad nerves. Maybe you should take something for it," she commented, not unkindly, after I'd tripped up the stairs and spilled half a bowl of soup.

"I'm just stressed out."

Her suggestion to medicate myself infuriated me because the genesis of my nervous disposition had been my upbringing. I suspected that her desire to medicate me was as much for her comfort as mine. To gloss over my deficiencies was to let her off the hook - something I was too bitter to do. I struggled not to wield my brokenness as a reproach.

My focus had to be on Mummy, because the end was drawing near. I wanted to help her prepare for death, for her to be calm and unafraid as she traversed this last stretch. I wanted to be her doula, providing support and guidance through this transition. I got her ready for her post-lunch nap and she seemed quieter than usual as I got her pillows fluffed and wheeled the oxygen tank into position.

"Are you okay, Mummy?"

She assured me that she was, without meeting my eye.

"Mummy?" I kept my eyes fixed on her until she returned my gaze. Her eyes filled with tears.

"I just hope God thinks I'm good enough for heaven."

The thought of this wee woman somehow not meeting the criteria was ludicrous to me, and my response came out before I had a chance to vet it.

"Well, if my daddy's there, you're a shoe-in."

In terms of compassionate responses, it was down there with, *You'll have to do this twice.* Even after all this time, she was still holding out for a completely different daughter to the one she had.

"I'm being facetious – you will be with Daddy and the boys on the other side. That is where 'home' is. You're just going home, like all of us do."

She nodded, still downcast. I realised that nothing I could say would help, that she needed to remember herself as an eternal being and understand that death is just a doorway - not a full stop, but a comma.

"Would you be open to having a session with a spiritual healer?"

She eyed me suspiciously. The Bible expressly warns against fortune tellers and the like. She had tried to do the right thing all her life, and here she was, inches away from heaven and here I was, potentially setting up a last-minute hurdle to trip on.

"It's not…evil, is it?"

"No Mummy. She just lays her hands on you, and you just relax. You might even fall asleep."

She reluctantly agreed and I arranged a session with my friend, Saffron, later that week. Saffron arrived at my house and we hugged hello. She was immaculately turned out as usual, her bright copper hair curled and framing her pale face and striking green eyes. She is a West Belfast girl, and, ever the chameleon, I immediately lapsed into my Belfast accent and affectations.

"Ack, hiya love! Do you want a bit of lunch here first or would you rather do the session first?"

"I've to do the session now, love. They were telling me on the way down that she's tired."

I loved the way she chatted about those on the other side unselfconsciously, regardless of her audience. I walked her down to the apartment, where Mummy was indeed dozing off in her chair. Saffron gave her a hug hello and helped her into the bedroom to lie down for her healing.

"Are you okay, Mummy?"

She nodded, but I could see she was nervous. Saffron soothed her.

"Now, you're not to worry, love, okay? You're in good hands. I'm looking after you. Just relax."

Mummy nodded, smiling weakly, a little embarrassed that her reticence was showing and might cause offence to this girl who had travelled all this way for her. I left them to it and tiptoed down the stairs to go home.

"Well? How did it go?"

"Your mummy is tired. I'd leave her on her own for a wee while just to absorb what happened. She's crying, but it's happy tears. Give her

twenty minutes or so. She can tell you herself what happened - it's not for me to say."

I could barely wait to get over to her. When I did, she was sitting up in bed, lit up with amazement.

"What happened, Mummy? Was it good?"

"I can't explain it, Peggy. I don't know how to explain it."

"Start at the start!"

"Well, you know I was nervous -"

"Oh, were you? I hadn't noticed."

"Give over, you! Well, she put her hands on my shoulders and I just said the Lord's Prayer into myself, just in case it wasn't right, what she was doing, and then when I'd finished that, I said, 'The Lord is My Shepherd' and then -"

"The Rosary?"

"Stop it, you!"

"Then?"

"Then I just felt this wave of peace come over me. And I felt…I felt…God. Does that sound stupit?"

"No, Mummy."

"I felt God! And just for a second – just as soon as I'd noticed – they were gone again – your daddy and the boys. Right there!"

She pointed to the corner of the room. It was exactly as I had hoped. She had relaxed enough to make space for them.

"See, Mummy? They are waiting for you. You are going home."

She nodded, amazed.

"I just don't have the words."

"The two worlds overlapped. Mummy. They are never far. You were just able to see that today."

And from that moment on, she was content, sometimes even giddy. She took each day as it came, as a gift to be with us, taking her one day closer to her boys, who she knew were waiting for her, ready to embrace her.

One morning, a carer was helping her wash as she sat on the shower stool. My sister was in the living room of the apartment, playing with Sia. Jeanette heard the carer switch the shower off, and Mummy say, in a strangled, panicked voice –

"It's gone! My leg has gone!"

Jeanette jumped up and ran to the doorway, where she saw the carer reaching away from Mummy to get a towel for her. Mummy sat on the shower stool, her face blank as she pitched forward without putting her hands out to save herself, and landed with a sickening thud, all of her weight on her forehead on the cold, tiled floor.

I was in the playroom at the back of the house as Jeanette ran up the garden screaming,

"Call an ambulance! Get Sia! Call an ambulance!"

For one dizzying moment I thought something had happened to my girl. I couldn't function. I was looking at the phone and didn't know how to use it. Then I saw Sia – alive, intact – running after Jeanette and crying. I threw my phone at Phil.

"Phil – phone an ambulance!"

I sprinted to the apartment with no idea of what I was going to find.

There she was, lying on the freezing floor, her body covered with a towel. The carer looked panicked and asked for help getting Mummy into the recovery position. A huge purple blue lump stuck out on her forehead. I tried to turn her over as gently as I could, but as she moved air rasped up through her throat, sounding like a laboured exhale. I took this as evidence of life and cradled her head in my hands. I stroked her face and spoke to her, unsure if she could hear me, but knowing that if she was conscious, she would be in pain.

"Ah, Mummy. I've got you, love. Ah, love. I've got you, darling. You're alright, sweetheart. Ah, love. I love ya. I love ya, sweetheart."

On and on I went, stroking her soft cheeks, kissing her, talking, in soft tones and using terms of endearment I had never used for her before. She seemed to watch me, her eyes brimming with unshed tears, fixed on mine. I noticed her tongue was growing darker, inside her ears becoming purplish and then I realised she wasn't seeing me at all. Her spirit had left.

The end was so sudden. She had simply stood up from the stool in the shower and her leg had given way from under her in a violent iteration of her collapse at Martin's funeral, except this time, instead of leaving him, she was making her way back.

The paramedics arrived. They understood that this was a seventy-two-year-old woman with a terminal cancer diagnosis, who had been thus far unresponsive to CPR, and asked if we - Jeanette and I - wished for them to continue with resuscitation attempts. I was in shock and had no understanding of the rigours of resuscitation. I only saw strangers looming over me in their green and fluorescent yellow uniforms as I sat shivering on the sofa, asking me if I wanted to let my mother die, waiting impatiently for an answer. I tried to imagine what Mummy would want me to say and remembered her determination to undergo radiotherapy to extend her life, remembered her disappointment that further treatment was not being offered. She had wanted to live. In those fraught moments, saying no felt like a betrayal. Half an hour earlier I had been baking banana bread and planning to share it with her that afternoon - this can't be it. I nodded, then looked up, searching their faces for whether my affirmation was what they had hoped to hear, but they gave no indication and simply closed the door to shield us from what was about to unfold. I heard the defibrillator power up, instructions to clear and counting rhythmical compressions. It seemed to go on for ever, this relentless assault on my poor mummy, four foot eleven and a half of skin and bone, pressed against the unyielding cold tile. A thought occurred - we were bringing her back to spend the rest of her days in a hospital bed in pain from her shattered femur, to count down the days until cancer reduced her to the horrifying husk it had left Daddy. This wasn't a kindness. Suddenly, the work of these broad paramedics seemed ghoulish, as though they were mortifying a corpse, dishonouring the dead. I couldn't stand it.

"Please, let her go, she has suffered enough! We have to let her go!"

But they had detected the very faintest of pulses and were duty bound to carry through the resuscitation process, pummelling and shocking her fragile shell until all signs of life, however feeble, were gone. I sat, horrified, drenched in remorse as they continued going through the motions behind the thin door. At last, at last, they called it, and in a horrible reversal of my feelings just moments before, I felt relief.

They lifted her into her bed and covered her with the duvet I had bought for her just four weeks before. I sat beside her, stroking her soft cheek as the warmth subsided, love and grief interrupted by horror at the blue and purple bulge on the top left of her forehead, a garish reminder of the violent impact, then pity as her top lip kept curling back to expose a tooth. I was grateful to be able to cry some, but even in this entirely appropriate situation for tears, it still felt indulgent.

Suddenly it seemed very important to tend to the admin of death. I phoned close family, trusting myself to keep a steady voice and put their feelings before mine.
"Are you sitting down? I'm sorry to have to tell you…It was quick, at least she doesn't have to suffer like Daddy did…"

It was safer territory, doing things properly and giving people their place. Going through the motions, tracking down the nail polish remover.

She died just over a fortnight after my son's first birthday. I imagined her with Daddy in the space between lives, gloating that her grandson would bear her beloved's name because she had beat the cut-off date by fifteen days, and that her last days made sure of Big Ben's legacy.

Later that night, Jeanette and I sat in my living room shell-shocked and exhausted, nursing cups of tea on adjacent sofas. The room grew dark around us as night closed in. I flicked on a side lamp, which did little to dispel the gloom as we stared off blindly, lost in our own thoughts.

"*Do you know what was weird?*"

Jeanette startled.

"*What?*"

"*When I was holding Mummy at the end, when I was talking to her, I was calling her darling, sweetheart, love. I've never called her anything like that in my life, but it just kept coming. It reminds me of what she said about that time she fell off a ladder and Daddy held her and kept saying, Aw, darling. Aw, love. I've got you, sweetheart. I've got you.*"

Jeanette paused.

"*Peggy, maybe you heard Daddy talking to you. You've picked up on him reassuring you as you sat with Mummy.*"

Part of this resonated with me, but part of it didn't. And then I felt the white light and I realised.

"*No, that's not it. I heard him and I was repeating him, but he wasn't talking to me. He had caught Mummy on the other side and was talking to her.*"

And I knew, I felt in my very essence that it was true. As she passed from this world into the next, Daddy held her in the embrace she had dreamed of so many times since he had died, and I cradled her head as her broken body lay on the floor, while we chanted incantations of our love for her, like an echo song, sung in rounds, like a responsive prayer.

Thirty-Two

Mummy died the day before Jeanette was due to fly home. When Jeanette purchased her ticket to go home in a month's time, little did we know that Mummy would be leaving us too.

"At least she didn't have to suffer like Daddy did," was my mantra to shut down dialogue with well-meaning friends, but it didn't reflect the complexity of my true feelings.

I was relieved that she didn't have to suffer, and relieved that we could circumvent the harrowing experience of watching her waste, terrified, sick, in pain, starving and gasping like Daddy, head flopping like a fish until the doctors finally relented and gave a decent dose of morphine, post-trauma, after the *'eloi eloi lama sabachthani'* had sullied our recollections. But the violence of her end was sickening. My tiny, afraid mother felt her femur crumble and had cried out in horror and pain. She had been aware - briefly, I hope - of her weak heart, sputtering and stuttering to a stop. I pray she was unconscious for the keeling forward, for the crack of bone on tile. I told no one that I had intrusive visions of the end - Mummy with her mouth open, her tongue grey.

A few days later, Sia sat on the floor in front of me as I rested on the sofa and lay her head back on my lap. When she looked up at me, her eyes were Mummy's eyes looking at me, but not seeing, brimming with tears. I wouldn't say aloud that I had been a cunt in the days leading up to her death - tired from the never-ending merry-go-round of cooking, serving, washing up and managing children, too fond of venting and lamenting to make any kind of successful martyr. Perhaps if I had chosen more compassion, I wouldn't be eaten up by regrets. She died on a Sunday. I regretted that our last Friday night takeaway had been Mexican, which I knew she wouldn't be keen on, instead of her favourite scampi and chips. I regretted that I started the day before she died by complaining to her about how I'd scheduled a day of activities I could well do without. I regretted that I didn't call over that evening around eight, as I normally did, for an hour of companionship. Instead, I procrastinated and finally forced myself over at her bedtime to tend hurriedly to her bedsores. I regretted that I didn't visit at all on Sunday morning, instead making banana bread in the glorious isolation of my kitchen, like some carefree person who didn't have a dying mother thirty metres away, with her last hours, minutes and seconds counting down. I served the banana bread at her wake.

These thoughts stayed my own. I didn't want to tell my friends of my failures and have them respond with *You did plenty!* because it felt like soliciting reassurance -

pointless reassurance because who is really going to tell someone whose mum just died that they had fucked it?

I dissociated. It wasn't a choice, more a reflexive survival tactic to combat overwhelm, but this numbness was an old friend I was happy to embrace. I was no use to anybody crying and consumed with self-pity and self-recrimination.

Mummy's funeral was peaceful. The church seemed to be suffused with tranquillity, a quiet gratitude that this gentle spirit had been released from a hard innings. I felt at peace as I walked away from the grave where she had been lowered, knowing they were all together. I was freed from carrying the grief of others.

The house needed cleared for the housing executive to repossess, providing me with the solid ground of practical tasks. Memories blossomed in this vacated space. The silver stick-on numbers on the front door - the four at a rakish angle to the two. Daddy had intended it to look whimsical. When I first saw it, I asked sincerely if his hand had slipped. Mummy had rolled her eyes in a silent *Trust HIM!* and Daddy looked sheepish. The phone by the door brought memories of Daddy earwigging from his chair waiting for me to say something incriminating, so that he could swoop in and save me from corruption. That living room had witnessed our many incarnations: the chair Martin and I squeezed into to watch the funnies, which later became Daddy's chair, his profile turned away from the room and towards the news, or a book, or the paper. The window beside the chair, once broken by the sonorous boom of a bomb, and Mummy's jubilation when it was replaced with our first double-glazed windows. The little bathroom at the top of the stairs where I locked myself in to cry in peace. The tiny back hall where we played on rainy days as kids and how it once stank of shit and piss the time we acquired a puppy which destroyed Daddy's padded gym equipment with its tiny teeth in the few days it stayed before going to live on a farm on White Mountain. The pitying look on Daddy's face when I asked, nearly twenty years later, to which farm Claudius had been sent. Ghosts everywhere. The eyes of so many versions of me watching this exact moment with curiosity. I realised that as I grew up, I was watching my parents grow up, too.

I started with Mummy's clothes, choosing to experience this landmark event mindfully. I smelled each jumper, felt gratitude that it once kept her warm and then set it carefully in a bag for charity, hoping that it would go on to warm others. After about twenty minutes of this, I soon realised that I hadn't seen her wear many of these jumpers and began to suspect that she may have had a secret addiction to the Edinburgh Wool Mill, whereupon my mindfulness and gratitude process was replaced with dumping piles of jumpers into bags and bidding them a hastily muttered *"good luck in your future endeavours."* After this, the coat closet gave me pause. Expensive coats, many with the tags still on. I remembered noticing similar items after Daddy died - expensive clothes, bought for birthdays or Christmases, kept for good, waiting for the prestigious outing that never transpired. Those coats were not practical purchases but expressions of love - the quality of the leather, the expert tailoring expressing affection and esteem in lieu of words. Money spent was their love language. I remembered being sent to school in the correctly fitting blazer with the handcrafted leather satchel. Because they knew poverty, they bestowed material gifts like benedictions. My friends lived in a world where having your basic needs met was a given, their love came in words and physical affection. Little then did I understand that to those for whom food on the table and clothes on your back could not be counted upon, words were wind.

Our different beginnings had set us at odds, theirs stranding them at the bottom of Maslow's Triangle of needs, the upper echelons an out of reach frivolity. They bought warm coats, stylish coats, greatcoats, leather coats, because as children they had so little that they lay under other people's coats to stay warm in bed, coats that were taken off them and put on the fathers' backs in the morning, while they themselves were sent off to school in threadbare hand-me-down ones. I folded and bagged up these coats, smiling for each token of love until I ran out of bags and exclaimed, *"Jaysus, okay, you loved each other, enough bloody coats,"* into the emptiness.

I had to decide what got auctioned, what went to charity, what few items I might keep and what, devastatingly, must be binned. Furniture, clothes, photographs, bric-a-brac, there was a logical destination for such items which helped take the emotional sting out of the process, but one category of items gave me immense pain; those things kept to remind them of their sons. Little remained of these boys' lives, but every facet of their deaths had been saved: newspaper clippings, letters and cards of condolence. Grief was packed into shoeboxes, albums and drawers, from where it had seeped throughout the house, like damp. They had reached the end of their utility when my parents reached the end of their lives.

Two items remained, the boys' trophies, which stood sentry for decades in the living room. Billy's Memorial Trophy with the little boxer figure at the top, and Martin's Football Trophy, engraved with the names of previous winners, with Martin's name at the bottom, the full stop on the list of celebrations. I left these until the end of the week, eyeing me reproachfully from the mantle. Mercifully, Martin's best friend Chris said he'd be glad to take his trophy as a lasting reminder of their friendship. He had grown into a gentleman who carried his grief as an honour instead of a wound. Only Billy's trophy remained. It had graced our home my whole life, a symbol of a devastation that I hadn't witnessed, but which clung nonetheless. I offered Jeanette the trophy – to my mind, Billy had been her brother as Martin had been mine – but she didn't want it, for the same reasons I hadn't wanted Martin's. When I lowered the tall boxing trophy into the bin, trepidation gave way to immense relief. It was over.

That was my final act in my childhood home. I locked up and got into my car to drive away from this house for the last time, no longer the daughter of broken, heart-sore parents, the daughter who stayed behind and stuffed the pain down because my loss could never compare. I felt like my slate had been wiped clean and I was finally free to be my own person. I felt lighter.

Out of everything, I kept Mummy's singer sewing machine and her locket with a picture of the boys on each side, Daddy's well-worn boxing gloves, his sturdy study desk and the wooden chess board he'd taught us all to play on. It made me wonder which material items will be kept when I go. Of all the things I love and touch and use (assuming the correct order of things is observed, and I go first, *please God*) - which will my children choose as memento? A life, distilled, an item as epitaph.

Thirty-Three

I had gone from being somebody's child to nobody's child, an orphan at thirty-eight. Liberation and vulnerability buttressed together uncomfortably, jostling for supremacy. The frenetic chapter of running back and forth between Mummy's apartment and the house had ended, but though the stress of caring for a dying parent had eased, anxiety remained. I labelled it repressed grief and having no time to grieve with two children to tend to, I put myself on a waiting list for bereavement counselling. The promise of counselling was really a justification to evade grief in the meantime. I didn't know how to grieve properly and part of me was content to remain in this dissociative state where pain was remote behind a glass wall, a window that I waved through and mouthed promises to visit later.

Realisation dawned that I have always been stressed and cross, only the circumstances which I blamed changed. It wasn't Daddy's illness, Mummy's illness or punishing toddler sleep schedules. It was me, porting my stress microclimate around. Adverse childhood experiences hardwired my system for stress; my cortisol levels remained high, a survival mechanism which had me on red alert for a danger which had long passed. I couldn't shake the feeling of impending doom because it was dictated by the chemicals in my brain that just wanted to keep me alert and safe. I was the perfect storm for poor parenting. Biologically, I was hardwired for stress, which bequeathed a short fuse and knee-jerk reactions, while the environment I had grown up in meant that my default behaviours around parenting were blame and punishment rather than empathy and guidance. I wanted to be a good parent, but what I knew about it was learned from books and my conditioned responses were at odds with what I now knew was best. I was in a constant state of inner civil war, as the fractious parent tried to wrestle control from the learned one.

There were only enough hours in the day to attend to one of the three broad responsibilities of domestic motherhood: either I looked clean and tidy, or the children did, or the house did – never all three at once and rarely two, if ever. Perfectionism dictated attempting a rough gallop at all three, crashing out, and bemoaning my failure. If the house was tidy, we were all still in our pyjamas at noon, if we had to leave the house we would look presentable but be returning to a house with apocalyptic proportions of mess. Those were good days without the curveballs of tummy bugs or bumps; on the bad days I could be relied upon to go into a state of near apoplectic terror. My relationship was beginning to suffer too. Phil returned from work each evening unable to make even a vague reference to any kind of frustration he'd experienced during his day, because I would be primed to one-up him, *"Oh – you think YOUR day was bad?!"*

I noticed that I had marginally greater control over my behaviour in public places than when I was at home, unfettered by fear of the judgement of strangers, so I took the children out frequently. Going out became a safety behaviour. We went for nature walks on the beach or forests, to parks and soft play areas. My conditioning to not make a scene was at odds with my conditioning to react punitively, but the perceived social shame of being publicly mean to my children could usually be relied upon to shackle my worst impulses. Whether through biology or environment, Sia was fairly obedient, as I had been, but Ben wouldn't bend the knee. One day we were in a soft play centre, and it was time to go home for lunch.

"Ben, it's time to go!" I sang, with the forced cheer of a children's TV presenter.

"No!" he replied and darted off in the direction of an area of soft play that I could only enter if I lost two stone or became a contortionist.

I remembered that a better way to navigate transitions with a child is to give them a five-minute warning to allow time to adjust.

"Okay, five more minutes, and then we have to go!" I called, still upbeat.

"No!" he called over his shoulder as he attempted to break the land speed record.

I knew I was making arbitrary decisions on his behalf and understood it would be frustrating for him. Transitions can be hard for all of us but most of all for children who do not have control over decisions governing their lives. I had ostensibly announced, *No more fun for you!* and foolishly expected him to be fine with it. I shook off the embarrassment of my defiant child and reminded myself that I had five more minutes to work out how to navigate getting an unwilling Ben out of soft play and into the car.

"It's lunchtime and we must go home to eat in five minutes. You can play for five more minutes, then we will go," I called to no one in particular, because at this point, I was undeniably alone.

I congratulated myself on compromising the five minutes and explaining why we had to leave. Good parenting, I thought. Five minutes passed, long enough for Ben to have forgotten the plan and have wandered back into my vicinity.

"Okay, Ben, five minutes are up. It is time to put on your shoes."

"No. I want to stay."

"Ben, it's lunchtime. It's time to go."

"I don't want to!" he screamed.

This might have been embarrassing for another parent, but not me, a Public Supermum. I was determined to remain calm.

"I understand you don't want to. It is hard to go when you are having fun, isn't it?"

Empathy. What a parent.

"Now, time for shoes."

"NO!"

I could feel the flush in my cheeks as my heart rate increased. My mask started to slip.

"Ben, if you don't put your shoes on, there will be no Friday treat this week."

He relented, but it didn't feel like a victory. In threatening to withdraw a treat, I had reinforced extrinsic motivation – he only chose to put his shoes on to avoid punishment. Ideally, he would be intrinsically motivated - putting on his shoes because he wanted to. I was irritated. Perfectionism prickled in a sudden sweat.

As we walked out, Ben attempted to wrestle back control and wring some last moments of joy from the outing by insisting that he climb the stairs solo and instructing me to take the lift to the ground floor with Sia. I'm not a normal human being who can content myself with a quick calculation of the risk of child abduction in a public place peppered with CCTV units; I'm more likely to expect an opportunist child abductor to be loitering around stairwells in the hope of exactly this scenario. I looked at my son, who has had just about enough of my fun-quenching shit and wagered that relenting to this one request might mean the difference between a child on the first floor who takes my hand and walks happily to the car, and one who must be carried past people, kicking and guldering his indignation directly into my earhole.

As Sia and I got into the lift, Ben was smiling and buoyant, ready to tackle the stairs when the doors closed and not a moment before. Intrusive thoughts began immediately - *someone could grab him at the bottom of the stairs and take him to the changing rooms, shave his head, put on a different coat and have him crossing the border within the hour, or mess with him in a changing cubicle, or get him upstairs and lift him to a car before the slowest lift in the fucking universe creaks up two metres and finally opens these slow, bastard doors. Or maybe he got upstairs moments ago, assumed I had left without him and has darted outside to find our car, straight into traffic. The doors will open, and he won't be there.* My heart rate raced, and I began to sweat.

Of course, he was there. My relief was suffocated by frustration – why the inner histrionics? Being me was exhausting. He took my hand, but the high of his recent solo trek up the steps has worn off and he issued renewed objections as he realised that we were definitely heading home. We were moments away from the eyes of strangers, and metres from the solitude of the car, so I stopped interacting and focused deep within myself - remote, untouchable, ruminating. It felt unfair. I had explained, I had compromised, I had even capitulated to the stairs at great personal cost to my already unsteady equilibrium. My inner Gollum muttered that earlier I used threats to force him to relent, so really, I wasn't that great a parent to begin with. By the time we got to the car, I was furious with both of us; me for failing, and him for pushing me to it.

In the car, Ben continued to expel the full weight of his frustration by yelling. I closed the car door and my socially dependent restraint collapsed spectacularly in our relatively soundproofed car, unfettered by prying eyes.

"Enough! Shut up! No more of this noise!"

I shouted so loudly that my throat rasped, words of rage sandpapered my throat. Ben froze in shock. He hadn't the run of himself any more than I did - we were two toddlers tantrumming, but some primal survival instinct in Ben kicked in as my rage registered as dangerous. I noticed this change in his affect and knew I had scared him into submission. I started the car and pressed ahead on this low road, voice deep, tone menacing, countenance darkened. I hiss and growl, mouth-watering, rabid-dog-salivating and suddenly remember Daddy, foam on his lips, flecking spit as he swore and raged when the monster overtook him. Now I am the monster.

"Shut. The. Fuck. Up."

I am channelling the familiar unfettered viciousness, spewing evil, a fountain of rage. When Daddy became angry, did he remember his own father in the same way as I was remembering him, and feel this disgust? Did it matter? Whether he was conscious of the similarities or not, the fact was that both of us were performing iterations of abuse. Our respective developmental adversities led to this chronic dysregulation. Did either of us deserve forgiveness?

Ben cried - no longer cries of rage, but fearful tears, hurt tears. I know I've gone too far, but I just need the noise to stop. His cries are a reproach, his rage an affront. I am utterly overstimulated and just want it to end.

"Stop fucking crying! I have had enough! Enough!"

My poor son hiccoughed into a terrified silence as my child-self had done so many times. That expensive silence provided space to remember what it felt like to be yelled at to stop crying, hiccoughing through silent tears, yearning for comfort and to have my pain acknowledged by the very person who had just inflicted it. Such moments were the birthplace for my lack of self-compassion, when I was made to understand that my feelings didn't matter, and when I became intolerant of my own tears. I was programming my son to have the same beliefs.

There's a cacophony in my head in this silent car.

This familiar rage - is it nature or nurture? Is the Bell temper something that passes genetically, a defect in the frontal lobe, an impulse control issue? Or did each generation simply learn these behaviours, modelled by the last?

These are my thoughts in the eerily quiet car, all the while knowing that these psychological musings are moot because the outcome is the same: emotional damage. I didn't need an explanation; I needed a cessation. I drove towards home, silence ringing post-detonation. I got my silence, but at the terrible price of passing on my wounds and my darkness. I was relinquishing responsibility to heal the wounds that had passed down through too many generations and leaving the work to Ben instead. My parents didn't know enough to do the work, but I do. Know better, do better. I know that I must be the cycle-breaker, not Ben. The passing on of wounds had to stop with me. If I continued being unable to manage myself, I was hardwiring them for stress, normalising anxiety and conditioning them to end up like me. Fuck that. I wouldn't wish that on anyone.

I became human again, feeling remorseful and receptive. We parked outside the house.

"I'm sorry for shouting," I say, quietly.

Both children eagerly accepted my apology, trying to manage me by being agreeable, and my heart hurts that they feel the need to overlook their own pain to remain safe and loved by the one person supposed to keep them safe from harm.

Sia nodded her wide-eyed acceptance of my apology, keen to escape the fog of unpredictable rage and bring us back to safer ground. Ben looks mournful; in his childish innocence he had allowed me to displace the blame onto him. He nods too, and says, *"it's okay,"* the s sounding slushy over his wee wet lips. It looks like good behaviour, but it is fear. I opened Ben's door and reached in to hold his soft, forlorn face in my hands.

"I'm sorry, wee love. I'm sorry for being mean."

"It's okay, Mummy."

Except it wasn't, and he collapsed into hurt weeping before he has even got the words out, relieved that it is finally over and that the danger has passed, clinging to the person who inflicted the hurt. I lifted my son and let his little face burrow into my shoulder and soak my neck with his tears. When we got inside, I sank into a chair and held him, rocked him as I kissed his little head.

His hair smelled like Martin's. I wiped his sad tears and looked into his little face, so trusting.

"*I'm sorry, my love. I love you. I'm sorry I was mean and that is not okay.*"

I'm sickened with myself though, not only for what I've done but because even as I speak these words, I notice other thoughts lurking on the periphery, urging me to tell him that his behaviour caused my anger, because if he understands this, he may resist crossing me again, giving him the responsibility not to trigger me. I don't want to make this child responsible for an adult's behaviour. I had been parented with fear and control, with anger and justifications and it had seeped into my bones. It was hard, fighting myself like this, but I circumvented the low road and wouldn't blame him for the pain he suffered at my hands.

I was finally ready to admit that I was playing with a stacked deck and that no amount of determination was enough to enable me to manage myself. I began to consider the possibility that medication could help. It felt like failure. Needing chemical intervention to function like a normal person felt like weakness. Phil had suggested the possibility several times before - poor Phil watching the merry-go-round of stress, snapping, remorse and resolve playing out in our home with our children front and centre, absorbing it all. We all deserved better. And yet, some treacherous little voice inside my head muttered, *he doesn't care about you, he just wants his life to be easier. The only time your suffering matters is when it impacts others.* I remembered Mummy and her observation of my 'bad nerves' and my refusal to get help so that she could see the results of the harsh parenting I had experienced. I wore my anxiety like a fuck you. But who was I really hurting? It was like swallowing poison and expecting the other person to die.

Enough was enough. Time was passing and every day that I elected to remain un-medicated was another day with a high likelihood of unnecessary stress for all of us; another formative year of my children absorbing tension and learning that the world, and love, was unpredictable and unsafe. I made a doctor's appointment and started on an antidepressant used for anxiety, Sertraline. It wasn't long until the medication made a difference. After a week or so, I had a longer fuse. Situations that once had me tense and fractious were more easily managed. Instead of waking up and anxiously anticipating the challenges scheduled for the day, I woke up looking forward to what the day had in store. I was enjoying my life. Is this how other people felt? Was this normal? I began to feel content, and only then did I realise the extent of the underlying dread which had previously permeated my days.

Taking medication made sense. Within weeks I was a convert, a medication evangelist. If I was playing a computer game with a massively disadvantaged avatar and had the opportunity to 'level up', I wouldn't think twice. If my suspicions were correct and I am a spiritual being learning and growing in Earth school, it didn't make sense to allow biological or psychological issues to impede my progress if there were available options to help me overcome them. My genetic and conditioned characteristics, my specific weaknesses were holding me back and there was neither honour nor wisdom in continuing a solo struggle against a stacked deck.

This calmer mind gave me space to observe and reflect before reacting. I could see that my default strictness was conditioned and that I could choose differently. I thought of Daddy, static and hardened, and felt sad. Our relationship had been collateral damage. It had never been personal.

As the medication did its work smoothing over my frayed nerves, it became apparent that Phil had taken on much of my burden. I was cooking at the counter and Phil sat some distance away, on the sofa at the other end of the kitchen, when Ben spilled his drink. Phil reacted.

"Ben! You have made a mess on the floor!"

I looked up and saw that Phil had leapt to his feet, scolding Ben and preparing to sweep him out of the room in an attempt to manage the situation so that I didn't have to, so that I didn't become overwhelmed with having to cook, and mop, and manage unruly children. So that I didn't lose my shit. I saw him clearly, perhaps for the first time. He was modelling his parenting on mine – overreacting, doing what I would do so that I wouldn't have to. I didn't like what I was seeing in this mirror. Sertraline had made me less fraught and therefore less reactionary.

"It's okay, Phil. Ben – come and grab a towel and we will mop the spill together. It's okay, chum. Wee accident."
Phil scrutinised me, looking confused.
"I take it the Sertraline has kicked in, then? Oh shit…am I the mental one now?"

It certainly wasn't linear, but gradually I was providing a much calmer environment for the children. Sertraline gave me a longer fuse, space to reflect rather than react. In a nutshell, psycho-pharmaceuticals have made me a better parent. I'm not perfect, but children don't need a perfect parent, just a happy one, occasionally making human mistakes and being accountable for them, apologising and making amends, modelling healthy behaviour. Trauma is passed from generation to generation until someone is equipped to address it, and I straddle two worlds, feeling the pain of the last one while working towards a better one, so they don't have to.

Epilogue

Re-living some parts of this book re-opened old wounds and at times I wondered how this story could ever be of any use. I wondered if committing these experiences to paper was pointless - not even a simple exercise in catharsis, but instead the writing of one long suicide note explaining to my children why they are better off without me, this flawed, damaged individual with so much potential to inflict harm. However, my gut, my Head Letterbox guidance, my white-light moments remind me: I am here to be a cycle-breaker. This ancestral trauma, the pain that has been passed down through the generations must stop somewhere. It's why I'm here.

Writing was often a struggle. I frequently became ill for a few days after recounting difficult events - sometimes my throat ached, like when I was a child and suppressed tears sent pain down my gullet. I got throat infections and it seemed as though the words I had suppressed for so many years had festered into poison. Often, I just felt too worn out to function in my everyday life. The cost of an hour or two of writing was exhaustion that made me a less patient and present parent. Ironically, in the course of processing trauma, in order that my children didn't have to feel it, I wasn't as tuned in to their needs - the very thing I berated my parents for, and I questioned whether these absences were too high a price to pay. In another way, every illness felt like a little bloodletting, a tap releasing pockets of poison so that they didn't accumulate and mutate into a cancer that could kill me further down the line. If Adverse Childhood Experiences are considered predictors of illness and early death, then perhaps feeling these traumas in bite-sized chunks from the safety of my laptop might circumvent something worse.

As Epictetus wisely observed, it isn't events but our perception of events that makes us happy or unhappy. I hope that my story illustrates that our exact circumstances teach us specific lessons, the exact lessons we came here to learn. I can't say for sure whether Earth is a schoolroom, I can't say for sure that we chose our obstacles to learn, or that those who have left us are cheering us on from the other side, but I get to choose my perspective, and this is the one that rings true for me. I also get to choose whether these events ripped holes in the fabric of my being or whether they were the forge in which I grew strong. On bad days, when I feel damaged and disconnected, I declare the forge analogy a delusion and suspect I am being held together by my belief in a lie. But then, by that logic, the ripped fabric analogy is also a delusion. All perspectives are delusions and all we can do is choose our delusions wisely and use them to steer and stay the course or be tossed in seas of confusion until we are begging for mercy. As I said to dear, lovely Jill: it's all bullshit perspective. Does it matter if others declare your beliefs nonsense if those beliefs have kept you afloat?

All beliefs must be delusions. Was this the latest life taken on in the conscious evolution of my spirit or just a flash in the pan, my consciousness a pointless evolutionary blip? Were the various experiences of the unmanifest visitations from spirits or delusions generated by stress or grief? Are some experiences and events predetermined, or are we buffeted about on the stormy waters of random happenstance? Is eliciting a narrative arc from the events that have occurred in my life evidence of being tuned in, or spiritual bypassing?

All I can offer is anecdotal evidence that these things occurred, along with a perspective that drawing forth meaning from my experiences has facilitated a kind of self-acceptance. I cannot say for sure whether it is a spiritual or biological imperative, but I know that we are driven not only to survive, but to thrive. We have an innate need to know that there is a point to all of this, to elicit a 'why', as expressed so profoundly by Viktor Frankl in Man's Search for Meaning:

"A man who becomes conscious of the responsibility he bears toward a human being who affectionately waits for him, or to an unfinished work, will never be able to throw away his life. He knows the 'why' for his existence and will be able to bear almost any 'how'."

-Viktor Frankl

So, regarding the biggest question of life – *Why?* - the best we can do is state our opinions with the caveat – this is my belief, my delusion and I am free to amend it at any time in accordance with whichever evidence I choose to give credence to, and secure enough in myself not to need hoards to agree with me.

Sia looks like my mini-me. There's nothing of her daddy in her, except her feet - which is a mercy otherwise a paternity test could be on the cards. She's all me - large brown eyes behind glasses to remedy her squint, unruly hair - things I hoped she wouldn't have as she grew in my tummy, before she gave me a reason to love myself. Every time I look at her, I see myself looking back, a reminder to be gentle. She is also a trigger, so like me that at times I apply the same perfectionistic standards that I had been held to. She's a talker. She doesn't know what she thinks until she hears it coming out of her mouth and I have to resist the urge to tell her to stop gabbling on, as I was told as a child. When I see her face - my face - our face looking back at me, I stop myself from inflicting wounds that take too long to heal.

That's our contract. She is my teacher, and a brave and loving soul she is to show up for that assignment. Through loving Sia, I am learning to love me. When I was young, my neural networks for love were underdeveloped, but with practice, with neuroplasticity, those capabilities have emerged. Yes, trauma changes the brain, but so does healing. Sia taught me to love. When she was in utero, hiding her gender with her crossed legs, I wanted a boy to replace the boys we had lost, but deep down I knew nothing would replace them and I had latched on to this convenient fiction to hide the fact that I was afraid to have a girl. Being born a girl forced my awareness of the cultural narrative but being the mother of a girl forces me to engage with it. I don't have the luxury of debating the rights and wrongs of society's attitude towards women on a theoretical level, lamenting misogyny but merely managing the symptoms and taking preventative measures. Sia has given me righteous indignation and fire to live the truth that some things are not to be withstood.

Recently, she accompanied me to my aunt's funeral and, despite only having met her once, wept copiously throughout the service. Big tears rolled down her cheeks and her breath was ragged. Because I have been conditioned to believe there is a hierarchy of grief, to push down my feelings because others have it worse, I was a bit embarrassed, but my overarching feeling was of gratitude that she is open and tender. Giving her space to feel her feelings is a gift I didn't get, but I have given it to her. Then I noticed she was wearing purple nail polish and it felt like a little nod from the universe, a reminder that I'm doing something right when my daughter can feel her feelings without having to stifle or present in a certain way.

Sia and Ben are the same difference in age as Jeanette and Billy. That triggered me for a long time. I feared that I was predestined to live my mummy's life, that after a lifetime of judging her harshly for not being the mother I wanted her to be, I was destined to find out how a bereaved mother loses part of herself when she loses a child, and to thereby understand that the failings I saw in her were not her fault. But through looking at my life through this fear filter, I was doing what I criticised my parents for – I was forgetting Kahlil Gibran's *your children are not your own*, forgetting that each day is a gift to be cherished. As Osho said, *you can appreciate the flower, but when you pick it to own it, it dies*. Today is all we have, and when we fear the future, it poisons the day. Parenting well is to live in the eternal now.

Of course, parenting mustn't be the be-all and end-all. These little spiritual beings chose to have their human journey with me as their mother, and I take that very seriously and try to be a conscious parent, but my childhood experiences taught me that being the centre of your parents' universe is a heavy load. To maximise their chances of achieving their potential by accomplishing the spiritual quests they chose before incarnating, I can't just sit and pontificate about it. I need to show them how it is done by setting an example. In other words, the best thing I can do as a parent is to strive to be self-actualised. I have to be seen to discover my reason for being and lean into my truth, so that they know how to do it when their time comes.

In writing this book, I wished to portray an example of generational trauma, but I hope that throughout the narrative, you have also been able to see that generational strengths exist too, something that I have only come to understand during the writing process. Daddy passed on his insatiable thirst for knowledge and answers. His love of philosophy and his talent for writing became the catalyst for mine. Mummy's faith drew my attention to a world beyond the one we can see, and her grace in somehow continuing to put one foot in front of the other showed her to be the bravest of us all. With hindsight, I can see that Mummy was a gabbler, just as I was and just as Sia is, and if it wasn't for gabbling on, where would this book be? I am everything I am because of them, and my children will thrive because of that.

I hope, as I once did as a journaling student, that this story of overcoming will become someone else's survival guide.

About the Author

Peggy Bell lives in Bangor, a seaside town in Northern Ireland with her husband, Phil Johnston, two children, Sia and Ben, two fluffy dogs called Teddy and Barney, and two ex-battery hens - Joseph and Lola. She is a former teacher and CBT therapist.

She can be found on Instagram *@interior_alchemy*

Family Photographs

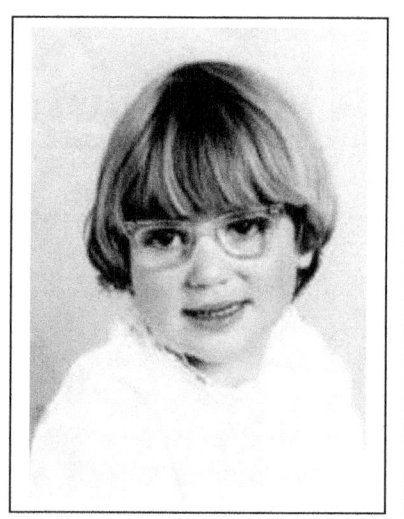

Peggy - with glasses

Martin

Left: Mummy, Jeanette and Billy; Above: Jeanette and Billy

Above and below: Mummy and Daddy, Tates Avenue

Daddy

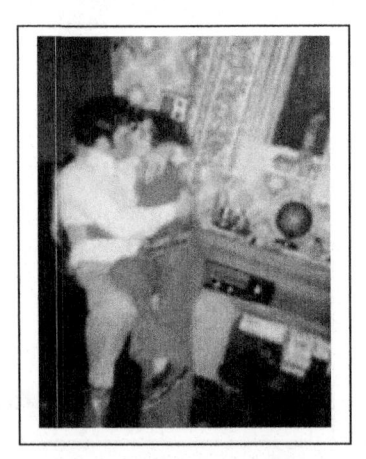

Mummy and Jeanette with Billy's Trophy

Daddy, Hughie, Janet and Tucker

Above and Below: Aunt Lily's wedding with Mummy as bridesmaid

Bella Bell

Above: Uncle Billy, Mummy, Granda Bob, Uncle Jamesy and Aunt Lily

Granny Martha on the left

Daddy as a schoolboy, on right

Phil and Peggy

Above: Clare, Melanie and Julie

Left: Peggy, Sia and Ben

Tribute to Martin in the local paper

Acknowledgements

Huge thanks to Phil, who looked after weeks-old baby Ben and toddler Sia so that I could write, write, write when the urge became irrepressible.

Heartfelt gratitude to my first reader, Cathal Tierney, for constant enthusiastic encouragement and thoughtful feedback.

Thanks to my sister Jeanette - where do I even start? Near or far, you are my lifelong constant, my witness, my soft place to land. You revisited painful places so that I could understand better. You jumped off the pedestal I placed you on, to put your arm around my shoulder and speak of times gone by.

Big love to my lifelong best friends Julie Atkins, Melanie Anderson and Clare Aughey, who formed - and continue to form - essential parts of my narrative.

Thanks to my Queens - Alison Cherry, Corinna Keenan, Emma Bryans, Donna Bloye, Lucy Wallace, Sarah Etheridge and Shelley McDonald - a motley crew of blow-ins, all but one! My sounding boards, cheerleaders and inexhaustible sources of love and support throughout these writing years. Now that I'm done, there will be more time for kitchen discos and sinking our faces into wheels of Brie.

Much appreciation to my editor and publisher Heather Shields, who coaxed out my very best efforts - on the dance floors at uni as well as during the editing process.

But most of all, thank you, Sia and Ben, for showing up for this assignment - you cracked my heart wide open so that I could spill the contents onto a page.

Finally, love and gratitude to Reggie, who showed up when it mattered, and who whispered missives into my Head Letterbox.

Index

Throughout this book you will meet with colloquialisms and favoured Northern Irish slang. For anyone not from the North of Ireland, this is what it means:

'eloi eloi lama sabachthani' "My God, my God, why hast Thou forsaken me", 541

aul' old, 17, 91, 167, 172, 224, 233, 357, 405, 482, 516

bangled when one has taken many hard substanc es and is feeling 'beyond mangled' - as in to have lost control, 294

beak face - pronoun ced bake, 95

craic enjoyable conversa tion or social activity, 65, 225, 285, 305

cribby kerb, 23

feg cigarette, 149

foutered dithered, not getting on with it, 118

frightening the bejaysus out of

to frighten or annoy someone very much, 380

gurny gub cry baby, 236

hafta have to, 197

hauched Ulster Scots term to cough up phlegm to clear the throat, 205

jipped cheated, 94

lacrimonious prone to sadness, 417

marleys marbles, 23

nai now, 56, 59, 78, 103, 150

poke ice-cream cone, 261

snides an unpleasant or underhand person, 264

stupit *stupid*, 508, 534

*W*eemen women, 119

Printed in Great Britain
by Amazon